Sacred
Ground

**Americans
and Their
Battlefields**

D1509782

Sacred Ground

Americans and Their Battlefields

Second Edition

Edward Tabor Linenthal

Foreword by Robert M. Utley

University of Illinois Press

Urbana and Chicago

Illini Books edition, 1993

© 1991, 1993 by the Board of Trustees of the University of Illinois

Manufactured in the United States of America

P 5 4 3 2 1

This book is printed on acid-free paper.

Library of Congress Cataloging-in-Publication Data

Linenthal, Edward Tabor, 1947–
   Sacred ground : Americans and their battlefields / Edward Tabor
Linenthal ; foreword by Robert M. Utley.
     p.   cm.
   Includes bibliographical references and index.
   ISBN 0-252-01783-8 (cl)
    1. Battlefields—United States—History.   2. United States—History, Military.
   3. Historic sites—United States—Psychological aspects.   I. Title.
E181.L36   1993
973—dc20   93-23925
                                              CIP

First edition available in cloth (ISBN 0-252-01783-8) from the University of Illinois Press.

For Robert S. Michaelsen,
with respect and affection

Contents

Foreword by Robert M. Utley   ix

Acknowledgments   xiii

Introduction   1

1 "The Pivot on Which the World Turns"
Lexington and Concord   9

2 "A Reservoir of Spiritual Power"
The Alamo   53

3 "A Joint and Precious Heritage"
Gettysburg   87

4 "A Sore from America's Past That Has Not Yet Healed"
The Little Bighorn   127

5 "Rust and Sea and Memory in This Strange Graveyard"
Pearl Harbor   173

Conclusion   213

Epilogue   219

Index   251

Illustrations

Lexington and Concord, *following pages 14, 30, and 38*

The Alamo, *following pages 64 and 74*

Gettysburg, *following pages 94 and 110*

The Little Bighorn, *following pages 140 and 158*

Pearl Harbor, *following pages 186 and 196*

Foreword

Sacred Ground not only afforded me a fascinating and instructive reading experience but also brought into focus some memorable events that had swirled around me during the 1960s and 1970s. As the assistant director of the National Park Service concerned with historic preservation, I was personally involved with four of the five battlefields discussed in this book. These and others in the national park system attracted the kind of struggle for symbolic possession that Edward Linenthal describes. Promoters of competing ideologies—usually, as Linenthal's case studies suggest, the orthodox and the heretical—enlist these sacred spaces in their diverse crusades.

The sacred space that stirred the greatest contention, as chronicled in chapter 4, was the Custer Battlefield National Monument. Demands and complaints of the Indian activists, on the one hand, and the Custer loyalists, on the other, cascaded onto my desk in Washington. The entire episode climaxed with painful directness during the centennial ceremonies at the battlefield in 1976, when I contested the speaker's platform with red power champion Russell Means.

My speech, which followed Means's incendiary rhetoric, was a plea to view the battle and its participants on their own terms, to refrain from perverting history, the battlefield, and the anniversary in the service of modern political and social agendas, however valid their aims. But as Edward Linenthal gently observes—and demonstrates in every chapter—anniversary ceremonies have always served precisely this purpose. The minutemen of Lexington and Concord were summoned to validate the war for the Union and, more recently, America's missile defenses. Anniversary speeches at the Alamo mobilized the "freedom fighters" of 1836 in support of the contras in Nicaragua. Russell Means clearly knew the power of sacred space in advancing his cause.

During my years as a National Park Service historian, I (and my associates) conceived our mission as essentially twofold. First, we were to care for "historic resources" and guard them from whatever forces, natural or human (including our own managers), endangered them. The historic resources of battlefields are the terrain, vegetative cover, road systems, buildings, and other structures that have survived from the time of the battle. Second, we were to "interpret" these resources through museums, films, publications, lectures, tours, and other media, to give the visitor an understanding and appreciation of the resources and the events being illustrated.

A third purpose sometimes intruded, although we tended to resist it. This was commemoration: to memorialize the achievements and sacrifices of the people who acted out the events we were interpreting. Memorialization took many forms, but too often, we thought, it involved homage that approached worship. This we felt to be unhistorical. We favored education over veneration. We wanted to tell it and show it as it was, as dispassionately and objectively as possible. We looked on the places charged to our care as historic properties where people came to be informed, not as shrines where people came to worship.

Purity demanded that our battlefields be as uncluttered by commemorative monuments as possible. Those inherited with the older battlefields, such as Gettysburg and Vicksburg, could be rationalized as themselves historic, as testaments to what earlier generations believed a battlefield should be. But in developing new parks, such as Pea Ridge and Wilson's Creek, we fended off most proposals for memorials. We had less success in blocking the new memorials at the old parks that sprang from the commemorative fervor of the Civil War centennial celebrations.

In *Sacred Ground,* Edward Linenthal does not invalidate our professional attitudes, but his case studies strongly suggest our insensitivity to a robust current in American thought. Commemoration has always been a powerful motive, perhaps the most powerful, for preserving historic places. People approach these places not only as vestiges of the past, as vehicles for enlightenment, but also as shrines, as temples for veneration. The custodians of historic places may frown on excesses of commemoration, but this is not likely to change the public's instinct to look on these places as shrines.

The shrine aspect of historic sites, especially battlefields, makes them ideal arenas for the kind of struggle over symbolic possession discussed in this book. For site managers, the messages implicit in these case studies should be understood and heeded. First, such struggles are inevitable and should be anticipated. They can even be viewed as healthy symptoms of democracy, demonstrating the depth of public feeling about the nation and its heritage, promoting public discourse on fundamental issues. Second, in such struggles no single point of view should be allowed to prevail. The orthodox and the heretical should have equal access to the "free market of sacred space." To orchestrate contending interpretations while denying exclusive domination to any single contender, to fashion an "official" interpretation that acknowledges all while remaining true to professional canons, is a formidable task. That for the most intensely contested symbolic battlegrounds it may be impossible does not lift the obligation to search constantly for the elusive balance. In a democracy there should be no prescribed orthodoxies.

At the Custer Battlefield National Monument in 1976, my speech represented the orthodox speaking to the orthodox. In that setting, Russell Means represented the heretical. To the discomfort of all, he managed to gain access to the free market of sacred space. The conflict that day was but one skirmish in a long war for symbolic possession of the battlefield. If the National Park Service handles its stewardship with sensitivity, the war will never be won, but the visitor should come away with an understanding of the competing viewpoints and, more important, their true roots in history. Perhaps indicative of the times, Russell Means and I now share membership on a committee to oversee erection of an Indian memorial on the Custer battlefield.

Sacred Ground is an instructive essay for historic preservationists. More significantly, however, it is a thoughtful, provocative excursion in intellectual history, an illuminating treatise for those who treasure both the tangible and the intangible expressions of our nation's heritage.

Robert M. Utley

Acknowledgments

Part of the pleasure of working on this project has been the opportunity to meet a great number of interesting people, some of whom have become good friends and all of whom have contributed in important ways to this book. I thank them for assistance cheerfully and graciously given. Four of the five battlefields I have written about are National Park Service sites, and beginning with my first research trip to the Little Bighorn in 1980, I have profited immensely from the help of a number of people associated with the NPS. In particular, I would like to thank Robert M. Utley, former assistant director and chief NPS historian; Edwin C. Bearss, the current chief NPS historian; and James P. Delgado, maritime historian, who helped greatly with the Pearl Harbor chapter and, with his wife, Mary, extended a gracious invitation to stay with them during an important week of research in Washington, D.C., in July 1989. I would like to thank as well Kathleen Georg Harrison and Robert Prosperi, NPS historians at Gettysburg National Military Park; James V. Court and Neil Mangum, former superintendent and historian, respectively, at the Custer Battlefield National Monument; and Douglas C. McChristian and Mardell Plainfeather, current historian and former historian/ranger, respectively, at the Custer Battlefield National Monument. I also wish to thank Mark Hertig, former museum curator at the USS *Arizona* Memorial. There are many other NPS people who helped with this project; their names appear below.

Although I was able to visit the Little Bighorn on the anniversary of the battle and to attend a Patriots' Day celebration at North Bridge in Concord, Massachusetts, I was able to attend a major anniversary celebration only at the Alamo, in San Antonio, Texas, on March 6, 1986, the sesquicentennial of the fall. The previous summer I had visited the Alamo for research purposes and met three people who deserve special thanks: Bernice Strong, former archivist at the Daughters of the Republic of Texas Library at the Alamo, helped me in many ways during the past six years and I greatly appreciate her kindness. I also wish to thank Dr. William E. Green, who is a walking library of information on the Alamo. Along with hundreds of others, we stood in Alamo Plaza in the chilly, early morning hours of March 6, 1986, exactly 150 years after Santa Anna's attack, and shared the excitement of the Dawn at the Alamo ceremonies. Together we also visited John Wayne's Alamo, roughly three hours from San Antonio. And Bill Green introduced me to chicken fried steak in his favorite San Antonio restaurant, which makes my return to that city inevitable. During one of my trips to the Alamo, I had the good fortune to meet Professor Margit Nagy of Our Lady of the Lake University in San Antonio, whose painstaking work in uncovering the fascinating story of the Japanese monument at the Alamo deserves wide recognition. Professor Nagy graciously extended an invitation for me to stay at the university during a subsequent research trip and, without my asking, videotaped the baseball All-Star Game while I dutifully read microfilm at the San Antonio Public Library—for this act alone, she deserves the highest praise. Finally, I wish to thank Kevin Young, technical director for the film *Alamo: The Price of Freedom* and himself a battle reenactor. Our discussions about the controversial film and about the culture of battle reenactment were most helpful, as was his assistance with visual materials.

For assistance on the Lexington and Concord chapter, I wish to thank Marcia E. Moss, curator, Concord Free Public Library, Concord, Massachusetts; the reference staff of Cary Memorial Library, Lexington, Massachusetts; Linda Ziemer, prints and photographs division, Chicago Historical Society; Jill Erickson, Sara Morgan, and Harry Katz, of the Boston Athenaeum; the Lexington Historical Society; the reference staff of the Massachusetts Historical Society; Superintendent Fred Szarka, Steven Neth, and Teresa Wallace, of Minute Man National Historical Park; the reference staff of Widener Memorial Library at Harvard University; Col. Robert F. Baker, director, Institute of Heraldry, U.S. Army; Mary Bogda and Joan Elchlepp of Sentry Insurance; Jeanne Bracken, reference librarian, Acton Memorial Library, Acton, Massachusetts; Elizabeth S. Conant of the Acton Historical Society; Professor Robert A. Gross, director of the American studies program, College of William and Mary; Klein Post Card Service, Hyde Park, Massachusetts; Jason Korell of Concord, Massachusetts; Henry M. Narducci, Ph.D., historian, Headquarters Strategic Air Command, Offutt Air Force Base, Nebraska; Joe Ofria, The Image Inn, Arlington, Massachusetts; Pat Pate of GTE; Marilyn Phipps, historical archives librarian, Boeing Corporation; and Dr. Raymond L. Puffer, chief historian, Headquarters Ballistic Missile Office, Norton Air Force Base, California.

At the Alamo, I wish to thank the reference staff of the San Antonio Public Library; Professor Félix D. Almaráz, Jr., University of Texas-San Antonio; Bruce Avrett, assistant to the curator at the Alamo; Steve W. Beck, former curator at the Alamo; Anastacio Bueno; Sharon Crutchfield, former director of the Daughters of the Republic of Texas Library at the Alamo, and other members of the library staff, especially Martha Utterback; Gilbert R. Cruz; Gary Foreman; Edwin M. Gearke, former assistant to the curator at the Alamo; Henry Guerra; Professor Gilberto Hinojosa, University of Texas-San Antonio; Rev. Balthasar Janacek; Edith Mae Johnson; Carol Jova, public relations department, Liggett Group; Professor Arnoldo De León, Angelo State University; Patricia Osborne; Frederic Ray; the Texas Historical Commission; Ray Sanchez; Tom Shelton, library assistant, Institute of Texan Cultures; Aristeo Sul; Ron Tyler and George B. Ward, editor and managing editor, respectively, of the *Southwestern Historical Quarterly;* Professor Lalo Valdez, University of Texas-San Antonio; and Judy Zipp of the *San Antonio Express-News.*

At Gettysburg, I wish to thank Professor Emeritus Robert Blum, Gettysburg College; John Fiedor, NPS; William A. Frassanito; Professor Gary W. Gallagher, Pennsylvania State University; Edward Greenlee; Edward Guy; Scott Hartwig, NPS; Thomas Harrison; John Heiser, NPS; Daniel Kuehn, former superintendent of the Gettysburg National Military Park; Nancy Massengill, Napoleonic Tactics, Inc.; Clem Murray, director of photography, *Philadelphia Inquirer;* James Roach, chief of interpretation and visitor services at the Gettysburg National Military Park; Loring Schultz; and Dave Stemrich and Donna Willson of the Stock Advantage, Allentown, Pennsylvania.

At the Little Bighorn, I wish to thank the reference staff of the Billings Public Library, Billings, Montana; the members of the Little Big Horn Associates, for their hospitality at the annual meeting in Billings in 1983; Barbara Booher, superintendent of the Custer Battlefield National Monument; Dr. Lawrence Frost; Vincent Gleason, chief of the publications division, NPS; Professor Walter Gulick, Eastern Montana College; Michael Koury; Joe Medicine Crow; Elliose Pease; Heath Pemberton, NPS; LeAnn Simpson, executive director of the Custer Battlefield Historical & Museum Association; Harold Stanton; Lorna Thackeray of the *Billings Gazette;* R. N. Wathen, Jr.; John Whiteman Runs Him; and Robbie Yellowtail.

At Pearl Harbor, I extend thanks to the reference staff of the Hawaii State Archives; the American Philatelic Research Library; Gary K. Beito, executive director, USS *Arizona* Memorial Museum Association; James H. Charleton, NPS historian, whose provocative comments added immeasurably to this chapter; Michaelyn P. Chou, Ph.D., head of public services, Special Collections, University of Hawaii-Manoa Library; Gary T. Cummins, former superintendent, USS *Arizona* Memorial; William K. Dickinson, former superintendent, USS *Arizona* Memorial; Robert J. Du Bois; Ray Emory of the Pearl Harbor Survivors Association; Professor Brian Hayashi, Koryo College, Japan; George Lang of KGO-TV in San Francisco, California; Daniel J. Lenihan, chief of the Submerged Cultural Resources Unit, NPS; Richard C. Malley, curator of the Mariners' Museum; Daniel A. Martinez, historian at the USS *Arizona* Memorial; Janet Michaelieu, librarian, Arizona Historical Society; Professor Franklin S. Odo, University of Hawaii-Manoa; Gary L. Price, journalist, USS *Missouri;* Ted Przychoda, for his kindness in sharing some of his magnificent collection of visual materials; Sandy Saunders of the Pearl Harbor Survivors Association; Michael Slackman, whose own work on the USS *Arizona* Memorial was very helpful; Professor John Stephan, University of Hawaii-Manoa; Lt. Mark Walker, public affairs officer, USS *Missouri;* Herschel Whittington, development director, and Loretta Rodriguez, executive secretary, of the Confederate Air Force.

I also wish to acknowledge others who have helped me in various ways: Don Weber, director of grants, and the Faculty Development Board at the University of Wisconsin-Oshkosh, which made it financially possible for me to travel to the various battlefields; and Professor Paul Boyer of the University of Wisconsin-Madison, who offered insightful comments on early chapter drafts, as did Professors Michael Sherry of Northwestern University and David Chidester of the University of Cape Town, South Africa. David's provocative work in religious studies has been a great help to me, and I will cherish as well the memory of having been the best man at his wedding. Bruce Craig, cultural resources coordinator for the National Parks and Conservation Association, offered interesting materials that were helpful in the Gettysburg and Little Bighorn chapters, while Erin Czech, interlibrary loan librarian at the University of Wisconsin-Oshkosh, always greeted my mountains of requests with a smile, and with efficiency. David Muench provided the magnificent photograph that graces the jacket. Thanks also to William C. Davis, editor in chief of the National Historical Society; Professor John W. Dower, University of California-San Diego; Professor J. B. Harley, University of Wisconsin-Milwaukee; Barry Mackintosh, NPS historian; Professor John K. Roth, Claremont-McKenna College; Professor Tony Sherill, University of Indiana-Indianapolis; Professor Jerry Stark, Department of Sociology, University of Wisconsin-Oshkosh; and Michael D. Watson, chief of the Division of Interpretation, NPS—all of whom made thoughtful and provocative suggestions about this book at various stages of its development.

Finally, some personal words of thanks to those people who made the years I spent on this project livable ones. For memories that I will hold forever, I thank Bo Schembechler, Glen Rice, Rumeal Robinson, et al. To the Board of Directors, I am proud to be a member. To Dr. Arthur J. Linenthal and Violet B. Linenthal, congratulations for receiving the Family

Proofreaders of the Year Award. To Elizabeth G. Dulany, Theresa L. Sears, and the staff of the University of Illinois Press, heartfelt thanks for all your efforts. Little did I realize when I met Liz in 1985 that I would eventually publish two books with the Press. Nor did I realize what an immensely pleasurable experience it would be. To Professor Emeritus Thomas E. White and my colleagues in the Department of Religious Studies at the University of Wisconsin-Oshkosh, my thanks for providing a supportive environment in which to write. And to my wife, Ulla, and our sons, Aaron and Jacob, a very big thank you for putting up with my long absences.

Introduction

This book is about the processes of veneration, defilement, and redefinition that have characterized public attitudes toward America's most famous battlefields: the Lexington Green and Concord's North Bridge, the Alamo, Gettysburg, the Little Bighorn, and Pearl Harbor. These battlefields function in diverse ways. On the one hand, they are ceremonial centers where various forms of veneration reflect the belief that the contemporary power and relevance of the "lessons" of the battle are crucial for the continued life of the nation. Furthermore, many people believe that the patriotic inspiration to be extracted from these sacred places depends not only on proper ceremony but on a memorialized, preserved, restored, and purified environment. On the other hand, these battlesites are civil spaces where Americans of various ideological persuasions come, not always reverently, to compete for the ownership of powerful national stories and to argue about the nature of heroism, the meaning of war, the efficacy of martial sacrifice, and the significance of preserving the patriotic landscape of the nation.

With the exception of Native American peoples, Americans are not used to classifying their land as "sacred." Holy land is elsewhere, usually thought of in connection with the centers of Judaism, Christianity, and Islam. Hence, many people have no trouble perceiving Jerusalem, Rome, and Mecca as sacred ground, but they would not think to elevate America's battlefields to the same status. Yet, like all other peoples, Americans do not—indeed, could not—live in a cultural environment in which all space is perceived to have the same value. Even the Puritans, immediate inheritors of the Reformation ideology that denied the sacredness of certain places, betrayed such belief in practice. The Puritan meetinghouse, for example, stood at the symbolic center of Puritan towns; and these same Puritans, through the "rhetoric of paradise"—which celebrated the opportunity to find or build the New Jerusalem—and the "rhetoric of wilderness"—an ominous, chaotic, often evil space to be conquered physically and spiritually—provided generations of Americans with images of the New World as sacred space.

In the formative years of nation building, the natural landscape of America became dotted with places considered sacred. The first half of the nineteenth century found religious groups such as the Shakers using the rhetoric of paradise as they established communes where earthly and heavenly space could meet, where earthly space could be transformed into the New Jerusalem. The Mormons believed that the Garden of Eden was to be found in the United States. John Sears, in his study of tourist attractions of the nineteenth century, argues that Niagara Falls, Mammoth Cave, Yellowstone, and Yosemite, for example, were perceived as sacred environments, places of power where God chose to manifest himself through the spectacular beauty of the natural order. Tourists went to these places with the same kind of expectations medieval pilgrims carried on their journeys to sacred sites. According to Patrick McGreevy, to see Niagara Falls "was to glimpse the power and majesty of God, and perhaps to be transformed by the encounter."[1] In his poem "A Sabbath at Niagara," Abraham Cole exclaims:

> If, in th' immensity of space,
> God makes one spot his special dwelling-place,
> That spot is this.[2]

Pope Pius IX also called attention to the power of this particular space when he chose in 1861 to establish a pilgrim shrine at the falls.

At the same time that Americans were celebrating the presence and power of the divine in such natural shrines, they were constructing a complex patriotic landscape. Wilbur Zelinsky notes that visitation to many of these power points was fueled by "the rise of historic preservation, monument building on a grand scale, the institutionalized celebration of the national past, improved transportation, and greater affluence."[3] The most obvious example is Washington, D.C., which was consciously designed as the ceremonial center of the nation. John F. Wilson characterizes Washington as the American Mecca for "pilgrimage on behalf of the American polity." Certainly, the monuments and memorials and the neoclassical architecture of the capital express the grandeur of the American experiment and the power of patriotic inspiration. Speaking of the Washington Monument, for example, Wilson asks, "What is one to make of the 'father of his country' when he is commemorated by an outsize phallus dominating the landscape? Could it be appropriate except to celebrate a nation whose reach spans the continent and whose mission girdles the globe?" He also notes that the Lincoln Memorial is clearly a "classic temple, raised in commemoration of the charismatic leader" who was engaged in the "struggle to preserve the sacred American Union."[4]

The patriotic landscape extends far beyond the nation's capital. Patriotic pilgrims visit the site of primal origins, Plymouth Rock, and the site of the political birthplace of the nation, Independence Hall, with its treasured relic—displayed in its own building—the Liberty Bell. Birthplaces and burial sites of national saints dot the land: Mount Vernon, Monticello, Lincoln's birthplace and tomb, the gravesite of John F. Kennedy, marked by an eternal flame, and the gravesite of the Reverend Dr. Martin Luther King, Jr. The recently refurbished Statue of Liberty and the newly restored complex of buildings on Ellis Island express the enduring power of the "Promised Land." Pilgrims are also attracted to places transformed by cataclysmic public events: Ford's Theatre in Washington, D.C.—the site of the assassination of Abraham Lincoln—and the house across the street, where the president died and in which visitors can see the blood-stained pillow on which his head rested; and the Texas School Book Depository in Dallas, the infamous building from which Lee Harvey Oswald fired the shots that killed President Kennedy.

These famous pilgrimage sites represent only some of the most recognizable features of this landscape. American domestic and commercial space—the places where people do their daily living—are saturated with various kinds of patriotic symbols, including the widespread display and enduring veneration of the American flag, which, Zelinsky argues, has "preempted the place, visually and otherwise, of the crucifix in older Christian lands." Similarly, Zelinsky analyzes the popularity of various cultural uses of the American eagle, which "has yet to reach its peak as a decorative accent on the exterior and grounds of the American house."[5]

Dominating the patriotic landscape are various places that memorialize war. Beyond memorial halls, auditoriums, and veterans hospitals, this martial landscape consists of street names, memorial highways—Monument Drive in Richmond, Virginia, being one obvious example—memorial parks, military cemeteries, war museums, and monuments ranging from whole memorial complexes—the Indiana War Memorial Plaza in Indianapolis, for example—to thousands of statues in cities and towns throughout the nation. Martial pilgrimage sites represent some of the most popular attractions in the country: for example, the Tomb of the Unknown Soldier in Arlington National Cemetery, the Marine Corps War Memorial (popularly known as the Iwo Jima Memorial) and the Vietnam Veterans Memorial in Washington, D.C., and Valley Forge.[6]

Conspicuous by their presence on the martial landscape are battlefields, prime examples of sacred patriotic space where memories of the transformative power of war and the sacrificial heroism of the warrior are preserved. These sites, symbolically transformed by the events that took place there, are visited by those who seek environmental intimacy in order to experience patriotic inspiration. The civic importance of such intimacy was clearly articulated in the mid-nineteenth century by persons interested in the preservation of George Washington's revolutionary war headquarters at New-burgh, New York: "If the love of country is excited when we read the biography of our Revolutionary heroes . . . how much more will the flame of patriotism burn in our bosoms when we tread the ground where was shed the blood of our fathers, or when we move among the scenes where were conceived and consummated their noble achievements."[7]

Like visitors to the sacred natural sites of the nation, visitors to battle-fields often use religious language to express their awe, having stood on ground sanctified by the "blood of our fathers." In 1886 J. Howard Wert remarked in his guidebook to the Gettysburg battlefield that "those who have traversed with us these rock-crowned cliffs have gone over the most consecrated ground this world contains, except the path of the Savior of the world as he ascended the rugged heights of Calvary." During his visit to the Little Bighorn in 1957, J. R. Kelly exclaimed, "I remained alone at the 'monument,' memories flooded my mind. . . . I thought of another bleak and barren hill . . . and of a MAN who stood there long, long ago—His garments stripped from his body. I thought of an old parable: 'Take the shoes from off thy feet—you stand on sacred ground.' "[8]

The evocative power of battlefields has engendered various forms of veneration: patriotic rhetoric, monument building, physical preservation, and battle reenactment. Patriotic rhetoric reveals a persistent faith in the inspirational powers of words. As we will see, it is made up of "fixed" translations of the patriotic canon and serves to establish and continually reinforce the primal themes of patriotic orthodoxy: war as holy crusade, bringing new life to the nation and the warrior as a culture hero and savior, often likened to Christ. This is the language of conservation; it asks people to preserve, protect, perpetuate, reawaken, revitalize, and rededicate them-selves to the ideals for which sacrificial warriors died. The heroic era of the battle and the heroism displayed in the battle itself are perceived as "re-positor[ies] of precedents,"[9] and continued adherence to these precedents is deemed crucial to the life of the nation.

Because one of the functions of monuments is to "make it worthwhile to be a descendant,"[10] guardians of patriotic faith also engage in monument building on battlefields. Generations of Americans have established endur-ing statements of patriotic faith, from the Revolutionary Monument on Lexington Green, erected in 1799, and the USS *Arizona* Memorial in Pearl Harbor, dedicated in 1962, to the battlefield at Gettysburg, where more than thirteen hundred monuments and markers reveal our continued fas-cination with this form of veneration. However, as we will see, the contro-versies that have erupted over the design, placement, and treatment of martial monuments illustrate the intense desire of diverse groups to dom-inate in an enduring manner these sacred spaces.

Patriotic rhetoric and monument building are designed to ensure continued allegiance to patriotic orthodoxy. Physical preservation is designed to preserve the sanctity of the site itself and to separate sacred space from surrounding secular space. There are often attempts to restore or to "freeze" the natural landscape of the battlefield as it was at the time of the battle so that visitors can reflect on the meaning of the epic event in an "authentic" landscape. Those who believe in inviolate boundaries around such sacred space often clash with those who prize land for commercial purposes and resent what is to them the wasteful veneration of prime property.

Battle reenactment is another form of veneration, especially for those who feel that merely being present on the battlefield is not enough. Reenactors seek imaginative entry into the heroic past, re-creating the total environment of the time of the battle and thus paying meticulous attention to the authenticity of the clothes they wear and the food they eat. Many reenactors study the history of the battle in which they will take part, in order to bring the "real" past to life and to help spectators "see" the battle as it occurred. Sometimes these reenactments spark considerable controversy, as was the case with the numerous reenactments that took place during the Civil War Centennial in the 1960s and continued through April 1990, when the end of the 125th anniversary of the war was celebrated in Virginia. Are such reenactments "educational," as proponents claim? Do they really motivate spectators to learn about American history? Or, as critics argue, are they activities that continue to present the dangerous illusion that war is glamorous activity?

These forms of veneration are both an articulation of patriotic orthodoxy and a symbolic defense against various forms of ideological defilement (heresy) and physical defilement. Patriotic rhetoric persistently warns that the danger of falling away from the ideals of the culture heroes who died in battle is always present, and the weakening of patriotic resolve, clearly apparent in any unwillingness to obey the nation's summons to arms, is considered clear evidence of indifference to or hostility toward the welfare of the nation. Inevitably, patriotic rhetoric warns, such attitudes are heretical: they make the blood sacrifice of past generations of American warriors meaningless. Those concerned with maintaining the purity of the sacred environment struggle against other forms of contamination as they work to protect sites against inauthenticity in museum displays and gift shop items and as they contend with the forces of modernity—suburbs and shopping centers, for example—that threaten to penetrate the boundaries and permanently alter (hence defile) the sacred ground. For some, the attempt to redefine the meaning of the battle is itself perceived as an act of heresy.

Attempts at redefinition have taken place as the voices of "outsiders" have begun to be heard in American culture. Some of these outsiders have done battle with the guardians of patriotic faith, declaring, "You don't own these symbols, we do." For example, the Peoples Bicentennial Commission claimed that the official ceremonies in 1976 had perverted authentic revolutionary war tradition, a tradition of dissent in which their protest at Concord was consciously rooted. Some Mexican Americans reject the heroic creation myth of Texas as an Anglo-American gloss over imperialistic acts, while others seek to restore to their rightful place the Tejanos (Mexican Texans) who fought *in* the Alamo. At Gettysburg, diverse ceremonies at the 125th anniversary in 1988 revealed different readings of the meaning of the Civil War. Growing sensitivity to less-heroic interpretations of the Anglo-American conquest of the frontier has profoundly altered the National Park Service's interpretation of the significance of the battle of the Little Bighorn. And at Pearl Harbor, the Park Service is charged with interpreting a site that for many is still an "open wound." Further, the NPS must construct an appropriate set of fiftieth anniversary ceremonies at Pearl Harbor in 1991, ceremonies that must be provocative and still palatable to ideologically diverse audiences.

David Chidester reminds us that the sacredness of symbols is "directly related to the energy generated when people appropriate them, invest in them, and fight over them in the always contested struggles over ownership."[11] The energy expended over the contested spaces of these American battlefields, revealed in the processes of veneration, defilement, and redefinition, offers graphic evidence of their enduring significance as sacred ground.

Notes

1. John Sears, *Sacred Places: American Tourist Attractions in the Nineteenth Century* (New York: Oxford University Press, 1989), esp. pp. 12–30, 31–48, 122–55, 156–81; Patrick McGreevy, "Niagara as Jerusalem," *Landscape* 28, no. 2 (1985): 29.

2. Quoted in McGreevy, p. 29.

3. Wilbur Zelinsky, *Nation into State: The Shifting Symbolic Foundations of American Nationalism* (Chapel Hill: University of North Carolina Press, 1988), p. 95. Zelinsky's chapter entitled "Nationalism on the Landscape" is an excellent survey of the patriotic landscape of the nation.

4. John F. Wilson, "The Status of 'Civil Religion,'" in *The Religion of the Republic*, ed. Elwyn A. Smith (Philadelphia: Fortress Press, 1971), p. 4.

5. Zelinsky, pp. 196, 201.

6. The primary virtue of James M. Mayo's *War Memorials as Political Landscape: The American Experience and Beyond* (New York: Praeger, 1988) is his detailed compilation of the various elements of the martial landscape in America. Each of the popular pilgrimage sites I mention deserves treatment in its own right. And certainly some of these have been the scenes of the kinds of struggle over symbolic ownership

that have taken place at American battlefields. The sensitivity regarding martial monuments is perhaps best revealed in the celebrated controversies over the Vietnam Veterans Memorial. For a thorough introduction to this story, see Jan C. Scruggs and Joel L. Swerdlow, *To Heal a Nation: The Vietnam Veterans Memorial* (New York: Harper and Row, 1985). There have been similar controversies regarding Vietnam veterans monuments throughout the nation. For an introduction to such monument-building activity, see Jerry L. Strait and Sandra S. Strait, *Vietnam War Memorials: An Illustrated Reference to Veterans Tributes throughout the United States* (Jefferson, N.C.: McFarland and Co., 1988). See also Elizabeth Hess, "Vietnam: Memorials of Misfortune," in *Unwinding the Vietnam War: From War into Peace,* ed. Reese Williams (Seattle: Real Comet Press, 1987), pp. 262–79. For an insightful treatment of the development of Valley Forge as a sacred site on the patriotic landscape, see Barbara Powell MacDonald, "The Most Celebrated Encampment: Valley Forge in American Culture, 1777–1983" (Ph.D. diss., Cornell University, 1983).

7. Quoted in David Lowenthal, "Past Time, Present Place: Landscape and Memory," *Geographical Review* 65, no. 1 (1976): 13.

8. Wert, quoted in Reuben M. Rainey, "The Memory of War: Reflections on Battlefield Preservation," in *Yearbook of Landscape Architecture,* ed. Richard L. Austin (New York: Van Nostrand, 1983), p. 72; J. R. Kelly, *The Battle of the Little Big Horn: Requiem for the Men in the Shadows* (n.p., 1957), p. 16.

9. Eric Hobsbawm, "The Social Function of the Past: Some Questions," *Past and Present* 55 (May 1972): 13.

10. Barrie B. Greenbie, *Spaces: Dimensions of the Human Landscape* (New Haven: Yale University Press, 1981), p. 247.

11. See David Chidester, "Shots in the Streets: Religion, Violence, South Africa," ms., author's files, p. 25.

1

"The Pivot on Which the World Turns"

The road to Lexington and Concord began in Boston. Although Gen. Thomas Gage and some thirty-five hundred British troops had occupied that rebellious city since May 1774, they were powerless beyond Boston. In the spring of 1775, after his spies reported that military supplies were being stockpiled in Worcester and in Concord, Gage seized the opportunity to launch a surprise attack on the closer of the two towns. On April 18, 1775, he sent approximately eight hundred men, led by Lt. Col. Francis Smith and Maj. John Pitcairn, to destroy military stores in Concord and capture resistance leaders there. There would be no surprise, however, for on the way to Concord the British had to pass through Lexington, and Paul Revere, on his fabled midnight ride, had already stopped at the Reverend Jonas Clarke's house to sound the alarm. As the town bells pealed, Lexington minutemen gathered on the Green under the command of Capt. John Parker.

By two o'clock that morning the British had not yet appeared, so the Lexingtonians dispersed until shortly before daybreak, when approximately seventy men spread out in two thin lines to face the British on the Green. Pitcairn remembered that he "instantly called to [his] soldiers not to fire but to surround them and disarm them." Captain Parker also gave an order "to disperse and not to fire." But somebody did fire, prompting the British troops to break ranks and begin shooting at will. The result, Parker said, was that the British killed "eight of our party, with out receiving any provocation therefor from us." As shocked and grieving onlookers came forward to retrieve the bodies of their loved ones and treat the wounded, the British fired a victory volley and continued on to Concord.

Alerted in the early morning hours by Dr. Samuel Prescott, the sleepy citizens of Concord scrambled to disperse the precious military stores. Maj. John Buttrick assembled a company of minutemen at the Wright Tavern as the alarm spread throughout neighboring communities and beyond. With dawn approaching on April 19, approximately one hundred fifty men gathered in the center of Concord. Some marched out to meet the enemy but retreated in the face of the "red coats and glistening arms." As the British approached the town, Col. James Barrett led his men to high ground on the west side of the North Bridge.

The British were able to uncover and destroy only modest caches of military equipment. Then they set about burning down the town's liberty pole. The blaze ignited the courthouse roof, and while the fire was quickly put out, clouds of smoke could be seen by the four hundred minutemen now gathered beyond the bridge. Convinced that the British intended to burn Concord to the ground, the minutemen resolved to stop them and set off in pairs toward the bridge. After a half-hearted attempt to render the North Bridge uncrossable, the three British companies on the east side fired a volley at the approaching men. Capt. Isaac David of the Acton minutemen fell dead, as did Acton's Abner Hosmer. Major Buttrick then declared, "Fire, fellow soldiers, for God's sake, fire," and the ensuing shots wounded several British soldiers, three of whom died.

Two hours later the British began their tortuous fifteen-mile march back to Boston along the Battle Road. Besieged at every turn by minutemen who used the natural cover of the countryside to inflict heavy losses, the British troops fled back to Lexington in a panic. They were saved only by the appearance of Sir Hugh Percy's First Brigade.

The fighting at Lexington Green and at Concord's North Bridge lasted no more than a few minutes. But those famous minutes sanctified the ground on which American patriots died.

Lexington and Concord

A MID THE RUSTIC BEAUTY of the stately New England towns of Lexington and Concord are two sacred martial centers that symbolize the birth of the nation on April 19, 1775. Both Lexington Green, where Capt. John Parker and the minutemen offered themselves as martyrs to the revolutionary cause, and Concord's North Bridge, where the first British soldiers died in battle, are familiar sites on the American patriotic landscape.

Commemorative events in Lexington and Concord provided the occasion for various forms of patriotic veneration. These rituals celebrated the creation of a republic that had come into being through the agency of holy war and that symbolized the most profound revolution in human affairs the world had yet witnessed. In both towns, consequently, various forms of veneration centered on the warriors who had brought about this birth. Emerging from such veneration was the public construction of a uniquely American image of warriors, the minutemen, described by Ralph Waldo Emerson in 1835 as "poor farmers who came up that day to defend their native soil," acting "from the simplest instincts."[1]

These instinctive warriors were ceremonially perceived as men whose New England origins nurtured republican principles that protected them from the moral pollution of old-world warriors. Consequently, the minuteman became a powerful cultural model for generations of Americans at war and at peace: from Billy Yank and Johnny Reb in the Civil War to the doughboys of World War I and the GI's of World War II; from the rightwing Minutemen of the 1960s to a more recent transformation into the Minuteman intercontinental ballistic missile.

Patriotic rhetoric portrayed the minutemen as Christ-like saviors, and citizens of Lexington and Concord were proud that these new-world warriors drank from the wellsprings of liberty which, they believed, ran especially deep in their towns. Yet these same commemorative events witnessed the use of rhetorical strategies of the jeremiad, brooding over the ever-widening gap between the principles the minutemen fought for and the sorry condition of contemporary American society. Accordingly, patriotic celebrations often became ceremonies of rededication. Yet only occasionally, after the Civil War, for example, were there events powerful enough for celebrants to believe that, like the minutemen of the Revolution, they too had endured the crucible of holy war and successfully navigated the patriotic rite of passage.

The veneration of the minutemen also found expression in attempts to memorialize or alter the patriotic landscape: monument building in both Lexington and Concord; the recent construction of a "commemorative" bridge on the site of the old North Bridge in Concord; and the ongoing efforts of the National Park Service (NPS) to re-create the physical environment of 1775 along the Battle Road (on which the British retreated from Concord to Boston), an effort that called for the rerouting of a major highway (Route 2A).

Beyond the ever-present threat of failing to measure up to the principles embodied by the minutemen, the specter of defilement appeared in other ways. Beginning in rancorous debate in the 1820s, a number of citizens of Lexington and Concord claimed that *their* town was the authentic birthplace of the nation. Each was accused of falsifying the national creation story by refusing to grant this sacred status to the other. Controversies that at first glance seemed to be part of a quaint and amusing New England family argument revealed, on closer inspection, a passion that has not been fully spent to this day. Where did the Revolution begin? Where was the first battle? If the encounter on Lexington Green was not a battle but a massacre, were the martyred minutemen really the first models of how Americans die in war or just further examples of colonial victims? And if they were only victims, could that affect popular perception of the potency of their sacrifice? Or, as Lexingtonians argued, had Concord partisans conveniently and arrogantly overlooked the first battle of the war (Lexington) and, in the process, overlooked the first real sacrifice of Americans at war.

On occasion, what some people perceived as defilement, others viewed as creative attempts to redefine the meaning of the events of April 19, 1775. Both the Vietnam Veterans Against the War and the Peoples Bicentennial Commission understood Lexington and Concord to be sacred ground when they held separate protests on the Battle Green and at the North Bridge in the mid-1970s. In their view, the purpose of protest was not desecration of a sacred spot, for they believed the *real* defilement had been perpetrated by a new class of American Tories who had severed the link between revolutionary war principles (especially the principle of dissent) and contemporary American life. Each group believed that its protest would spark the recovery of the American revolutionary tradition, which was viewed as crucial to the resuscitation of authentic American values that had fallen into disrepair because of public apathy.

Citizens of Lexington began promptly to commemorate the bloody confrontation between the minutemen and the British regulars on Lexington Green. In 1776 Rev. Jonas Clarke, Lexington's influential minister, started the practice of annual memorial sermons. By 1791 citizens had been frustrated in their requests to Congress for funds to build a monument to the revolutionary martyrs, but by 1797 the Massachusetts General Court had agreed to provide the town with such funds. On July 4, 1799, a monument was dedicated. The names of the eight minutemen who died on the Green were inscribed in stone, as were the words of Rev. Jonas Clarke, words that over the centuries would remind visitors that "the Freedom & Independence of America [is] Sealed & Defended with the Blood of Her Sons." The events of April 19, 1775, were also celebrated in patriotic rhetoric in Fourth of July festivities throughout the early decades of the nineteenth century. The first Nineteenth of April celebration in Lexington took place in 1822, when twenty survivors helped reenact the battle. William Munroe, who had formed the line of minutemen on the Green in 1775, did so again and attested to the accuracy of the famous words attributed to Capt. John Parker (and later inscribed on a commemorative boulder marking the line of battle):

Stand Your Ground
Don't Fire Unless Fired Upon
But If They Mean To Have A War
Let It Begin Here

As Munroe noted, "Them is the very words Captain Parker spoke."[2]

On April 20, 1835, the remains of the minutemen were moved from the Old Burying Ground in Lexington to a stone vault in the monument. "A lead box containing a history of the Battle, orders of the day, names of those present, and a program of the ceremonies of 1835" was deposited with the sarcophagus. "All flags were at half mast during the funeral service, and a procession from the First Parish Church to the new burying place included twelve survivors of the original 19. Guns echoed in a series of salutes."[3]

In 1850 a joint seventy-fifth anniversary celebration with Concord was held at the North Bridge. Doris L. Pullen and Donald B. Cobb describe the activities: "The two towns worked out a monumental union celebration to which representatives of all the towns that had sent men to the Battle in '75 were invited. Special trains brought visitors from Boston. . . . At 11:00 A.M. a procession marched to the monument beside the Concord River [the granite obelisk erected in 1836 on the spot where the British soldiers fell] and then back to the center of Concord to a huge pavilion erected for the banquet and orations." Concord homes were brightly decorated in national colors, and bells and cannon salutes added to the cultivation of martial spirit. During the festivities, two survivors of the events of April 19, 1775, were introduced, ninety-two-year-old Jonathan Harrington and ninety-four-year-old Amos Baker, who were greeted with a "succession of cheers upon cheers."[4]

Lexington and Concord held massive but separate ceremonies on the centennial in 1875.[5] In his history of the town, Charles Hudson writes, "Before '75 Lexington still celebrated in her own quiet, delightful way." The centennial was anything but quiet or delightful for residents, however, as more than a hundred thousand visitors braved freezing weather to attend the ceremonies. Hudson notes that there were "crowded trains that wouldn't move" and "hungry mobs that raided private larders and invaded the most sacred precincts of our homes." Despite this, David B. Little assures us, "houses were decorated, historic spots marked." Many of the relics on display at Lexington—Captain Parker's musket, a British musket, a cannon ball, various portraits of the battle, and the autograph of Jonathan Harrington—attracted a great deal of attention.[6] After his visit to Concord, Pres. Ulysses Grant, Vice Pres. Henry Wilson, and a host of other political dignitaries made their way to Lexington to attend patriotic observances in a tent, located on the Battle Green, that held some seven thousand guests.

Ceremonies between 1875 and the turn of the century were largely local affairs. Inevitably, perhaps, festivity became more and more intertwined with sober commemoration. Grand balls (initially held in 1855), elaborate parades, concerts, and patriotic instruction for children were regular parts of commemorations during this period. Significantly, April 19 finally became a legal holiday—Patriots' Day—in Massachusetts in 1894.[7] That year, more than forty thousand visitors came to Lexington. According to Pullen and Cobb, "When 'Paul Revere' rode through town at midnight, he was followed by some 200 bicycle riders. The newly formed Lexington Drum Corps and the school color guards marched over the Paul Revere route at 5:00 A.M. . . . At sunrise and sunset bells were rung and salutes fired, and children were entertained in the Town Hall. . . . During the afternoon there were two band concerts on the Green and a Town Hall banquet."[8]

The Captain Parker Monument (also called the Lexington Minuteman), the work of sculptor Henry H. Kitson, was dedicated on the 125th anniversary of the battle in 1900. Standing on the edge of the Green, the monument was designed, according to one observer, to teach its "silent lesson" to the "wayfarer who stops to read its story . . . to the children coming home from school; to the workman going to their labors, to the worshippers returning from their devotions." As such, it joined the 1799 monument and several commemorative boulders as permanent statements of patriotic faith. The Lexington Minuteman changed the Green, according to a 1959 report by the Boston National Historic Sites Commission, from

The Revolutionary Monument (1799), on Lexington Green.
(Joe Ofria, The Image Inn, Arlington, Mass.)

The Lexington Minuteman, also known as the Captain Parker Statue, on Lexington Green. (Joe Ofria, The Image Inn, Arlington, Mass.)

The Minuteman Boulder, on Lexington Green. (Boston Athenaeum)

Ralph Waldo Emerson's "Concord Hymn" was read at the dedication of this monument at the North Bridge, in Concord, on July 4, 1837. The monument stands on the east side of the river, where the British soldiers fell. (National Park Service)

The North Bridge was restored in time for the Centennial in 1875. Photograph by A. W. Hosmer. (National Park Service)

The North Bridge was again restored, in 1950. (National Park Service)

Daniel Chester French's Minuteman Statue, near the North Bridge.
(Concord Free Public Library, Concord, Mass.)

The Acton Monument (1851), which honors Isaac Davis. (Acton Historical Society, Inc., Acton, Mass.)

An arch was erected at the entrance to Lexington Green for the centennial celebration in 1875. (Concord Free Public Library, Concord, Mass.)

This drawing of a civil and military parade during the centennial celebration in Concord appeared in *Frank Leslie's Illustrated Newspaper*. Drawing by Harry Ogden and E. R. Morse. (Concord Free Public Library, Concord, Mass.)

A sizable crowd gathered at North Bridge for centennial services in 1875. Photograph by A. W. Hosmer. (National Park Service)

a "casually maintained open space for the common use of the inhabitants into a monumental park."[9]

Throughout the nineteenth and twentieth centuries elaborate programs took place every twenty-five years, with smaller commemorations in most other years. In 1956 a Town Celebrations Committee was made responsible for future Nineteenth of April activities in Lexington, and during the 1960s a recognizable pattern emerged. The town conducted private ceremonies for its own citizens in the morning. At six o'clock the "alarm" was rung in the Old Belfry, as it had been in 1775, followed shortly thereafter by the pealing of Lexington's church bells. A sunrise parade began at seven o'clock and one hour later descended on the Green, where the American flag was raised. Later, the men who portrayed the minutemen in the parades or battle reenactments placed a wreath at the base of the Captain Parker Monument. At about the same time various athletic events began. Public ceremonies in the afternoon consisted of parades and speeches, and there was a Patriots' Ball in the evening.

Before the Marquis de Lafayette visited Concord in 1824, "little note was taken of the anniversary."[10] On April 19, 1825, the prestigious orator Edward Everett delivered a commemorative address, a task he would also carry out in Lexington in 1835. In 1875 the centennial celebration in Concord was as elaborate as the one in Lexington. One newspaper reported that the processions in both towns "were of an imposing order, each being nearly two miles long, and composed of Minutemen, companies of ladies and gentlemen dressed in ancient costume, besides delegations in carriages from most of the towns that responded to the alarms of a century ago. There was a profusion of decorations . . . salutes of a hundred guns at sunrise and sunset.[11] Oration and banquet tents were erected, Ralph Waldo Emerson and James Russell Lowell spoke, and the thousands of visitors suffered through the same miserable conditions as those in Lexington. The principal event of the Concord centennial was the unveiling of Daniel Chester French's Minute Man Statue at the North Bridge.

As in Lexington, almost every celebration in Concord of an additional twenty-five years evolved into an elaborate and festive occasion. The *Middlesex Patriot* reported that at the 125th anniversary celebration on April 19–20, 1900, there were ten thousand visitors. The first day of activities was highlighted by commemorative services at the various churches, the marking of graves, and parades, concerts, and a patriotic meeting. On the second day there was a parade to the bridge and a reenactment of the battle. A letter from Prescott Keyes, chairman of Concord's Nineteenth of April Committee, to "invited guests" details the drama that would unfold: "Several companies of Provincials . . . will march down this hill, ahead of the parade, and attack the British holding the Bridge. The Provincials will drive the British from the Bridge, this clearing the way for the parade, personifying All America, to cross."[12]

In 1925 a number of towns joined Concord in the 150th anniversary festivities. Gen. John J. Pershing and Vice Pres. Charles G. Dawes journeyed to both Lexington and Concord. Activities, in addition to traditional events, included the issuance of commemorative stamps and coins. In Lexington the celebration extended into summer, highlighted by the three-night presentation in June of playwright Sidney Howard's *Lexington*. No other joint ceremonies were held until 1961, when fourteen towns, including Lexington and Concord, held a three-day celebration. That year the ceremonies began on April 18 with a military ball and militia drill exercises. At 1:30 A.M. on April 19 there was a "mobilization of the spirit of '61" at Wright Tavern in Concord, with the reenactment of Dr. Samuel Prescott's early morning warning to Col. James Barrett, commander of the 1775 militia, that the British were marching. According to the program of events, "On order . . . the bells will ring in the town square with rolling of drums and assembly bugle call. The merchants . . . will light up their stores for thirty minutes."[13]

At approximately 5:30 that morning, as the sun rose, the celebration continued with an artillery salute by the Concord Independent Battery which accompanied the flag raising at North Bridge; this was followed by religious services and a pancake breakfast sponsored by the Lions Club. At 9:00 a large parade made its way to the North Bridge for the main ceremonies: the singing of Emerson's "Concord Hymn," the reading of a message from the governor, a variety of speeches, wreath laying at the graves of the British soldiers and at the Minute Man Statue, a series of musket volleys, and the playing of taps. The parade then returned to Monument Square in the center of Concord and gathered around the Civil War Memorial for a short service in honor of Concord's Civil War veterans. Various other short dedication ceremonies took place at important spots along the Battle Road. Even the high school track meet was held within a commemorative atmosphere. The master plan for the celebration indicated that the "track meet will be opened by brief ceremony by color guard and American Legion Posts . . . in honor of Concord High School boys who gave their lives in World War II for whom memorial trophies and medals are named."

Throughout the rich history of commemorative activity in Lexington and Concord the dominant figure has been the minuteman. Early-morning ceremonies reenact the dramatic warnings brought to neighboring communities by Paul Revere, William Dawes, and the aforementioned Samuel Prescott. Occasional battle reenactments in the nineteenth century prefigured the popularity of Civil War reenactments beginning in the 1960s. A group of minutemen was organized in Lexington in 1874 and outfitted in Continental uniforms; the group was disbanded in 1876, then reactivated permanently in 1910. In 1962 in Concord, the town selectmen and the Concord Ceremonies and Celebrations Committee called for the "mustering of a new company of militia to be known as the Concord Minute Men . . . and that this company be formed as a representative body of modern-day Concord." Volunteers would be expected to perform at various town ceremonies and reenactments and to aid in teaching colonial history to children. On January 12, 1963, over a hundred men turned out for the first muster; by 1964 members had learned to play the fife and drum and were outfitted in homespun uniforms.[14]

Both the Captain Parker Monument and French's Minute Man Statue idealize this unique American warrior. However, the articulation of the nature, function, and legacy of the minuteman is nowhere so clear as in the patriotic speeches attached to this figure. Such rhetoric has helped establish a patriotic orthodoxy designed to satisfy the inquiries of the faithful and the curious: Who were these men? What were their motives? What exactly did they do? What did it mean? The model for these speeches was set in Boston, in 1771, when the city inaugurated an annual lecture on the anniversary of the Boston Massacre. Richard Brown remarks that such speeches "repeatedly described the virtuous patriot and self-consciously tried to exemplify his character, pointing with alarm to the standard ways in which tyranny conquered or seduced a free people."[15]

William Emerson, the Concord minister who watched the battle from his house near the North Bridge, had earlier characterized as holy warriors those who were prepared to resist the British. On March 13, 1775, during a sermon to the town militia company, he spoke of the character of the virtuous soldier: ". . . then we may hope that the Lord God of Israel will go forth with you into the field; then we shall expect you will be enriched in the Arms of God's protecting providence." Lexington's anniversary sermons often identified the minutemen in this way. For example, in a 1782 sermon Rev. Phillips Payson told his audience that a Christian soldier "is a noble character. . . . to your martial address, you will be careful to add the ornaments of our holy, holy religion, and take to yourselves the whole armour of God."[16]

Unlike other warriors of the Lord, the minutemen were viewed as unique. Like their martial father, George Washington, they were "perfectly balanced" fighting men who killed not out of hate but out of the forceful inspiration of the love of liberty. Such moral balance was highlighted even more when the patriot press accused the British of atrocities. Isaiah Thomas's *Massachusetts Spy* of May 3, 1775, declared: "AMERICANS! Forever bear in mind the BATTLE OF LEXINGTON! Where British Troops, unmolested and unprovoked, wantonly, and in a most inhumane manner fired upon and killed a number of our countrymen." Ezekiel Russell published a "Revolutionary Extra Edition" of the *Salem Gazette, or Newbury and Marblehead Advertiser* on April 21, 1775, in which he accused the British of "circumstances of cruelty not less brutal than what our venerable ancestors received from the vilest of savages of the wilderness." The *Essex Gazette* reported that the minutemen were guilty of no such barbarities: "We have the pleasure to say, that, notwithstanding the highest Provocations . . . not one Instance of Cruelty . . . was committed by our victorious Militia; but listening to the merciful dictates of the Christian Religion, they 'Breathed higher Sentiments of Humanity.' "[17]

Edward Everett, the featured orator at Lexington's sixtieth battle anniversary, underscored the belief that the key to the minutemen's victory was their moral condition. They were inspired, he said, not by the "ambition of power, the hope of promotion, nor the temptation of gain" but by "a plain, instinctive sense of patriotic duty." The power of their discipline and duty was celebrated by Rev. Grindall Reynolds during the centennial of the Concord battle when he noted that "in all human history there is no more noble instance of the subordination of passion to duty than the silence, until the lawful order came, of those four hundred muskets at North Bridge." Likewise, during the Lexington centennial Richard Henry Dana remarked that Lexington's sons were "intentionally and intelligently martyrs."[18]

The enduring image of the humane warrior of the New World was cultivated in commemorative rhetoric during the second century of celebration. In 1885, speaking at the 250th anniversary of the incorporation of Concord, George Frisbie Hoar declared that the minutemen "measured their duty with the deliberation and calmness that became men who were to establish constitutions and men who were to preserve them. . . . Every step they took was premeditated, measured, firmly planted and without a retreat. . . . They valued the old-fashioned virtue of consistency, and they practised the old-fashioned virtue of constancy. They detested and rebuked exaggeration." In its 1984 handbook, the Lexington Historical Society told readers that the minutemen were warriors in "whose hands was placed the sublime service of firing the first shot for American freedom, and a Republic of human equality."[19]

Patriotic rhetoric also declared that these unique warriors gave shape to an unparalleled revolution. During the Concord centennial celebration, for example, Rev. Grindall Reynolds insisted that the American Revolution stood alone in world history, for the same "moral and spiritual convictions" had certainly not been present in the Spanish Revolution nor in the French "carnival of blood." The minutemen, he emphasized, were builders, not destroyers. In 1825, during the fiftieth anniversary at Concord, Edward Everett noted that the "liberty achieved, the institutions they [the minutemen] founded, shall remain one common eternal monument to their precious memory."[20]

Only rarely was the unique character of the minutemen and of the Revolution perceived as being attached to a certain race, but the fact that some commemorative events became the occasion for the rhetoric of exclusion is telling. For example, George Curtis's centennial speech at Concord—which was blasted by the editors of the *Boston Pilot* as the "utterance of a person too small in heart and brain to grasp the significance of the Concord centennial"—revealed nativist fears of the day: "We will enter into the second century of the Republic with responsibilities which neither our fathers nor the men of fifty years ago could possibly foresee. Think of the changes wrought by foreign immigration. . . . This enormous influx of foreigners has added an immense ignorance and entire unfamiliarity with republican ideas." On April 18, 1875, the *Boston Courier* declared that the minutemen showed that they had the "indomitable spirit of the Teutonic race, from which they sprang." Sidney Howard's "pageant drama of American freedom," presented during Lexington's celebration in 1925, tells the story of the evolution of freedom through World War I and calls for the chronicler of these events to be of the "fine Anglo-Saxon type." Howard also speaks of "soldiers of freedom out of the past of the race" and notes that out of the battle "came a nation and a nation's race and a race's vision of freedom."[21]

Both towns took pride in the institutions that had nurtured the minutemen. During the Concord centennial, Curtis characterized each New England town as a "small but perfect Republic" and the town meeting as the "nursery of American independence." Indeed, he said, the Revolution was most "fully embodied" in the New Englander. Speaking at Concord's 110th anniversary, James Russell Lowell declared, "It was over that bridge that the town meeting, that *democracy*, in short, in its purest and most beautiful form, marches on to the field of cosmopolitan politics." Likewise, in Lexington in 1913, James Phinney Munroe argued that the battle was fought "in defense of the Town-Meeting, that instrument which in the hands of freemen, is the basis of all efficient government." Munroe characterized the minutemen as simply carrying out "at the foreordained moment the instructions which they had received, Sunday after Sunday, and in town meeting after town meeting, from the voice and pen of their great spiritual leader."[22]

Patriotic rhetoric also noted the significance of what the minuteman had done. He was not only portrayed as a Christian warrior fighting in the sublime cause of liberty, but he was also venerated as a sacrificial figure, bringing the new republic into being through the power of his sacrifice. Lexington's Jonas Clarke, who, like so many of his ministerial colleagues, preached about the moral duty to resist unjust authority, emphasized this theme in his 1776 first-anniversary sermon. The eight minutemen who had died that morning did so, he said, for noble sentiments, "not in their own cause only, but in the cause of the whole people—in the cause of God, their country and posterity." In 1783 Rev. Zabdiel Adams reminded his audience that the minutemen's sacrifice had been Christ-like: "Your friends and townsmen died in so good a cause, that they fell the first victims, and were made a sacrifice for the good of their country." During centennial activities Richard Henry Dana declared that it was Lexington's "felicity" to be "consecrated to the world's use by the blood of her own sons."[23]

Speaking in Concord in 1885, Massachusetts governor George Dexter Robinson noted the efficacy of the minutemen's sacrifice when he spoke of a "joint current of blood from Lexington and Concord, uniting in one Grand Force the power of patriotic devotion to America." In 1961 Maj. Gen. E. N. Harmon (ret.), president of Norwich University, reminded his Concord audience of the tenuous nature of blood sacrifice. American heritage was "bought by blood," he said, but this heritage of sacrifice would have been purchased in vain "if we are overrun and forced into the Communist mold." Similar sentiments were expressed in commemorative rhetoric at Lexington on the occasion of the bicentennial of the battle in 1975, when some thirty thousand spectators gathered on the Battle Green for a modest reenactment. They heard Gov. Michael Dukakis declare that the "richest legacy the world ever received was inscribed in lines of blood upon the battleground of Lexington."[24]

What did this sacrifice mean? One of the most enduring themes of patriotic rhetoric at Lexington and Concord has been that of birth. The parallel to Christian imagery is clear: just as Christ died so that sinners could be reborn, the minutemen died so that a new world could be born. During his visit to Concord in 1796, Timothy Dwight, the eminent Congregational clergyman, president of Yale University, and grandson of Jonathan Edwards, remarked on the birth that was the legacy of the minutemen: "From the plains of Concord will henceforth be dated a change in human affairs, an alteration in the balance of human power, and a new direction to the course of human improvement. Man, from the events which have occurred here, will in some respects assume a new character, and experience in some respects a new destiny." Echoing similar sentiments, Edward Everett, speaking in Concord on the fiftieth anniversary of the battle, reminded his audience that the clash was "one of the elemental occasions in the world's affairs."[25]

During the centennial celebrations in both towns the imagery of a new world emerging from the sacrifice of the minutemen was obvious. In Lexington a large triumphal arch stood at the entrance to the Battle Green, bearing this inscription: "Welcome to the Birthplace of American Liberty." In Concord, after the Rev. Mr. Reynolds asked for divine preparation for the "sacred influences which shall steal into our hearts," James Russell Lowell read his "Ode to Concord," which includes this stanza:

> Yet the earth heard,
> Nor ever hath forgot,
> As on from startled throne to throne,
> Where superstition sate or conscious wrong,
> A shudder ran of some dreadful birth unknown.
> Thrice venerable spot!
> River more fateful than the Rubicon!

Following Lowell, George Curtis compared America's birth in Concord to Christ's birth. Just as angels sang "Glory to God in the highest, for Christ is born," on April 19, Curtis said, they "whispered . . . Good-will to men: America is born."[26]

During Concord's incorporation anniversary in 1885, the "President of the Day," the Honorable John S. Keyes, greeted those assembled at the North Bridge and spoke graphically of the travail of birth. Concord, he insisted, was indeed the "birthplace of American liberty; for if in Boston was the conception, and in Lexington the agonizing throes of deadly pain, here the blessed child was born." This birth was also celebrated in Allen French's 1935 stage play, "The Drama of Concord: A Pageant of Three Centuries." The play reviewed the history of Concord, from the early treaties with the Indians and the hardships of King Philip's War to the uprising against Gov. Edward Andros in 1689, the battle with the British in 1775, and the great literary history of the town in the nineteenth century. During a scene dramatizing colonial times the Spirit of History declared that liberty took root in Concord well before the American Revolution: "There has been liberty in the world before, but this is its new home. For mankind this is a fresh beginning." And after the events of 1775 the Spirit of Concord exclaimed, "Not a man, not a boy, not a woman or child, but begins a new life from this day." This birth image is found even in recent publications of the National Park Service. For example, a 1984 brochure declares, "A thin line of armed Americans, drawn up across Lexington Green on the morning of April 19, 1775 marks the beginning of a new era in world history."[27]

Both the nobility of their character and the decisiveness of their deeds made the minutemen popular cultural models for succeeding generations.

They were the primal patriots. On the centennial anniversary the *New York Communal Advertiser* remarked that the "country should stand with uncovered head before the statue of the Minuteman of Lexington, who left his home at duty's call and taught the world how a free man could die." Yet the minuteman was not only a model of martial sacrifice but also a symbol of unchanging verities in the midst of the never-ending threat of the erosion of patriotic fervor. Consequently, patriotic rhetoric has consistently emphasized rededication to the unchanging principles of the Revolution, embodied by the minuteman. Such allegiance, it has often been proclaimed, provides the surest form of civic orientation in an increasingly problematic world.[28]

Nostalgia for the resurrection of revolutionary principles grew stronger as the ranks of surviving minutemen grew smaller during the first half of the nineteenth century. Even while these venerable figures were still alive, however, orators warned audiences that they must remain attentive to the minuteman's lessons. After witnessing the reinterment of the Lexington minutemen in 1835, Edward Everett turned to the survivors and exclaimed, "Venerable Men! We gaze upon you with respectful emotion." He then reminded the audience that the blood shed "must not sink uncommemorated into the soil."[29] Evidence of patriotic nostalgia was also evident when Jonathan Harrington, the last survivor of the Lexington battle, died in 1854. His funeral was described by the *Boston Post* on March 31, 1854: "A large concourse of people were present" and "streets . . . and yards swarmed with omnibuses, coaches, and carriages of various descriptions." The size of the crowd, estimated at ten thousand, was appropriate, "for no common death had taken place." Numerous speeches were given, and Harrington's life was described as "eventful beyond that which could belong to any other."[30]

George G. Forgie characterizes those who came of age between the end of the Revolution and the opening of the Civil War as the "post-historic" generation. They saw themselves as inheritors or preservers of the democratic inheritance given to them by their revolutionary forebears, but the perception that their lives were less "eventful" than the lives of their heroic ancestors made them uncomfortable. Patriotic rhetoric at Lexington and Concord often asked, uneasily, if those paying their respects "measured up," and if they did not, was it because of laziness or, worst of all, because they were unable to perform heroic deeds, the ultimate form of patriotic impotence.[31]

Failure to perform heroic deeds—almost always understood to mean heroic deeds in battle—did not simply mean that the heirs of the revolutionary tradition would be guilty of the ultimate heresy of consigning the sacrifice of the minutemen to oblivion through contemporary impotence.

It also meant that such heirs feared they would fail to reach civic maturity, would fail to become patriotic fathers themselves. Commemorative rhetoric consistently has portrayed the battles of Lexington and Concord as rites of passage, bringing a transformation not only from colonies to nation but from sons to fathers, from Englishmen to Americans. In 1826, on the fifty-first anniversary of the Lexington battle, William Emmons remarked that the battle had "no parallel on the records of history" and that "boys became men at the approach of an invading foe . . . the aged became fired with the vigor of youth." In 1885, at Concord's incorporation anniversary, George Frisbie Hoar declared, "At the moment of John Buttrick's word of command American national life began. . . . The order was given to British subjects. The order was obeyed by American citizens."[32]

With elderly survivors Jonathan Harrington and Amos Baker in attendance, Robert Rantoul delivered a spirited speech at the Union Celebration at Concord in 1850. He spoke of the deeds of the nation's forebears, of "occupying such a continent, receiving it consecrated by the toils, and [of the] sufferings and outpouring of ancestral blood. . . . how delightful is the duty which devolves on us to guard the beacon-fire of liberty whose flames our fathers kindled." With the approach of the Civil War, the duties of the sons seemed more onerous, and the end of the republic for which the fathers died seemed imminent. In 1860 Samuel Ripley Bartlett, in "Concord Fight," asked bluntly about the sons' adequacy:

> Oh! Can it be that we degenerate sons,
> False to our blood that from such sources runs,
> Have ceased to pray by word, by deed, by thought;
> Base heirs to glory which our Fathers bought?

Bartlett then comforted his readers, assuring them that the sons would indeed act, for the spirit of Concord would revitalize them, as it did their revolutionary fathers:

> Here still in Concord sleeps the ancient force;
> Here rebels wild, fanatics fierce, we find,
> Who war against a tyranny more dread
> Than that of old, the thraldom of the mind.
> What the old spirit dead? No, No!—it lives."[33]

The minutemen became models for both the North and the South during the Civil War. On the eve of that divisive conflict, Southerners looked to the spirit of the American Revolution as a model of their own aspirations for independence. William L. Yancey of Alabama thought that the South should "produce spirit enough . . . to call forth a Lexington, to fight a Bunker Hill." The trauma of the Civil War was, paradoxically, a relief for those who worried about their own patriotic potency, since the postheroic generation would now also have the chance to give birth to a nation purified through the crucible of war and boys again would have the opportunity to become men through the test of battle. "Whatever else it did or failed to do," George Forgie writes, "the war brought the post-heroic age to a close by ending the psychological thralldom to the past that defined it." In April 1867 Concord's Soldiers' Monument, which commemorates those who fought and died in the Civil War—the inscription reads, "The Sons Defended What the Fathers Won"—was completed in Monument Square. Dedication ceremonies took place during the ninety-second anniversary of the town's revolutionary war battle. The Soldiers' Monument Committee reported that the monument rested on a "solid foundation"—a stone from the abutment of the North Bridge—and that the heroes of 1775 could now "admit to their fellowship the men who in their turn have offered their lives for their country, for freedom and the rights of mankind."[34]

According to one report, "thousands came from near and far to share in the impressive ceremonies of the day." People "marched to the old battleground and around its monument, and from thence to the front of that Town-House where the exercises took place." John S. Keyes gave the opening address and declared that, just as the revolutionary ancestors had proved their patriotism, the Soldiers' Monument was dedicated to others whose "lives . . . deeds . . . deaths, we enshrine." The ensuing prayer of thanksgiving offered grateful praise that in a new time of trial brave men were found who came "from all our peaceful homes, our husbands and brothers, our fathers and sons." Then Samuel Ripley Bartlett offered this ode:

> Beneath the shadow of the elm, where ninety years ago
> Old Concord's rustic heroes met to face a foreign foe,
> We come to consecrate this Stone to heroes of to-day,
> Who perished in a holy cause as gallantly as they."[35]

The ceremonies continued with a speech by Ralph Waldo Emerson in which he reminded those in attendance that the 1836 monument at the North Bridge, which purported to symbolize the American Revolution, was flawed, for it "overlooked the moral law" and "winked at a practical exception to the Bill of Rights." By contrast, the Soldiers' Monument pointed to the "arrival of the nation at the new principle." Emerson also drew on the established traditions of patriotic rhetoric to honor Concord's Civil War heroes. "It is," he said, "an interesting part of the history, the manner in which this incongruous militia were made soldiers." Before the Civil War, Emerson declared, "our farmers went to Kansas as peaceable, God-fearing men," but they saw such brutalities there that they were transformed by a rage and "became on the instant the bravest soldiers and the most deter-mined avengers." Another speaker, William Schouler, also drew the audi-ence's attention to the parallels between Civil War soldiers and their revo-lutionary fathers. "Our boys were good boys. . . . They did not go there with their hearts full of hatred. Six years ago today . . . our Sixth Regiment was attacked in the streets of Baltimore, and the first blood was shed in defence of the American Union as it was, on the same day, in 1775."[36]

Satisfaction in having met contemporary patriotic trials in the Civil War was also evident in the rhetoric of the revolutionary war centennial cele-brations in 1875. George Curtis told a crowd gathered in Concord that the deaths of Concord men in the Civil War made the sacrifices of 1775 un-derstandable. "Now we *know the secret* of those old hearts and homes. We can *measure the sacrifice,* the courage, the devotion; for we have seen them all." The *Cheshire Republican* reflected on the meaning of the Civil War in light of the centennial events and told its readers that if the Civil War had split the nation permanently, "the guns of Concord [would be] a reminder of our infidelity to the memories of our Fathers, rather than the announce-ment of the advent of a new life." After recounting in his 1885 speech in Concord the dramatic baptism of fire of the revolutionary fathers, George Frisbie Hoar blessed the Civil War generation and declared that the most recent baptism of blood proved "the spirit of the Fathers has descended to the children."[37]

This same spirit was perceived to have descended on future generations who went to war, including the doughboys of World World I. In 1916 the *New York Herald* listed the virtues of contemporary minutemen, "united in the spirit of alertness to danger, of devotion to country, of determination to defend their rights and principles." When troops from Concord prepared to march off to war in 1917, the *Boston Transcript* remarked that "old Con-cord showed . . . that the spirit of the men of '76 yet lives in the hearts of their descendants and of all its citizens." The *Boston Sunday Herald* declared that while the "science of conflict has utterly changed," the "Concord Min-ute Men are ready to perform their full duty," for the village possessed a "latent power that requires only the electrifying current of a national emer-gency to release its forces."[38]

Townsend Scudder's history of Concord quotes the *New York Tribune's* tribute to Concord's spirit during the war: "The Spirit of Concord is not merely a glorious memory—it is a living fact. Of five generations that sep-arate April 1775 from May 1898, three have marched. From father to son there has been handed down not a tradition but an example, there has been transmitted the lesson that life, liberty, and the pursuit of happiness, are not easy inheritances . . . but rather that they are the fruits of an ancient sacrifice, to preserve which there is demanded of Concord boys a service, and there may be demanded a future sacrifice as well. This is the spirit of Concord and it lives." After the war, the *Concord Enterprise* quoted from Mary Pride's "Welcome Home Concord" and remarked that the poem should be part of every household, for it put the sacrifice of the modern minutemen in its proper symbolic context.

> From the Bridge whereon you bled
> The Road to the Meuse lies far
> But straight the way as when you led
> And Liberty called to war
> . . . .
> And they, the gold-starred, who never
> Will reap what they have sown,
> Concord will keep them forever,
> Her Dead are her very own.[39]

The symbol of the minuteman was widely used in World War II as well. On June 3, 1943, the *Concord Journal* proudly noted that the battle in 1775 was a "symbol for victory in our Present day fight against tyrants." The newspaper reminded its readers that Daniel Chester French's image of the minuteman appeared on "every Victory Bond, Victory stamp and every advertisement of war loans." During the war years, Nineteenth of April ceremonies became occasions for celebrating the sacrifice of the modern-day minutemen. The Patriots' Day announcement of 1944, for example, declared that the holiday was designed to help "insure perpetuation of the privileges inherited from the determination, planning, struggles, and sacrifices of the Colonial Patriots." Those lessons, the announcement added, "are at this minute up for confirmation or for destruction." Even some combatants perceived themselves as guardians of the sacrificial tradition. On Iwo Jima in 1945, a marine captain said that "from Lexington and Concord to Cologne, Manila, and Iwo Jima the line of succession is unbroken, and it will continue unbroken as long as Americans value their heritage of liberty enough to die for it."[40]

In addition to becoming a model of redemptive sacrifice for those Americans who would go to war, the minuteman became a model of civic virtue and a never-ending reminder of the danger of falling away from the ideals that the revolutionary war generation had supposedly embodied. The popularity of the minuteman was certainly evident in American popular culture at the turn of the century, as best-selling dime novels featured a series called "The Liberty Boys of '76," which began in 1901 and lasted until 1925. The series followed a "brave band of American youths who were always ready and willing to imperil their lives for the sake of helping along the gallant cause of Independence."[41] Patriotic rhetoric at twentieth-century Nineteenth of April celebrations continued to turn consistently to the minuteman as an inspiration for cultural renewal.

Charles J. Bonaparte, who delivered Concord's commemorative oration in 1900 before ten thousand visitors at the North Bridge, spoke of the sorrowful state of civilization. He told the audience, "If you see too often in our public life but a swinish scuffle for sordid gain . . . [if] you are sickened by the greed . . . the grossness which degrade and poison our national being, I bid you look to the minute-man!" In 1936 Judge Francis J. Good delivered a speech in Concord in which he declared that the minutemen would be disgusted by various forms of "lax public morality." For example, he said, if the minutemen knew of the "conduct of millions of motorists [they] would surely urge upon us a campaign to bring the common rule of politeness to the highway." The *Boston Sunday Herald* reported on April 18, 1948, that a scroll containing "The Minute Man Resolve of 1948," passed by the Massachusetts legislature, was handed to Henry B. Cabot of Boston by six-year-old Michael B. Wood, a descendant of early Concord settlers, in a ceremony at the base of the Minute Man Statue in Concord. Cabot was to deliver the scroll to the mayor of Chicago to mark the beginning of World Government Week, which would focus attention on the need to "secure the world against conquest by atomic and similar modern weapons."[42]

More traditional memories of the minuteman were used in the formative years of the cold war. "Peace through Preparedness" was the theme of Lexington's 1948 ceremony. In 1950 the minuteman image was also used in a speech delivered by Massachusetts senator Leverett Saltonstall, who told a hundred thousand people gathered in Lexington that America was in conflict with a "godless tyranny called Communism," a conflict that "affects every single one of us in every aspect of our daily lives." In light of this clear and present danger, Saltonstall insisted, "we are the Minutemen of 1950 just as surely as were our forebears the Minutemen of 1775." Gov. Christian Herter's Nineteenth of April proclamation in 1953 addressed the significance of the war in Korea, arguing that the United States had to lead in the spread of democratic principles and "support and defend those principles with specific acts." In the midst of a "brutal and bloody war," the governor said, the nation must defend itself against "foreign beliefs" that were "contrary to those to which the Patriots of Concord and Lexington dedicated themselves." Two years later Herter's message continued in the same vein, declaring that in a world "half slave and half free," other Lexingtons and Concords "will have to come elsewhere in the world before all people can walk uprightly in the spirit of freedom."[43]

In 1961 the "mobilization of the spirit of '61" was accomplished by paying obeisance to the guiding spirit of 1775. The Concord Committee on Public Ceremonies and Celebrations, in planning the day's events, was concerned about what it believed was a sense of cultural alienation and disorientation from the cherished principles of the Revolution. "There are many indications," the committee noted, "that we as a people desire renewal of our spiritual capacities, and hunger for the security and serenity that comes with knowledge of 'where we came from.'" Nineteenth of April ceremonies should, the committee declared, help people deal with modern "fears, anxieties, and uncertainties" by renewing "memories of our nation's past." Various civic groups were involved in this patriotic revival, including the West Concord Garden Club, which began a campaign to "encourage display of the national emblem by families and places of business on 19 April 1961, Memorial Day and on other appropriate occasions." Orators were asked to provide patriotic instruction that would "educate our youth in the tradition and history of their country." Gov. John A. Volpe noted that the minutemen were "working men, like your fathers, or older brothers or uncles." He also spoke about his own profession of politics and asked that the audience "dedicate [itself] to the establishment of clean, honest government, a government that, if the dead heroes of the Revolution could see it, would be a government they deemed a worthy reason for their sacrifices."[44]

To be sure, the fear of nuclear weapons and the constant state of cold war that transformed every citizen into a potential warrior was also present in Nineteenth of April ceremonial rhetoric. In 1961 Brig. Gen. Charles J. Terhune, Jr., USAF, the vice commander of the Electronic Systems Division at Hanscom Field, remarked that to Paul Revere's signal of "one if by land and two if by sea," citizens must "add another, 'three if by air.'" This third lantern, he argued, made up "the warning systems which alert us concerning the threats to our national security," because "for the first time" the nation was vulnerable to "destructive surprise attack." Terhune also spoke of the need for modern minutemen ready to do battle in the arena of technological development. "In this electronics and aerospace era," he said, "Lexington, Concord and the route 128 area are still the battle grounds."[45] Some anticommunist groups took such declarations seriously. For example, in June 1960 Robert DePugh founded the Minutemen, a heavily armed group that practiced guerrilla warfare in anticipation of the coming invasion of the United States by communist forces. DePugh claimed to have been inspired initially by a speech by John F. Kennedy in which the president called for a "nation of minutemen" who were not afraid to take up arms in the country's defense. H. S. Riecke of New Orleans, founder of the Paul Revere Associated Yeomen, Inc., also sought to locate militant anticommunism within the American revolutionary tradition.[46]

The actions of the minutemen also sanctified the ground on which their sacrifices were made. As at other battle sites, the urge to venerate these places went beyond verbal consecration. At Lexington the construction of the Revolutionary Monument in 1799, the 1835 reinterment in the monument of the eight martyrs, the erection of the Captain Parker Monument in 1900, and the various commemorative boulders and markers that have been placed on the Green are evidence of the desire to set that area apart as sacred ground. The perceived need for physical veneration, to establish the "tone" of the place, led F. Lauriston Bullard to comment in 1912: "It is good to see that many of the pilgrims who come here in scores every summer day . . . feel deeply the significance of the place. Heads are bared before the monuments."[47]

Activity designed to transform Lexington Green into a commemorative landscape continued in the decades that followed. In 1921 eight elm trees were planted on the Common in memory of the Lexington men who were killed in World War I. In anticipation of the 1975 bicentennial, trees, shrubs, and flowers were planted. This, the *Lexington Minuteman* reported, was an altogether fitting memorial, because the "first liberty tree planted in Lexington was cut down by the British before they left for Boston."[48] The goal was to provide the proper physical context for the annual ceremonies and to impress on visitors, through natural beauty and monumental impact, the drama of the birth of the nation. During the bicentennial reenactment of the battle the narrator, using Walter Cronkite's "You Are There" formula, told the crowd where the old buildings and the line of minutemen had stood and reminded them that "this *very common* became the birthplace of American liberty."[49]

The same sense of awe was apparent in earlier times. When the road leading to the site of Concord's Old North Bridge was abandoned in 1793, Ezra Ripley, who replaced William Emerson as Concord's minister, bought the road and "loved to tell the story of that famous happening on his own ground." In 1829 Ripley spoke reverently about the North Bridge: "The spot, the site of ground, appears to us little less than holy, and really consecrated by Heaven to the cause of liberty and the Rights of man." Rev. Grindall Reynolds's centennial speech characterized Concord as "one of the great centres, not only of intellectual life, but also of political influence and power." Concord, he said, offered the nation the "choice spirits of the country" and the "high sons of liberty." Reynolds then drew his audience's attention to the North Bridge, for "within the bounds of the original thirteen States there is no spot more interesting than the two secluded green slopes . . . where the soldiers of the king and the soldiers of the people met in military array and exchanged fatal volleys."[50]

As was the case in Lexington, citizens of Concord wanted to erect a monument to their battle. In 1825 Concord joined the Bunker Hill Monument Association, whose purpose was to build monuments in Charlestown and Concord. On April 19, 1825, a cornerstone for a monument was laid in Concord's town square. The inscription reads: "Here on the 19th of April, 1775, began the war of that Revolution which gave Independence to America." Despite the fact that sixty survivors gathered with others and "listened to eloquent word painting of their deeds from the lips of Everett," townspeople ridiculed the placement of the cornerstone so far from the battlesite; during the winter months, some of them dramatized their displeasure by putting boards around the cornerstone and setting them ablaze. In 1827 the *Yeoman's Gazette* suggested a spot for a monument near the site of the old bridge and looked forward to a "splendid and durable monument [which will] rise on that site of ground." Ripley offered land to the town if it would agree that the monument be "erected near the site of the ancient bridge; and that a monument be erected within three years from the fourth of July next."[51]

The monument was designed by Solomon Willard, the architect of the Bunker Hill Monument. Construction began in 1836, and the monument was dedicated on July 4, 1837. Ralph Waldo Emerson, although not present at the ceremonies, wrote the "Concord Hymn" to be read at the dedication. The *Yeoman's Gazette* declared that "no land could be more appropriate, as . . . the spot on which the first of the enemy fell," and it looked forward to a time when the monument would "draw more pilgrims than ever journeyed to any . . . single shrine of monkish superstition." Still, the controversy over placement of the monument continued. Some citizens felt strongly that it should not be situated on the side of the river on which the British troops had taken their stand. Their argument was bolstered by the fact that since 1793 no bridge connected the land on which the British had fallen with the west bank, where the minutemen had come to contest the enemy. The situation went unresolved until a Concord farmer, Ebenezer Hubbard, who had seen the battle bridge as a child, bequeathed the town $1,000 when he died in 1870, the money to be used to "build a monument . . . on the spot where the Americans fell, on the opposite side of the river from the present Monument." Stedman Buttrick, grandson of Maj. John Buttrick, who had led the Concord minutemen at the battle, gave the town a piece of land for the express purpose of housing a monument, and in 1874 a bridge was built that joined the east bank to Buttrick's land on the west.[52]

A town committee recommended that a statue of a Continental minuteman be erected, and it selected Daniel Chester French, one of its own, as the sculptor. Congress gave the town ten condemned brass cannon to use in the casting. In *The Story of the Minuteman*, Roland Wells Robbins argues that French created the statue to resemble Capt. Isaac Davis of Acton, the first minuteman to die at the bridge. French finished the figure

Sentry® Insurance

This image of the Captain Parker Statue is used by
Sentry Insurance. (Sentry Insurance)

This image of the minuteman
is used by GTE. (GTE)

Defense contractors often used the image
of the minuteman, as in this decal from
the late 1960s. (Ballistic Systems Division,
Norton Air Force Base, Department of
the Air Force)

During its tour of the nation in 1960, the Minuteman missile stood next to its namesake on the Lexington Green. (Boeing Company Archives)

A different view of the Minuteman missile and the Captain
Parker Statue. (Boeing Company Archives)

The cover of a 1974 issue of the Boeing Company's *Minuteman Service News*. (Boeing Company Archives)

in September 1874, and on March 24, 1875, the base and inscription were completed. Five days later the statue arrived in Concord from the Ames Foundry in Chicopee. The committee thought it "spirited, lifelike . . . alert and ready for action." The Concord Minuteman was unveiled on April 19 during the major centennial parade as the carriage carrying Pres. Ulysses Grant approached. At the appropriate moment William Emerson "pulled the cords, the flags dropped away from the bronze and the splendid youthful figure leaped forth in the fullness of his life and vigor." Then "a cannon boomed, the crowd cheered, and the procession moved on."[53]

Admirers of French's work certainly would disagree with J. B. Jackson's remark that the statue suggests "no particular line of conduct." On April 19, 1875, the *Springfield Republican* called the statue the "ideal embodiment of the genius of the Revolution," adding that its features were "strongly marked and bear the energy, the self-command, the ready shrewdness, the immediate decision, and, above all, the air of freedom that belongs to the New England face." Prior to the official unveiling, Charles H. Brigham delivered a speech at the Unitarian Church of Ann Arbor, Michigan, in which he commented on the nature of such monuments and on the virtues of French's statue in particular: "These martial monuments are the truly religious monuments, symbolizing the truth, the courage, the faith and the hope which ought to be immortalized in the soul of the Nation." French's statue, he thought, showed "resolution and faith," not just to Americans, but also to the "heathen . . . from lands on the other side of the world." Innumerable visitors' comments express similar reverence. In 1893, for example, a tourist remarked that the Concord Minuteman was a "splendid statue. The pose makes your nerves tingle. It is not metal—it is flesh, bone, will, spirit—You'd swear that young farmer in bronze could draw a bead on an Englishman yet." A 1908 book introducing visitors to various sites in Concord and Lexington notes that French's statue "admirably depicts the character of the early colonial fathers."[54]

In the late 1950s the United States Air Force named its newest inter-continental ballistic missile (ICBM) the Minuteman and used likenesses of French's statue to popularize the weapon's mission. Raymond L. Puffer, chief historian of the Ballistic Missile Office at Norton Air Force Base, notes that the name was the result of "suggestions from Air Force, support and contractor personnel" and is "particularly apt," for the first solid-fueled ICBM could be launched much more quickly than liquid-fueled missiles. Dr. Puffer writes that "the missile was literally standing guard over the nation, sleeplessly in its silos, waiting to spring into action at a moment's time." Brigadier General Terhune, in his April 19, 1961, anniversary speech, also thought the name appropriate, because "our military forces must be constantly trained and prepared to act at a minute's notice like the Minute

Men of the American Revolution." Contractors, too, clarified the missile's purpose. According to a Boeing Corporation publication, "The people of Boeing know that the better job they do, the less chance there will be for some future poet to modify the words of Ralph Waldo Emerson . . . 'Here the embattled farmers stood and fired the shot *reaching* round the world.' "[55]

Concord closely guards this enduring image of the "embattled farmers," which it feels so typifies the spirit of the town. In 1973, for example, a Bedford High School student notified the police that he heard a ticking sound coming from a bag resting at the base of the statue. Four sticks of dynamite, set to go off at 11:00 A.M., were discovered inside the bag. Subsequently, the town made an exact mold of the statue, to assure that if anything did happen the statue could be recast. In 1984 Concord selectmen denied the Air National Guard permission to construct a replica of the statue for its new headquarters building at Andrews Air Force Base, even though the Guard had used the minuteman as its symbol since 1960. Col. Fred Helms tried to convince those at the town meeting that the Guard's request should be granted, noting: "Folks, I'm your next door neighbor. I'm no foreigner. . . . when the time comes, I put my tools down and pick up my gun." The historical district commission chairman simply responded, "It would be like saying to Russia, 'Go ahead, use the statue of liberty.' " Nevertheless, likenesses of French's famous statue have been used by the military and also in business advertising.[56]

Besides the Concord monuments, the bridge (or, more accurately, the memory of the ancient structure that had stood over the river in 1775) was venerated by townspeople and visitors alike. The battle bridge, built in 1760, had long since washed away. But as Alfred Sereno Hudson notes, "Its name and memories will remain forever; and every pilgrim who visits the site of it will naturally glance backward into the past for an imaginary glimpse of those grim old timbers which were hewn by the Fathers, and pressed by the feet of the Patriots as they pursued the retreating foe on April 19, 1775." In preparation for the centennial celebration, Concord built a new bridge in 1874. A citizens' committee insisted that the new bridge resemble the old one, though they did add half-arbors with seats in the middle (having decided that the old structure was too simple). According to Hudson, the bridge became a "mecca of multitudes, and it may be said that all roads lead to it."[57]

The new North Bridge also washed away, in 1888, and was replaced by yet another bridge, which lasted until 1909. In its next reincarnation the bridge was built of concrete, but it, too, had to be replaced, in 1955, when it was damaged by a hurricane. The present bridge was built in 1956 to replicate the bridge that appears in Amos Doolittle's 1775 engraving of the battle. This bridge was consciously designed as a commemorative bridge as well, for the townspeople were aware that the concrete bridge it replaced had given a "shortsighted and inaccurate impression . . . [to] the 150,000 or more persons who come every year" and had "irritated historical-minded citizens attempting to visualize the original rude wood bridge." At the dedication ceremonies on September 29, 1956, Governor Herter stated that the new wood bridge was a "symbol throughout the world of man's eternal fight for freedom"; a visitor noted that "no concrete anachronism jars sensibilities."[58]

Lexington's Battle Green and Concord's North Bridge are, in their own ways, "preserved" environments, intentionally set apart in order for sacred sites to function as ceremonial space. Although the Green sits near downtown Lexington, there has been little tension between preservation and commercialization forces. Visitors are impressed by the Green's stately and serene reminder of past glories, secure in its stature amid a small yet bustling affluent community. Curiously, there appears to be no need for buffers from traffic or other elements of modernity, which seem so aesthetically destructive at other battle sites. The monuments in Lexington draw our attention but do not dominate the area. Amid the tone of modern life, the Green manages to exude the same ineffable presence that is found at other martial centers. By contrast, the North Bridge has been the focus of sporadic attempts to preserve the patriotic landscape from the ravages of modernity. For the sixty-third anniversary in 1838 the citizens of Concord planted some two hundred trees on the road to the Revolutionary Monument. And in 1929 the Old North Bridge Protection Association was formed to "protect the approaches to the famous Concord battleground, and to afford to the visiting thousands who come every year . . . means for their instruction and comfort."[59]

For some people the modest size of both sites was troublesome. One disgusted visitor wrote to the *Boston Globe:* "Is that tiny area all the space in Lexington and Concord you have to spare to commemorate the epic events that occurred there?" The congressional answer to this question was "no," for three years later, on September 21, 1959, Public Law 86–321 established Minute Man National Historical Park. The park includes the North Bridge area and a four-mile strip of land alongside Route 2A, the Battle Road, from Meriam's Corner in Concord to Fiske Hill in Lexington, but not Lexington Green. The National Park Service was charged with the "preservation and interpretation" of the events of April 19, 1775, which were noted to be of "great importance in American history." In a meeting on March 11, 1963, Concord entered into an agreement whereby the NPS would administer the North Bridge site but it would still be owned by the town.[60]

While the North Bridge and Lexington Green have remained relatively free from environmental defilement in the eyes of preservationists, the same is not true of the Battle Road. Since 1959 the Park Service has spent more than ten million dollars on preservation of the landscape and restoration of a number of historic structures. Nevertheless, an NPS report from the early 1960s stresses the danger: economic growth in the area that threatens to bring "shattering changes in the historical landscape and the irrecoverable loss of historical values." Similarly, a 1983 NPS report notes that the "most historic stretch of road in America . . . is disappearing under a sea of cars and asphalt." Proposals for wider roads to accommodate the heavy commuter traffic on Route 2A and plans for new hotels and offices would, according to the NPS, "irrevocably destroy what remains of the Battle Road's historic character."[61]

As at other battle sites, the National Park Service and concerned citizens assumed a crucial link between the environment and patriotic ideology. If the landscape could be adequately frozen in time, they said, then the contemporary significance of the site could be adequately presented and its lessons appreciated. However, if modernity was allowed to pollute the site, the extinction of patriotic virtues was assured. To strengthen the link, and at the request of the NPS in 1984, thirteen students from the Department of Landscape Architecture at Harvard University produced a booklet entitled *Alternative Futures for Minute Man National Historical Park*. Their study became the basis for the Park Service's general management plan, which proposed a park that would emphasize the area's "1775 character." The plan states that visitors should be able to *walk* the Battle Road to "better . . . appreciate the events that led to the American Revolution and, specifically, the context in which the battle of April 19, 1775, occurred." Visitors would have to be protected from modern developments, "particularly traffic." The task before the NPS was to "preserve historic buildings," remove modern "visual intrusions," expand "signs and exhibits," and gradually restore the "historical appearance of The Battle Road."[62]

The NPS planned to carry out this restoration in three stages. First, it would begin altering the physical landscape through leasing of open fields, controlled burning of vegetation, and removal of "intrusions" such as "signs, utility poles, houses, and other modern structures"; it also would determine the exact location of several stretches of the original Battle Road. In the second stage historic buildings would be restored and the land would be shaped as closely as possible to resemble "conditions at the time of the battle." Initially, a small section of the road would be closed to traffic, pavement would be removed, and the road would be restored to its "1775 configuration." Because traffic noise and the like were perceived as a form of defilement, it was decided that "the park will work with the state officials to plan and install appropriate sound barriers. . . . This will include vegetative screening of the sound barriers themselves." The visitors center on the Battle Road, which had been dedicated on May 8, 1976, was also viewed as a modern intrusion and would be moved. In the final stage of the plan a four-mile stretch of Route 2A would be relocated, all traffic would be barred from the Battle Road, and the "historic alignment and surface [of the road would] be replicated as accurately as possible." In addition, hiking and bicycle trails would be established.[63]

Fred Szarka, the NPS superintendent at Minute Man National Historical Park, commented that the plan represented the most extreme preservationist view and that, on completion of the project in the early twenty-first century, the NPS could declare that it had "put the public in the field." He hoped, too, that the restoration of the Battle Road would help visitors appreciate the British experience. Thomas Boylston Adams, treasurer of the American Academy of Arts and Sciences and former president of the Massachusetts Historical Society, as well as a direct descendant of John Quincy Adams, characterized the NPS plan as the "uncovering of history." It was especially significant, he thought, that visitors would be able to see forgotten sacred spots that had been hidden by natural growth as well as by the processes of modernity. For example, Lincoln's William Thornton, while engaged with the British in the battle, had taken cover behind some boulders and had killed two of the retreating troops. Once the area was restored, said Adams, the public would be able to see what used to be called the Minuteman Boulders, as well as the knoll that was known as the Soldiers' Graves. This not only would help people appreciate the "peril of plain citizens who take on a disciplined, well-armed and organized tyranny" but would remind them that "independence and freedom are bought at a high price."[64]

The Park Service's plan for Minute Man National Historical Park stirred up a controversy between those who perceived such battlesites as sacred ground, to be venerated through restoration and preservation, and those who did not. For opponents the land was an economically valuable commodity, and the idea of undoing progress, especially by relocating a busy commuter highway in the midst of a high-tech area, was nonsensical. Frances Cabot, chairwoman of the Concord Board of Selectmen, characterized the townspeople as being "shocked and dismayed" by the plan. A resident of the Battle Road area commented angrily: "This is the 20th century—I don't see people going along with a dirt road. I don't see all the need for taking all this land for this."[65]

An even more enduring controversy has occupied some citizens of Lexington and Concord since 1824: namely, which town can rightfully claim to represent the birthplace of the nation. During Lafayette's visit to Concord in 1824, Samuel Hoar's public address reminded him that the first "forcible resistance" to the British was made in Concord. Similar claims were made by Ralph Waldo Emerson and other citizens of Concord, which raised a "storm of protest" among Lexingtonians. The industrious Elias Phinney began to collect depositions from the elderly Lexington minutemen, and his pamphlet, a vigorous defense of Lexington as the home of the first "battle," appeared in 1825. Phinney noted that "inhabitants of Lexington feel it to be particularly incumbent on them to lay this statement of facts before the publick, on account of some recent publications stating that 'at Concord the first blood was shed between the British and the armed Americans.' " Concord, Phinney argued, was not the first battle, and it was Lexington's duty to leave a correct memory of those whose "blood became the first offering upon the altar of their country's freedom."[66]

Phinney's spirited defense of Lexington aroused Concord's redoubtable Ezra Ripley, who collected his own set of depositions and published a refutation in 1827. Ripley thought it *his* duty to reveal the "present pretensions and claims of the citizens of Lexington," who made an "unjust claim upon the public faith" and attempted to "wrest from the inhabitants of Concord . . . the legitimate honors which their brave and patriotic fathers achieved and bequeathed to them." Lexington, he said, was a "massacre." Phinney's depositions notwithstanding, Ripley argued, the British were not fired upon by the minutemen on the Green but by those gathered at the North Bridge. Thus, in Ripley's opinion, the nation correctly traced the "progress of civil liberty and national freedom in various parts of the world" from the events in Concord. Lexington's minutemen deserved the "highest praise for their courage and love of country and liberty," he said, but "we deny that they returned the fire of the British at the time."[67]

Neither side could sway the opinion of the other, and as the centennial approached the *Hudson Pioneer* reported that the "rivalry between the towns is injuring and belittling the whole centennial." The *Boston Globe* declared that unless the rivalry was settled it would "interfere with the excellently made programme which has been arranged for the centennial." It also advised that there was no reason for this "warm dispute as to which is entitled to the honor of being first in the great struggle," for there was certainly "enough glory . . . for all concerned." Nonetheless, the two towns conducted separate centennial celebrations. In Lexington, Richard Henry Dana claimed "beyond doubt" that the "first shots fired back by our troops at theirs" were fired on the Green. While French's Minute Man Statue was being installed in Concord—and was itself the occasion of partisan rhetoric—Lexington residents nervously awaited the imminent arrival of two statues (as opposed to one, they were quick to point out), of John Hancock and

Samuel Adams, to be placed in the town's Memorial Hall. The *Boston News* reported that "the bronze Minute-Man which Concord is to have weighs 1250 pounds. Lexington people say, . . . Our men are worth sixty of him."[68]

Although active controversy between the two towns ceased after the centennial, occasional ill-chosen comments continued to engender prickly displeasure. In *The Story of Patriots' Day* (1895), George Varney raised the hackles of Concord residents when he claimed that at Lexington a "volley from the muskets of the minute men rang out in reply." And residents of Lexington were certainly not pleased when Harold Murdock claimed in a 1916 issue of the *Massachusetts Historical Society* that the fact the Lexington minutemen did not return the British fire was as "clearly proved as any historical fact need be," although he believed that "certain individuals belonging to the company or numbered among the spectators did before or after the British attack discharge their pieces." In 1962 William F. Buckley, assistant director of the Cary Memorial Library in Lexington, reawakened the controversy and fueled the fire when he created a diorama of the battle (which is still on display in the visitors center near the Green) showing the minutemen firing at the British. During the bicentennial a Lexington flyer noted that Concord was still "quite willing to overlook the fact that the first shot was not fired in Concord at all."[69]

Despite evidence to the contrary, the belief that the Lexington minutemen fired back at the British on the Green has become a crucial part of commemorative events. The "truth" of such invented traditions may be witnessed during battle reenactments, for these traditions fit perfectly into the heroic mythologies of the battle. Since the stories have become an accepted part of the patriotic canon, folk wisdom "knows" that they are true, historians' protestations notwithstanding. Those who cast a skeptical eye on these sagas are deemed guilty of bad manners, at the least; some are viewed as defilers of patriotic tradition.[70]

Battle art also contributes to the perpetuation of invented tradition at Lexington. The earliest artistic depiction of the battle is by Connecticut engraver Amos Doolittle, who, after hearing news of the battle on April 21, 1775, volunteered to go to Cambridge with the Governor's Second Company of Guards. He spent approximately three weeks in Cambridge in early May, during which he traveled to Lexington and Concord collecting information for his sketches. Doolittle portrayed the minutemen in Lexington in disarray after the British opened fire; no patriot is shown firing back. To be sure, such a scene had immense propaganda value. Ian Quimby writes: "Doolittle saw no need to embroider the account by showing the outnumbered Americans making a glorious stand; it served better to depict a vastly superior military force slaughtering American farmers on their home ground."[71] However, an 1830 painting by John Pendleton shows patriots standing fast against the British, firing and reloading. Similarly, a Hammett Billings sketch in 1857 shows a number of patriots firing back.

Henry Sandham's mural *The Dawn of Liberty,* an influential depiction of the battle, was completed in 1886. The painting portrays an organized skirmish line of minutemen engaged in an exchange of volleys with the British. The Lexington Historical Society thought this was an accurate representation of the battle, as did Rev. George E. Ellis, president of the Massachusetts Historical Society, who called it "adequate and realistic." A committee appointed by the Society to buy the painting praised Sandham's work because it represented "the determined attitude of the colonies at that time," symbolized by Sandham's minutemen, the "type of sturdy Fathers of New England" who demonstrated an "unyielding courage . . . in defense of their rights." Furthermore, the committee members said, the painting demonstrated the "individuality of the minute-men, as compared with the line of disciplined troops." *The Dawn of Liberty* cost the city $4,000, but it was worth it, for its "educating influence . . . cannot be overestimated."[72] The Sandham mural now hangs in Lexington's Cary Memorial Hall.

Lexington and Concord were not the only towns to claim the right to be honored as the birthplace of the nation. In his address during Acton's centennial celebration on July 21, 1835, Josiah Adams complained that Phinney and Ripley ignored the *real* hero of the day, Capt. Isaac Davis of Acton, one of the minutemen who died at the North Bridge and who, reputedly, had urged the minutemen to march down the hill and face the British. Adams declared that "if the honor belongs to Lexington, it is because the British gave the brave company there the first opportunity. If the first blood was shed at Concord, the men of Acton arrived in season to shed it." Adams also bristled at Concord's claim that the spirit of resistance had been born there. "The truth is . . . when Captain Davis arrived on the ground, no one would agree to go in front. When he arrived, they took courage."[73]

In 1850 Adams continued his quest for proper recognition of Acton's contributions. He criticized Shattuck's history of Concord, in which Davis's action at the bridge was hardly mentioned, as "derogatory to the character and services of Captain Davis of Acton." The book, he thought, was designed to focus on "the services and conduct of the officers belonging to Concord." At the Union Celebration in Concord in 1850, Acton's Deacon Hayward was even more direct. "Concord," he said, "found the *ground* and Acton the men!" The centrality of Davis and Acton was emphasized at the town's October 19, 1851, dedication of the Isaac Davis Monument, the "tomb of

A hand-colored engraving by Amos Doolittle, after a drawing by Ralph Earl, of the battle of Lexington. (Chicago Historical Society)

The "invented tradition" of the Lexington minutemen firing at the British is evident in this 1830 painting by John Pendleton. (Lexington Historical Society)

The "tradition" was carried on in this 1856 painting by Alonzo Chappel. (Boston Athenaeum)

"The Battle of Lexington," from a drawing by Hammatt Billings. (Boston Athenaeum)

Henry Sandham's mural "The Dawn of Liberty" (1886), portraying the minutemen in a pitched battle with the British, hangs in Cary Memorial Hall in Lexington.
(Joe Ofria, The Image Inn, Arlington, Mass.)

This diorama of the battle of Lexington is on display in the Lexington Visitors Center. (Klein Post Card Service, Hyde Park, Mass.)

Plate III. The Engagement at the North Bridge in Concord.

1. The Detachment of the Regulars who fired first fired. 2. The Provincials headed by Colonel Robinson & Major Buttrick 3. The Bridge.
on the Provincials at the Bridge

A hand-colored engraving by Amos Doolittle, after a drawing by Ralph Earl, of the engagement at the North Bridge. (Chicago Historical Society)

A large crowd witnessed the protest at the North Bridge during Pres. Gerald Ford's bicentennial visit. (National Park Service)

the first martyred officer of the Revolution." Frederick Noyes complained that through Concord's attempts to ignore Davis's heroics the "spiritual significance" of the Acton story had been "belittled." Noyes even commented on the significance of the patriotic landscape in Lexington and Acton, and how peripheral it seemed in Concord: "Both villages have grown around their Revolutionary monuments. The tomb and battlefield dominate the every-day life of the villages. On the other hand, one might motor into Concord Square, and never find the distant battlefield."[74]

Acton, like Lexington and Concord, sought to commemorate the deeds of Isaac Davis and the other Acton minutemen through the preservation of the patriotic landscape, in this case, the Isaac Davis Trail, the road the minutemen had taken to reach Concord. The original route was surveyed in 1897 by members of the Children of the American Revolution (CAR) and Lucy Emily Noyes, a descendant of Isaac Davis and the first president of the Old North Bridge Society. Mrs. Daniel Lothrop, founder of the CAR, remarked that the trail was "too important to American History ever to be forgotten." In 1959 the Capt. Isaac Davis chapter of the Daughters of the American Revolution (DAR), led by project chairwoman Maria Davis Hunt, announced its intention to preserve the line of march of the Acton minutemen. Furthermore, the chapter planned to continue the march to the North Bridge that had been begun by the Acton Boy Scouts in 1957. The DAR declared its intention to "retrace [the march] annually to the tune of the White Cockade, to mark it, to have bells rung once again and to have it a townwide celebration." By 1969 the Acton Historical Society was fighting a subdivision that threatened the trail, over which "thousands of people come from all parts of our state and nation each year on Patriots' Day to retrace the steps of the Acton Minutemen."[75]

Others lamented the "luck" of Lexington and Concord to be the towns in the right place at the right time. The *Bennington Banner* of April 22, 1875, argued that the first blood of the Revolution was really shed in Vermont. Quoting from B. H. Hall's *History of Eastern Vermont,* the paper's editors agreed: "It should never be forgotten, that on the plains of Westminster the cause of freedom received its first victim." In his 1907 report to the Peabody Historical Society, Thomas Carroll noted that two months before April 19 the minutemen of Salem turned back a British force, and it was by the "merest chance" that the first shot was not fired at the "Old North Bridge at Salem." Had that been the case, Carroll said, the first revolutionary monument would "commemorate the 26th of February instead of the 19th of April, 1775." He also pointed out that several men of Danvers (then part of Peabody) lost their lives while doing battle with the British during their retreat from Concord. Consequently, he argued, Danvers deserved to be known as the "centre of [the] patriotic movement," for these men were "the first martyrs in the cause of American liberty."[76]

As we will see in subsequent chapters, the struggle for symbolic ownership of a battlesite and its message usually involves attempts by those traditionally excluded from the story, or those who played the role of villain in the story, to redefine not only the history but also the meaning of the battle. The citizens of Lexington and Concord felt the need to locate their communities in the hierarchy of American patriotic space, yet the controversy that ensued was, by and large, minor compared to the often bitter conflicts at other battlesites. In the 1970s, however, in the midst of the Vietnam conflict and with the approach of the nation's bicentennial in 1976, several groups engaged in symbolic protest at Lexington and Concord to force citizens to rethink the meaning of these sacred martial centers.

For the most part, those opposed to the U.S. involvement in Vietnam generally failed to utilize potent American symbols. However, on May 28–29, 1971, the Vietnam Veterans Against the War (VVAW), declaring that it wanted to "publicize the parallels between the actions of the citizen-soldier during the Revolutionary War era and those of the Vietnam Veterans Against the War today," staged a protest as part of its Memorial Day activities. According to the VVAW, "this present hour in history is again a time when the people are trying to secure the liberty and peace upon which the country was founded." Vietnam veteran John Kerry, who was later elected to the U.S. Senate from Massachusetts, said that the purpose of the protest was to "force the country to admit the mistake it has made in Indochina in the name of democracy."[77]

Early on the morning of May 28, a lantern was placed in the steeple of the Old North Church; then, after a message was carried by jeep from Charlestown to Concord and on horseback from there to the veterans' campsite, the group marched the reverse of Paul Revere's famous ride. The next day, when approximately one hundred fifty veterans and supporters attempted to set up camp on Lexington Green, the town selectmen refused to allow the group to stay the night. Chairman Robert Cataldo, reportedly fearing a violent confrontation, declared that "no good purpose would be served" by the veterans' presence on the Green and thus obtained a restraining order from the Middlesex Superior Court that enjoined the VVAW to leave the area by 10:00 P.M. The assembled veterans and a growing number of sympathetic townspeople refused to leave; nor would they accept Cataldo's compromise to move to a nearby park. By early morning the crowd had swelled considerably, and several hundred people were subsequently arrested, including Kerry and Massachussetts Institute of Technology activist Noam Chomsky. VVAW organizers told the protesters to give their "name, serial number, date of birth—April 18 [*sic*] 1775." After being processed and released, they marched to the base of the Bunker Hill Monument, where more than a thousand Charlestown residents cheered their arrival. Then they moved on to the Boston Common for a peace rally featuring a speech by Sen. Eugene McCarthy.[78]

The VVAW sought to dramatize what it believed was the loss of the revolutionary tradition of active dissent in American culture. It did so by turning not only to the rhetoric of the Revolution but to the sacred places of the Revolution. If, as it argued, U.S. involvement in Vietnam was a symptom of a serious disease at work in America, then the prescription was, at least in part, a physical and spiritual journey to the wellsprings of the nation, to the locations that dramatized traditions of individual dissent. For supporters of the war, of course, these places symbolized other values as well: a sense of duty and a citizen's willingness to fight for and, if need be, die for the nation's principles. Fred Szarka of the National Park Service, speaking about the veterans' march, commented that "people who were minutemen would be appalled at what they do."[79]

As the bicentennial approached another group sought to utilize the patriotic environment of Concord to stimulate a reawakening of what it perceived was the lost revolutionary tradition. The Peoples Bicentennial Commission (PBC) was formed to offer the nation a choice of celebrations. "The White House and Corporate America," it claimed, "are planning to sell us a program of plastic Liberty Bells, red-white-and blue cars and a 'Love it or Leave It' political program." Jeremy Rifkin, one of the co-directors of the PBC, believed that the *real* bicentennial should introduce Americans to strategies by which they could regain political and economic power, not serve merely as a celebration of American affluence. Rifkin correctly understood that the political Left in America had abandoned "most of the symbols to which the great majority of American people can respond." Consequently, he thought, the New Left needed to use our revolutionary heritage as a "tactical weapon to isolate the existing institutions." Running throughout the PBC's literature was a nostalgia for a common civic language and a "shared vision of our Revolutionary promise." PBC members believed that Americans were in dire need of reattachment to this primal vision, and they hoped that widespread demonstrations at sacred sites would create a "mass Revolutionary consciousness in tune with the revolutionary legacy of 1776." Such demonstrations would also dramatize the PBC's resistance to official ceremonies, which would merely "commercialize, trivialize, and vandalize" this legacy.[80]

In November 1974 the PBC distributed throughout New England 100,000 copies of a broadside calling for a "major economic protest at

Concord Bridge" that would demand "democracy for the American economy." To that end, the PBC asked the National Park Service for permission to camp at the North Bridge and carry out their "educational activities," including readings from the nation's founders, music, speeches, and theater. Despite the efforts of Concord selectmen to dissuade them, on April 4, 1975, representatives of the NPS, who thought that refusal to grant permission would be a "truly terrifying prospect," grudgingly granted a permit. Approximately forty-five thousand people joined in the all-night celebration before the official commemorative activities began. The PBC waxed eloquent about the significance of the event: "Like the Minutemen of 200 years ago, these 45,000 patriots came to send a message . . . to Wall Street." Speakers, including Rifkin and Harvard professor George Wald, a Nobel Prize winner, called for a new American revolution and attacked the "new Tories" who were soiling the memory of April 19 with a "mini–Rose Bowl parade or Disneyland with the added attraction of America's military machine passing in review." Speakers also asked if affluent Americans *really* understood the revolutionary heritage or were simply titillated by the "superficial thrill of reenactment garb."[81]

Throughout the night complaints were lodged with the Concord Police Department about rowdy behavior and the misuse of alcohol and other drugs. By morning the crowd had shrunk to about twelve thousand, yet those who remained were determined to register their protest at the official ceremonies, which began in the early morning with a twenty-one-gun salute from the Concord Independent Battery. Following the parade to the North Bridge, a procession of limousines brought Pres. Gerald Ford to deliver a speech that celebrated the growth of the global power of the United States, at which PBC's adherents "booed, waved banners . . . and shouted obscenities." When the president crossed the bridge to place a wreath at French's Minute Man Statue, a few protesters waded into the river carrying banners. Others tried to force their way into the parade, "heckled Concord's honored guests," and made "obscene gestures." After the celebration the selectmen and the PBC traded charges. Concord town manager Paul Flynn accused the Peoples Bicentennial Commission of misleading the town about its plans. No one, Flynn stated, agreed to an "all night party approach." The PBC responded that the selectmen had used "every device at their command to curb the First Amendment rights of the PBC." The group blamed any rowdiness on the ignorance of local teenagers "who grew up in the towns that helped launch the American Revolution, [but] knew next to nothing about that Revolution—a sad tribute to the kind of community that the Board of Selectmen helped shape."[82]

Some critics viewed the PBC's protest at the North Bridge as a form of desecration. Francis Watson, for example, wrote that the real motive of the

PBC was agitation "for socialism in the United States on the model of that in North Vietnam and Cuba." The *Daily Journal* in Elizabeth, New Jersey, accused the Peoples Bicentennial Commission of a "new kind of dissent . . . dissent for the hell of it." The *New York Sunday News* characterized the PBC as "a bunch of stoned activists, mouthing coarse and drunken epithets." Such people, the editors said, "defile the spirit of the Revolution." Others saw the freedom to dissent at sacred sites as proof that the revolutionary tradition was still alive. Jason Korell, the editor of the *Concord Journal*, echoed the belief of many that the spirit of freedom endured in Concord. The clashing ceremonies proved, he said, that "democracy and the system still work. . . . there is still freedom to assemble, to express oneself without fear, and to differ yet compromise." The *Allentown Call* described the PBC activities as "orgiastic revels" that revealed how many "liberties this free country [allows] even rude hooligans." Still others noted the possibility that the PBC protest had raised important questions. The *Canton Repository*'s Don Oakley wrote: "For all their excesses and inanities, the Yankee Doodleheads of 1975 do reflect the existence of unresolved inequities and injustices in American society." Finally, an occasional editorial even questioned the appropriateness of the official ceremonies. In the *Birmingham News*, Vic Gold commented on the "undesired intrusion" of the PBC but also characterized the official ceremonies themselves as a form of "mild desecration."[83]

Whatever one thinks of the boorish behavior of PBC members and their arrogance in claiming that they knew and could speak for the "real" American revolutionary tradition, they were indeed acting out the role of ceremonial social critic at the North Bridge, as had so many before them. From the early years of commemorative activity in Lexington and Concord, patriotic rhetoric has expressed fears that the heirs of the minutemen were falling away from revolutionary principles; such rhetoric also bemoaned the degenerate condition of the times. The PBC, of course, was not enthralled by the martial virtues of the minutemen, but it did choose the revolutionary tradition of dissent as a way of legitimating its protest against contemporary American society. Like so many others who had come to these patriotic centers, the Peoples Bicentennial Commission sought to refashion an American identity out of the fabric of the generation of the minutemen. And like so many others, the PBC fancied itself the true guardian of the spirit of Lexington and Concord.

Lexington Green and the North Bridge are the primal martial centers in American culture. Americans of various ideological persuasions have turned to these places to claim for themselves membership in the traditions of the nation whose birth is celebrated here. And in the minutemen, these sites have provided the nation with enduring images of the nature of Americans at war. Certainly, the legacy of Lexington and Concord looms over perceptions of martial heroes at other American battlesites.

Notes

1. Ralph Waldo Emerson, *A Historical Discourse Delivered before the Citizens of Concord, 12 September 1835 on the Centennial Anniversary of the Incorporation of the Town* (Boston: W. B. Clarke, 1835), p. 35.

2. Munroe, quoted in F. Lauriston Bullard, *Historic Summer Haunts from Newport to Portland* (Boston: Little, Brown and Co., 1912), p. 85. Much of my understanding of the history of Lexington ceremonials comes from the brief but valuable survey by Doris L. Pullen and Donald B. Cobb, *The Celebration of April the Nineteenth from 1776 to 1960 in Lexington, Massachusetts* (Lexington, Mass.: Town Celebrations Committee, 1960).

3. Pullen and Cobb, p. 8. The reinterment of the Lexington minutemen antedates by almost a half century what Michael Kammen calls the national "obsession" with reburying revolutionary war heroes. This obsession, he argues, began when one of Thomas Jefferson's grandchildren petitioned Congress in 1882 to build a memorial in Washington and move Jefferson's remains there. See Kammen, *A Season of Youth: The American Revolution and the Historical Imagination* (New York: Alfred A. Knopf, 1978), p. 65.

4. Pullen and Cobb, p. 8. The *Boston Daily News* reported on April 20, 1850, that "the populations of these towns turned out literally en masse, added to which the thousands from the cities of Boston and Lowell, swelled the multitude present to a very numerous gathering."

5. On November 12, 1873, the Lexington Centennial Committee wrote to Concord's Board of Selectmen inviting the town to participate in a joint celebration. The board apparently declined the invitation. See David B. Little, *America's First Centennial Celebration: The Nineteenth of April 1875 at Lexington and Concord, Massachusetts* (Boston: The Club of Odd Volumes, 1961), p. 16.

6. Charles Hudson, *History of the Town of Lexington* (n.p., n.d.), pp. 63, 74; Little, p. 43; *The Morning Star* (Boston and Chicago), Apr. 28, 1875. The *New York Times* noted on April 20, 1875, that the relics on display at Lexington "bind us to an event lying close by the beginnings of our national history."

7. April 19 has been a sacred date since before 1775. On that date in 1689 the Concord militia marched to Boston to help depose Governor Andros. After 1775 the date was further enshrined when, following the fall of Fort Sumter on April 14, 1861, couriers in New England rode along Paul Revere's route on April 19 calling out regiments and were met with "the ringing of bells, the firing of cannon and the assembling of soldiers, as brave, true and prompt as those of olden times" (Pullen and Cobb, p. 9). In addition, the Sixth Massachusetts, en route to defend the nation's capital in 1861, was met by an unfriendly mob in Baltimore on April 19. In the early 1970s the Massachusetts legislature decided that Nineteenth of April ceremonies should be celebrated on the Monday closest to that date. However, residents of Concord voted to continue holding their celebration on April 19. See Ann Chang, "Patriots' Day in Concord, Mass., Where April 19 Is Always April 19," *AAA World* 3, no. 2 (Mar./Apr. 1983): 11–12.

8. Pullen and Cobb, pp. 16–17. Lexington residents complained during the 1890s about this carnival-like atmosphere.

9. Thomas Carroll, "Lexington Monument," *Twelfth Annual Report of the Peabody Historical Society, 1907–1908* (Peabody, Mass.: Press of C. H. Shepard, 1909), p. 12; *Interim Report of the Boston National Historic Sites Com-*

mission Pertaining to the Lexington-Concord Battle Road (Jan. 27, 1959), 86th Cong., 1st sess., H. Doc. 57.

10. *Concord '75: Centennial Celebration,* Concord Pamphlets, Concord Free Public Library, Concord, Mass. (hereafter CFPL). The *Concord Journal* noted on April 13, 1944, that "for fifty years the site of the battle lay neglected." An indispensable source for understanding Concord's history in revolutionary times is Robert A. Gross, *The Minutemen and Their World* (New York: Hill and Wang, 1976).

11. *The Morning Star* estimated the crowds at Lexington and Concord at fifty thousand each and noted the "interesting display of relics" (Apr. 28, 1875).

12. Although this letter is about the 125th anniversary, it is in "Papers and Correspondence—150th Anniversary—Concord Fight," CFPL.

13. Quotes in this paragraph and the next are from the program for the 1961 festivities, in "Events in Concord," vol. 12 (1958–62), CFPL.

14. *The Spirit,* 1970, Concord Pamphlets, 35–130, CFPL. In 1964 the Concord Minute Men joined other New England groups at the New York World's Fair, the inauguration of Pres. Lyndon Johnson, and many battle reenactments. Frank Kennedy, a Sudbury minuteman, said of his group: "Each fellow comes out to relive the spirit that made the men march two hundred years ago. . . . Corny? It's not corny. It's true" (undated quote from the *Tribune Review* [Greensburg, Pa.], in *History of the Modern Concord Minute Men,* Concord Pamphlets, 31–144, CFPL). By 1970 there were approximately twenty-one Massachusetts towns with their own groups of minutemen. In keeping with National Park Service guidelines, there have been no battle reenactments at the North Bridge since 1967, but the Concord Minute Men have taken part in Battle Road reenactments. See Sgt. John F. Denis, ed., *Handbook for the Order and Discipline of the Concord Minute Men* (Concord, Mass.: n.p., 1979). For a profile of Jason H. Korell, a prominent Concord minuteman, see Evan M. Wylie, "The Man Who Fires 'the Shot Heard Round the World,' " *Yankee Magazine* (Apr. 1983): 80–85+. Korell, whose house is only a few minutes' walk from the North Bridge,

speaks easily about the attraction of the place. Calling Patriots' Day a "religious experience," he mentions his frequent solitary visits to the bridge and how it is so quiet there that "you can almost hear the whispers of the ghosts. It gives you a funny feeling" (interview, May 26, 1988). See also Korell, "Now Who Are These Old Men Coming Down the Street?" *Yankee Magazine* (Apr. 1971): 64–65+.

15. Richard D. Brown, *Revolutionary Politics in Massachusetts: The Boston Committee of Correspondence and the Towns, 1772–1774* (Cambridge: Harvard University Press, 1970), p. 44.

16. Amelia Forbes Emerson, ed., *Diaries and Letters of William Emerson 1743–1776* (n.p., n.d), p. 70, in CFPL files; Phillips Payson, "A Memorial of Lexington Battle, and of Some Signal Interpositions of Providence in the American Revolution," in *Anniversary Sermons Preached at Lexington* (n.p., n.d.), p. 22, in the Lexington Room, Cary Memorial Library, Lexington, Mass. (hereafter CML).

17. Thomas, quoted in Francis G. Walett, *Massachusetts Newspapers and the Revolutionary Crisis, 1763–1776* (Boston: Massachusetts Bicentennial Commission Publication, May 1974), p. 39; *Essex Gazette,* quoted in Frank Luther Mott, "The Newspaper Coverage of Lexington and Concord," *New England Quarterly* 17 (Dec. 1944): 500. The original broadside of Russell's special edition of the *Salem Gazette* is at the Boston Athenaeum.

18. Edward Everett, *An Address, Delivered at Lexington, 19 April 1835* (Charlestown, Mass.: William W. Wheildon, 1835), p. 8; Reynolds, quoted in *Proceedings at the Centennial Celebration of Concord Fight, April 19, 1875* (Concord, Mass.: by the town, 1876), p. 55, Concord Pamphlets, W. W. Wheildon Collection, CFPL; Richard Henry Dana, *Oration at Lexington, April 19, 1875* (Boston: Lockwood, Brooks and Co., 1875), p. 5.

19. Hoar, quoted in *Celebration of the Two Hundred and Fiftieth Anniversary of the Incorporation of Concord, September 12, 1885* (Concord, Mass.: by the town, n.d.), p. 40; Lexington Historical Society, quoted in *Lexington: Birthplace of American Liberty* (Lexington, Mass.: Lexington Historical Society, 1984), p. 14.

20. Reynolds, quoted in *Proceedings at the Centennial Celebration*, p. 56; Edward Everett, *An Oration Delivered at Concord, April the Nineteenth, 1825* (Boston: Cummings, Hilliard and Co., 1825), p. 54.

21. Sidney Howard, *"Lexington": A Pageant Drama of the American Freedom* (n.p., 1924), pp. 19, 81, 83; Curtis, quoted in "Concord Fight—Centennial—1875," Pickard Family Home Collection, vol. 1, CFPL. The May 5, 1875, issue of *The Pilot* calls Curtis's speech "A Know-Nothing Appeal" by someone who had forgotten that not just Anglo-Saxons were good patriots. Hope for the nation lay in diversity, the editors thought. They added, "Mr. Curtis would celebrate the centennial of the Concord fight by the descendants alone of the men who fought there," while "tens of thousands of Irish and German soldiers, who died for the Union, cried from their graves a reproof to this ingrate who would defame their lives and forget their death."

22. Curtis, quoted in *Proceedings at the Centennial Celebration*, pp. 92, 93; Lowell, quoted in *Celebration of the Two Hundred and Fiftieth Anniversary*, p. 67; Munroe, quoted in James Phinney Munroe, *The New England Conscience* (Boston: Gorham Press, 1915), pp. 22, 57.

23. Jonas Clarke, "The Fate of Bloodthirsty Oppressors and *God's* Tender Care of His Distressed People," in *Anniversary Sermons*, p. 28; Zabdiel Adams, "The Evil Designs of Men Made Subservient by God to the Public Good; Particularly Illustrated in the Rise, Progress, and Conclusion of the American War," in ibid., p. 20; Dana, p. 4.

24. Robinson, quoted in *Celebration of the Two Hundred and Fiftieth Anniversary*, p. 57; Harmon, quoted in *19th of April 1961 Ceremony*, Concord Pamphlets, 35–118, CFPL; Dukakis, quoted in *Lexington Minute Man*, Apr. 24, 1975, p. 5. On Sunday, April 20, 1975, an estimated twenty-five hundred visitors celebrated the rededication of the Battle Green.

25. Timothy Dwight, *Travels in New England and New York*, ed. Barbara Miller Solomon. 4 vols. (Cambridge: Harvard University Press, 1969), 1:280–81; Everett, *An Oration Delivered at Concord*, p. 42.

26. *The Complete Poetical Works of James Russell Lowell*, Cambridge ed. (Boston: Houghton Mifflin Co., 1897), pp. 361–62; Curtis, quoted in *Proceedings at the Centennial Celebration*, p. 97.

27. *Celebration of the Two Hundred and Fiftieth Anniversary*, p. 14; Allen French, *The Drama of Concord: A Pageant of Three Centuries* (Concord, Mass.: n.p., 1935), pp. 8, 42. The Minute Man National Historical Park brochure is in "Minute Man National Historical Park," historical correspondence files, box 1, National Park Service, Washington, D.C. (hereafter NPS).

28. *New York Communal Advertiser*, Apr. 19, 1875. The monument referred to must be the Revolutionary Monument erected in 1799, for the Captain Parker Monument was not erected until 1900.

29. Quoted in Pullen and Cobb, p. 7.

30. The *Boston Post* article is in the Boston Athenaeum. Part of the frustration of those haunted by their fathers' glory was the fact that seemingly no opportunities now existed for the same kind of martial heroism. In his address at the dedication of the Bunker Hill Monument in 1843, Daniel Webster declared that "heaven has not allotted to this generation an opportunity of rendering high services . . . but we may praise what we cannot equal, and celebrate actions which we were not born to perform" ("An Address Delivered on Bunker Hill, on the 17th of June, 1843, on Occasion of the Completion of the Monument," in *The Great Speeches and Orations of Daniel Webster*, ed. Edwin P. Whipple [Boston: Little, Brown and Co., 1879], p. 138). The Civil War would soon give these sons ample opportunity for martial sacrifice and a new baptism of blood. It is ironic that the revolutionary generation was similarly haunted by the epic deeds of their Puritan ancestors, those who broke the geographical bond with England. The same tension is apparent in their rhetorical memories of their ancestors. See, for example, Catherine Albanese, "Our Fathers Who Trod the Wilderness," in *Sons of the Fathers: The Civil Religion of the American Revolution* (Philadelphia: Temple University Press, 1976), pp. 19–45.

31. See George B. Forgie, *Patricide in the House Divided: A Psychological Interpretation of Lincoln and His Age* (New York: W. W. Norton and Co., 1979).

32. William Emmons, *An Address in Commemoration of Lexington Battle, Delivered April 19, 1826* (Boston: n.p., 1826), p. 15; Frisbie, quoted in *Celebration of the Two Hundred and Fiftieth Anniversary*, p. 24. The sense that the revolutionary generation was unlike any other is found not only in commemorative rhetoric. Consider, for example, John Shy's remark about the United States in the 1970s: "Our lack of heart, and our paucity of imagination, are themselves symptoms of a 'present' that seems all the more disheartening when we look at the evidence of energy and brilliance two hundred years ago" (Shy, *A People Numerous and Armed* [New York: Oxford University Press, 1976], p. 8).

33. Robert Rantoul, *Oration by Robert Rantoul, Jr., and Account of the Union Celebration at Concord, Nineteenth of April, 1850* (Boston: Dutton and Wentworth, 1850), p. 74; Samuel Ripley Bartlett, *Concord Fight* (Boston: A. Williams and Co., 1860), pp. 10, 29.

34. Yancey, quoted in Richard Maxwell Brown, "Violence and the American Revolution," in *Essays on the American Revolution*, ed. Stephen G. Kurtz and James H. Hutson (Chapel Hill: University of North Carolina Press, 1973; New York: W. W. Norton and Co., 1973), p. 113; Forgie, p. 292; *Ceremonies at the Dedication of the Soldiers' Monument in Concord, Mass.* (Concord, Mass.: Benjamin Tolman, 1867), pp. 13, 15. Indianapolis's Monument Square also houses a monument to the dead of World War I, dedicated in 1924, a monument to the dead of the Spanish-American War, and a monument to those who perished in Korea, the Dominican Republic, and Vietnam. In his study of antebellum South Carolina, Harold S. Schultz notes that a group called the Minutemen organized to march on Washington to prevent the inauguration of Abraham Lincoln. See Schultz, *Nationalism and Sectionalism in South Carolina, 1852–60* (Durham: Duke University Press, 1950), p. 226.

35. "Events in Concord," vol. 3 (1921–27), CFPL; Keyes, quoted in *Ceremonies at the Dedication of the Soldiers' Monument*, p. 5; Bartlett, quoted in ibid., p. 11.

36. Emerson, quoted in *Ceremonies at the Dedication of the Soldiers' Monument*, pp. 31, 32, 35; Schouler, quoted in ibid., p. 65. An-other speech honored George Prescott, a Civil War minuteman from Concord who was born of the "sturdy stock of the yeomanry of Middlesex." Having grown up in Concord "under the influences of the church and the Sunday-school, the lyceum, the library, the town-meeting and the battle-ground," Prescott had "no love of battle" but was ready when the "trial" came (ibid., p. 21). He died a martyr in 1864.

37. Curtis, quoted in *Proceedings at the Centennial Celebration*, p. 90 (emphasis added); *Cheshire Republican* article, in "Concord Fight—Centennial—1875," vol. 2, CFPL; Hoar, quoted in *Celebration of the Two Hundred and Fiftieth Anniversary*, p. 24.

38. The *New York Herald* article is in "Events in Concord," vol. 1 (1877–1916), CFPL. A *Concord Enterprise* liberty bond advertisement on April 24, 1918, sponsored by the Concord National Bank, used the image of the city as a collective minuteman: "Concord's bells are rousing the people of Concord to help turn back the armies of Kaiser William."

39. Townsend Scudder, *Concord: American Town* (Boston: Little, Brown and Co., 1947), p. 323. World War I also gave the nation a popular new minuteman hero: Sgt. Alvin C. York, a simple, pious deadeye born to Appalachian mountain folk. See David Lee, *Sergeant York: An American Hero* (Lexington: University of Kentucky Press, 1985).

40. "Patriots' Day Message," Apr. 19, 1944, in "Events in Concord," vol. 6 (1937–44), CFPL; "A Significant 1945 Message Calling Attention to Pioneering Achievements of Patriots of Massachusetts Whose Legacy Is Our Inspiration," in "Pageants—Festivals—Celebrations," CML.

41. Edward J. Leithead, "The Revolutionary War in Dime Novels," *American Book Collector* 18 (Apr./May 1969): 18.

42. Bonaparte, quoted in *The Middlesex Patriot*, p. 2, in "Papers and Correspondence—150th Anniversary—Concord Fight," CFPL; Good, quoted in *Boston Globe*, Apr. 12, 1936.

43. "Address of Senator Leverett Saltonstall of Massachusetts, April 19, 1950 (Patriots' Day), Lexington, Massachusetts, 4:15 P.M.," in "Pageants—Festivals—Celebrations," CML; *Concord Journal*, Apr. 23, 1953; *Patriots'*

Day, April 19: A Proclamation by His Excellency Christian A. Herter, Governor, 1955, Concord Pamphlets, CFPL.

44. Material on the 1961 ceremonies in Concord is in *19th of April 1961 Ceremony*.

45. Ibid.

46. Harry Jones, Jr., *The Minutemen* (Garden City, N.Y.: Doubleday and Co., 1968); "The Minutemen," *Time* (Nov. 3, 1961): 19; "Armed Superpatriots," *The Nation* 163 (Nov. 11, 1961): 367, 372–75; James Ridgeway, "Don't Wait, Buy a Gun Now!" *New Republic* 150 (June 6, 1964): 9–10.

47. Bullard, p. 100.

48. *Lexington Minuteman*, Nov. 2, 1974.

49. "Bicentennial Celebrations," file drawers, CML.

50. Allen French, *Historic Concord and the Lexington Fight* (Ipswich, Mass.: Gambit, 1987), p. 19; Ezra Ripley, *Half Century Discourse Delivered November 16, 1828, at Concord, Massachusetts* (Concord, Mass.: printed by Herman Atwill, 1829), p. 24; Rev. Grindall Reynolds, *Concord Fight, April 19, 1775* (Boston: A. Williams and Co., 1875), pp. 5, 6, 22, 23.

51. The comment on Everett's speech is in "Concord Fight—Centennial—1875," vol. 2, CFPL; *Yeoman's Gazette,* Apr. 21, 1827. Information on the history of Concord monuments and the North Bridge, as well as the Ripley quote, appears in *Interim Report of the Boston National Historic Sites Commission*, pp. 84–95.

52. *Yeoman's Gazette*, Dec. 10, 1836.

53. Roland Wells Robbins, *The Story of the Minuteman* (Stoneham, Mass.: George R. Barnstead and Son, 1945); Little, p. 34; Margaret F. Cresson, *Journey into Fame: The Life of Daniel Chester French* (Cambridge: Harvard University Press, 1947), p. 97. A sealed copper box enclosed in the monument's pedestal contained a record of proceedings "relating to its erection," the names of various political dignitaries, a history of Concord, William Emerson's account of the battle, an account of the 1850 celebration, and the program of dedication at the Soldiers' Monument (see *Proceedings at the Centennial Celebration*). This is not the only time items have been placed inside the statue. In March 1975 the statue was removed for cleaning, and when it was returned, a local Girl Scout troop put a time capsule into the base, a "treasure of historic and contemporary memorabilia" (*Concord Journal,* Mar. 27, 1975). In 1878 Concord adapted French's statue for its town seal.

54. J. B. Jackson, *The Necessity for Ruins and Other Topics* (Amherst: University of Massachusetts Press, 1980), p. 94; Charles H. Brigham, "The First Battle of the American Revolution: A Discourse Delivered in the Unitarian Church in Ann Arbor, Michigan, on the Evening of April 18, 1875," *Argus*, Apr. 23, 1875; *Concord and Lexington* (Boston: Worcester Press, 1908), p. 3; visitor, quoted in *New England Sketches,* in "Events in Concord," vol. 1 (1877–1916), CFPL.

55. Letter from Dr. Raymond L. Puffer to the author, May 30, 1989; Thomas Riedinger, "The Meaning of the Master Missile . . . Minuteman," *Boeing Magazine* (Nov. 1959); Terhune, quoted in *19th of April 1961 Ceremony*.

56. *Concord Journal,* Nov. 29, 1973; "Events in Concord," vol 26 (1982), CFPL.

57. Alfred Sereno Hudson, *Colonial Concord: Middlesex County Massachusetts* (Concord, Mass.: Erudite Press, 1904), pp. 127, 128. Curiously, Concord town records do not reveal any interest in those "grim old timbers" as valuable relics in the same manner that others prized chunks of Alamo rock, wood from the copse of trees at the Angle at Gettysburg, or pieces of bone or spent shell casings at the Little Bighorn.

58. *Interim Report of the Boston National Historic Sites Commission*, p. 18. The quoted material in this paragraph is from "Concord Bridge of Revolutionary War Restored with Pressure Treated Wood," *Wood Preserving News* (Sept. 1956): 18.

59. *Concord Enterprise,* Jan. 16, 1929.

60. *Boston Globe,* July 15, 1956. The *Interim Report of the Boston National Historic Sites Commission* includes a recommendation for the "creation of a national historic park embracing portions of the traditional setting . . . that was traversed by the British," for on April 19 "man reached an important milestone in the eternal struggle to control and improve his estate upon earth" (p. 7).

61. The NPS brochure is in Concord Pamphlets, CFPL. See also *Battle Road: Memorial*

or Arterial? (Washington, D.C.: National Park Service, Oct. 1983).

62. *Environmental Assessment Land Protection Plan—Minute Man National Historical Park* (Washington, D.C.: Department of the Interior, National Park Service, n.d.), p. 31.

63. Ibid., pp. 34, 42, 47, 51.

64. Fred Szarka interview, May 25, 1988; Thomas Boylston Adams, "Uncovering Six Miles of American History," *Boston Globe,* June 4, 1988, p. 15. In a later editorial Adams informed readers that this particular area was "the most important piece of ground in the United States" (*Boston Globe,* Apr. 15, 1989, p. 23). On September 30, 1989, he again offered his support for the restoration plans, remarking that "the intent of the National Park Service is to make the past come alive by showing the truth" (*Boston Globe,* Sept. 30, 1989, p. 23).

65. Quoted in Daniel B. Wroblewski, "U.S. Proposes to Take Battle Road Back in Time," *New York Times,* July 17, 1988, p. 28.

66. Elias Phinney, *History of the Battle at Lexington, on the Morning of the 19th of April 1775* (Boston: Phelps and Farnham, 1825), p. 6. For a good summary of the controversy, see Harold Murdock, "Historic Doubts on the Battle of Lexington," *Massachusetts Historical Society* (May 1916): 361–86. See also Kevin Aylmer, "The Banker and the Battle: Lexington 1775," *American History Illustrated* 7, no. 6 (Oct. 1973): 12.

67. Rev. Ezra Ripley, D.D., *A History of the Fight at Concord on the 19th of April 1775* (Concord, Mass.: Allen and Atwill, 1827), pp. 24, 38, 41. Lemuel Shattuck also makes the case for Concord as the site of the first battle. See Shattuck, *A History of the Town of Concord* (Boston: Russell, Odiorne and Co., 1835).

68. *Hudson Pioneer,* Feb. 19, 1875; *Boston Globe,* Apr. 14, 16, 1875; Dana, pp. 16, 17; *Boston News,* Mar. 19, 1875. See Little, pp. 16–20, for the story of the last-minute arrival of Lexington's centennial statues.

Even the War Department took part in the debate between Lexington's and Concord's supporters. On April 3, 1924, Maj. Frank Geere recommended that the crest of the U.S. Army Reserve be changed to include French's image of the minuteman rather than Kitson's. He argued that Kitson's statue did not depict "the original Minuteman" and could be taken for "an early pioneer of the Daniel Boone period." By contrast, he said, French's statue "represents no individual person, and marks the spot where the *first organized force of American citizen soldiers used arms against and defeated an enemy.* It is . . . distinctly emblematic of and unequivocally characterizes the citizen-soldier—the first of his kind in our nation, who furnished the key to our traditional defense policy—the forerunner of the modern Reservist." An October 2, 1924, communication from the historical division of the U.S. Army War College supported Geere's conclusion: "It would appear that the Concord Minute Man is the one that should be used as a crest for the Organized Reserves." The adjutant general to whom Geere and the War College had appealed responded that there was merit to the argument for changing the crest and that "either the Lexington or the Concord statue might have been chosen. [But] the Lexington [figure] was selected because the Revolutionary War started on the site and the figure was a statue of Captain Parker who was killed there." I am indebted to Col. Robert F. Baker, director of the Institute of Heraldry, Department of the Army, for providing me with copies of relevant correspondence on this subject.

69. George J. Varney, *The Story of Patriots' Day* (Boston: Lee and Shepard, 1895), p. 34; Murdock, p. 383. On April 18, 1925, the *Independent* told its readers that Murdock's article and subsequent book about the Nineteenth of April destroyed the "myth" of the battle of Lexington, "perpetuated in the enthusiastic ignorances of a thousand orators" (p. 434). Arthur B. Tourtellot, in *Lexington and Concord* (New York: W. W. Norton and Co., 1963), is also hard on the Lexington boosters. He states that it was "less a battle or even a skirmish than an hysterical massacre at the hands of badly disciplined British soldiers" (p. 134). When I asked a staff member at the visitors center at Lexington if the diorama represented a historically accurate portrayal, since I had heard that the minutemen might not have fired back, I was told in no uncertain terms that they had and that the diorama was quite accurate. For an account of the diorama, see *Boston Globe,* Aug. 21,

1962. The Lexington flyer mentioned in the text is in "Bicentennial Celebrations," file drawers, CML.

70. See Eric Hobsbawm, "Inventing Traditions," in *The Invention of Tradition*, ed. Eric Hobsbawm and Terence Ranger (Cambridge: Cambridge University Press, 1983), pp. 1–14.

71. Ian M. G. Quimby, "The Doolittle Engravings of the Battle of Lexington and Concord," *Winterthur Portfolio* 4 (1968): 87.

72. This information is found among the boxed materials on revolutionary paintings at the Massachusetts Historical Society, Boston.

73. Josiah Adams, *An Address Delivered at Acton, July 21, 1835, Being the First Centennial Anniversary of the Organization of That Town; with an Appendix* (Boston: J. T. Buckingham, 1835), pp. 20, 24.

74. Josiah Adams, *Letter to Lemuel Shattuck, esq., of Boston, from Josiah Adams, esq., of Framingham in Vindication of the Claims of Captain Isaac Davis, of Acton, to His Just Share in the Honors of the Concord Fight* (Boston: Damrell and Moore, 1850), p. 7; Hayward, quoted in Little, p. 38; Frederick B. Noyes, *The Tell-Tale Tomb; or, The Acton Aspects of the Concord Fight* (n.p., n.d.), pp. 2, 5, 8.

75. Maria Davis Hunt, "Line of March," *Daughters of the American Revolution Magazine* (n.d.): 422–23, 426, in the Acton Memorial Library, Acton, Mass. All other quoted material in this paragraph is from two flyers, "Let's Save the Isaac Davis Trail" and "The Replica Scrolls: The Line of March of the Acton Minutemen to the Old North Bridge at Concord—April 19, 1775," in "Minute Man National Historical Park," historical correspondence files, box 1, NPS. Hunt wrote of a "reawakening of pride in the history of Acton," adding: "Scouts clear the old roads of the original Line of March. The Garden Club keeps flowers and plantings bright at the Isaac Davis Monument." Also, the "beautiful colonial red signs that now clearly mark the route . . . were . . . a community accomplishment. A lumber dealer provided the material, the high school voctional [*sic*] department built the signs and posts, an artist did the silver Minute Man and lettering, and the Boy Scouts and their Leaders placed the signs with the assistance of the town engineer" (p. 422). I am indebted to Jeanne Bracken, reference librarian at the Acton Memorial Library, for bringing this material to my attention.

76. Carroll, pp. 5, 7, 9.

77. *Lexington Minute-Man*, May 27, 1971; *Boston Herald Traveler*, May 31, 1971.

78. See the *Boston Herald Traveler*, May 31, 1971; "Special Events—Dedications, Anniversaries—Vietnam Veterans—5/31/71," National Park Service files, North Bridge Visitors' Center, Minute Man National Historical Park, Concord, Mass.

79. Szarka interview, May 25, 1988.

80. Peoples Bicentennial Commission, *America's Birthday: A Planning and Activity Guide for Citizens' Participation during the Bicentennial Years* (New York: Simon and Schuster, 1974), pp. 9, 11; Jeremy Rifkin, "Bicentennial," *New American Movement* (Nov.-Dec. 1971), in "Concord Fight—Bicentennial—April 19, 1975—200th Anniversary," document box 4, CFPL. See also the interview with Rifkin and John Warner of the American Revolution Bicentennial Administration in "Growing Controversy over the Bicentennial: Two Views," *U.S. News and World Report* 78 (Mar. 24, 1975): 35–37.

81. "45,000 Patriots Gather at PBC Rally for Economic Democracy," *Common Sense* 3, no. 2 (1975): 6–8, in Concord Pamphlets, 35–136, CFPL. The Concord selectmen tried to convince the Park Service to deny the PBC request. They outlined their worries about public safety and damage to the town and battlesite in a letter to David Moffett on April 1, 1975. After the decision, Philip H. Suter, chairman of the Concord Board of Selectmen, wrote to the secretary of the Interior Department to "register our protest . . . and request an immediate review of the action" ("Bicentennial Celebration, April 19, 1975: Report and Analysis," North Atlantic Regional Office, National Park Service, Minute Man National Historical Park, Concord, Mass.).

82. Ibid.; letter from Paul Flynn to Jeremy Rifkin, June 26, 1975, in Concord Pamphlets, 35–136, CFPL; PBC, quoted in "45,000 Patriots Gather."

83. Francis J. Watson, Jr., *The Destructive Program of the Peoples Bicentennial Commission: Analysis of Its Propaganda and Recommended Countermeasures* (Dunn Loring, Va.: n.p., 1975), p. 2; *Daily Journal* (Elizabeth, N.J.),

Apr. 22, 1975; *Sunday News* (New York), Apr. 27, 1975; Jason Korell, *Report of the 1975 Celebrations Committee,* Concord Pamphlets, 35–142, CFPL; *Allentown Call, Canton Repository,* and *Birmingham News* are quoted in "Concord Fight—Bicentennial—April 19, 1975—200th Anniversary."

Many critics point out that during the nation's bicentennial Americans were being asked to celebrate their past with the usual mixture of fable presented as history and crass commercialism. David Lowenthal commented that "not only are most of the landscapes touted by Bicentennial hawkers historically false, they are unconvincing either as imitations or as evocations of the past. No one really believes in them, but their popularity as entertainment lends support to the suggestion that the true Father of the modern United States is no longer George Washington but Walt Disney" (Lowenthal, "The Bicentennial Landscape: A Mirror Held Up to the Past," *Geographical Review* 67, no. 3 [July 1977]: 256).

2

"A Reservoir of Spiritual Power"

Encouraged by the Mexican government's offer of free land and no taxes, colonists from the United States poured into the vast Mexican province of Texas in the mid-1820s. The plan had been for them to help develop the area, but by the time Antonio López de Santa Anna assumed the presidency in 1832, tensions between the Mexican government and the colonists were running high. In 1835 Santa Anna sent troops under the command of his brother-in-law, Gen. Martín Perfecto de Cós, to San Antonio de Bexar to quash the rebellion. Cós occupied the town and made his headquarters in an old Spanish mission commonly known as the Alamo. In December of that year a small Texas army led by Benjamin Rush Milam drove Cos out of San Antonio, prompting an infuriated Santa Anna to declare that Texans would "soon learn their folly."

On February 23, 1836, the Mexican president and his army rode into San Antonio. Santa Anna discovered that a group of Texans, commanded by William Barrett Travis and a gravely ill Jim Bowie, had decided to make their stand at the Alamo. Allied with the Texans were a number of Tejanos, or Mexican Texans, who opposed the Mexican dictator, as well as Davy Crockett and his Tennessee Mounted Volunteers, recent arrivals who were prepared to fight for "the liberties of our common country." When Travis ordered that a single cannon shot be fired in reply to Santa Anna's demand for unconditional surrender, the siege of the Alamo began.

On February 24 Travis penned a message "to the People of Texas & all Americans in the world," asking for their help and pledging, "I Shall Never Retreat or Die." Twice James Bonham rode ninety-five miles to Goliad, where the four-hundred-man Texas army was encamped, to request assistance; twice he returned alone. Only the arrival of thirty-two volunteers from Gonzales cheered the Alamo defenders as the shelling increased during the last part of February and into early March. Finally, in the predawn hours of March 6, with the sound of the "Deguello" blaring from Mexican trumpets, Santa Anna ordered his troops to storm the former mission. Repulsed twice, the Mexican army eventually succeeded in breaching the walls. When the battle was over, all 183 of the Alamo defenders were dead. "It was a small affair," declared Santa Anna.

Almost immediately this "small affair" captured the attention of people throughout the United States and furnished the battle cry for Texas's victory over Santa Anna on April 21, 1836, at San Jacinto, thereby assuring Texas independence. The saga of the Alamo thus took its place in the American heroic tradition.

The Alamo

T HE CELEBRATION of the Texas Sesquicentennial in 1986 once again focused attention on the saga of the last stand of the Texas heroes at
the Alamo on March 6, 1836. The Witte Museum in San Antonio and the
DeGolyer Library at Southern Methodist University in Dallas had major
displays on the evolution of the old mission and on Americans' perception
of the battle. In addition, a replica of the Alamo, originally built for a 1960
John Wayne movie filmed in Brackettville, Texas, was refurbished in 1986
for the NBC-TV movie *The Alamo: Thirteen Days to Glory,* which aired on
January 26, 1987, and was advertised as a film about a time when "America
had real heroes."[1]

It would be a mistake to dismiss such attention as a sign of antiquarian
curiosity, or as part of a nostalgic impulse, or as an anachronistic attachment
to the minutiae of history. Rather, such vibrant cultural activity reminds us
of the care we take to cultivate symbols that link us to events perceived as
crucial both to the life of the nation and to our understanding of contemporary dilemmas. As Maj. Gen. H. L. Grills, commander of Lackland Air
Force Base, said in 1957, the Alamo belongs to "American history—and all
Americans must be allowed to share the pride of Texans in it." Many Texans
have indeed taken a tribal pride in the Alamo story, for it tells of the crucial
event in the creation of the Texas republic. Like the Exodus in ancient
Israel, the saga of the Alamo has become part of the patriotic canon, just
as its heroes and lessons have become the measure of each new generation
and each new set of crises.[2]

The Alamo, like other battlesites, has been the object of veneration and
defilement, and its enduring message of patriotic orthodoxy has been subject to redefinition. My survey of the symbolic history of the Alamo in the
twentieth century focuses not only on how this famous symbol has been
perceived but also on the struggle over who should speak for it. That is,
who are the legitimate owners of the "true" meaning of the symbol? A
discussion of the ideal types of attitudes of veneration, defilement, and
redefinition provides an appropriate beginning.

While the Alamo lay in ruins in the first decade after the battle, from 1836 until the U.S. Army occupied the site in 1847, visitors often responded to the scene with words of awe and fascination, mixed with regret that the heroes were not memorialized in a more fitting way. Many still use the language of veneration. Among them are the Daughters of the Republic of Texas (DRT), who have proudly and carefully maintained the Alamo as a "sacred Memorial to the heroes who immolated themselves upon that hallowed ground." Edith Mae Johnson, a former chairwoman of the DRT's Alamo Committee, described the awe that fills her every time she enters the famous chapel, the "shrine" of the Texas heroes. Speaking reverently of men who had the courage to die in war, she said she measures a man by his "willingness for self-sacrifice" in a heroic cause.[3]

The Alamo has also been venerated as an enduring model of patriotic behavior by popular television evangelist Pat Robertson, who broadcast his "700 Club" from there as part of the Texas Sesquicentennial celebration. Setting the tone for the show, Danuta Soderman, one of Robertson's co-hosts, asked him: "Was that sacrifice worth all those deaths? Was the Alamo worth dying for at that time?" In response, Robertson spoke of the importance of the sacrifice for those who later fought at San Jacinto, the battle that ended Mexico's rule of Texas. That battle was won, Robertson said, because Texans were "inspired by the nobility of those who had died for this cause." He asserted that "bravery and heroic actions in behalf of freedom have never been in vain" and that from this historic "moment of liberty" America must learn a truth repeated by many Texans: "Eternal vigilance is the price of liberty." Robertson warned that Americans cannot only enjoy "freedom, prosperity, and wealth" but must also "get involved." He urged citizens to bolster Mexico's "chaotic economy" and warned that the United States must not allow "Communist tyranny to take over nation after nation." For Robertson, the Alamo freedom fighters personify timeless values of American patriotic commitment. If we would learn from these heroes, he said, we would willingly help a "little outpost of freedom fighters down in Central America who are saying, 'We want to bring freedom and liberty to our country.' "[4]

The Alamo is an object of veneration as well for Gary L. Foreman, a member of several living-history reenactment groups and an amateur historian who moved from Chicago to San Antonio in 1985. For him, the patriotic truths nurtured at the Alamo are intimately tied to an accurate physical reconstruction of the Alamo complex as it was at the time of the battle in 1836. Foreman used the language of defilement to describe threats to the purity of the Alamo message from within and without. He believes that the DRT desecrated the site by turning a sacred place into merely a tourist attraction. For Foreman, the only solution is a return to historical authenticity in museum displays, reenactments, and even in the choice of items sold in the gift shop. Furthermore, according to Foreman and others, the threat of defilement also comes from the ominous growth of the city of San Antonio. In their view, the Alamo and its message can be preserved from the encroachment of uncaring modernity only by a commitment to the physical transformation of the bustling secularity of Alamo Plaza.[5]

Very different language was used by Rev. Balthasar Janacek, archdiocesan director of the Old Spanish Missions and pastor of Christ the King Church in San Antonio. For Father Balty, as he calls himself, the symbol of the Alamo is a vehicle of separation and bitterness between ethnic communities in San Antonio. Like Pat Robertson, he thinks about current events in Nicaragua; but for Father Balty, the muscular American imperialism that provided the impetus for the Mexican-Texan conflict, and that continues to provide the impetus for the rigid, simplistic anticommunism at work in Nicaragua, is a prime example of the American desire to "control events." Consequently, Father Balty tries to expand the symbol of the Alamo. Unlike other dissenters from traditional Anglo-American patriotic orthodoxies, he is not interested merely in restoring to their rightful place the Tejanos (Mexican Texans) who fought in the Alamo. Rather, he struggles to alter our perception of this symbolic landscape, bringing into view the Alamo's prerevolutionary past as a vibrant Catholic mission.[6]

Many visitors to the Alamo have shared the reverence of Edith Mae Johnson; and, like Pat Robertson, they are persuaded that lessons from the saga of the Alamo are relevant to contemporary situations. Occasions like the sesquicentennial recall the power of blood sacrifice and trace the life of republican virtue in a series of righteous American warriors: from the minutemen of Lexington and Concord and the heroes of the Alamo to more recent incarnations, even including the Nicaraguan "freedom fighters" supposedly inspired by the power of American ideals. Alamo commemorative rhetoric has declared that continuity with this heroic past is crucial. Only through adherence to the sacrificial model of the heroes of the Alamo, this rhetoric informs us, can contemporary citizens follow in the footsteps of these heroes, men like Col. William B. Travis, Jim Bowie, James Bonham, and Davy Crockett. Symbolic continuity with the past, celebrated in patriotic rituals, has been perceived in recent years as even more important because of widespread fears that the nation has lost the commitment of these primal heroes. Consequently, commemorations have become opportunities for jeremiads, warnings of danger from within and without if a process of rededication does not begin soon.

The fear of broken connections has been expressed most clearly in Alamo commemorative rhetoric that emphasizes the continued efficacy of martial sacrifice. Rededication, it has been assumed, brings revitalization, a faith that the idealized attributes of the Texas frontier can provide models of contemporary public behavior. For those guided by such traditional messages, the symbol of the Alamo is complete; it needs no revision. Rather, it requires only that each generation's rededication is expressed in proper form. Failure to live up to the heroic ideal reveals a lack of personal commitment to the lessons of the Alamo, not a deficiency in the symbol itself. These traditional patriotic themes are most obvious in the rhetoric of military celebrants on Alamo Day or in Alamo pilgrimages speeches during San Antonio's Fiesta Week, which each April celebrates Texas independence. Fiesta Week was first celebrated in 1891, to honor the visiting president, Benjamin Harrison, and it has continued as a celebration of the Texans' victory at San Jacinto and the creation of the Texas republic. Fiesta Week pilgrimages to the Alamo began in 1927 as part of the schoolchildren's commemoration, but by the mid-1930s these pilgrimages had become an all-city event. Even as participants experience a "weeklong period of unprecedented hilarity," they remember to pause "in the twilight . . . to pay solemn and thankful tribute to Texas heroes."[7]

Curiously, throughout the nineteenth century there were no ceremonies at the Alamo on March 6, the day it fell. San Antonio newspapers usually mentioned the significance of the date, but even the fiftieth anniversary passed with only this comment from the *Daily Express:* "It is suggested that a society be formed, whose duty it shall be to see that the prominent anniversaries of Texas histories are properly observed." Formal anniversary ceremonies were not held in San Antonio until 1897, when the Daughters of the Republic of Texas began to conduct services at the grave of Benjamin R. Milam, who had died during the capture of San Antonio in December 1835. Although no formal services were held at the Alamo itself, visitors to the site could listen as a Texas veteran, Capt. Tom Rife, the custodian of the mission from 1885 to 1893, told the story "in a manner and a tone so impressive that the mind [would] unconsciously go back to the story of the Iliad." By 1909 formal anniversary services were being held at the Alamo and were so popular that in 1912 the *Express* proudly noted: "Even representatives of races the Anglo-Saxon world does not consider civilized have been moved by the story every stone in the old church tells."[8]

Familiar themes were repeated in a series of elaborate Texas centennial celebrations in 1936. Anniversary events were led by Texas governor James V. Allred and Gov. Hill McAlister of Tennessee (home of Davy Crockett's volunteers), with the support of religious, civic, military, and patriotic groups. Five bishops celebrated a pontifical high mass before a crowd of twenty thousand gathered in front of the Alamo, after which the Episcopal bishop of the diocese of west Texas, William T. Capers, gave an address. He declared that the Alamo heroes had died for the sacredness of the home, threatened in modern times by the forces of materialism. In what had already become a familiar tribute, the bishop asked, "Who could follow in the footsteps of Travis, Bowie, or Crockett?" Governor Allred told the assemblage that the Alamo was the crucial event in the birth of Texas, and Pres. Franklin D. Roosevelt sent a message that the battle was a "victory for principles of liberty." When Roosevelt visited the Alamo in June of the centennial year, he honored the men who had died there, declaring that "without the Alamo the great Southwest might never have become a part of the nation." He assured the crowd that "we have not discarded nor lost that virility [or] ideals of the pioneers."[9]

The crises of World War II brought renewed calls for adherence to the animating lessons of the Alamo. Writing in the dark days of 1942, Charlie Jeffries traced the spiritual inspiration of the Alamo heroes for generations of Texans who had fought in the nation's wars. He asked if Texans were now prepared for a war that would try them "as they have not been tried since the dark days of the Civil War." Could they, he wondered, stand the "baptism of fire"? He thought they could, for they had been "properly imbued for the ordeal." As the Alamo has served Texans in the past, he concluded, "the lights of the Alamo will shine on them, too." Anniversary speakers in 1943 and 1944 honored those who had died in the war that was still going on and declared that their courage was formed by allegiance to the principles for which the Alamo heroes had died. Evelyn M. Carrington noted that modern courage had its "roots and very being in the faith of [the] fathers." Samuel L. Terry declared that in troublesome times "we must go back to the original foundation from which we sprang."[10]

Commemorative rhetoric in the postwar years continually used the Alamo drama to interpret each new crisis of public faith. The tensions of the cold war brought renewed emphasis on the contemporary relevance of the lessons of the Alamo. For example, in 1948 Fleet Adm. Chester W. Nimitz pronounced that the sacrifice at the Alamo was a beacon to all Texans who had fought in other wars and that it served as a "warning to present-day dictators." A 1951 *San Antonio Express* editorial stated, "Should the aggressor begin a World War III, he would find the name and flame of the Alamo a force to reckon with." This militant rhetoric offered assurances that the evil forces of communism would never triumph in the United States because the moral force that provided the inspiration for the last stand at the Alamo was still a powerful one. In 1947 Texas governor Beauford H. Jester stated that against the menace of communism "our mightiest weapon is that Excalibur of the spirit handed down to us by Travis and his men." A 1953 speech by Adj. Gen. Kearie L. Berry of Texas emphasized the moral orientation that the Alamo could provide in an otherwise chaotic world.

"As the growing menace of Communism seeks to enslave the world," he said, "free men everywhere must 'Remember the Alamo.' "[11]

Although warnings of doom and degeneration are prevalent in commemorative rhetoric, the emphasis has been on the importance of maintaining continuity with the heroic past. Heroism in war is celebrated as a revelation of the animating spirit of the Alamo. In 1952 Lt. Gen. William L. Hogue, Fourth Army commander, declared that the "performance of our soldiers in Korea proves that there has been no weakening of our spiritual fibre since the Alamo." In 1953 Texas attorney general John Ben Shepperd called forth the heroes: "Look down Travis! Crockett, . . . Bowie, Bonham. Look down! Yes, we are keeping the faith. We kept it at Normandy, at Okinawa, and we are keeping it in Korea." In a 1962 speech, Col. Armin F. Puck traced the history of the First Battle Group of the Texas 141st Infantry and asked, "Are we like our forefathers? I believe yes." Puck asserted that battles fought at San Jacinto, by Hood's Texas Brigade in the Civil War, at the Meuse-Argonne during World War I, at Salerno, Italy, and in France during World War II justified "placing into our custody the sacred trust of the streamer for the Battle of the Alamo."[12]

Alamo rhetoric also presents communism as a spiritual challenge to the resources of America. Each eruption of military conflict during the seemingly endless cold war gave patriots a chance to "examine the American spirit." Such stocktaking in 1963 was, declared Lt. Gen. Carl H. Jark, commander of the Fourth Army at Fort Sam Houston, analogous to the contemplative discipline of the Alamo heroes who searched their "innermost selves" for the answer to Colonel Travis's challenge to cross the line. Thus did one of the Alamo's most enduring tales provide the occasion for a renewal of the nation's patriotic covenant.[13]

According to this particular legend, when all hope was gone, Travis, as cavalier of the Alamo, drew a line on the ground with his sword and challenged the men under his command to cross it and thereby face certain death in order to "buy time" for the beleaguered Gen. Sam Houston. All but Moses Rose did so. William P. Zuber, who claimed that Rose told the story at his family's house when Zuber was a little boy, made the story public in the *Texas Almanac for 1873*. It was eventually popularized in the first three editions of Anna M. J. Hardwicke Pennybacker's *New History of Texas for Schools* (1888). Skeptics were often able to delete the story from the school history canon, and following the example of George P. Garrison's *Texas: A Contest of Civilizations* (1903), the last three editions of Pennybacker's history book did not mention it either.[14]

The story is not so easily expunged from popular history, however; in fact, over the years it has spurred fairly acrimonious debate. For some it symbolizes Texans' courage and should not be debunked even if it is not historically accurate. Noted Texas folklorist J. Frank Dobie has declared that no amount of research will ever diminish the "Grand Canyon cut into the bedrock of human emotions and heroical impulses" provided by the story of Travis's line. In a letter to the editor of the *Southwestern Historical Quarterly,* J. K. Beretta, a member of the Texas Centennial Control Commission, warned of the danger to the nation of whittling away at heroes. Thinking the tale so crucial to the patriotic canon of the Alamo, and in the absence of definite proof that Travis did *not* draw the line, he argued: "Let us believe it . . . [in order to] keep our illusion of . . . Texas heroes as patriotic, loyal, and good citizens." Former DRT president Martha Rash has remarked, "These stories were handed down for an awful long time, and whether they're true or not, I want to believe them." In 1989 the DRT installed a plaque in the ground directly in front of the Alamo that reads: "Legend states that in 1836 Lt. Col. William Barrett Travis unsheathed his sword and drew a line on this ground before his battle-weary men stating: 'Those prepared to give their lives in freedom's cause, come over to me!' " And in the *Handbook of Production Information* for the 1988 film *Alamo . . . The Price of Freedom,* director Kieth Merrill quotes J. K. Beretta to justify dramatizing the legend. Merrill was aware of the controversy regarding the story's authenticity but remarked, "When we had to choose, we have opted always on the side of heroism and idealism and the spirit of the Alamo."[15]

The tale of the Alamo heroes crossing Travis's line has been acted out innumerable times, including during the Texas sesquicentennial celebration on Alamo Plaza. It is, in fact, a required part of the "conversion" drama, for it was at this point, guardians of the patriotic faith argue, that men from various states and countries became Texas and American heroes and revealed their distinctive American courage and determination. The line crossing, accompanied by a crescendo of music, is clearly the emotional high point of the film *Alamo . . . The Price of Freedom,* with the spectacular battle scenes that follow serving simply to dramatize the inevitable. The power of the story was not lost on the actors or the production crew. Kevin Young, who was the film's technical director and who also portrayed an Alamo defender, recalled: "Our movie Travis [actor Casey Biggs] commences his lines. As he tells us that help will not come for the Alamo and that he is prepared to give his life for freedom, suddenly the reality of it all comes down upon us. Even if this moment did not take place like some historians believe, it is nevertheless the very reality of what the Alamo is all about . . . when 189 people stop being New Yorkers, Illinoisians . . . and become Texians. . . . Our Travis finishes, and . . . a cheer comes up from the crowd; our Travis can not speak and tears roll from his eyes. For a split second, we have become the men of the Alamo."[16]

The Travis legend is often used to express a model of patriotic conversion required of each generation of Americans. Like the heroes of the Alamo, we are told, Americans will continue to face individual moments of truth. For example, in 1954 John Ben Shepperd asked, "Can we say . . . that not one Texan has turned Communist? Can we say we have not surrendered a single ideal or compromised a single principle?" In 1964 Lt. Gen. Robert W. Burns, commander of Air Training at Randolph Air Force Base, declared that everyone "has had to, or will have to, answer the question: Are we prepared to die for the cause of freedom?" In a pilgrimage speech in 1975, Lt. Gen. Allen Burdett, Jr., commander of the Fifth Army at Fort Sam Houston, stated that even though the fact of the line could not be proved, "each man [at the Alamo] had crossed a line in his heart." This same decision, he believed, was being faced by Americans in 1975. In 1980 the crises in Iran and Afghanistan moved Gen. Bennie L. Davis, also a commander of Air Training at Randolph Air Force Base, to suggest that such lines must be drawn once again. "Crisis revives the spirit of this nation," he declared, observing that as a nation we faced the "crossroads of our destiny." The spiritual reality of Travis's line was echoed by John H. Collins, Jr., director of Presidio La Bahia in Goliad, where Gen. Antonio López de Santa Anna had slaughtered more than four hundred Texas soldiers upon their surrender shortly after the Mexican victory at the Alamo. In a 1989 speech at the 153rd anniversary celebration, Collins said: "I have not seen the line. You have not seen the line. The line is drawn across our hearts."[17]

Rhetorical commemorations of the thirteen-day siege at the Alamo tend to follow a common pattern. These recitations emphasize the heroism of the besieged, which is identified in various ways: acts of defiance in the face of the "no quarter" flag raised by Santa Anna; the voluntary return of James Bonham after two unsuccessful attempts to gather recruits; the dash of the volunteers from Gonzales through enemy lines to the Alamo; and the volunteers' heroic last stand. Direct application of the lessons of the Alamo could be made because of the continued potency of blood sacrifice—blood spilled in defense of liberty, making possible the birth of the Texas republic. There are still ideals worth dying for, this rhetoric declares. Furthermore, modern America's insidious loss of the will to sacrifice makes the historical analogy all the more important.

Even in the shadow of the nuclear age, Alamo rhetoric has defiantly celebrated the power of blood sacrifice in war. In 1955 Dr. W. S. McBirnie of Trinity Baptist Church in San Antonio noted that while the mushroom-shaped "ominous cloud" of the hydrogen bomb rose to threaten all, the Alamo was there to remind citizens that "some things never change." Whenever Americans require faith in freedom and God, McBirnie declared, they need only say, "Remember the Alamo." In 1984 Lt. Gen. John R. McGiffert, commander of the Fifth Army at Fort Sam Houston, delivered the Alamo Day address and warned of the danger of believing that nothing was worth dying for. "It seems almost sacrilegious," he said, "to whisper those words, let alone speak them within earshot of the Alamo." As a nation, McGiffert declared, we have honored those who were willing to die for freedom, integrity, family, and country. "We honor all who believe that freedom is worth dying for. That is why we Remember the Alamo."[18]

Texas sesquicentennial events also emphasized the creative power of the Alamo heroes' sacrifice. Gathering with others outside the former mission at 5:30 A.M. on March 6, 1986, to commemorate the moment of the final Mexican assault, San Antonio mayor Henry G. Cisneros declared that the fallen Alamo heroes had sacrificed themselves "in order that we modern Texans may enjoy what we do." Later in the day, standing before a large crowd in Alamo Plaza, amid the flags of the states and countries from which the volunteers had come, Texas historian T. R. Fehrenbach delivered his address as a part of the patriotic worship service. He noted that the modern age would be "baffled" by the Alamo if it did not understand courage and honor. The Alamo, he declared, was a "fearful symbol for any age that hopes to eradicate risk . . . for it is [a] symbol of a thousand battles . . . fought by men prepared to make the supreme sacrifice." In his anniversary speech in 1987, Dr. Jack Hooper, minister of the Alamo Heights United Methodist Church, asked, "Is anything really worth dying for?" The answer, he said, must be yes, unless Texans wanted to surrender "even the claim to greatness." He declared that "honor, goodness, devotion, freedom and love demand readiness for self-sacrifice as the inherent and ultimate risk."[19]

Such emphasis on the necessity of sacrifice is not incidental. Traditional patriotic observance must make coherent symbolic connections between heroic sacrifice in the past and its potential viability in the modern world. In the United States our perception of the efficacy of sacrifice in war has been questioned at least since the later years of the Civil War. During the Vietnam conflict this perception underwent a striking transformation, with sacrifice being seen by some as a blood payment for the *sins* of the nation— a stunning inversion of the traditional interpretation, which claims blood sacrifice as the key to the *life* of the nation. Renewed emphasis on the horrors of nuclear war in the late 1970s, particularly in terms of the meaninglessness of the mass death that would result from such a conflict, threatened heroic interpretations of sacrifice and thereby led a frontal attack on the essence of the symbol of the Alamo: namely, that sacrifice in war is a product of human choice made by courageous and principled individuals. In response to this attack, Alamo celebrants have intensified their insistence that the nation must look to the heroes of 1836 as patriotic archetypes who set forth the ideal to which every future age must aspire.[20]

The sacrifice of the Alamo heroes was not only perceived as a creative event that brought life to the Texas republic and gave future generations patriotic orientation; it was also an expenditure of lives, a body count for freedom that placed future generations forever in the debt of these heroes. More than at any other battlesite, patriotic rhetoric at the Alamo has focused on the price these men paid. As one enters the movie theater to watch *Alamo . . . The Price of Freedom,* the soft strains of a country and western song declare, "The price of freedom is not free." Alamo rhetoric proclaims that citizens must, in the crises of their own time, repay the heroes of the Alamo; they must be willing to "pay the price," which has almost always been understood as blood sacrifice in war. There seem to be few other ways to work off the debt owed to those who crossed Travis's line.[21]

Many Americans, among them Gary Foreman, might agree wholeheartedly with the patriotic orthodoxies celebrated in Alamo commemorative events, but they also worry that the sacred environment has been contaminated. Fears of such defilement have endured since the Alamo lay in ruins after the battle and have led to various attempts either to immortalize the sacrifice by erecting monuments or to reconstruct the environment as it was in 1836.

Visitors to the Alamo after the battle saw "real and shocking evidence of the . . . carnage as well as the ruined Alamo buildings." The immediate threat of additional Mexican incursions into the city prevented any attempt at preservation of the site, and this official neglect continued throughout the nineteenth century. A part of the original mission now called the Long Barrack, the site of fierce fighting, passed into private hands in the 1870s. In the early years of the twentieth century the historical authenticity of the Long Barrack was questioned by two groups of the Daughters of the Republic of Texas. The women of the Alamo Mission chapter, led by Clara Driscoll, argued that the scene of the most significant fighting was the chapel. They believed that the ruins of the Long Barrack did not date from the time of the battle and should be torn down. Members of the other group, led by Adina De Zavala, granddaughter of the first vice president of the Republic of Texas, characterized the Long Barrack as the "scene of the greater part of that memorable martyrdom" and were aghast at Driscoll's plan to tear the walls down. This controversy grew so bitter—in fact, it is often referred to as the "second battle of the Alamo"—that Gov. O. B. Colquitt was forced to intervene. In a meeting at the St. Anthony Hotel in San Antonio on December 28, 1911, the governor declared that despite

The existing chapel and part of the Long Barrack are the only recognizable features of the original Alamo compound. Those concerned with the physical integrity of this sacred space wish to restore the entire compound as it appears in this drawing. (Frederic Ray and the Daughters of the Republic of Texas Library at the Alamo, San Antonio)

C. B. Graham's lithograph of the ruins of the Alamo
Chapel, San Antonio de Bexar, modeled after a
drawing by the army artist Edward Everett.
(Daughters of the Republic of Texas Library
at the Alamo, San Antonio)

The first Alamo monument, made of Alamo stone
by Joseph Cox and William B. Nangle, was almost
completely destroyed in the Texas capitol fire of
November 9, 1881. (Daughters of the Republic of
Texas Library at the Alamo, San Antonio)

The Alamo as it appeared in the early 1890s, with the Hugo & Schmelter building atop the Long Barrack. This desecration of sacred space helped spur the DRT's successful bid for custodianship of the Alamo. (Daughters of the Republic of Texas Library at the Alamo, San Antonio)

Christmas at the Alamo, 1890s. (San Antonio Conservation Society and the Institute of Texan Cultures at San Antonio)

COPYRIGHTED 1912 by A.A. BRACK

Alfred Giles's proposed Alamo Heroes Monument (1912). (Daughters of the Republic of Texas Library at the Alamo, San Antonio)

Crowds filled Alamo Plaza during the Fiesta San Jacinto parade, April 1931. (*San Antonio Light* Collection, Institute of Texan Cultures at San Antonio)

Pres. Franklin Delano Roosevelt and his entourage in front of the Alamo during Texas's centennial celebration, June 11, 1936. (*San Antonio Light* Collection, Institute of Texan Cultures at San Antonio)

Representatives of various organizations laid wreaths in honor of the Alamo heroes, April 19, 1938. (*San Antonio Light* Collection, Institute of Texan Cultures at San Antonio)

The Alamo Heroes Cenotaph, designed by Pompeo Coppini in 1939. (Daughters of the Republic of Texas Library at the Alamo, San Antonio)

The chiseled figures of the Alamo Heroes Cenotaph are superimposed over the familiar outline of the Alamo Chapel. (Daughters of the Republic of Texas Library at the Alamo, San Antonio)

The long rifle, a sacred relic of the battle, is on display in the Alamo Chapel.
(The Alamo, Daughters of the Republic of Texas, San Antonio)

The interior of the Alamo Chapel, or, as it is usually called now, the Shrine.
(The Alamo, Daughters of the Republic of Texas)

the fact that a commercial building had been erected above the walls of the Long Barrack, he wanted to restore the historic building to its 1836 condition.[22]

The famous Alamo Chapel, originally owned by the Catholic church, was leased to the army and later, in 1883, was sold to the state. In 1885 the city of San Antonio assumed control of the chapel. Twenty years later it relinquished control to the DRT, which began its guardianship of the historic building. Since 1905 attention has focused on the cultivation of the Alamo Chapel as a shrine to the Texas heroes and on the development of an entire square block that includes a gift shop and a library.

The failure to preserve the Alamo in the years immediately following the battle—including a delay in burying the bones and ashes of the Alamo's defenders—made informal veneration all the more important.[23] In 1840 the San Antonio Town Council was so indifferent to the ruins that it allowed citizens to buy Alamo stone at five dollars per wagon load to build their homes. At the same time various kinds of relics and carvings made from Alamo rock were popular and kept attention focused on the drama of the battle. Bone fragments, pieces of cannon, and entire human skeletons (probably from prerevolutionary times), found during construction projects in the nineteenth century, were especially treasured. Veneration of these artifacts made the official neglect of the Alamo all the more obvious and led to public declarations of bad conscience. Some people used the language of defilement to express their anger at the treatment of such a holy site. In 1881 a letter to a Galveston newspaper expressed these common sentiments:

> You cannot imagine my amazement and disgust upon this my first
> visit to the old church fortress of the Alamo at finding the structure,
> so famous not only in the history of Texas but the annals of liberty
> and the record of the world, filled with sacks of salt, stinking
> potatoes, odorous kerosene and dirty groceries generally. It's a
> strange, very strange mingling of fame and sourkraut [sic], and still
> stranger the fact that the great State of Texas . . . should permit a
> historic building like the Alamo, once consecrated to deity and
> latterly baptized in blood of heroes like Travis and Crockett, slain in
> the cause of liberty and democracy, to become a grocery
> warehouse.[24]

As is the case with any sacred site, the ground itself was perceived to have been transformed by the heroic acts that took place on it. Expressions of this veneration abound. In 1947 Mrs. Floyd V. Rogers dug soil from the Alamo to place around a flagpole in Eagle River, Wisconsin, that raised aloft the Texas Lone Star. In 1954 A. Garland Adair, executive director of the Texas Heritage Foundation, gave a small piece of Alamo block to each of the 254 Texas counties; attached to each piece was a replica of Travis's famous letter appealing for aid, in which he declared: "I shall never surrender or retreat. . . . Victory or Death."[25]

More recent complaints about the physical preservation of the site are similar to those voiced in the late nineteenth and early twentieth centuries. The growth of San Antonio itself has been viewed with ambivalence by Alamo celebrants. While the high-rise buildings and active construction can in one sense be understood as the fruits of the heroism of those who died at the Alamo, in another sense the city itself becomes a threatening presence. As modern San Antonio has grown around and dwarfed the Alamo, it has blurred the boundaries between sacred center and secular city. For many Alamo visitors there is no satisfying passage from city to ceremonial center, no satisfactory markers to frame the site. One persistent response to such aesthetic defilement was the call to construct a monument in Alamo Plaza, the city-owned area in front of the Alamo.

This desire to memorialize the heroes in stone is another form of veneration, another attempt to respond to the neglect of the physical site. Reuben Marmaduke Potter, whose song "Hymn of the Alamo" (1836) and heroic account "The Fall of the Alamo" (1860) aroused nationwide interest in the Alamo story, commented that "neither at the Alamo itself, nor at the forgotten grave of its defenders, does any legend or device, like the stone of Thermopylae, remind the passer by of those who died in obedience to the call of their adopted country." In 1841, during a visit to San Antonio, Potter had occasion to speak with two men, stonecutter Joseph Cox and artist William B. Nangle, who were "engaged in manufacturing, from the stones of the Alamo, various small mementos, such as vases, candlesticks, seals, etc." Cox and Nangle had constructed a ten-foot-high monument from Alamo stone, but when the poverty-stricken Texas republic could not afford to buy it, they carried it to several Texas cities by wagon and charged people to see it. The *Houston Morning Star* reported in July 1843 that the monument was "doubtless the most beautiful and impressive piece of sculpture ever completed in the Republic" and implored citizens who felt even a "single emotion of respect for the martyred heroes" to visit this "relic hallowed by the blood of martyrs." Cox and Nangle's monument passed through private hands until the state finally placed it in the vestibule of the new capitol and then purchased it in 1858. Unfortunately, only fragments of the monument survived a November 9, 1881, fire.[26]

Interest in the preservation of Texas history grew after the founding of the Texas Veterans Association in 1873 and the celebration of the nation's centennial in 1876. In San Antonio the preservation movement centered around the Alamo Monument Association, founded in 1879. For almost twenty years this group tried without success to raise money for a fitting monument. In 1887 the association adopted a proposal by architect Alfred Giles to build a monument on Alamo Plaza that would be 165 feet high, with an elevator stopping at a large balcony 100 feet above the ground, but nothing came of the project. By December 1909 the *San Antonio Daily Express* believed it was time to resurrect the idea, for "Alamo Plaza then would become the most beautiful spot in the world." Looking down from the balcony, the editors exclaimed, visitors would see the progress of civilization made possible by the "fearless sacrifice of life when a brave band of Texans made liberty in Texas possible by their devotion to duty and to the flag of the Empire State." Even after the formal demise of the Alamo Monument Association, ambitious—perhaps grandiose—proposals continued to be proferred. In 1912, for example, Giles envisioned a monument 802 feet tall and 85 feet square, the base of which would house museum displays and art galleries devoted to Texas history. The base of the monument would consist of twelve columns of Texas granite and 30-foot statues of Travis, Crockett, Bonham, and Bowie.[27]

The Texas Centennial in 1936 brought about renewed interest in erecting an Alamo monument. One newspaper editorial declared that if this opportunity should be missed, the "rich commonwealth [is] unworthy of its heritage." Finally, in 1939, ground was broken for the Alamo Heroes Cenotaph, to be made of Georgia marble with a base of Texas granite. When completed the monument consisted of a naked male figure, the Spirit of Sacrifice, consumed in flames and surrounded on all sides by imposing figures of the major Alamo heroes, along with a female figure representing the Texas republic. The inscription on the cenotaph praises the heroes for giving birth to the "Empire State" through their noble sacrifice. During a 1940 radio interview Italian-born San Antonio sculptor Pompeo Coppini said that patriotic memories evoked by such monuments are as "necessary as schoolbooks." Still, the monument did not please everyone. J. Frank Dobie, for example, remarked that it "looked like a grain elevator." Nevertheless, the cenotaph, supplemented by various plaques and markers in Alamo Plaza and in the Alamo complex, stands today as a permanent patriotic statement of faith.[28]

The erection of the Alamo Heroes Cenotaph did little to erase the threat of defilement from secular culture, mainly in the form of irreverent behavior and indifference to the sacredness of the site. Tourists have been taking souvenir chunks of Alamo rock or carving their initials into the walls since at least 1840, and Joseph Gallegly tells us that even in 1879 visitors remarked that they were both "surprised and indignant at the condition in which they found the shrine of Texas liberty." During those years Alamo Plaza was the scene of vendors selling wares and of "rollicking cow-hands." Since then there have been numerous complaints about the inappropriate clothing worn by tourists and the demeanor of plaza inhabitants. In the late 1940s and early 1950s women were not allowed to wear shorts in the Alamo; yet by 1958 a newspaper headline shouted, "Vendors, Nude Girls Battle for Tourists' Attention at Shrine." The paper also spoke out against the ice-cream vendors, beggars, and "characters" who populated the plaza. In 1968 a Michigan tourist complained that people entering the shrine were "talking loudly . . . wearing hats! . . . I had rather see the Alamo closed forever and fallen into decay than to see such desecration."[29]

Others have attacked the commercial desecration of the Alamo, complaining that the gift shop carried kitsch and that there were inauthentic items in the shrine itself. Columnist Bob Greene, for example, was outraged by the presence of John Wayne's Screen Actors Guild Award, "which officials of the Alamo displayed along with the genuine Crockett-Bowie-Travis memorabilia." He also commented disparagingly on the size of the building—"it felt like a tiny one-room schoolhouse"—and on the irreverence displayed by "young women wearing Walkman headsets, and young men carrying tape players the size of suitcases." Most of these critics took pains to point out that they were not unbelievers. Roddy Stinson of the *San Antonio Express* remarked that as he would pass the Alamo on the way to work, all his "smirks and jokes and irreverent quips give way to a deep breath, an unseen salute and a ripple of gooseflesh." Attorney Doug Harlan, another local columnist, expressed directly the underlying intuition behind the often lighthearted criticism of pseudo-patriotic commercialism: "The place itself should be more pure."[30]

Protests of various kinds, each adding to the sense of defilement, have occurred at the Alamo over the years. In 1980 and 1981, for example, members of the Maoist Revolutionary Communist party raised a red flag and declared that what the Alamo stood for was "offensive, not only to Chicano people, but to people all over the world. . . . It's a symbol of oppression, not freedom." The Ku Klux Klan responded by appearing, uninvited and unwelcome, on May Day in 1982 and again in 1983 to "guard" the Alamo from communist defilers; in 1983 the group was barred from Alamo property but for several years held parades that passed by the sacred shrine. Far more controversial were the nearly unmentionable desecrations that occurred at the Alamo in 1982: heavy metal rock singer Ozzy Osbourne urinated on the wall, after which the San Antonio City Council permanently banned him from performing in the city; and joggers threw paint on the cenotaph as a group gathered in the early morning hours of March 6 to commemorate the battle. Such acts were taken as proof of the degenerate state of modern American society.[31]

By 1987 the Daughters of the Republic of Texas was concerned about another kind of pollution, namely, the damage caused by exhaust fumes from tour buses that parked in close proximity to the Long Barrack. An editorial in the *San Antonio Express-News* noted that "tour buses don't drive up the front of St. Peter's Basilica in Rome, so why do they have some inalienable right to do it at the Alamo?" In March 1989 the *San Antonio Light* reported that in the future buses would be allowed to unload visitors in front of the Alamo but could not park there.[32]

One of the enduring fears at any American battlesite is the potential defilement of the land through the encroachment of modern development. Except for Gettysburg, this sense of aesthetic defilement is nowhere so evident as at the Alamo. Some critics cite the inadequacy of the physical context. It is impossible, they say, to imagine what the Alamo was like at the time of the battle when very little of the original mission is still standing and when the city of San Antonio looms over what remains. The enterprising owner of the now defunct Remember the Alamo Theater and Museum across the street from the chapel had suggested that, before beginning the illustrated walking tour, visitors avail themselves of a thirty-minute "multimedia experience" in his "specially designed theater." Such artificial visualization was necessary, he argued, because the Alamo is "surrounded by buildings of commerce hemmed in by arteries of traffic." It was pointed out that those who wanted to see the Alamo in a "pure" state should make the three-hour trip to Brackettville, Texas, where they could visit the "Alamo" that was built in the late 1950s for a John Wayne movie. This "Alamo" is often perceived as more "real" because there is no city around it to pollute the imagination.[33]

A restoration project offered by Gary Foreman constitutes the latest and most sophisticated manifestation of the desire to venerate the Alamo and its heroes by preserving the sanctity of the physical site. For Foreman and others, John Wayne's "Alamo" suffers one fatal flaw: it was not built on the ground sanctified by the Alamo heroes. There is only *one* sacred site, and this site must be purified, cleansed not only of the pollution of the city that has invaded the sacred boundaries but cleansed also of the pollution of inauthenticity in museum displays and the gift shop. In addition to marking off the sacred site from the homogeneity of secular space, Foreman's detailed plan seeks to restore and mark the Alamo so that people might have an "accurate" perspective of the past. Within the context of his proposal Foreman levels a series of charges against the custodianship of the DRT. There has been, he says, little "actual effort to recreate the original Alamo," and there certainly has been no attempt made to provide "actual demonstrations of clothing or weapons." According to Foreman the Long Barrack has been "badly violated with non-Alamo trivia and poorly designed displays." Furthermore, the "so-called museum [sells] cheap souvenirs" and "items from non-Alamo periods."[34]

Foreman's plan envisions a restoration of the 1836 grounds where possible and also the marking of significant sites that have fallen into private hands. Living-history groups would introduce visitors to the realities of life in the 1830s and would be complemented by displays of authentic artifacts, "tasteful" memorabilia and souvenirs, and an underground theater with a sound and light show that would convey a new "understanding" of the battle. Foreman selects from the multiple identities of the Alamo (it was first a mission and only occasionally a fort) the importance of the last stand and insists that *this* event, enacted on *this* site, must be forever frozen apart from its current physical surroundings.

Spirited opposition to the Foreman plan has come from many quarters. The DRT reminded him that the site was intended primarily as a shrine, not a historic site. To demonstrate the impracticality of Foreman's plan, Patricia E. Osborne of the San Antonio Department of Historical Preservation outlined what it would take to achieve consensus among city, state, and federal agencies to begin even moderate changes in Alamo Plaza, let alone the massive reconstruction Foreman envisions. She also criticized his "obsession with the battle" even as he ignores the rich history of the mission period. Eventually, she hopes, there will be some marking of the original boundaries of the mission and perhaps a limitation on traffic through Alamo Plaza, as well as various "beautification projects." She emphasizes, however, that Foreman's plan will never be carried out.[35]

Those who are involved in the production of Alamo ceremonies and are inspired by patriotic rhetoric, and those who are interested in an even more inspiring physical environment, have not usually questioned the truth of the patriotic orthodoxies celebrated at the Alamo. Yet such orthodoxies have evoked responses that take issue with Anglo-American interpretations of the Alamo drama. Not surprisingly, ambivalent responses to such interpretations have emerged from the Mexican American community. Ferocious racism during the time of the Texas Revolution transformed the war for Texas independence into a hatred of all things Mexican. In the wake of the last stand of the defenders of the Alamo and the slaughter of the Texas garrison at Goliad, the Anglo-American thirst for revenge broke the alliance that had existed between Mexicans and Anglo-Americans opposed to Santa Anna. According to Arnoldo De León, Texas quickly became " 'white,' spiritually, attitudinally, politically, socially, economically and demographically." Tejanos (Mexican Texans) came to be hated by the new American immigrants to Texas. To these immigrants all Tejanos were simply Mexicans, treacherous by their very nature. J. M. Parmenter's "Texas Hymn" (1838) declares:

> We'll never trust his honor, assassin he is bred.
> Brave Fannin and his warriors thus found a gory bed.
> And Travis with his heroes on San Antonio height,
> before the foeman legions fell in unequal fight.[36]

These negative images of Mexicans were strengthened during the Mexican War. To American soldiers gazing with awe at the physical beauty of Mexico and fascinated by the remnants of vanished civilizations, Mexicans appeared to be poor human specimens. Soldiers' comments revealed not only contempt but an optimism born of arrogance that an American culture at the apex of world civilization could elevate even the Mexicans. Many spoke of the "mongrelization" that the mixing of Spanish and Indian in Mexico had produced, with only the "evil qualities . . . retained," qualities fostered by the oppressive nature of the Mexican government and the Catholic church.[37]

Consequently, the battle at the Alamo was almost immediately perceived as a racial struggle between Anglo-Americans and Mexicans, rather than a battle waged by Tejanos and Anglo-American immigrants to Texas against the authoritarian rule of Santa Anna. Throughout the nineteenth century the symbol of the Alamo was an Anglo-American symbol of conquest. And by the early twentieth century, David Montejano notes, the "story of the Alamo and Texas frontier history had become purged of its ambiguities— of the fact that Mexicans and Anglos had often fought on the same side." Don Graham details how these images have shaped perceptions of the battle in film and literature. He maintains that novels of the nineteenth and early twentieth centuries present Alamo defenders as "upright Anglo-Saxon heroes . . . the Mexicans [as] craven outragers of everything that is good, pure, and decent." Films such as *Martyrs of the Alamo* (1915) also propagated these virulent racial stereotypes throughout the twentieth century, until *The Last Command* (1955) and *The Alamo* (1960) moderated such images.[38]

Of course, there are Mexican Americans for whom the Alamo is not an evocative symbol at all. According to Aristeo Sul, a San Antonio auto mechanic, for lots of folks the Alamo "doesn't really register." It is a "fuzzy little thing that happened," he said, and we should "just let it be history." Ray Sanchez, former dean of extended services at San Antonio College, disagreed: "You can't get away from the Alamo. It's there." Sanchez and Anastacio Bueno, who works for a publishing company in San Antonio, remembered how the Alamo became an oppressive symbol during their childhood. In a tone somewhere between bemusement and anger, Bueno commented, "We learned in the third or fourth grade that we killed the Alamo heroes." Nodding in agreement, Sanchez added that most of his Mexican American friends were ashamed that "they killed Davy Crockett."[39]

Many Mexican Americans have come to hate the Alamo, Montejano argues, because it is perceived as an "everyday symbol of conquest over Mexicans, as a vindication for the repressive treatment of Mexicans." The Mexican American community has responded to this oppressive symbol in a number of ways. Mexican American restorationists believe that a growing awareness of the patriotism exhibited by their Tejano ancestors would lessen racial antipathy and pave the way for greater acceptance of twentieth-century Mexican Americans in the United States. Others attack the essence of the symbol and look upon processes of restoration with contempt.[40]

Early histories of Texas gloss over the contribution of Tejanos who fought alongside the Anglo-Texan heroes of the Alamo and contributed much to the saga of the Texas Revolution. But by the mid-1930s Eugene C. Barker and a number of Mexican writers were resurrecting the history of people whom Arnoldo De León calls "anonymous souls in the history of Texas." At the time of the Texas Centennial in 1936, it was being argued that Tejanos had been patriotic allies of Anglo-Texans during the revolution. More recently, Gilberto Hinojosa and Gerald E. Poyo have suggested that about 3 percent of both the Anglo and Tejano populations fought in the Texas war for independence. Hinojosa has stated that "Tejano participants appear to have shared political ideals with their Anglo-Texan compatriots and exhibited acceptable if not equivalent determination to see Texas free of centrist rule."[41]

Some Mexican Americans believe that ignorance of this forgotten history is at the root of the ideological and cultural barriers that have created ethnic tensions between Mexican and Anglo-American communities in San Antonio. Félix D. Almaráz, Jr., argues that little effort has been made to "expand" the symbol so that both races might "learn and grow." Others have tried to use the language of restoration in Alamo ceremonies. Henry A. Guerra, the "Voice of the Alamo" and a respected radio figure at WOAI in San Antonio since 1939, has read the roll call of the Alamo heroes during commemorations since the mid-1960s, when the names of Tejanos who died defending the Alamo were added to the list. (In 1987 the name of Damacio Jimenes, another Tejano defender, was added.) For Guerra, incomplete representations of this chapter of Texas history result from a "lack of research," not from Anglo dominance of interpretations of the battle's significance. He believes that the Alamo is not a symbol of oppression but of the "commitment of the Hispanic population to independent Texas rule." The message, according to Guerra, is clear: heroic commitment to a cause and the virtue of sacrifice. Still, Guerra acknowledges that he has received complaints about his praise, during Alamo commemorative ceremonies, of the courage exhibited on both sides of the battle. Clearly, for some members of the Anglo community the patriotic canon is closed and should not be subject to revision.[42]

Others in the Mexican American community look upon the symbol of the Alamo as unalterably oppressive. For them the task at hand is to demythologize the Anglo saga of the battle. Rodolfo Acuña's *Occupied America,* for example, presents the view that Tejanos were not patriots but fought at the Alamo with Travis, Bowie, and Crockett because of vested economic interests. Acuña traces into colonial times the American desire to wrest Texas from Mexican control and argues that Anglo-Americans have not yet "accepted the fact that the United States committed an act of violence against the Mexican people when it took Mexico's northwest territory." He also stands the history of the battle on its head when he declares that "well-armed professional soldiers" in the Alamo faced "ill-prepared, ill-equipped, and ill-fed Mexicans." Tejanos were nothing more than collaborators, and to make heroes of them is, Acuña insists, like "making heroes of the Vichy government." In somewhat the same vein Lalo Valdez argues that the Alamo was "a bastion of racism and oppression" and that "Anglo-Texans were the first illegal aliens."[43]

Still others express indignation at the heretical idea that the Alamo is in any way tied to ethnic contentiousness. The Alamo story always has been quite clear, claims Edith Mae Johnson of the DRT: "I always knew Tejanos took part in the battle. These people were Texians [a term of self-identity used by Texans in the early nineteenth century]." Patricia Osborne also vehemently rejects the belief that the Alamo has been in essence an Anglo symbol. The problem, she says, can be found in "100 years of incorrect history." For her, the heart of the message transcends race and speaks to all people of "standing up and sacrificing lives for freedom."[44]

Only sporadically has Alamo rhetoric attempted to suggest that the Alamo symbolizes ethnic unity since men of both races fought side by side. In 1960 Gen. Edward T. Williams, commander of the Fourth Army at Fort Sam Houston, urged Texans to "be in the forefront of those who want to encourage Pan-American solidarity." In 1961 Lt. Gen. James E. Briggs, commander of Air Training at Randolph Air Force Base, suggested that the "blending of the culture of our two nations is evident throughout the southwest, but no more so than in San Antonio." In 1973 Gen. Patrick F. Cassidy, commander of the Fifth Army at Fort Sam Houston, declared that the Alamo heroes were precursors of a multiethnic Texas, for nowhere is ethnic unity "more prevalent and apparent" than in Texas. In 1985 Lt. Gen. Louis Charles Menetrey, commander of the Fifth Army at Fort Sam

Houston, spoke of his admiration for soldiers on both sides who "fought hard and desperately." And in 1988 the concept of restoration went even further, as a double wreath-laying ceremony honored the dead on both sides of the battle. T. R. Fehrenbach, a Texas historian, remarked on that occasion, "We should not see the Alamo in terms of the ethnicity of the participants. It is not a symbol of Anglo-American superiority nor of Mexican defeat. Brave men from many nations fought on both sides of these walls. We should, we must, see the Alamo battle in terms of the cause for which each side fought. . . . The Alamo is the triumph of spirit over death."[45]

The Texas Sesquicentennial engendered renewed interest in the processes of restoration and redefinition. Mayor Henry Cisneros, interviewed on ABC-TV's "Good Morning America" in early 1986, stated: "There were many Hispanics inside the Alamo. It wasn't a racial war. It was one against central government." Fr. Virgil Elizondo, offering mass at San Fernando Cathedral where Santa Anna's "no quarter" flag flew, spoke of his "profound gratitude" for the "efforts and sacrifices of our ancestors." This sacrifice, he argued, should motivate all to work for the elimination of poverty and injustice. According to Father Elizondo, the original purpose of the mission is unchanged: once it symbolized unity between Spaniards and Indians, and now it celebrates "the unity of Anglos and Tejanos in the cause of liberty." He also cautioned that to remember the battle in terms of victory and defeat would only serve to "keep old wounds alive, and kindle new fires of racism."[46]

Other activities during the sesquicentennial year emphasized the message of civic unity and focused some attention on the prerevolutionary past. As part of a more balanced presentation, a new Long Barrack museum display included a section on the history of the Alamo as a mission. Such subtle changes prompted Dr. Gilbert R. Cruz, a former National Park Service historian, to judge the sesquicentennial celebration more "mature" than the centennial celebration had been. "People pay obeisance to the old myths," he said, "but not too loudly." Nevertheless, Joe B. Frantz insisted that "it's an Anglo celebration. . . . It ignores the first 250 years."[47]

Fr. Balthasar Janacek also did his best to redefine the meaning of the Alamo, to make sure that the early mission period was not forgotten. In 1968, during the HemisFair celebration in San Antonio, he had hoped that the Alamo would be included in a tour of San Antonio's Spanish missions, but "they [the DRT] wouldn't even put up our posters." However, during the sesquicentennial's Semana de las Misiones (Week of the Missions) in August, Father Balty was able to present, inside the compound, an evening program about the mission period of the Alamo. The most interesting aspect of the program was that it did not mention the battle but instead asked visitors to look upon the Alamo in novel ways.[48]

Prof. Shigetaka Shiga's monument to the Alamo heroes. (Daughters of
the Republic of Texas Library at the Alamo, San Antonio)

Reenactors at the sesquicentennial Dawn at the Alamo ceremony, 5:30 A.M., March 6, 1986. (*Express-News* Collection, Institute of Texan Cultures at San Antonio)

The Alamo Cafe in San Antonio. (Daughters of the Republic of Texas Library at the Alamo, San Antonio)

The Alamo Coin Laundry in Willston, Fla. (Kevin Young and the Daughters of the Republic of Texas Library at the Alamo, San Antonio)

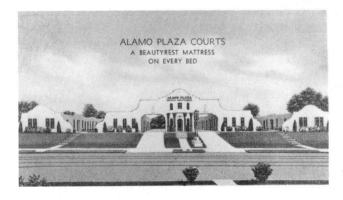

The Alamo Plaza Courts apartments in Little Rock, Ark. Photograph by Dwayne Jones, of Austin, Tex. (Texas Historical Commission)

A bicentennial advertisement by Liggett & Myers. The fine print offers a color poster of the Alamo, without commercial identification, in exchange for two proofs of purchase and seventy-five cents. (Liggett Group, Inc.)

Clearly, during the Texas Sesquicentennial various efforts were made to expand or redefine the symbolic meaning of the Alamo. Restorationists hoped that by reviving their version of the story they could claim some ownership of the symbol itself. Others, like Rodolfo Acuña and Lalo Valdez, wished to reject out of hand the heroic Anglo myth of the Alamo, which for them symbolized racism and the power of Anglo imperialism, an alien presence in conquered space. Still others, like Father Balty, perceived the Alamo as a sacred place for reasons that had nothing to do with the battle.

In the face of these attempts to alter the meaning of the Alamo within the context of present-day San Antonio, the appearance of the 1988 movie *Alamo . . . The Price of Freedom* revealed both the enduring power of the heroic Anglo-American interpretation of the battle and the bitter opposition engendered by the contemporary celebration of such orthodoxy. The moving force behind the movie was George McAlister, a successful Texas businessman, Marine Corps veteran, and former faculty member at Howard County Junior College. McAlister had written a book entitled *Alamo—The Price of Freedom: A History of Texas,* and in 1987 he announced plans to bring to the screen "a story that has not been told before." This ostensibly "new" Alamo story would cost $6.5 million to tell and would be permanently housed in San Antonio's Rivercenter, shown in a special IMAX theater on a screen six stories high. Production started in July 1987, and Academy Award–winner Kieth Merrill was chosen to direct the film.[49]

Like other Alamo movies, notably John Wayne's *Alamo,* that were intended to revitalize the spirit of American patriotism, McAlister wanted his movie to serve as a lesson that "where freedom exists . . . men have been willing to pay the supreme price." He also believed that *Alamo . . . The Price of Freedom* would be the first film to restore Tejanos to their rightful place in the Alamo saga. Not everyone agreed. On August 13, 1987, San Antonio City Council members Walter Martinez and Maria Berriozabal held a news conference to express their concern over McAlister's script, which they felt contained several scenes that were racially demeaning. In one, a Mexican girl was involved romantically with an Alamo defender; in another, the body of Jim Bowie was hoisted on Mexican bayonets. Martinez complained bitterly that, far from restoring Tejanos to their rightful place in the story, scenes like these portrayed Tejanos as "subservient, of loose morals, less involved, less active, less heroic than their non-Hispanic counterparts." McAlister wrote to Councilwoman Berriozabal to ask that she and Martinez withhold judgment until they had seen an uncut version of the film. He also wrote that he was proud to identify and "give credit to Damacio Jimenes for bringing the 18-pound cannon to the Alamo"; he was proud to be the "first to recognize Toribio D. Losoya and the fact that he had been born in the Alamo and was willing to die there"; and he was proud that he had "made into a human interest drama the fact that Gregorio Esparza fought with the Tejanos; and his brother, Francisco, fought with Santa Ana." McAlister also noted that his was the "only film to identify the one black defender, Private John."[50]

Despite McAlister's claim of restorative success, controversy swirled as the film moved toward its debut on March 6, 1988, the 152nd anniversary of the battle. Writing in the *San Antonio Express-News,* Ricardo Sanchez labeled the film an "insensitive and racist product" and declared,

> [It] has grave implications for a significant segment of U.S. society, and those implications are troubling—especially at a time when there is deep economic crisis as well as the effects of overzealous fanaticism in the land. . . . Are we to return to that jingoistic era of tyrannosaurian thinking? Are the children again to be made to feel shame for being born other than Anglo? Are we to repeat the past, to return to the same degradation just because someone wants to make a buck at the expense of cross-cultural dialogue?

He also found certain scenes insulting: "Why is Bowie . . . ruthlessly bayoneted . . . in a scene which is pure fiction? Why is Davy Crockett again shown . . . fighting to the very death . . . when serious scholars subscribe to the notion that he was captured and executed?"[51]

In an editorial in the *San Antonio Light,* Severo Perez argued that it was "impossible to make a worthy myth of the bald jingoism, racism and greed that led to the forming of the Texas Republic." Texans, he said, had for some time been trying to "dress up their aggression as a mythology of freedom." Douglas Beach, a managing partner of Rivertheater Associates, wrote an opposing editorial in the *Light* in which he characterized the film as a "45 minute docu-drama built on the concurrent themes of courage and freedom." It "blatantly cheers Alamo defenders, both Texan and Tejano," he claimed, and "makes a point to feature Tejanos as defenders of the Alamo, to portray the emotional dilemma caused as Tejanos fought against their own brothers and countrymen in defense of Texas liberty."[52]

In December 1987, after forty Mexican American community leaders viewed the uncut version of *Alamo . . . The Price of Freedom,* Councilman Martinez characterized the film as an "insult to all Texans" and "potentially damaging [to] ethnic progress in San Antonio." McAlister told the *Dallas Morning News* in January 1988 that he was "dumbfounded to be accused of demeaning anyone with this movie. . . . It bewilders and hurts me." Félix Almaráz, who served with DRT Library archivist Bernice Strong as one of the historical advisers to the movie, commented, "The First Amendment to the Constitution has not been suspended and, therefore, I see all this as a monologue from City Hall . . . an attempt to censor a movie." Almaráz also accused Martinez of "political barnstorming." Willie Velasquez, president of the Southwest Voter Registration Education Project, perceptively declared that "the net effect is . . . a film that gets Mexican-Americans and Anglos again at each others' throats."[53]

On opening night protestors marched in front of the theater calling for a boycott of *Alamo . . . The Price of Freedom.* Several groups also called for a boycott of Pace Foods, Inc., and Luby's Cafeterias, major sponsors of the film. Cruz Chavira, a member of the League of United Latin American Citizens (LULAC), pulled out a sword and drew an imaginary line in front of the theater, stating, "All of you who will join in our boycott of Luby's and Pace, cross the line." Others continued to decry what they believed would be the damaging social effects of the film. Inside the theater the audience listened to the rhetoric of restoration. Director Kieth Merrill insisted that his intent was to "animate and preserve the spirit of the Alamo and *all* its defenders." This film is not about ethnic conflict, he said, "it is a film about freedom."[54]

Curiously, vocal criticism of the film quickly subsided. It is difficult to determine whether this was because the protests had failed to halt the production and subsequent screenings or because many who saw it decided it wasn't as biased as others had claimed. Clearly, however, the making of another heroic Alamo film had touched a raw nerve in San Antonio. Perhaps people were disillusioned and angered because the film promised a new treatment of the Alamo but was in fact the traditional story of Anglo heroes. Perhaps the film served to bring to the surface simmering discontent about other social issues that had nothing at all to do with the symbol of the Alamo. What cannot be denied, in my view, is that *Alamo . . . The Price of Freedom* is an impressive retelling of the orthodox story, with spectacular battle scenes that capture as no other Alamo movie has the early morning fury of the last stand.

There is no reason to doubt the sincerity of McAlister, Merrill, or any of the other people associated with the film who claim that they tried to restore the Tejanos' part in the Alamo saga. Tejanos *do* appear in the film, though all too briefly; and important figures such as Juan Seguín—a captain in the Texas army who played a prominent role in the defeat of Santa Anna at the battle of San Jacinto and the last Mexican mayor of San Antonio (1840–42) until Henry Cisneros took office—*are* physically present, though they take on no real identity. Still, the real heroes in *Alamo . . . The Price of Freedom* are Anglos: Travis, Bowie, Crockett, and Bonham. In his insightful commentary in the *Express-News*, Gilberto Hinojosa reminded readers that the orthodox interpretation of the Alamo saga is not a heroic one for Mexican Americans but one that justifies "the slaughter of Mexican soldiers at San Jacinto, the killing of civilians by Texas volunteers during the Mexican

War, the dispossession of Mexican-Americans of their property under a rule of terror in the 1800s, and the discrimination and exploitation in the 20th century." In his opinion, the movie failed to transcend this message because it did not develop Tejano characters. They "should have been given prominent roles in the development of the story and should have been shown fighting as bravely as Travis and Crockett."[55]

Protestors seemingly were torn between two different messages. Councilman Martinez and others were angered apparently because in their view Tejanos had once again been slighted. They were not publicly attacking the heroic saga, only asking for it to be expanded. Still others saw the saga itself as racially exclusive and wanted to bring about the destruction of what was for them a pernicious Anglo-American interpretation of the battle. Some Mexican Americans thought that the first step toward the destruction of this orthodoxy was a change in the physical and symbolic ownership of the Alamo. Jose Garcia de Lara, the state director of LULAC, declared that the group would petition the state to become the caretaker of the shrine, replacing the DRT. "The Daughters have had it long enough," he said. "After all, we [Mexicans] were the ones to build it." Ramon Vasquez y Sanchez, chairman of LULAC's arts and humanities committee, justified the attempt to take control of the Alamo by calling attention to the "thousands of lives lost by defenders of the mother country [i.e., those who attacked the Alamo]. . . . Where is their history on the walls of the Alamo?"[56]

Eventually, LULAC backed off. Group members argued that they really were interested in greater accountability in the expenditure of surplus funds at the Alamo (a subject of some controversy in 1988). Yet they continued to attack the DRT, which they believed perpetuated "myth and omission" and made the Alamo Chapel a "symbol of oppression." Such statements struck a raw nerve among the guardians of patriotic faith. A letter to the *Houston Chronicle* declared that this was a "major attempt by liberal historians and Hispanics to discredit the history of the battle and to paint the Mexicans in a better light." Giving control of the Alamo to LULAC made "about as much sense as giving control of the Pearl Harbor Memorial to the Japanese." Writing in the *Houston Post* in April 1988, Felton West declared that "the Anglos have it, and aren't going to give it back." Charles Edgren of the *El Paso Herald Post* believed that "entrusting one of the more important chapters of American history to such a group would be unwise in the extreme."[57]

The various struggles over the physical and symbolic ownership of the Alamo reveal the enduring significance of such martial sites in America. At the Alamo, Anglo-Americans celebrate the creation epic of Texas; the Alamo defenders are perceived as men of principle, models of civic virtue for the ages. From the beginning, however, the symbol of the Alamo has often been used as a racist symbol, and when minority voices came to be heard more clearly in twentieth-century America, the existing patriotic orthodoxy did not go unchallenged. To be sure, the Alamo will continue to inspire curiosity, reverence, and awe because of the almost universal fascination with last stands and the lessons they are perceived to offer to contemporary culture. Processes of veneration, defilement, and redefinition will continue to be in evidence as the struggle for control of the symbol reveals the need for a usable past to legitimate contemporary ideological positions. Yet the Alamo has also become the focus of a different kind of redefinition, even as it retains its traditional character as a shrine: it has served as a center for rituals of reconciliation.

Standing on the grounds of the Alamo near the Long Barrack is a five-foot-high granite marker that reads, "To the Memory of the Heroes of the Alamo," and below that, "Prof. Shigetaka (Juko) Shiga, Tokyo, San Antonio, Texas, September 1914"; the rest of the inscription is in Chinese. The English inscription on the back of the marker reads, "Stone from the native province of Suneemon Torii, the Bonham of Japan; in the province is Nagashino, the Alamo of Japan." For almost seventy-five years this curious monument stood uninterpreted for the millions of visitors who flocked to the Alamo. In 1984 Margit Nagy, president of the Japan America Society of San Antonio, asked the DRT for permission to prepare a brochure about the monument for San Antonio's Japan Week. During the next five years, after the brochure was completed, she continued to research the story of the Japanese monument, struggling to re-create the efforts for intercultural friendship symbolized by Shigetaka Shiga's gift.[58]

In *Remembering the Alamo Japanese-Style,* Nagy describes the Waseda professor as a "world traveler, popular writer and eminent geographer." She says that he visited the United States in 1912 and was troubled by the anti-Japanese attitudes he encountered on the West Coast. Determined to build stronger bonds between the two nations, Shigetaka Shiga, who was fascinated by the similarities of the battles of Nagashino (1575) and the Alamo, decided to visit San Antonio for the purpose of erecting a monument to the heroes of both battles.[59] Nagy reports that he was greeted warmly in San Antonio and that the dedication of the monument on November 6, 1914, was hailed as an "unprecedented event for showing Japanese-American friendship. Every newspaper recorded the exchanges of goodwill." Judge J. E. Webb, a spokesman for the Daughters of the Republic of Texas, told Shigetaka Shiga:

> It is natural for men to differ. . . . but on the subject of patriotism,
> love of country, home, friends, kindred and family there can be no

difference between us—we meet on common ground. . . . You . . .
have left your native land, friends and loved ones, and have
journeyed more than six thousand miles across sea and land,
attracted by deeds of patriots of foreign blood; and to them honor—
we bless and thank you for the sacrifice. . . . At last we have the
proofs . . . that although there may be wide divergencies between
men on account of race, education, environment, and religion, there
is, nevertheless, unity in the brotherhood of man and the fatherhood
of God.[60]

The gift attracted little attention until the Japanese attacked Pearl Harbor on December 7, 1941. The following day it was defaced. As racial hatred
intensified during World War II, there were public discussions about what
to do with the monument. In 1943 the *Alamo Height News* noted the "public
clamor for removal of the obnoxious shaft" but added that the monument
was not worded "in the Jap language." The monument survived the war
and was largely forgotten until Margit Nagy took an interest in it. After
completing the monument brochure in 1984, she worked on behalf of the
Junior Ambassadors Friendship Mission from Musashino City, Japan, to
obtain permission for Shigetaka Shiga's son to donate a portrait of his father
to the DRT, on August 4, 1986, for display in the Alamo. On November
15, 1989, a formal commemoration of the seventy-fifth anniversary of Shigetaka Shiga's visit celebrated the "sense of shared values transcending
cultural differences that was so evident in 1914 when a truly appreciative
San Antonio received Dr. Shiga's tribute to the Alamo heroes." Nagy perceived the monument and the ceremony of rededication as part of the "road
to peace." What is important to remember, she declared, is that "every
country has people willing to fight and die for principles of justice. . . . what
is especially important to remember, this one man couldn't change the
climate of prejudice that existed between the Americans and Japanese alone,
but he decided to do something to make a difference." Elsewhere she commented, "We have remembered Pearl Harbor, we have remembered Hiroshima. . . . Now, we have a new reminder so different, a reminder of our
commonality."[61]

Amid the bustling modern landscape of downtown San Antonio, the
Alamo stands not only as a reminder of the creation saga of Texas but as
a reminder of the power of the guardians of patriotic faith, those who
defend the physical and ideological purity of the place. For them the Alamo
has crucial contemporary relevance. It serves as a symbol of patriotic education and revitalization. The guardians of such orthodoxies are locked in
a struggle with those who want to expand the symbol, to make a place for

other heroes in the retelling of the story. The guardians of such orthodoxies must also face those who say that the saga itself is not heroic but simply a story of imperial conquest. Because the Alamo is such a powerful symbol, it is also a contentious one. Yet even in the midst of the struggles for "ownership" of the symbol, people like Margit Nagy see the shrine of Texas liberty as a place where the enduring appeals of battle can engender mutual respect among former enemies. Hence, the Alamo is not a static symbol that conveys one meaning to everyone. It is alive and changing. It will continue to be consecrated through processes of veneration, defilement, and redefinition.

Notes

Portions of this chapter appeared in an earlier form in Edward T. Linenthal, "A Reservoir of Spiritual Power: Patriotic Faith at the Alamo in the Twentieth Century," *Southwestern Historical Quarterly* 91, no. 4 (April 1988): 509–31.

1. "Remember the Alamo: The Development of a Texas Symbol, 1836–1986," an exhibit prepared by William Elton Green for the Witte Museum in San Antonio, opened in February 1986 and was due to close in August, on the birthday of Davy Crockett. The exhibit was so popular, however, that the closing date was extended until November. *Alamo Images: Changing Perceptions of a Texas Experience* (Dallas: DeGolyer Library and Southern Methodist University Press, 1985), a companion catalog for the DeGolyer display, was prepared by Susan Prendergast Schoelwer with Tom W. Gläser. John Wayne's "Alamo" in Brackettville, Texas, was also used for the filming of *Alamo . . . The Price of Freedom*, which debuted in 1988 in San Antonio.

2. Grills, quoted in "Pilgrimage to the Alamo," in "Historic Sites—Alamo," San Antonio clippings file, Daughters of the Republic of Texas Library at the Alamo (hereafter DRTL).

3. *Message of Governor O. B. Colquitt to the Thirty-third Legislature Relating to the Alamo Property* (Austin: Von Boeckmann-Jones Co., 1913), p. 95; Edith Mae Johnson interview, July 18, 1986.

4. Author's transcription of the Mar. 6, 1986, broadcast of "The 700 Club" from the Alamo, San Antonio, Texas.

5. See Gary Foreman, "Remembering the Alamo," in "Historic Sites—Alamo," DRTL.

6. Balthasar Janacek interview, July 16, 1986.

7. *San Antonio Express*, Apr. 23, 1946 (hereafter *Express*). The anniversary was not officially recognized by the state until 1960, when Gov. Price Daniel designated March 6 as Alamo Day. See *San Antonio Light*, Mar. 1, 1960 (hereafter *Light*); *San Antonio Express-News*, Mar. 1, 1960 (hereafter *Express-News*).

8. *San Antonio Daily Express*, Mar. 6, 1886 (hereafter *Daily Express*); *Express*, Mar. 6, 1890, and Mar. 6, 1912. I wish to thank William Green for the opportunity to read his manuscript "Remembering the Alamo: The Development of a Texas Symbol." My understanding of the Alamo's nineteenth-century background relies heavily on his thorough examination.

9. "Holidays—Texas Centennial," general clippings file, DRTL; Roosevelt, quoted in *Light*, June 12, 1936.

10. Charlie Jeffries, "The Lights of the Alamo," *Southwestern Historical Quarterly* 46 (July 1942): 8; Evelyn M. Carrington, "Alamo Day Address, 1943," in "Alamo Day Addresses—Alamo Historic Sites," San Antonio clippings file, DRTL; Samuel L. Terry, "Alamo Day Address, 1944," ibid.

11. *Express,* Apr. 20, 1948, and Mar. 6, 1951; *Light,* Apr. 22, 1947; *Express,* Mar. 6, 1953.

12. *Light,* Apr. 22, 1952; *Express,* Apr. 21, 1953; Armin F. Puck, "Alamo Day Address, 1962," in "Alamo Day Addresses—Alamo Historic Sites," DRTL.

13. Newspaper clipping, Apr. 22, 1963, "Pilgrimage to the Alamo," DRTL.

14. Mary Ann Zuber, "An Escape from the Alamo," *The Texas Almanac for 1873, and Emigrant's Guide to Texas . . .* (Galveston: Richardson, Belo & Co., [1872]), pp. 80–85; Anna J. Hardwicke Pennybacker, *A New History of Texas for Schools . . .* (Tyler, Tex.: n.p., 1888); George P. Garrison, *Texas: A Contest of Civilizations* (Boston: Houghton Mifflin Co., 1903). The other two editions of Pennybacker's history in which the story appears were published in Palestine, Texas, by Percy V. Pennybacker (1895) and in Austin, by Mrs. Percy V. Pennybacker (1900).

15. J. Frank Dobie, Mody C. Boatright, and Harry R. Ransom, eds., *In the Shadow of History.* Publications of the Texas Folklore Society, no. 15 (Hatboro, Pa.: Folklore Associates, 1966), p. 14; J. K. Beretta, "Debunking and Debunkers," *Southwestern Historical Quarterly* 43 (Oct. 1939): 252, 253; *Dallas Times,* Apr. 18, 1988; *Handbook of Production Information,* in the press packet for the film *Alamo . . . The Price of Freedom,* DRTL. For a fascinating account of the history of the Zuber story, see Llerena Friend, "Historiography of the Account of Moses Rose and the Line That Travis Drew," in William Physick Zuber, *My Eighty Years in Texas,* ed. Janis Boyle Mayfield (Austin: University of Texas Press, 1971), pp. 255–62.

16. Young, quoted in *Handbook of Production Information.*

17. *Light,* Apr. 20, 1954; *Express,* Apr. 21, 1964; *Light,* Apr. 22, 1975; Davis, in "Pilgrimage to the Alamo," DRTL; *Light,* Mar. 7, 1989. Clayton Williams, the 1990 Republican party nominee for governor of Texas, made good use of the story of Travis's line in a fundraising letter. He declared that modern-day Texans faced a "similar fateful decision," that the line "has been drawn. It's me against . . . the liberals, rallying behind Ann Richards [the Democratic party nominee]." Recipients of the letter were asked to cross the line via a campaign donation that would allow them to become a "Williams Ranger." I wish to thank Kevin Young for bringing this letter to my attention.

18. *Express,* Mar. 6, 1955; *Express-News,* Mar. 7, 1984.

19. Cisneros, quoted in the author's notes from the Dawn at the Alamo Celebration, Mar. 6, 1986; Fehrenbach, "Alamo Day Sesquicentennial Address, 1986," in "Alamo Day Addresses—Alamo Historic Sites," DRTL; Hooper, quoted in "Rites and Ceremonies, 6 March 1987—Alamo Historic Sites," San Antonio clippings file, DRTL.

20. The symbolic transformation of martial sacrifice is explored more thoroughly in Edward Tabor Linenthal, *Changing Images of the Warrior Hero in America: A History of Popular Symbolism* (New York: Edwin Mellen Press, 1982); in Linenthal, "Restoring America: Political Revivalism in the Nuclear Age," *Religion and the Life of the Nation: American Recoveries,* ed. Rowland A. Sherrill (Urbana: University of Illinois Press, 1990), pp. 23–45; and in David Chidester, "Saving the Children by Killing Them: Redemptive Sacrifice in the Ideologies of Jim Jones and Ronald Reagan," paper delivered at the annual meeting of the American Academy of Religion, Nov. 1989.

21. This notion of expenditure in schemes of sacrifice is developed in a most provocative manner by Chidester in "Saving the Children."

22. Green, "Remembering the Alamo," chap. 2, p. 2; De Zavala, quoted in L. Robert Ables, "The Second Battle of the Alamo," *Southwestern Historical Quarterly* 70 (Jan. 1967): 383. For a detailed discussion of this controversy, see Ables, pp. 372–413. For Colquitt's discussion, see *Message of Governor O. B. Colquitt,* pp. 136–40.

23. Santa Anna had ordered the bodies of the Alamo defenders burned, and the remains were not interred until February 1837. See Green, "Remembering the Alamo," chap. 2, pp. 2–4.

24. The letter is quoted in ibid., chap. 4, p. 23.

25. *Express,* Mar. 11, 1947; *Express-News,* Dec. 7, 1954.

26. Reuben Marmaduke Potter, "The Fall of the Alamo," *Magazine of American History* 11, no. 1 (Jan. 1878): 20; remaining quotes from C. W. Raines, "The Alamo Monument," *Quarterly of the Texas State Historical Association* 6 (Apr. 1903): 303, 304, 306.

27. *Daily Express,* Dec. 12, 1909. For a further description of Giles's plans, see Mary Carolyn Hollers Jutson, *Alfred Giles: An English Architect in Texas and Mexico* (San Antonio: Trinity University Press, 1972), pp. 157–60.

28. Newspaper clipping, n.d., in "Texas Centennial, 1936—Holidays," general clippings file, DRTL; "Cenotaph," KTSA radio transcript, Jan. 23. 1940, in "Alamo Historic Sites," San Antonio clippings file, DRTL; Dobie, quoted in *Light,* Nov. 19, 1939.

29. Joseph Gallegly, *From Alamo Plaza to Jack Harris's Saloon: O. Henry and the Southwest He Knew* (The Hague: Mouton, 1970), p. 27; *San Antonio News,* Nov. 11, 1958 (hereafter *News*); *Express,* Sept. 26, 1968. In 1989 a San Antonio city ordinance banned the sale of T-shirts and trinkets from the area directly in front of the Alamo, prompting vendors in Alamo Plaza to move only a few feet to the side.

30. Bob Greene, "Remember the Alamo?" *Esquire* (Apr. 1984): 12–14; Stinson, quoted in *Express-News,* Jan. 12, 1986; Harlan, quoted in ibid., Mar. 2, 1986. See also Stephen Harrigan, "The Alamo? Sure, Two Blocks, Turn Right, and It's Right Across from the Five and Ten," *Texas Monthly* 3 (Sept. 1975): 58–60, 112–23.

31. *Light,* June 17, 1980; *Express-News,* Feb. 23, 1982; *Light,* Mar. 7, 1982.

32. *Express-News,* July 18, 1987; *Light,* Mar. 21, 1989. For information on the problem with tour buses, see *Light,* Feb. 28, 1987.

33. *Alamo Visitors Guide* (San Antonio: R. Jay Casell, 1981), unpaginated.

34. "Foreman Plan," in "Alamo Historic Sites," DRTL.

35. "The Daughters of Texas Have a Curt Rebuke for a Yankee Who Remembers the Alamo—Forget It," *People* (June 4, 1984): 46–47; Patricia E. Osborne interview, July 15, 1986. For other responses to the Foreman project, see *Express,* Dec. 8 and 14, 1983; *News,* Dec. 9, 1983; *Light,* Feb. 2, 1984; *Austin American Statesman,* Mar. 2, 1984; *Waco Tribune-Herald,* Mar. 4, 1984.

36. Arnoldo De León, *They Called Them Greasers: Anglo Attitudes toward Mexicans in Texas, 1821–1900* (Austin: University of Texas Press, 1983), p. 13; Parmenter, quoted in Mark E. Nackman, *A Nation within a Nation: The Rise of Texas Nationalism* (Port Washington, N.Y.: Kennikat Press, 1975), p. 92.

37. Robert Johannsen, *To the Hall of the Montezumas: The Mexican War in the American Imagination* (New York: Oxford University Press, 1985), p. 22.

38. David Montejano, *Anglos and Mexicans in the Making of Texas, 1836–1986* (Austin: University of Texas Press, 1987), pp. 223–24; Don Graham, "Remembering the Alamo: The Story of the Texas Revolution in Popular Culture," *Southwestern Historical Quarterly* 89 (July 1985): 46. See also Graham, *Cowboys and Cadillacs: How Hollywood Looks at Texas* (Austin: Texas Monthly Press, 1983), pp. 41–53; Schoelwer, pp. 104–62.

39. Aristeo Sul interview, July 14, 1986; Ray Sanchez interview, July 15, 1986; Anastacio Bueno interview, July 16, 1986.

40. Montejano, p. 305.

41. Arnoldo De León, *The Tejano Community, 1836–1900* (Albuquerque: University of New Mexico Press, 1982), p. 2; Gilberto Hinojosa interview, July 14, 1986; *Light,* Apr. 6, 1986. For a good history of Tejanos in the early period of Texas history, see De León, *Tejano Community.*

42. Félix D. Almaráz interviews, July 14 and 18, 1986; Henry Guerra interview, July 16, 1986.

43. Rodolfo Acuña, *Occupied America: A History of Chicanos.* 2d ed. (New York: Harper and Row, 1981), pp. 3, 9; Acuña, quoted in Arnoldo De León, "Tejanos and the Texas War for Independence: Historiography's Judgement," *New Mexico Historical Review* 61 (Apr. 1986): 143; Lalo Valdez interview, July 14, 1986.

44. Edith Mae Johnson interview, July 18, 1986; Patricia Osborne interview, July 15, 1986.

45. Remarks by Williams, Briggs, Cassidy, and Menetrey are in "Pilgrimage to the Alamo," DRTL; Fehrenbach's remarks are in

"Rites and Ceremonies, 6 March 1988—Alamo Historic Sites," DRTL.

46. Cisneros, quoted in *Express-News*, Feb. 22, 1986; Elizondo, quoted in ibid., Mar. 3, 1986.

47. Gilbert R. Cruz telephone interview, July 16, 1986; Frantz, quoted in the *New York Times*, Mar. 16, 1986.

48. Janacek interview, July 16, 1986.

49. George McAlister, *Alamo—The Price of Freedom: A History of Texas* (San Antonio: Docutex, 1988); *Express-News*, Aug. 2, 1987. A certain amount of hubris accompanied the marketing of the film. The casting call for reenactors declares, "This film will stand as the 'Last Word' on the Alamo." It notes that Alamo Village in Brackettville was being repaired and that reenactors, carefully dressed in historically correct outfits, would use words known to have been spoken at the Alamo. See "Alamo: The Price of Freedom," DRTL.

50. *Express*, July 27, 1987; *Light*, Aug. 13, 1987; letter from George A. McAlister to Maria Berriozabal, Aug. 17, 1987, "Alamo: The Price of Freedom," miscellaneous papers, DRTL. I am indebted to Bernice Strong for bringing this material to my attention. Clearly, McAlister sees the Alamo as a heroic model through which Americans should read contemporary history. In his book he says the Alamo is a "clarion call [that] would echo through the canyons of time and inspire future generations of Texans and other Americans as they defended freedom on Battlefields all over the world" (p. 186).

51. *Express-News*, Oct. 11, 1987. Like the Travis legend, the Crockett story has become a jealously guarded part of patriotic orthodoxy. No one familiar with Walt Disney's Davy Crockett in the 1950s will forget the immortal Crockett, never falling, swinging his rifle butt to the very end, exhibiting the same courage in the face of certain death that Errol Flynn's Custer did in 1941. Nevertheless, Carmen Perry's translation of the diary of José Enrique de la Peña, who fought with Santa Anna at the Alamo, sheds new light on Crockett's supposedly heroic death in the heat of the battle:"Some seven men had survived the general carnage and, under the protection of General Castrillon, they were brought before Santa Ana. Among them . . . was the naturalist David Crockett. . . . Santa Ana answered Castrillon's intervention in Crockett's behalf with a gesture of indignation and, addressing himself to . . . the troops closest to him, ordered his execution. The commanders and officers were outraged at this action and did not support the order. . . . but several officers who were around the President and who, perhaps, had not been present during the moment of danger . . . thrust themselves forward . . . and with sword in hand, fell upon these unfortunate, defenseless men just as a tiger leaps upon his prey. Though tortured before they were killed, these unfortunates died without complaining and without humiliating themselves before their torturers" (de la Peña, *With Santa Ana in Texas: A Personal Narrative of the Revolution*, trans. and ed. Carmen Perry [College Station: Texas A & M University Press, 1975], p. 70). When McAlister was asked why he had disregarded the information in de la Peña's diary, he said that he doubted its validity because it indicated that "Crockett was a coward" (quoted in *Express-News*, Aug. 2, 1987). In 1978 Dan Kilgore, a past president of the Texas State Historical Association, wrote a book based on various eyewitness accounts of Crockett's death, including de la Peña's. He concluded: "Not one report of an eyewitness has been found by Alamo scholars to support the popular notion that Crockett went down while desperately clubbing Mexican soldiers with the barrel of his shattered rifle" (*How Did Davy Die?* [College Station: Texas A & M University Press, 1978], p. 39). Like Perry, Kilgore was subjected to various forms of harassment, among them a letter received in May 1978 that reads in part, "How dare you degrade Davy Crockett. . . . I want you to know that we know the reason for this. This is one of the Communits [*sic*] ploys to degrade our hero's [*sic*]. 'He's still King of the wild frontier.' " On May 17, 1978, the *Houston Chronicle* ran a syndicated column from Roger Simon of the *Chicago Sun Times* commenting on Kilgore's book. Simon declared, quite inaccurately, that Kilgore judged Crockett "a flop and a fink and maybe a coward to boot." A letter to the *Chronicle* on that same day insisted that Kilgore's book was part of an attempt to "discredit and disgrace all prominent white Americans who helped to build

our state and nation. Perhaps Dan Kilgore . . . will bravely lead the American charge if any, when Omar Torrijos, Fidel Castro and all the Russians, Mexicans, Hindus, Chinese, Vietnamese, Iranians, Nigerians, Arabs and South Americans make official their invasion of America and overthrow of our democratic republic." For more on the reaction to Perry and Kilgore, see Barbara Paulsen, "Say It Ain't So, Davy," *Texas Monthly* (Nov. 1986): 129; Bill Walraven, "Historian Finds Truth about Crockett Hurts," *Corpus Christi Caller,* May 2, 1978; ibid., Oct. 23, 1986; *Houston Chronicle,* May 7, 1978 (hereafter *Chronicle*). I am indebted to Dan Kilgore for bringing these articles to my attention.

52. *Light,* Dec. 15, 1987.

53. *Express,* Dec. 30, 1987; *Dallas Morning News,* Jan. 10, 1988; *Express-News,* Jan. 23, 1988; *Chronicle,* Mar. 5, 1988.

54. *Light,* Mar. 7, 1988; Merrill, quoted in "Alamo: The Price of Freedom," DRTL.

55. *Express-News,* Mar. 27, 1988. During the controversies, McAlister and Merrill reminded the public that not everything could be covered to everyone's satisfaction in a forty-five-minute film. The original screenplay contained a more prominent role for Juan Seguín and also a role for the only black defender of the Alamo. However, these scenes were not included in the final version of the film. I thank Bernice Strong, a historical consultant on the film, for bringing this information to my attention.

56. *Chronicle,* Mar. 5. 1988; *Express-News,* Mar. 15, 1988. The proposal was made shortly before the highly publicized attempt by Rep. Ron Wilson, a Houston Democrat, to have control of the Alamo transferred to the Texas Parks and Wildlife Department. A bill to that effect (HB 2259) was filed in the Texas legislature in March 1989.

57. *Chronicle,* Oct. 12, 1988, and Mar. 15, 1989; *Houston Post,* Apr. 20, 1988; *El Paso Herald Post,* Apr. 23, 1988. The debate over actual and symbolic ownership of the Alamo also became intertwined with other controversial issues. For example, the *San Antonio Light* reported on Nov. 12, 1988, that leaders of the Official English Movement supported the DRT and that the American Ethnic Committee wanted legislation to protect the DRT from LULAC.

58. I am indebted to Margit Nagy, associate professor of history and intercultural studies at Our Lady of the Lake University, for bringing this fascinating story to my attention. She kindly shared with me her research on this subject during a visit to San Antonio in 1986 and again in August 1989. Much of the material in this section is based on her report "Remembering the Alamo Japanese-Style: Shigetaka Shiga's Monument as Tribute to the Alamo Heroes," no. 2 (San Antonio: Institute for Intercultural Studies, Our Lady of the Lake University, 1989).

59. Nagy, p. 2. In both battles, according to Nagy, defenders were greatly outnumbered. At the battle of Nagashino, Suneemon Torii, like James Bonham at the Alamo, left the besieged fortress to seek help. Unlike Bonham, who returned and died in the battle, Suneemon Torii was captured upon his return and killed, after shouting to the defenders of Nagashino castle that help was on the way (pp. 4–5).

60. Nagy, p. 11. She also notes: "One fascinating feature of Shiga's memorial is that it links the defenders of the Alamo with their counterparts in both China and Japan. The Chinese characters on the front offer poetic eulogy to the Alamo heroes. The text was composed in classical Chinese literary style (*kanbun*) by Shiga, who from his youth had a fondness for Chinese poetry and was known as a fine poet. The text . . . gives parallels for Crockett, Bowie, and Bonham not with Nagashino warriors but with the brave defenders of the Battle of Suiyang in eighth-century China" (p. 8).

61. *Alamo Heights News,* Apr. 29, 1943; Nagy, p. 20; *Light,* Nov. 14, 1989. Nagy's remarks about Pearl Harbor and Hiroshima are in an *Express-News* clipping, n.d., "Japanese Monument—Alamo Historic Sites," San Antonio clippings file, DRTL. How ironic that a symbol that is still so divisive also has provided the opportunity for renewed joint declarations of friendship between two peoples struggling to form appropriate human perceptions of one another. John W. Dower, in *War without Mercy: Race and Power in the Pacific War* (New York: Pantheon Books, 1986),

writes that racist perceptions continue to haunt Japanese and Americans in the post–World War II years, and "it is predictable that harsher racist attitudes reminiscent of the war years will again arise at times of heightened competition or disagreement" (p. 312). What draws Japanese and Americans together at the Alamo, however, is the recognition of heroism and sacrifice present in each culture.

3

"A Joint and Precious Heritage"

There was little reason for Northern optimism in the Virginia theater of war in June 1863. Robert E. Lee's Army of Northern Virginia had crushed the Army of the Potomac at Fredericksburg in December 1862 and again at Chancellorsville in May 1863. Desperately searching for competent military leadership, on June 28, 1863, Pres. Abraham Lincoln appointed George G. Meade commander of the Army of the Potomac.

Earlier in June, Lee had decided to invade Pennsylvania to draw Union troops away from Richmond, to strengthen a growing peace movement in the war-weary North, and to gather needed supplies. On June 30 Union cavalrymen skirmished just north of Gettysburg with Confederates. On July 1 the battle of Gettysburg began in earnest as Confederate reinforcements poured into the area, pushing badly outnumbered Union troops through the town to defensive positions on Cemetery Hill and Cemetery Ridge. On July 2 the great armies were massed at Gettysburg.

The key to winning the battle was control of a partially wooded, rocky spur called Little Round Top, which stood in the shadow of the slightly larger Big Round Top. Confederates under the command of Gen. James Longstreet attacked here, to the left of the Union line. As savage fighting raged in Devil's Den, and subsequently in the Wheatfield and the Peach Orchard—names that ever after would recall the ferocity of the day's battle—Confederate troops started to ascend Little Round Top. Gen. Gouverneur K. Warren, the Union army's chief engineer, was shocked to find the spur almost undefended and rushed troops and cannon to the summit. The fighting was desperate. Gen. Joshua L. Chamberlain, commanding the Twentieth Maine, recollected that "blood stood in puddles in some places on the rocks." The Union troops held their ground on Little Round Top, as well as on Culp's Hill, at the other end of their defensive line. After two days of battle, neither side could claim victory.

On July 3, at one o'clock in the afternoon, a determined Robert E. Lee ordered 140 Confederate cannon along Seminary Ridge to open fire. The air, one Union soldier declared, "was all murderous iron." Shortly after three o'clock, approximately twelve thousand Confederate troops, a "sloping forest of flashing steel," led by three brigadier generals—George E. Pickett, J. J. Petti-grew, and Isaac R. Trimble—set out across more than half a mile of open ground separating them from Cemetery Ridge. A continuous wall of Union fire decimated the advancing men, no more than half of whom survived. Only a few hundred Confederates, led by Brig. Gen. Lewis A. Armistead (who would himself fall mortally wounded) managed to temporarily breach the Union lines at the Angle before being turned back. As one Union soldier described the scene, the "jostling, swaying lines on either side boil, and roar, and dash their foamy spray, two hostile billows of a fiery ocean."

After three days of intense fighting, the battle was over. The broken Confed-erates retreated. Coupled with the fall of Vicksburg on July 4, the high water mark of the Confederacy had passed. Gettysburg, consecrated by the blood of a war-torn nation's fighting men, had become truly sacred ground.

Gettysburg

ONE OF THE GREAT IRONIES associated with American battlefields is that they are often quite beautiful and, except at the height of the tourist season, quite peaceful. Many visitors to Gettysburg comment on how difficult it is to think of great violence taking place on such picturesque pastoral ground. During a visit to the battlefield on May 11, 1909, George S. Patton, Jr., then a student at West Point, wrote: "The trenches are still easily seen and their grass grown flower strewn slopes agree ill with the bloody purpose for which they were designed and used. . . . There is to me strange fascination in looking at the scenes of the awful struggles which raged over this country. A fascination and a regret. I would like to have been there too." I suspect that most visitors would feel deprived if Gettysburg were *not* beautiful; indeed, the field on which one of the greatest dramas of the Civil War was acted out *should* be physically inspiring as well as spiritually profound. The processes of veneration, defilement, and redefinition that have taken place at Gettysburg—called by some the symbolic center of American history—have created what Reuben M. Rainey refers to as "preservation of a preservation," for Gettysburg is a rich cultural archive of various modes of remembrance.[1]

During his brief address at the dedication of the Soldiers' National Cemetery on the Gettysburg battlefield on November 19, 1863, Abraham Lincoln declared that the living could not further "consecrate" nor "hallow" the ground, for "the brave men, living and dead, who struggled here have consecrated it far above our poor power to add or detract." Despite the president's claim that the sanctification of the field had been completed by heroic actions, feverish attempts to establish appropriate modes of remembrance began immediately after the battle and continue to this day. Although the cemetery was the earliest focus of traditional veneration, some people wanted the battlefield itself to serve as a permanent memorial to the heroism of the Union troops and the righteousness of their cause. Only three weeks after the battle ended, on July 25, 1863, David McConaughy, a Gettysburg lawyer, wrote to Gov. Andrew Curtin of Pennsylvania about his plan to buy portions of the field to be retained in the "actual form and condition they were in, during the battles." On August 19, in a plea for public support that appeared in the *Adams Sentinel,* McConaughy declared that there could be "no more fitting and expressive memorial of the heroic valor and signal triumph of our army" than preservation of the field of combat.[2]

This desire to provide a permanent commemorative landscape also found institutional expression in the charter of the Gettysburg Battlefield Memorial Association (GBMA), founded in September 1863 and chartered in April 1864. The association's goal was to "hold and preserve the battle-grounds of Gettysburg . . . with the natural and artificial defences, such as they were at the time of said battle, and by such perpetuation, and such memorial structures as a generous and patriotic people may aid to erect, to commemorate the heroic deeds, the struggles, and the triumphs of their brave defenders."[3]

Through their impressive preservation activities, McConaughy, the GBMA, and a legion of other individuals and organizations practicing various forms of veneration sought to freeze the meaning of Gettysburg in a simple and enduring patriotic orthodoxy, developed in the 1880s as Americans sought to recover the epic excitement of the Civil War and to forget its horror. Gettysburg became a place where, in the words of Angus W. McLean, a former governor of Virginia, Union and Confederate veterans alike could celebrate "a joint and precious heritage." In reunions, patriotic rhetoric on numerous ceremonial occasions, and monument building, many Northerners—and many Southerners, as well—came to celebrate Gettysburg as an "American" victory. Because it was believed that the bravery and heroism shown by the contending Union and Confederate forces revealed a uniquely American form of commitment to heartfelt principle, Gettysburg became a heroic landscape, one that was seen, in McLean's words, through a "golden mist of American valor."[4]

Beginning in 1863 those entrusted with the care of the battlefield have tried to contain this "golden mist" through careful preservation of the site. As defenders of this sacred ground, they battled fiercely with those who perceived the battlefield in secular terms and threatened to defile it. They also battled against the view that this "golden mist" was a distorting rather than an ennobling aspect of the processes of healing and reconciliation, indicative of a moral myopia that ignored the real legacy of the battle and the war. Some Civil War veterans expressed concern about the adequacy of such seemingly effortless healing. John Anderson, a former Union soldier, visited with a Southern family shortly after the war ended and wrote that the "only friendship possible was based upon a tacit ignoring of what was deepest in our hearts. And what sort of friendship was that?"[5]

Because rituals of reconciliation between Northern and Southern veterans at Gettysburg relied on this tacit forgetfulness, it was all too easy for veterans to lose themselves in camaraderie with friend and foe, and all too easy for Northern veterans to accept Southern claims that the war was *really* about arcane constitutional issues such as states rights, rather than about the moral issue of slavery. By the 1890s many Northern veterans had become more sympathetic to Southern views on blacks and, in consequence, these rituals of reconciliation became rituals of exclusion that ignored the history of black Americans after the Civil War and prevented them from taking part in the healing process. Some GAR encampments in the South barred black members, for example; and in 1899 the United Confederate Veterans cited the Spanish-American War and the recent Philippine insurrection—both categorized as conflicts with people of color—as reasons why Northerners should meet with Confederate veterans experienced in the ways of such people, in a "spirit of inquiry" and not "rebuke."[6]

Critics of reconciliation based solely on heroic recollections of battle understood that they were involved in a struggle for culturally significant memories of the Civil War. They believed that veneration at Gettysburg, or at any other Civil War battlefield, would never be authentic until commemorative events included sober reflection on slavery and on the enduring problem of racism. Such critics reminded Americans that "polite" memories, those that honored everyone, were dangerously flawed. The *real* purpose of veneration, they argued, was contained in Lincoln's famous address: that Gettysburg must serve to inspire the living to be "dedicated . . . to the unfinished work which they who fought here have thus far so nobly advanced." Frederick Douglass remarked in 1894, "I am not indifferent to the claims of a generous forgetfulness, but whatever else I may forget, I shall never forget the difference between those who fought to save the Republic and those who fought to destroy it." Nearly seventy years later John Hope Franklin wrote that Civil War commemorative events were "false and iniquitous," for they failed to confront the fact that sectional reunification was realized only because the nation chose to continue to exclude people of color from full participation in the "reborn" Union. In Franklin's view these celebrations failed to remind Americans that "while the war is over the battle to free man's mind and his actions of hatred and racial bigotry has not been won."[7]

The earliest attempts to sanctify the battlefield at Gettysburg took place in a setting that had been profoundly altered by the power of war. John Vanderslice, a Philadelphia lawyer and an active member of the Pennsylvania chapter of the Grand Army of the Republic (GAR), a powerful veterans' organization, reported that the "smoke of battle had scarcely cleared away before thousands of patriotic people were thronging to the place, with supplies and comforts, to render what aid they could to the wounded and help bury the dead." Eyewitness accounts of the battle and its aftermath detailed the gruesome scene. Mrs. Tillie Alleman wrote that immediately after the battle "the stench arising from the fields of carnage was most sickening. Dead horses, swollen to almost twice their natural size, lay in all directions, stains of blood frequently met our gaze, and all kinds of army accouterments covered the ground. Fences had disappeared, some buildings were gone, others ruined. The whole landscape had been changed, and I felt as though we were in a strange and blighted land." In 1903 a Western Maryland Railway Company publication estimated that the 200,000 visitors who annually came to Gettysburg still could see graphic evidence of the battle: "Houses everywhere retain the old shutters punctured with . . . shot, and door frames . . . retain the scars of the minié balls."[8]

In a journal entry dated July 7, 1863, only four days after the battle ended, John B. Linn remarked that the "smell of putrified blood" coming from the field where members of the Twelfth South Carolina Volunteers had fought and fell "was very disagreeable to me." The dead "were only lightly covered with earth and you could feel the body by pressing the earth with your foot." A visitor from Philadelphia who arrived on July 10 shared Tillie Alleman's sense of the place as a horrific new world that "no words can depict." "In some places," she said, "bodies, caught in the thickets as they fell, were still hanging midway between the summit and the hill's foot, dense clouds of insects hovering over them." Another eyewitness to the aftermath of the carnage watched exhausted surgeons operate on the wounded in makeshift field hospitals and later recalled seeing "legs and arms falling from the table to the floor beneath [which] were raked out . . . and carried away for burial."[9]

Clearly, the immediate postbattle perceptions of Gettysburg did not focus on a "golden mist of American valor." There was, and still is, however, a primal attraction to scenes of destructive power, to the shattered landscape and shattered people that bear witness to such events. And it is this attraction that has led people like David McConaughy to feel instinctively the urge to sanctify these places.

The first form of veneration at Gettysburg was directed toward the Union dead. According to John S. Patterson, "the creation of the Soldiers' National Cemetery on the 'sacred' ground . . . was an event that captured the attention and engaged the emotions of men and women throughout the Union." Northern visitors to the battlefield could step over the shallow Confederate graves without a trace of indignation, but it was decided that the remains of the Union heroes, now in temporary graves, would suffer no such indignity. David Wills, a Gettysburg attorney who played a key role in the creation of the cemetery, thought that it should be located at the apex of the fighting on Cemetery Hill, for it was most appropriate "to bury the victims of that battle in its contested and hallowed soil, already stained with the blood of the fallen." Representatives of the various Union states wanted their dead buried in distinctive state plots, but William Saunders, the landscape architect who designed the cemetery, wisely chose to honor all the dead equally.[10]

The laborious, gruesome process of exhumation began in mid-October 1863 and was completed on March 19, 1864. Samuel Weaver, hired by Wills to oversee the transfer of bodies, meticulously searched among the dead and in the end declared: "I firmly believe that there has not been a single mistake made in the removal of the soldiers to the cemetery by taking the body of a rebel for a Union soldier." (Such firm beliefs notwithstanding, several Confederates were reportedly buried in the cemetery.) The *Adams Sentinel* later noted that Southerners, not content to let their fallen relatives and friends lie in shallow Northern graves for eternity, visited the battlefield almost every day "for the purpose of recovering the bodies of the slain, with a view to having them removed and taken to their homes . . . for re-interment."[11]

Beginning in the 1870s and continuing until 1894, the Pennsylvania chapters of the GAR held reunions at Gettysburg. By the early 1880s a variety of reunions of Union troops, occasionally joined by Confederate veterans, also occurred with regularity. One of the moving forces behind such reunions was Col. John B. Bachelder, who until his death in 1894 was considered *the* authority on the battle. Bachelder arrived in Gettysburg shortly after the "great battle" ended and spent the next eighty-four days on the field, familiarizing himself with every aspect of the conflict that had taken place there. He became one of the directors of the Gettysburg Battlefield Memorial Association and wrote one of the first battlefield guidebooks. Throughout the 1880s he worked diligently to bring back both Union and Confederate veterans to help mark the lines of battle.[12]

Such modest reunions eventually became elaborate rituals of reconciliation, celebrated during commemorative ceremonies. These events offered the opportunity to dramatize the ideology of reconciliation, which judged the sacred causes of North and South to be equally just since soldiers on both sides were perceived to have demonstrated laudable martial valor inspired by a heartfelt commitment to their respective causes.[13]

The construction of an ideology of reconciliation began as the nation moved from bitter sectional hatred to what Paul Buck calls a "union of sentiment based on integrated interests." Wallace Davies notes that in the 1870s Union rhetoric emphasized the South's "criminal responsibility." He adds that "warnings not to lose the fruits of victory quickly followed nearly every profession of friendship; offers of forgiveness depended upon the South's admission of how grievously it had sinned." Although neither side fully "extinguished their resentments," as Lincoln had asked, when Rutherford B. Hayes became president in 1877 and began restoring white rule in the South, rituals of reconciliation became fashionable. In that year, for example, Hayes went to Tennessee to celebrate Memorial Day, making visible at a national level the joint celebrations that certain veterans groups had been commemorating in Northern and Southern communities for several years. Gerald Linderman believes that this spirit of reconciliation was fueled in large part by Northern nostalgic images of the prewar South. "Troubled by the decline of small-town communities wrought by urbanization and industrialization," he argues, Northerners "felt the empathy of a people confronting a 'disappearing civilization' of their own." Cruce Stark maintains that "the acceptance of the Southern soldier into the fraternity of arms was a necessary final distillation of the soldier into a distinct element of society. The line of separation . . . was not now between North and South, but between those who had tested their manhood in the fire of battle and those who had not."[14]

Joint veterans' reunions at Gettysburg reflected this national movement toward reconciliation and revealed that the celebration of Northern and Southern martial valor was more important than reflection on the causes of the war. In August 1869 Walter Harrison, the adjutant general for Confederate general George E. Pickett's division, met with Union officers in Gettysburg to begin marking Union and Confederate lines; by August 27 they had driven in 224 stakes. In July 1887 several hundred veterans of Pickett's and James J. Pettigrew's famous charge on the third day of the battle met with 1,000 veterans of the Philadelphia Brigade, which had manned the Union lines on Cemetery Ridge during the charge. John Bachelder walked with the veterans over the famous field on which the Confederates had advanced, stopping at the Angle, the low stone wall where the great armies had met in hand-to-hand combat. Bachelder reported: "The Southerners marched up to the right of the Northern column and halted, and above the explosion of . . . roman candles, sky rockets and the blare of red lights . . . by a common impulse of American Humanity . . . the two commands moved forward and spontaneously grasped each other's hands." Col. William R. Aylett, who had assumed command of a Confederate brigade during the dramatic charge, celebrated the symbolic reconciliation by telling his fellow veterans, "Above the ashes left by the War . . . we have created a new empire." Such dramatic meetings, especially the handshake at the Angle, would figure prominently in all future reenactments of the Pickett-Pettigrew charge.[15]

Confederate dead at Rose Woods, Gettysburg. Photograph by Alexander Gardner, July 5, 1863. (National Park Service)

Makeshift museums like this one displayed relics of the battle. (National Park Service)

Delegates badges worn at the fiftieth reunion in 1913 became prized souvenirs. (National Park Service)

Alfred R. Waud, a sketch artist for *Harper's Weekly,* visited Gettysburg shortly after the battle and was one of many artists to dramatize the Pickett-Pettigrew charge. In this scene Waud focused on the final moments of Brig. Gen. Lewis Armistead as he penetrated the Union lines on Cemetery Ridge. (National Park Service)

To commemorate the Pickett-Pettigrew charge, on July 3, 1913, a line of veterans marched through the field near the Angle. (National Park Service)

Members of the Philadelphia Brigade Association and Pickett's Division Association shook hands over the wall at the Angle during the fiftieth anniversary celebration in 1913. (National Park Service)

Two aged veterans shook hands over the stone wall near the Angle during the seventy-fifth anniversary celebration in 1938. (National Park Service)

Veterans camped out on portions of the battlefield during the fiftieth anniversary celebration in 1913. (National Park Service)

Ceremonies during the 125th anniversary at the Angle, July 2, 1988.
(National Park Service)

The Eternal Light Peace Memorial was unveiled by Confederate veteran A. G. Harris
and Union veteran G. M. Lockison on July 3, 1938. (National Park Service)

The Soldiers' National Monument.
(National Park Service)

Evidence of the monumental landscape at Gettysburg: the Angle and Hancock Avenue on Cemetery Ridge, seen from Ziegler's Grove Tower, 1954. (National Park Service)

The Virginia Monument, dedicated
in 1917. (National Park Service)

The North Carolina Monument, dedicated
in 1929. (National Park Service)

The 26th North Carolina Marker, dedicated on October 2, 1986, was the first advanced regimental marker ever placed on the field. It was situated thirty-five yards beyond the point at which Pickett's Virginians had been turned back from the Angle on July 3, 1863. (National Park Service)

The High Water Mark Memorial and the sacred copse of trees. (National Park Service)

A portion of Paul Philippoteaux's cyclorama, now housed at Gettysburg.
(National Park Service)

On the twenty-fifth anniversary of the battle in 1888, amid the dedication of a number of Union monuments, patriotic rhetoric again celebrated the ideology of reconciliation. For example, Maj. Gen. Daniel E. Sickles, who lost a leg during the battle and later, as a New York congressman, would provide the impetus for the legislation entrusting the battlefield to the War Department, proclaimed: "To-day there are no victors, no vanquished. As Americans we may all claim a common share . . . in the new America born on this battlefield." However, not all shared in the spirit of reconciliation. Some considered Confederate participation in reunions at Gettysburg an act of heresy. Addressing the encampment of a Pennsylvania chapter of the GAR in 1888 at Little Round Top (the site of fierce fighting during the battle), Bvt. Brig. Gen. J. P. S. Gobin angrily declared that he was "tired of this gush and pretense for the glorification of the veteran simply because he wore a gray uniform with a Southern flag printed on his badge. That badge meant treason and rebellion in 1861, and what it meant then it means now. . . . I want it to be distinctly understood, now and for all time, that the men who wore the gray were everlastingly and eternally wrong."[16]

The ideology of reconciliation dominated the fiftieth anniversary of the battle in July 1913 when over fifty-five thousand Union and Confederate veterans came to Gettysburg for a four-day celebration. The veterans were housed on the battlefield in more than sixty-five hundred tents spread across almost three hundred acres. Temporary water and sewer systems had been constructed, along with 173 kitchens, staffed by more than two hundred cooks. Army doctors and the American Red Cross cared for the veterans, whose average age was seventy-two years, in five makeshift hospitals. The speeches and ritual activity emphasized collective heroism and the importance of healing from sectional strife. Capt. Bennett H. Young, commander of the United Confederate Veterans, spoke out in defense of the South's purity of motive, one of the crucial elements of the ideology of the Lost Cause that had developed in the postwar South. "We both fought for principles," he said, "and you won, not because we lacked courage, but because we lacked further resources." Alfred B. Beers of the GAR responded that "time has removed the scars of fraternal strife." Other participants lauded the "revolutionary" nature of old foes meeting in such friendship on a battlefield.[17]

Among the dignitaries present on July 3 was Speaker of the House Champ Clark, who attended a reenactment of the Pickett-Pettigrew charge along with Vice Pres. Thomas Marshall and a number of governors. The events of the day moved Clark to declare: "Cold must be the heart of that American who is not proud to claim as countrymen the flower of the Southern youth who charged up the slippery slopes of Gettysburg with peerless

Pickett, or those unconquerable men in blue, who through three long and dreadful days held these . . . heights in face of fierce assaults. It was not Southern valor nor Northern valor. It was, thank God, American valor." Gov. James B. McCreary of Kentucky took the opportunity to personalize the drama of reconciliation. He told the assemblage about his former bitterness toward the North and added that, since his son had married a Northern girl, he considered his grandchildren to be "just a little bit smarter and . . . better all around because of that mixture of Northern and Southern blood."[18]

For many, the most stirring moment of the reunion came when 120 survivors of the Pickett-Pettigrew charge "formed a line on the Stone Wall at the Bloody Angle, while fifty feet north of the wall stood one hundred-eighty men of the Philadelphia Brigade Association . . . with the Stars and Bars and the flag of the Second Corps flying. Then both standard bearers advanced and crossed their flag-staffs over the stone wall while a color bearer ran forward with the Stars and Stripes and held it above the two battle flags." Veterans, "their hair silvered, some on crutches, some with empty sleeves, . . . who had fought at this identical point, clasped hands and buried their faces on each others shoulders." This act of reconciliation was accompanied by a "mighty shout of praise [which] burst forth from the thousands of interested spectators."[19]

The celebration came to an end on July 4 with a speech by Pres. Woodrow Wilson, the lowering of flags to half-mast, five minutes of silence for the dead, an artillery tribute, and the playing of taps. The national significance of the reunion was not difficult to discern. The *Literary Digest* declared that the veterans in attendance embodied the "disappearance of the old and the birth of the new." The reunion was necessary to "seal up finally the book of the past." Veteran Walter H. Blake believed that the reenactment drama that took place at the Angle, where the "best blood of America had soaked the sod," would result in "a new state of feelings. . . . All the old sores of by-gone days will be healed. The North and the South will understand each other as they never did before." The *Outlook* called the reunion an occasion for the demonstration of a "great spiritual fact," namely, that each side had been devoted to a different ideal of civil liberty.[20]

Those who expected that the 1913 reunion would be the last major gathering of veterans at Gettysburg were mistaken. Although their ranks were thinning, almost fourteen hundred Union veterans and five hundred Confederate veterans attended the Last Reunion of the Blue and the Gray in 1938, a celebration that attracted nationwide attention.[21] In the spirit of healing the *Christian Science Monitor* declared that the gathering held promise for the "disappearance of a remnant of sectionalism and the emergence of a wider sense of patriotism that forgives—and forgets—the separating bitterness of 1861–1865." Opening ceremonies, held at the Memorial Field at Gettysburg College on July 1, included an address by Harry H. Woodring, the secretary of war. Woodring drew on the ideology of reconciliation when he stated that those who fought in the war were *American* soldiers and that "each was fighting for principles that he sincerely believed to represent the eternal truth."[22]

The nation's effort to rid itself of intersectional strife was recognized during the seventy-fifth reunion ceremonies with the dedication of the Eternal Light Peace Memorial. Sentiment for such a memorial had been generated during the fiftieth anniversary celebration, at which time Andrew Cowan, president of the Society of the Army of the Potomac, joined with others in support of a proposal to erect a monument "higher than any other." On July 3, 1938, as "scores of automobiles and buses were wheeling into the already overpacked town of Gettysburg over the nine highways that converge in the center of this community," approximately one-quarter million people gathered on Oak Hill, ground occupied by both sides during the battle, for the unveiling. An urn on top of the memorial was to carry a flame dedicated to "Peace Eternal in a Nation United." The ceremony, which began at 6:30 P.M., was broadcast nationwide on the radio. Pres. Franklin D. Roosevelt, who delivered the main address, characterized Gettysburg as a shrine of American liberty and reminded his audience that Lincoln's wisdom was a good prescription for a range of contemporary problems.[23]

The Last Reunion of the Blue and the Gray ended on July 4. Military parades, aerial demonstrations, an artillery drill, and a tank drill all impressed visitors with their "startling contrast" to the "lumbering mortars and howitzers of 1863." Aside from a growing nostalgia over the dwindling number of veterans (the average age of those in attendance was ninety-four years), the reunion echoed familiar themes: the fruits of reunification and the regenerative power of sacrifice. One newspaper editorial noted that the four-day celebration bore witness to a nation "reunited in peace, rededicated to liberty, revitalized by faith in its ability to solve its own problems." Readers were reminded that in a world again troubled by rumors of war, "the meaning of Gettysburg is that no sacrifice is too great for the preservation of a united Nation and the defense of its priceless guarantees of individual freedom."[24]

During the 1950s elements of a distinct Civil War subculture took shape in America. History buffs populated Civil War Roundtables (discussion groups begun in Chicago in 1940) and a growing number of people sought to "experience" the war and its times. For those interested in living history, it was enough to re-create nineteenth-century life (food, dress, and modes of transportation) on a small scale. For battle reenactors, immersion in the culture of a previous time provided the proper setting for the climax—namely, a grand reenactment of the battle itself. Other Civil War enthusiasts included relic hunters, collectors, and "war-gamers," who played complex and lengthy board games that reproduced actual Civil War battles.[25]

In the late 1950s, amid growing racial tensions, the nation began its preparations for the Civil War Centennial. In 1957 Public Law 85-105 created the United States Civil War Centennial Commission, chaired by Maj. Gen. Ulysses S. Grant III, grandson of the Civil War general and former president. On February 26, 1958, the executive committee of the commission agreed to exercise great caution in its selection of blacks as advisory council members "to avoid political nuances or . . . the risk of bringing embarrassment to the commission." In April 1961, when a member of the New Jersey Centennial Commission was denied a hotel room in Charleston, South Carolina, during a meeting of the national commission, Pres. John F. Kennedy responded by moving the commission meeting to a U.S. naval base outside of Charleston. The Pennsylvania Centennial Commission declared that it would "insist upon the equality of opportunity . . . in connection with Civil War Centennial observances" at Gettysburg. Rather than a commemoration of the battle, the Pennsylvania commission believed that the centennial celebration should be devoted to "national unity and ideals and keeping peace through international understanding."[26]

The centennial celebration began on June 30, 1963, with an address by former president and Gettysburg resident Dwight D. Eisenhower. In his speech on July 1, John A. Carver, Jr., the assistant secretary of the Interior Department, declared that Gettysburg was the place where "the ideals expressed by the Emancipator became possible of realization." But there was work to be done, he added, for "the equality defined on this field has been withheld from millions of our fellow citizens." Gov. William W. Scranton of Pennsylvania hastened to reassure visitors that those who had fallen at Gettysburg had not died in vain because, despite the existing racial problems, "our nation today is great enough to keep trying."[27]

The battlefield burst with activity during these days of celebration. On July 1 governors of twenty-seven of the twenty-nine states that had sent troops to participate in the battle took part in a wreath-laying ceremony. There were separate ceremonies at various monuments, as well as the first-day issue of a commemorative stamp with a picture of Civil War soldiers locked in bayonet combat. For the entire three days the National Park Service (NPS) sponsored a living-history program that re-created some of the personal dramas associated with the battle: for example, the pathos of brother capturing brother, or acts of kindness between combatants. The goal of the NPS was to draw viewers into history in an intimate way, so they might "capture for [themselves] the actual scene at Gettysburg 100 years ago."[28]

On July 2 visitors witnessed several events: the rededication of the Virginia and Alabama monuments and the dedication of the South Carolina monument. Gov. George Wallace of Alabama participated in his state's ceremony and offered a defiant interpretation of the meaning of the monument when he declared that Americans "look to the South to restore . . . the rights of states and individuals." Ross Barnett of Mississippi called on Americans to note the "legitimate differences in problems of the states." Limited state sovereignty, he argued, should be "fully preserved." Other governors also took the opportunity to make convenient connections between the legacy of Gettysburg and contemporary issues. Harold E. Hughes of Iowa stressed that some of the problems over which the battle had raged were still alive, among them "strife between men of differing races, religions and nationalities." Hughes came close to patriotic heresy by questioning whether the sacrifice of Union soldiers at Gettysburg had been in vain, arguing that the goal of equality, "for which so many men fell at Gettysburg, eludes us." A similar message was communicated by Edmund G. (Pat) Brown of California, who thought that as Americans we should "remind ourselves that peace between the races . . . has not been secured."[29]

Visitors to Gettysburg on July 3 witnessed the "Reunion at High Water Mark," a dramatization of the Pickett-Pettigrew charge. This time, though, there would be no "struggle or slaughter." According to the program, "The 1,000 men will join in brotherhood and amity to pledge their devotion to the symbol of their common unity—the Stars and Stripes!" The heroes of the charge were portrayed by members of the Sons of Union Veterans and units of the North-South Skirmishers Association. With approximately forty thousand spectators looking on, some five hundred Confederate reenactors crossed the famous field and, as they approached the crowd, stopped and lowered their flags in tribute to those who had died. Then, accompanied by "pre-recorded sound effects of rifle fire, rebel yells, battle cries and music, giving a realistic impression of the din of battle," the Confederate troops proceeded to the Angle, where there was a "sudden silence." Over the low stone wall "the men who had been representing both sides became 'present day' Americans." Together they marched to the Armistead marker, where they joined in a salute and sang the national anthem.[30]

Rhetorical brooding over the unfinished business of uniting Americans of different races continued during other commemorative events in the centennial year, as did the insinuation that the martial heroism and death exhibited in the Gettysburg battle would find real meaning *only* as Lincoln's ideals were realized. On November 19, 1963, during Dedication Day services in Gettysburg to commemorate Lincoln's famous address, E. Washington Rhodes, the black publisher of the *Philadelphia Tribune* and president of the National Newspaper Publishers Association, spoke of racial tensions as a "melancholy fact." Unless action was taken, he said, the "government of the people, by the people, and for the people, will soon be endangered beyond repair." Former President Eisenhower, a man not unfamiliar with the necessity of martial sacrifice, echoed Rhodes's message. Lincoln's work was still "unfinished," he said, adding that Lincoln knew "to live for country is a duty as demanding as is the readiness to fight for it."[31]

Prior to the commencement of Civil War centennial celebrations, Bruce Catton, the popular Civil War historian whose writings helped spark widespread interest in the war during the 1950s, had delivered a speech at Gettysburg College on Dedication Day 1962 that raised deep-seated concerns about the shallowness of planned festivities.[32] Catton worried that a "sentimental haze will cloud the landscape" and people will "fail to see the deep, tragic issues and profound lessons" that such events should communicate. He was especially critical of battle reenactments, which he said "require us to reproduce, for the enjoyment of attendant spectators, a thin shadow-picture of something which involved death and agony for the original participants." Battles were not waged in a "spirit of fun," Catton argued, but were "desperately real and profoundly, if unforgettably tragic." A battle was not just a "tournament in which brave men did gallant things for the admiration of later generations." Echoing the concerns of those who believed that Civil War commemorations were being trivialized and sanitized to make them entertaining, Catton declared that the Civil War was fought, above all, over "shattering issues," notably slavery, and that no other place besides Gettysburg offered Americans "so good a vantage point for that long look back into our past to find the meaning that lies beneath the tragedy."[33]

Catton died well before the lengthy festivities in 1988 marking the 125th anniversary of the battle of Gettysburg. Had he lived, he would have witnessed two quite different ceremonies—one celebrating the power and pageantry of the battle, and the other attempting to utilize the memory of war to inspire sentiment for world peace. The official ceremonies opened with the 121st celebration of Memorial Day, including a procession of fifteen hundred schoolchildren scattering flowers over the graves of the veterans.[34] Battle reenactments, prohibited on the field itself, took place from June 24 through June 26 on private land. Scenes from J. E. B. Stuart's cavalry fight with Brig. Gen. David M. Gregg's horse soldiers,[35] the fierce fighting in Devil's Den, and of course the Pickett-Pettigrew charge attracted more than ten thousand reenactors and one hundred thirty thousand spectators. Reenactors came from forty-four states as well as Canada, Great Britain, West Germany, and Singapore.

From the earliest reunions at Gettysburg through the 1938 reunion—the Last Reunion of the Blue and the Gray—visitors could convince themselves that they were witnessing the essence of the battle. Not only were they on the field at the exact time of day that the battle had been fought, but they were also in the presence of those who had been the combatants. The palpable nostalgia present in the early reunions grew more desperate as the veterans became fewer in number and these last links to the battle passed away. It was as if the death of these veterans also signaled the death of a heroic past—a past that many believed the nation dare not forget. Consequently, certain modes of veneration that initially were commemorative in nature became primary strategies for reviving the past. Battle reenactment was one such strategy.

Despite the inauthenticity of the location (on private land rather than the actual battlefield) as well as the timing (late June rather than early July), even those who disdained reenactments were impressed by the spectacle of thousands of men in blue and gray massed against one another. For some of the participants this was the only way to bring back the past. Twenty-year-old Rodney Sweeney of Richmond, Virginia, described his feelings during the reenactment of the Pickett-Pettigrew charge: "I felt the collapse of time—as if I was there. . . . Later, I thought of the South and what it stood for, and I felt honor for my parents." For others, reenactments were a way to deepen the appreciation of history. Thirty-seven-year-old Chuck Hillsman, of Amelia County, Virginia, said, "It's not that we pretend that this is real, but it gives you an even greater respect for those men who really endured it. We can never reproduce what war was like, nor should we want to, but our endeavor is to never allow the sacrifices made by those who have gone before us to be forgotten."[36]

Those who view reenactments as "time trips" and those who believe reenactments are more commemoration than reproduction agree that authenticity in the way the battle is reenacted and in the reenactors' "impression" (their uniforms and other equipment) is crucial. John Heiser, a National Park Service engineering draftsman at Gettysburg who has been active in battle reenactments for more than a dozen years, believes that those who are dedicated to proper reenactments not only must look right but must take the right approach, that is, the right spiritual attitude, toward reenactments. In his view the reenactor's "impression" is not authentic if it deals only with what is worn. Heiser spoke with anger and contempt about "farbs," a term of derision used to characterize reenactors whose dress is not authentic or who sleep in hotels, eat hot dogs, and generally practice twentieth-century behaviors during the attempt to excavate the essence of a crucial past moment. *True* battle reenactors are obsessed with detail.[37]

Prior to the battle reenactments at the 125th anniversary celebration, Rita Mae Brown of the *New York Times* commented on this obsession with detail: "Naval and equine equipment, very difficult to duplicate, is accurate down to the pant legs, down to the stirrup leathers. If the reenactment is of a battle fought later in the war the men acting as Southern soldiers will go so far as to fight barefoot and in ragged clothing. Some combatants take on the identity of a man and will fall where he fell, reproducing his wounds when possible." Like Catton, Brown feared that the pageantry of the reenactments would draw attention away from the unresolved issues over which the war had been fought. Noting the horror of post–Civil War life for many blacks, she asked, "When will we have the guts to reenact that period of our history?" Brown's question notwithstanding, the focus of activities on June 24–26 was the aesthetic delight of battle. Spectators gathered to "experience" the Civil War they had only read about. It was beautiful, exciting, and clean. And most of all, it was fun.[38]

The National Park Service, bracing itself to deal with the hundreds of thousands of visitors to the battlefield on July 1–3, offered living-history presentations of military life in the Civil War period. On July 2, Reunion Day, the governors of Pennsylvania, New York, and Virginia met at the Angle, where they shook hands and presented original regimental battle flags to representatives of the NPS's newly renovated Museum of the Civil War. On July 3, traditionally reserved for dramatic ceremonies at the Angle, the theme was instead "Peace Eternal in a World United." The goal of the Gettysburg Peace Celebration Commission was to "unite all aspects of our community's life in the search for peace. By virtue of the national significance of the Battle and the Eternal Light Peace Memorial [which was being rededicated], we hope to draw the attention of our nation and the world to this important celebration."[39]

Following a picnic featuring international foods, the Morgan State University Choir and the Peace Child Choir (with children from around the world) sang on the steps of the memorial. The rededication ceremony, in the form of an ecumenical worship service, included readings from Lincoln's Gettysburg Address by Immanuel Iithete, former assistant to the bishop of the Evangelical Lutheran Church of Namibia. Dr. Joseph E. Lowery, president of the Southern Christian Leadership Conference, was unable to deliver his sermon as planned (due to travel complications). The major address was delivered by the renowned astronomer and antinuclear activist Carl Sagan, of Cornell University, who reminded his audience that the carnage of Gettysburg was minimal compared to the devastation that had been—and might in the future be—wrought by nuclear weapons. "It is time," he said, "to learn from the sacrifice of those who fell here. And it is time for us to act." The real triumph of Gettysburg was not the outcome of the battle, Sagan insisted, but the reunion of 1913, when the veterans met in "celebration and solemn memorial." Now, the nations of the world must emulate these veterans, "not after the carnage and the mass murder, but instead of the carnage and the mass murder." Following Sagan's speech, the memorial was unveiled and the flame relit.[40]

Despite the official attempt to shift attention away from the battle, an unofficial reenactment of the Pickett-Pettigrew charge took place on July 3. The NPS had planned a "modest ceremony" at the Pennsylvania monument before transporting spectators in shuttle buses to the main ceremony at the Eternal Light Peace Memorial. However, between eight hundred and one thousand reenactors decided to conduct their own ceremony to commemorate the famous charge. In consequence, approximately three thousand spectators stayed behind to watch Confederate reenactors walk across the battlefield toward the Union lines on Cemetery Ridge, where they shook hands with Union reenactors. Robert Prosperi, an NPS historian who witnessed the event, said it was "easier to let it happen . . . than [to] try to stop it." He also noted that there was physical damage to the stone walls and earthworks at the Angle as people climbed over them. The chief historian of the NPS, Edwin C. Bearss, commented: "The result was that considerable attention was diverted from the Peace Light ceremonies, a number of overweight re-enactors suffered from heat exhaustion, and many egos were bruised."[41]

Two quite different kinds of ceremonies thus characterized the 125th anniversary of the battle of Gettysburg. The first, privately sponsored in late June, celebrated the enduring appeal of battle and did not encourage participants or spectators to reflect on what Catton called the "meaning behind the tragedy," for the reenactment itself was not tragic in any respect. Just as veterans at early reunions had been enraptured by the "golden mist of American valor," to the exclusion of important reflections on the nature of reconciliation, so too were current reenactors and spectators enthralled by the pageantry of war. The essential challenge of Gettysburg, stated clearly by Lincoln, remained unspoken during this ceremony. However, the other ceremony, the rededication of the Eternal Light Peace Memorial, sought to deepen and universalize the ideology of reconciliation fostered on the field by earlier reunions. The interracial and international flavor of the commemoration embodied the fruits of the sacrifice of so many and served to make visible on the battlefield the enduring challenge of Gettysburg.

Reunion and reenactment have not been the only forms of veneration at Gettysburg. On August 19, 1863, David McConaughy made public his desire for Pennsylvanians to enshrine the battlefield, and a group of local citizens responded that the battle deserved to be commemorated in "every way in which such triumphs can be consecrated." The Gettysburg Battlefield Memorial Association, founded in September 1863, would provide the institutional impetus for the formative work of physical veneration. Kathleen Georg Harrison, an NPS historian at Gettysburg, writes that in the fifteen years following the battle the GBMA had the power to purchase land, to "repair and preserve the grounds, . . . to construct and maintain roads and avenues, to improve and ornament the grounds and to erect or promote the erection of commemorative markers, monuments and memorials."[42] What the GBMA did not have was sufficient funds to ensure that the grounds on which the battle was fought would be preserved in any systematic manner. Fortunately, Maj. Gen. Daniel E. Sickles, a Union veteran who had lost a leg at Gettysburg, emerged as an important champion of this cause. Elected to Congress from New York, Sickles worked tirelessly for federal funding for preservation.

On May 25, 1893, Secretary of War Daniel S. Lamont appointed a three-man commission to oversee the expenditure of a congressional appropriation of $50,000 for the preservation of the battlefield. The commission was initially made up of Bachelder, former Confederate Brig. Gen. W. H. Forney, and Col. John P. Nicholson, a Union veteran of the battle. Forney and Bachelder died soon after being appointed and were replaced by Charles A. Richardson, a Union veteran of the battle, and Confederate veteran William M. Robbins. On December 18, 1894, Sickles introduced a bill into Congress to authorize the War Department to accept ownership of 522 acres of land and all other assets of the GBMA. Its nurturing work completed, the GBMA disbanded after Pres. Grover Cleveland signed an amended bill on February 11, 1895, that was the establishing legislation for the Gettysburg National Military Park. The commission then undertook the task, as directed by the War Department, of placing historical tablets at "positions occupied by the various commands of the Armies of the Potomac and of Northern Virginia on that field."[43] Between 1895 and 1905 the battlefield was marked in detail: narrative tablets were erected to denote positions of troops, cannon were accurately placed, roads and fences were built, and thousands of trees were planted.

Until 1878 monuments commemorating the Union dead were placed only in the cemetery: the Soldiers' National Monument, a marble urn dedicated to Minnesota veterans, and the famous statue of Maj. Gen. John Fulton Reynolds, who died instantly from a bullet to the head as he led his men against Confederate forces. As the GAR grew stronger and military units that had participated in the battle were invited to erect memorials on the battlefield, a new era in monument activity began. In 1878 and 1879

Pennsylvania GAR posts erected memorials to Col. Strong Vincent and Col. Charles Taylor. The monument of the Second Massachusetts Regiment, dedicated in 1879, was the first regimental monument on the field and the first to honor living veterans in addition to serving the traditional funerary function. By the time of the twenty-fifth reunion in 1888 the landscape had been transformed by more than three hundred monuments. According to the *Gettysburg Compiler,* the field was a "forest of marble and granite, iron and bronze."[44]

From 1884 until 1894 monument dedications almost always took place during the anniversary of the battle. By the twenty-fifth anniversary many Northern states had passed (or were in the process of passing) bills authorizing state funds to erect monuments at Gettysburg. In 1887 the battlefield commission developed certain guidelines: that monuments had to be of granite or bronze and had to provide information about the unit—its position, strength, and casualties; that statues had to face enemy lines; and that careful attention had to be given to the monument's foundations and the natural setting, for the "pleasing effect of a beautiful monument may be entirely neutralized by untidy surroundings." On March 3, 1893, Congress declared that all tablets marking lines at Gettysburg should carry a "brief historical legend, compiled without praise and without censure." Recent policy does not substantially deviate from these early statements. Today, the approximately thirteen hundred martial megaliths that seem to emerge naturally from the ground are an enduring statement of patriotic veneration—in Stephen Vincent Benét's words, "startling groups of monumental men."[45]

Early monuments represented efforts by veterans to memorialize their own heroism and to honor the sacrifice of their martyred comrades. At dedication ceremonies speakers often assured those gathered that even though contemporary society might seem indifferent to the veterans' former role as saviors, the monuments would stand for all time, despite the corroding forces of commercialism, forgetfulness, or historical revisionism. Whether they were designed to honor regiments, individual common soldiers, or generals, these monuments of bronze and granite would remind future generations of the power of heroism and unchanging principles on the battlefield. During the dedication of the First Maine Infantry Monument on October 3, 1889, Bvt. Maj. Gen. Charles H. Smith, who had commanded that unit, assured listeners that future visitors to Gettysburg would rely on these monuments to tell the story of the battle. "These monuments, their emblems and legends that mournfully decorate this great battlefield . . . will become [future visitors'] interpreters and assistants," he said. According to Gettysburg hero Daniel E. Sickles, who spoke at the dedication of the Forty-Second New York Infantry Monument on September 24, 1891, these monuments also served as permanent reminders to the nation of the need for martial revitalization. He noted, "There is no better way to prepare for the next war than to show your appreciation of your defenders in the last war. No nation can long survive the decline of its martial strength. When it ceases to honor its soldiers, it will have none."[46]

The ideology of reconciliation also fostered growing pressure to mark correctly the Confederate lines and dictated that Southern veterans be invited to raise their own monuments on the battlefield. Only two Confederate monuments—one of which stood near the Angle and honored Brig. Gen. Lewis Armistead—were erected prior to 1888. On May 2, 1886, members of the GBMA and the Second Maryland Confederate Infantry visited the field to select a spot for their monument. The Confederate veterans wanted to place it where they had penetrated the Union lines on Culp's Hill on the second day of the battle, but the GBMA objected, claiming that the "erection of an ex-Confederate monument within the Union lines [would set] an important precedent." After much discussion a site was mutually agreed upon. The *Gettysburg Compiler* noted on November 9, 1886, that the monument "arrived last week and was put in place." The *Baltimore Sun* reported that approximately two thousand people attended the dedication ceremonies on November 19. In his dedication address Capt. George Thomas celebrated the fact that the Gettysburg story was no longer "half told." The new era of good feeling, he said, had "thrown wide the door to the survivors of the Confederate commands to complete the record." Coming generations, he cautioned, must guard the field as a "joint heritage of the North and South."[47]

For many, such modest Confederate monumentation still left the story half-told. In 1893 the battlefield commissioners began an ambitious program designed to mark Confederate lines of battle (rather than lines of furthest advance, as advocated by many Confederate veterans). William Robbins, himself a Confederate veteran and park commissioner, met little success in his attempts to arouse enthusiasm among his fellow veterans for more elaborate monuments. Understandably, they were disinclined to expend energy marking a Pennsylvania battlefield that symbolized the demise of their cause. This attitude would prevail until the ideology of reconciliation had taken firmer root in the early years of the twentieth century.[48]

One of the earliest signs of reconciliation through monumentation was the erection of the High Water Mark Monument on Cemetery Ridge in 1892. While the entire Gettysburg battlefield was considered sacred ground, the "holy of holies" was certainly this particular point on Cemetery Ridge where the dramatic conclusion of the Pickett-Pettigrew charge was played out and, in popular memory at least, where the Union was saved. In *Pickett's Charge,* George Stewart declares: "If we grant that the Civil War furnishes the great dramatic episode of the history of the United States, and that Gettysburg provides the climax of the war, then the climax of the climax, the central moment of our history, must be Pickett's Charge."[49]

Shortly after the war John Bachelder invited a member of Pickett's staff to visit Gettysburg, and they "spent several hours under the shade cast by the copse of trees [on Cemetery Ridge]." Bachelder remarked to the visiting colonel that, "as the battle of Gettysburg was the crowning event of this campaign, this copse of trees must have been the high water mark of the rebellion." From that time on, Bachelder noted, "I felt a reverence for those trees." He proudly declared that the "thought of naming the copse of trees the 'High water mark of the rebellion,' and the idea of perpetuating its memory by a monument, was mine." On a subsequent visit to the field he was "shocked" to find that the owner of the land was cutting down these sacred relics, "a dozen or more already lying on the ground." Bachelder convinced the owner that he would make more money if he let the trees stand as a tourist attraction. Unfortunately, this brought its own form of commercial defilement, for as the trees' "historic importance became known, relic-hunters commenced to cut their branches for canes."[50]

Bachelder failed to convince the GBMA in 1885 and again in 1886 that a protective iron fence should be erected around the trees. He was, however, successful in 1887, when the association unanimously passed his resolution. On September 25, 1888, the GBMA passed another resolution sponsored by Bachelder stating "that a bronze tablet be prepared indicating and setting forth the movements of troops at the copse of trees." Bachelder originally envisioned a small tablet on the fence but soon was immersed in planning the construction of a large monument. When completed, the monument included

> five distinct legends, cast in the statuary bronze. One bears the names of the confederate divisions, brigades and regiments which marched in the charging column. The second; the names of the union regiments, batteries, brigades and divisions which met and repulsed it. The third; the story of the assault, with the names of the organizations that made it, and of those that supported them. The fourth; the story of the repulse, the names of the organizations that made it, and also the names of the batteries which engaged the enemy on either flank and assisted in the repulse. And the fifth; the names of the states which contributed to erect the monument.[51]

The dedication of the High Water Mark Monument took place on June 7, 1892. The universal importance of the site was noted in a speech by Edward McPherson, who said that when the armies came together at Gettysburg, "all thoughtful men realized that a supreme moment in the history of the human race had come." In his address James A. Beaver, a former governor of Pennsylvania, remarked that Gettysburg monumentation played a crucial role in national reconciliation. These monuments, he said, "provoke no jealousies. They harbor no resentments. They are eloquent in their mute appeal to patriotism and to duty. They have a mission and they meet its requirement well." Visitors to the Angle should admire the courage of the "men who made the charge" as well as those who "received its momentum," for such admiration would eventually lead to the "utter destruction of sectionalism in all its forms and phases." Beaver concluded his speech with an eloquent plea for more Confederate monumentation on the battlefield.[52]

By the middle of the 1890s there was widespread feeling, in the North at least, that the monumental landscape at Gettysburg should more fully tell the Confederate story. In 1896, for example, the *Philadelphia Times* stated that no "sectional passions" could interfere with attempts to "tell the whole story of the matchless courage of American soldiers." For some, the entire story was necessary in order to appreciate fully the holy crusade of the Northern troops. The *Gettysburg Compiler* declared in 1903 that a fully monumented field would show that the "God of battles gave the victory for the preservation of the Union" and that the battle was evidence of "immortal Anglo-Saxon bravery."[53]

On June 8, 1917, Virginia became the first former Confederate state to erect a monument at Gettysburg, dedicating the equestrian statue of Robert E. Lee looking over the field of the Pickett-Pettigrew charge from Seminary Ridge. In his dedication address Henry Carter Stuart, the governor of Virginia, continued the Southern tradition of ignoring the moral issue that surely was at the heart of the war, remarking instead that the conflict had arisen over "divergent views of [the] Constitution." Stuart declared that Lee was the "supreme example" of the South's "convictions and principles" and remained a model for those "rallying to the defense of our liberty against the aggression of a foreign foe." Leigh Robinson, in another dedication address, went further than the traditional defense of Southern righteousness and the rhetorical celebration of national unity. First he pointed out to the gathering that Lee and the entire state of Virginia viewed slavery with distaste—consequently, their motives in the war were pure—then he preposterously argued that Southern whites, not blacks, bore the real burden of slavery. Robinson insisted that the governing of a "race incapable of self-government" brought a "greater benefit to the governed than to the governors."[54]

A dozen years passed before another former Confederate state—North Carolina—raised a monument at Gettysburg. Alabama followed suit in 1933. The remaining states of the Confederacy did not begin to place monuments on the battlefield until the 1960s: Georgia, in 1961; Florida and South Carolina, in 1963; Texas, in 1964; Arkansas, in 1966; Louisiana and Mississippi, in 1971; and Tennessee, in 1982.

Despite the growing popularity of the ideology of reconciliation, controversy attended the construction of Southern monuments at Gettysburg. During the planning for the Confederate Soldiers and Sailors Monument, dedicated on August 8, 1965, Frederick Tilberg, the Gettysburg park historian, objected to an inscription that characterized the Confederates as defenders of their country. He noted that the opposite was closer to the truth, namely, that "they came rather near to disrupting their country." In a similar vein, George F. Emery, the park superintendent, questioned the Mississippi Gettysburg Memorial Commission's use of the phrase "righteous cause" on the monument it intended to dedicate on June 11, 1971. Emery hoped that "a substitute could be found or perhaps [the phrase] could simply be eliminated," neither of which happened. For their part, some Southerners thought that the Confederate monuments, once erected, were not being treated with the same care as Union monuments. A 1965 visitor wrote to the National Park Service about conditions at the North Carolina monument: "Imagine our dismay and indignation upon finding the North Carolina section partly encircled by a dingy clothesline type rope, limply strung through lead pipes which were lopsidedly driven into the ground." This, the visitor thought, was a "desecration of the memory of our fighting ancestors" and an example of the South "being slapped around again."[55]

A related issue was the positioning of monuments on the field. As part of its goal to safeguard the integrity of the monumental landscape, the GBMA (and later the battlefield commissioners) successfully resisted attempts to place Confederate markers at the points of greatest penetration of Union lines (the stone marker where Brigadier General Armistead fell at the "high water mark" representing the only deviation from this policy). However, debates over spatial contamination were not confined to North versus South. In 1888, for example, the survivors of the Seventy-second Pennsylvania Infantry, which had plunged forward to help throw back the Pickett-Pettigrew charge, insisted that their monument be placed at the point where the unit had engaged Confederate forces. The GBMA wanted them to position the memorial twenty feet farther away from the Angle, since another Pennsylvania unit had also seen combat at that forward position. In the summer of 1888 members of the Seventy-second defied the GBMA, broke ground for a monument at their chosen spot at the Angle, and were arrested for trespassing. The case eventually made its way to the Pennsylvania Supreme Court, which on April 2, 1891, decided in favor of the veterans. At the dedication of the monument on July 4, 1891, Capt. William Kerr's address revealed the importance for survivors of proper location. After a dramatic description of the hand-to-hand fighting, Kerr declared: "To this place, this unknown spot, you have given name and fame. It is recorded in history 'The Bloody Angle at Gettysburg.' "[56]

Southerners also engaged in internecine struggles over appropriate locations for their monuments. Shortly after the battle Southern newspapermen, led by the influential Peter Alexander, provided reports on the battle to the *Savannah Republican* and the *Mobile Register*. They lionized Pickett and his Virginia troops and minimized the contribution that soldiers from other states, notably North Carolina, made in the Pickett-Pettigrew charge. Such favoritism was not easily forgotten. On August 24, 1921, Walter C. Clark, chief justice of the North Carolina Supreme Court, gave a speech to the Confederate Veterans Association and noted that Pickett commanded only three Virginia brigades in his division. There was, said Justice Clark, "no reason why the assault should have ever been styled 'Pickett's Charge.' " He emphasized that troops from North Carolina had advanced "80 yards further to the front," and while there was "glory enough for all, the North Carolinians beyond all question went farthest to the front at Gettysburg."[57]

Like the squabbles between New England towns over where the first "true" battle of the American Revolution took place, the state rivalries over the scope and positioning of Gettysburg monumentation were passionate affairs and were taken seriously by those who sought to preserve appropriate patriotic memories for coming generations. The placement of a monument a few feet in front of or behind that of another state or another regiment conveyed, for those concerned, a message about the impact of that particular unit or state on formative events. In consequence, there was an ongoing struggle to attain bragging rights at Gettysburg—that is, a struggle to dominate ceremonial space and gain permanent symbolic hegemony through the strategic placement of monuments. On October 2, 1986, more than 123 years after the battle, North Carolinians were able to erase what they perceived to be an injustice when they dedicated the Twenty-sixth North Carolina Monument, the furthest advanced regimental marker on the field. The *Raleigh News and Observer* smugly noted that this four-ton monument, which sits thirty-five yards ahead of the spot where Pickett's Virginians were turned back, would "redraw [the] popular notion of the 'high water mark of the Confederacy.' "[58]

Monument building and dedication at Gettysburg have been enduring forms of patriotic veneration. Construction of heroic statues of military leaders, dramatic monuments of soldiers in action, and grand allegorical memorials to the ideals of peace and reconciliation were the veterans' way of memorializing their own heroic action, symbolizing their desire to heal

Interpretive signs help modern-day visitors envision the battle, in this
case viewing the scene of the Pickett-Pettigrew charge from
Union positions on Cemetery Ridge. (National Park Service)

A group of reenactors participate in the restaging of the
Pickett-Pettigrew charge during the centennial celebration,
July 3, 1963. (National Park Service)

In late June 1988 more than ten thousand reenactors took part in a three-day reenactment of the battle of Gettysburg. This photograph shows Confederates marching off to fight at McPherson's Ridge.
(The Stock Advantage; ©1988 by David Aretz)

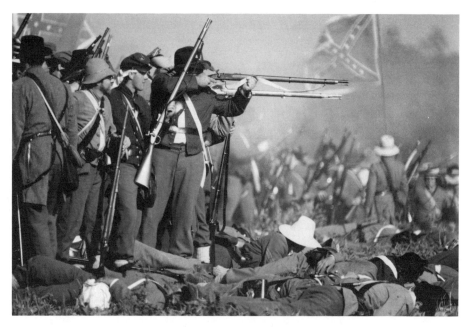

An estimated crowd of one hundred thousand witnessed scenes of combat like this one at the 125th anniversary celebration. (The Stock Advantage; ©1988 by Hub Willson)

Reenactors engaged in combat at the Wheatfield. (The Stock Advantage; ©1988 by Bob Hahn)

The Pickett-Pettigrew charge. (The Stock Advantage; ©1988 by Bob Hahn)

The Pickett-Pettigrew charge as seen from behind the Union line. (The Stock Advantage; ©1988 by Hub Willson)

A reenactment of camp life. (The Stock Advantage; ©1988 by Hub Willson)

Confederate and Union reenactors pay close attention to details, especially in their clothing. (The Stock Advantage; ©1988 by Hub Willson and Bob Hahn, respectively)

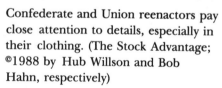

Desecration of the sacred environment of Gettysburg in the guise of the Gettysburg Electric Railway. (National Park Service)

Modern-day commercialization crowds portions of land where the battle took place. (National Park Service)

The controversial Gettysburg Tower. (National Park Service)

the wounds of war and enshrining the hope that peaceful reunification would emerge out of such healing. Monuments also were intended to stand as a constant reminder to younger generations of the heroism of the moment and the power of martial sacrifice. However, no monuments on the field offered a challenge to patriotic orthodoxy similar to the occasional heresy of questioning the meaning of sacrifice present in the patriotic rhetoric.[59]

Commemorative activity, whether in the form of patriotic rhetoric at anniversary celebrations or monument building and dedication, reminded participants that the ground they were standing on had been transformed by the potency of battle. Consequently, it became crucial to preserve, protect, and restore the field at Gettysburg, to freeze the landscape in its 1863 form. When Congress established the Gettysburg National Military Park in 1895, it gave the battlefield commission authority to purchase land according to a map prepared by Daniel E. Sickles. However, it failed to provide federal boundary legislation. The Sickles Plan called for a maximum procurement of almost four thousand acres, but a broader interpretation of the plan gave the government the authority to purchase more than fifteen thousand acres. As modernity, in the form of housing developments and commercial properties, began encroaching on the park, preservationists lobbied to incorporate into the park portions of the battlefield that were becoming indistinguishable from the rapidly developing secular landscape. They argued that the establishment of appropriate boundaries would preserve endangered land, define points of contact between sacred and secular environments, regulate such contact, and serve to protect the environment from physical or aesthetic defilement.[60]

In 1974 the National Park Service submitted to Congress a proposal for new park boundaries. Critics of the proposal felt that it left out crucial areas. The controversy came to a head in 1986 when the Gettysburg Battlefield Preservation Association (GBPA), a private, nonprofit organization, tried to donate to the NPS thirty acres of land on which fighting between Union and Confederate troops had taken place. Since the land was outside the park boundaries, and since there was no legislation authorizing the NPS to accept donations of private land, the offer had to be rejected. Largely as a result of this incident, in 1988 Congress requested that the NPS conduct yet another boundary study.[61]

The size of the battlefield at Gettysburg has always been a source of tension between administrators of the park—first the War Department and then, since 1933, the National Park Service—and residents of the town. Because the battle raged over vast areas, including the town itself, residents have often felt threatened by the expanding boundaries of the park, just as battlefield preservationists have often felt threatened by the lack of local zoning regulations, the creeping tentacles of freeways, and the growth of new housing developments. The recommendations of the newest boundary study only served to increase some local residents' fears of living in an "island town" in a vast sea of commemorative space. In 1980 William F. Goodling, a Republican congressman from Pennsylvania, spoke for the prodevelopment forces, as well as for a secular interpretation of the battlefield, when he said that the government should not be obligated to buy "every piece of land where a Union or Confederate soldier stepped."[62]

Another area of concern for preservationists has been the visual sanctity of the battlefield—in other words, the need for it to look historically accurate (an integral element in veneration). During the twenty-fifth anniversary trees were planted in Ziegler's Grove to restore its 1863 appearance. Similarly, in 1909 the battlefield commission declared that an important part of its task was "to preserve the landmarks and appearance of the field as it was during the war, and with this purpose in view trees have been replanted in positions where they existed at that time, [and] undergrowth has been cut out."[63]

Altering the physical landscape for the purpose of partially restoring the battlefield did not please everyone. In 1980 a controversy arose over the removal of trees in Devil's Den, an area of heavy fighting during the battle. Several local residents who valued the area for recreational reasons complained that a beautiful picnic area was being ruined for no good reason. In response to these and similar complaints, Kathleen Georg Harrison, the park historian, argued that "most visitors come to see the battlefield and not the trees." Furthermore, she declared, the battlefield was not a "city or county park" but belonged to all Americans "whose ancestors bathed these fields with blood and glory." It was the duty of the National Park Service, she continued, to "perpetuate [the] historic scene" as it "prevailed during the historic period." William Frassanito, the author of an acclaimed photographic history of the Gettysburg battlefield, contended that this particular restoration offered an authentic aesthetic entry into the time of the battle. He was "shocked, stunned, and even awed" when he rode through Devil's Den and saw it as it had been. According to Frassanito, removal of the trees offered a "unique chance of a lifetime to experience Devil's Den the way it was in 1863." Opponents countered that if historical authenticity were so important, "houses on the battlefield used by NPS personnel would have their electricity, telephones and indoor plumbing removed."[64]

Restoration and preservation of the battle landscape has always been one of the chief concerns of the National Park Service. The 1937 master plan of the Gettysburg park superintendent, James R. McConaghie, noted that the primary purpose of the park was to "preserve an area of great historical value in such a manner as to *permit the visitor to visualize conditions of the day*." The "Battlefield Area Restoration Policy," formulated that same year, outlined the manner in which the NPS would eliminate undesirable "modern encroachments," namely, anything that introduced a "jarring note" and hampered the visitor's ability to visualize the battle. Such concerns were still in evidence in 1982. That year's NPS general management plan detailed procedures for constructing "living screens 60 to 75 feet high" to shield visitors from the sight of "undesirable modern developments" beyond the boundaries of the field.[65]

One of the first major threats to the sacred environment of Gettysburg came in 1891 when the Gettysburg Electric Railway Company began construction, on private land that ran through the Devil's Den area, of a roadbed and train tracks. The company halted its work in the face of strong public opposition, but it refused to sell the land. In his report to the secretary of war on May 25, 1893, Maj. George B. Davis, judge advocate of the United States, described the contamination of the field:

> The ground has been torn up for about two miles across the fields charged over by Pickett's Division. . . . The rough glade in front of Little Round Top known as the Valley of Death, had been crossed, and the high rocks in Devil's Den that were so bitterly fought over on the second day of the battle, have been cut through, and such as were encountered in the work of construction have been destroyed. The fighting at this part of the line was so bitter and obstinate and the losses so great, as to associate with the spot only the sad and gloomy memories of the great tragedy which was enacted there. It should never have been made convenient of access to parties of mere pleasure seekers, and it was as startling an impropriety to cross it with an electric railway as it would have been to cross the grounds of a National Cemetery with a similar construction.[66]

On June 8, 1894, the U.S. attorney general began condemnation procedures, in an attempt to take control of the land for the park. In April 1895 the U.S. Circuit Court ruled in favor of the railroad, only to be overturned unanimously by the U.S. Supreme Court in *United States* v. *Gettysburg Electric Railway Co.* (1896). The brief filed for the United States argued that it was "common in all ages to preserve battlefields and mark them in some appropriate way. The ground whereon great conflicts have taken place, especially those where great interests or principles were at stake, becomes at once of so much public interest that its preservation is essentially a matter of public concern. The prevention of such uses as would either profane the ground or destroy its topography is necessarily a matter of public rather than private concern." Such special places expressed embodied principles, the brief noted, and Gettysburg embodied "the national idea and the principle of the indissolubility of the Union." While there were practical reasons for preserving the battlefield—marking lines of battle, fostering a "martial spirit of the people," providing students of military science with a field of instruction—sentiment alone would be enough to engender the protective cloak of the government, for a feeling of reverence for such patriotic sites "is one of the means of promoting 'the general welfare,' and providing for 'the common defense.' "[67]

Speaking for the Court against the railway company, Justice Rufus W. Peckham noted the crucial link between inspirational memory of the battle and preservation of the field of battle and, echoing the arguments presented in the government's brief, tied both to the general welfare of the nation. "Can it be," he said, "that the government is without power to preserve the land, and properly mark out the various sites upon which this struggle took place? Can it not erect the monuments . . . or even take possession of the field of battle in the name and for the benefit of all the citizens of the country for the present and for the future? Such a use seems necessarily not only a public use, but one so closely connected with the welfare of the republic itself as to be within the powers granted Congress by the constitution for the purpose of protecting and preserving the whole country."[68]

By its ruling the Supreme Court set a legal precedent for the belief of many that protection of sacred patriotic environments contributes to the welfare of the nation and, conversely, that commercialization or other forms of physical intrusion contaminates these sacred environments and weakens the civic health of the nation. Subsequent preservation controversies at Gettysburg, as at other battle sites, bear witness to the importance attached to the restoration and preservation of the physical landscape as a form of patriotic veneration.

Despite the efforts to establish enduring park boundaries, Gettysburg has been subjected to an irreversible process of commercial defilement. In 1939 the *Gettysburg Times* declared it unfortunate that on the land over which the "actual battle raged with bitter fury . . . land over which Pickett's brave men charged, there are now unsightly and incongruous objects—automobile dumps, miserable shacks, tourist camps and hot dog stands." Michael Frome's 1959 travelogue article in *American Forests,* in which he characterized Gettysburg as an "irresistible object of pilgrimage in our era of mobility," reminded potential tourists not to "overlook the scope or the damage of the new battle of Gettysburg, in which commercial development—motels, spreading subdivisions, souvenir stands, beer parlors, automobile graveyards—is advancing in strength against rather weak defense lines." With the coming of the Civil War Centennial, increased interest in battlefields brought about a growing awareness of the ravages of modernity that threatened fragile historic environments. The *Cleveland Plain Dealer* echoed the sentiments of many when it remarked: "Pickett's men would be able to see the one landmark over all others—and squarely in the path of their march. It is a tall neon landmark, crimson and bright. It says 'cafeteria.' " Later, the *New York Times* complained that by allowing a "barrage of fried chicken stands and commercial wax museums in one form or another, the meaning of this great battlefield has already been muddied."[69]

Certainly, the most celebrated preservation battle at Gettysburg took place over developer Thomas R. Ottenstein's plan to build a 307-foot observation tower, which he argued would provide a unique "educational experience" for those wishing to learn about the battle. Construction began on November 7, 1972, after several years of bitter fighting between Ottenstein, the state of Pennsylvania, and the Park Service over the location of the tower—and, for that matter, the appropriateness of *any* tower that would dominate the horizon of the battlefield. The controversy served as a lightning rod for the widespread concern over the commercial and aesthetic desecration of Gettysburg. Columnist Russell Baker bitterly observed that the tower was a symbol of the "sinister nature of the American soil. . . . Fertilize it with the blood of heroes and it brings forth a frozen-custard stand." The *Frederick Post* reported that Mrs. Marian Smith wanted her husband's body removed from the Soldiers' National Cemetery since the tower loomed over it. George Will called the tower "an affront to the living as well as the dead" and claimed that it distorted "the visitor's entire perception of the history-making topography."[70]

For those like Will who were angered by the distortion imposed on visitors' perceptions by the infamous tower, it was not enough for visitors to know that they were standing on transformed soil. Rather, the entire physical environment ought to be pure, unsullied by modernity in *any* form. Only then could visitors gain intimate entry into the past, their imaginations aided by the restoration of the 1863 landscape and supplemented by the inclusion of appropriate, meaningful monumental architecture. According to the interpretive canons of the National Park Service, such "grounded imagination" was necessary to fully "experience" the battle. Since the early years of its stewardship at Gettysburg, the NPS has provided descriptive commentary on the battle along with occasional remarks on its legacy (what it calls "interpretation"). Previously, aside from formal ceremonies on commemorative occasions, visitors had to rely on the oral traditions of veterans, some of whom joined a growing number of battlefield guides.[71] Guidebooks, visitors centers, and various other modes of interpretation later sought to orient and properly immerse visitors in the sacred environment.

Formal descriptive activities sponsored by the NPS began in 1941, with an orientation to the battle at the Rosensteel Museum, located near the cemetery and housing the famous "electric map" display. In the spring of 1942, despite resistance from the guides, the NPS staff developed materials for seven field exhibits, including interpretive and directional signs on the battlefield. Each exhibit had orientation maps, locations of battle lines, photographs, and a caption that informed visitors of the significance of the spot. In October 1942 the park superintendent, J. Walter Coleman, called for a historical tour that would "aim to put forth a clear, uninterrupted chronological narrative of events, readily understandable to visitors." He complained that there were too many entrances by which visitors could come into the park and that the vast size of the park allowed them to "wander around," obtaining "no concrete picture of the conflict." Coleman thought that visitors should go through the museum, tour the battlefield, and only then, in conclusion, view the drama of the Pickett-Pettigrew charge in the famous Gettysburg cyclorama. The "heroic and tragic realism depicted in this painting should be carried away by the visitor and remain uppermost in the memories of Gettysburg," he declared.[72]

The goal of various attempts at preservation, restoration, and interpretation is, in the words of the Park Service's 1982 general management plan, to "foster understanding and appreciation of the battle through interpretation of the events leading up to the battle and its aftermath and effect on the course of the Civil War." Park visitors "should be stimulated to reach their own conclusions about the moral, social, and political implications of the Civil War, and the role that Gettysburg played in the nation's history."[73] However, visitors to Gettysburg cannot "reach their own conclusions" in a neutral landscape, for within the sacred environment of the battlefield are several power points, places where ceremonies have sought to focus and refocus attention on the essential message of the battle.

One such power point is the Angle, the scene of the climax of the Pickett-Pettigrew charge on July 3, 1863. There is an almost irresistible attraction to the Angle, popularly perceived as the place where the fate of the nation hung in the balance and the valor of all Americans was displayed for the world to see. Like so many visitors before and since, George S. Patton, Jr., was captured by the power of this place during his visit to Gettysburg in 1909:

> This evening . . . I walked down alone to the scene of the last and fiercest struggle on Cemetery hill. To get in a proper frame of mind I wandered through the cemetery and let the spirits of the dead thousands laid there in ordered rows sink deep into me. Then just as the son [*sic*] sank . . . I walked down to the scene of Pickett's great charge and seated on a rock just where Olmstead and two of my great uncles died I watched the wonder of the day go out. The sunset painted a dull red the fields over which the terrible advance

was made and I could almost see them coming growing fewer and fewer while around and beyind [*sic*] me stood calmly the very cannon that had so punished them. There were some quail calling in the trees near by and it seemed strange that they could do it where man had known his greatest and his last emotions. It was very wonderful and no one came to bother me. I drank it in until I was quite happy. A strange pleasure yet a very real one.[74]

The various strategies of imaginative entry into the past—including battle reenactments and the cyclorama—commemorative veneration of the past—including patriotic rhetoric at anniversary celebrations or monument construction and dedication—and attempts to freeze the site "as it was" are all designed to help the imagination achieve aesthetic fulfillment, to "almost see them coming." Whether at the Angle or Devil's Den or Little Round Top, or at the site of the impressive Confederate state monuments on Seminary Ridge, the object is to *be* in the scene *as it was;* indeed, this has been one of the long-standing goals of the NPS interpretive programs. As a result, visitors to the sacred environment of Gettysburg can be seduced by the pageantry and drama and can easily ignore the enduring legacy of the Civil War.

Occasional attempts to disabuse people of the seductive appeal of battle include use of the dramatic story of Gettysburg by the Park Service's interpreters to communicate a more sober picture of war. For example, when Scott Hartwig takes people on a tour of the battlefield, his goal is to describe the events of the battle *and* to "deglorify war." He wants to help people understand that war is a "savage, violent affair." They should not gaze over the field of the Pickett-Pettigrew charge and then leave thinking, "Damn, that must have been really neat." And yet, as this sacred center remains "uppermost in the memories of Gettysburg," there is the danger that the fascination with martial spectacle will obscure the other, quite different messages about the meaning of the battle of Gettysburg, the Civil War, and contemporary civic responsibility.[75]

In the cemetery stands the Soldiers' National Monument, whose cornerstone was laid on July 4, 1865, near the spot where Abraham Lincoln delivered his Gettysburg Address.[76] Lincoln sought to give meaning to the horror of the battle in a most profound way, by placing the battle in the context of a long struggle. He challenged facile conceptions by declaring that such sacrifice would *only* be made meaningful as Americans struggled to reach the ideal of equality. The tension between these two powerful memories—of the battle itself and of Lincoln's challenge—were apparent in the separate celebrations that took place at the 125th anniversary in 1988. The huge battle reenactments revealed the enduring appeal of battle, as thousands of reenactors sought to stand for a moment in "real" history and thousands of spectators strained to participate in the re-creation of events perceived as bringing the nation once again to life through the cataclysmic power of war. For critics, such spectacles bore witness to the power of the ideology of reconciliation and trivialized the horror of war. Fixation on the battle itself, played out in the extreme in battle reenactments, celebrated American martial courage and ignored the more profound legacy of the battle and the war.

The ceremonies held at the Eternal Light Peace Memorial were of a quite different nature and sought to respond to Lincoln's challenge by turning public attention from the battle to, in the president's words, the "unfinished work which they who fought here have thus far so nobly advanced." In its celebration of the ideal of global racial harmony, and in a warning that reconciliation in the nuclear age must take place before (not after) war, the Park Service sought to deepen the spirit of reconciliation that had motivated Northern and Southern veterans to dedicate the memorial in 1938.

Those moved by the martial valor displayed at the Angle and by Lincoln's challenge perceive Gettysburg as a sacred environment, one that must be preserved and restored so that the landscape can speak its eloquent message to all who visit. Consequently, struggles will continue with those who perceive the park as wasted economic space, or who at least begrudge the expansion of the park. Yet what is it that is preserved within the park? Gettysburg is the site of diverse and visible attempts to venerate the nation's Homeric times. It does not, however, function only as an enshrined battlesite, nor only as an example of the enduring cultural memory of the Civil War. Gettysburg also functions as a place where contending perceptions of war and martial sacrifice can be ritually expressed. It is, and will continue to be, a place where we can be wrapped in the "golden mist of American valor." Still, it could become an even more provocative sacred environment if it asked visitors to draw inspiration from Lincoln's enduring challenge that there is a "great task remaining before us."

Notes

1. George S. Patton, Jr., *The Patton Papers 1885–1940*, ed. Martin Blumenson (Boston: Houghton Mifflin Co., 1972), p. 173; Reuben M. Rainey, "The Memory of War: Reflections on Battlefield Preservation," *Yearbook of Landscape Architecture* (New York: Van Nostrand, 1983), p. 79.

2. Quoted in Kathleen R. Georg, "A Fitting and Expressive Memorial," ms., Gettysburg National Military Park Library (hereafter, GNMPL).

3. Gettysburg Battlefield Memorial Association charter, GNMPL files, 11–30.

4. McLean's comments were made during

a speech at the dedication of the North Carolina monument on July 3, 1929. See "North Carolina Monument," GNMPL files, 17–58.

5. Quoted in Paul H. Buck, *The Road to Reunion, 1865–1900* (Boston: Little, Brown and Co., 1937), pp. 44–45.

6. Wallace Evans Davies, *Patriotism on Parade: The Story of Veterans' and Hereditary Organizations in America, 1783–1900* (Cambridge: Harvard University Press, 1955), p. 255. John S. Patterson notes that in 1869 blacks were barred from a procession to the Soldiers' Cemetery in Gettysburg on Decoration Day, although no one took responsibility for giving such an order. He also points out that during the 1870s and 1880s separate processions to the black cemeteries took place on the morning of Decoration Day. See Patterson, "A Patriotic Landscape: Gettysburg, 1863–1913," *Prospects* 7 (1982): 315–33.

7. John Hope Franklin, "A Century of Civil War Observances," *Journal of Negro History* 47, no. 2 (Apr. 1962): 107; David W. Blight, "For Something Beyond the Battlefield": Frederick Douglass and the Struggle for the Memory of the Civil War," *Journal of American History* 75, no. 4 (Mar. 1989): 1156.

8. John M. Vanderslice, *Gettysburg Then and Now* (Dayton, Ohio: Press of Morningside Bookshop, 1983), p. 36; Mrs. Tillie Alleman, *At Gettysburg; or, What a Girl Saw and Heard of the Battle* (New York: W. Lake Borland, 1889), pp. 82–83; *Gettysburg, Past and Present* (Baltimore: Western Maryland Railway Co., 1903), p. 49.

9. Linn diary, in "Early Visitation," GNMPL files, 11–50; "Four Days at Gettysburg," *Harper's Weekly* (Feb. 1864): 381, 382.

10. John S. Patterson, "Shrine Making: The Creation of the Soldiers' National Cemetery," in John W. Busey, *The Last Full Measure: Burials in the Soldiers' National Cemetery at Gettysburg* (Hightstown, N.J.: Longstreet House, 1988), p. xxxvi; Wills, quoted in Kathleen R. Georg, " 'This Grand Enterprise': The Origins of Gettysburg's Soldiers' National Cemetery and the Gettysburg Battlefield Memorial Association," ms., GNMPL. (I wish to thank Kathleen Georg Harrison for bringing this paper to my attention.) See also Patterson, "Patriotic Landscape."

There is a fine 1865 description of the cemetery in *Hours at Home:* "It is inclosed with a neat substantial railing, the gateway being inscribed within the names of the States represented within the ground, and surmounted by the American eagle on bronze. The crown of the hill is the site of the projected monument; and around this, in semi-circular slopes, lie the honored dead, each man separately coffined, and the men of each state together, in distinct sections. The divisions between the States are marked by alleys leading from the monument to the outer circle; the coffined rows are divided by continuous granite blocks about six inches in height, upon which the name and regiment of each soldier, so far as ascertained, is inscribed, as for his proper headstone. But many a grave bears the simple, touching mark: 'Unknown' " ("National Cemetery at Gettysburgh," *Hours at Home* 11 [Dec. 1865]: 183).

11. Weaver, quoted in Frank L. Klement, " 'These Honored Dead': David Wills and the Soldiers' Cemetery at Gettysburg," *Lincoln Herald* 74, no. 3 (Fall 1972): 132. See also *Adams Sentinel*, Dec. 5, 1865; "Reunions and Veterans Meetings at Gettysburg," GNMPL files, 11–60.

12. See Richard A. Sauers, "John Badger Bachelder: His Life and Work," in "Biographical Info.: GNMP Commissioners," GNMPL files, 11–34A.

13. It would be a mistake, of course, to assume that this theme of reconciliation was not bitterly opposed by some. For example, the *Grand Army Review* of 1887 was critical of intersectional reunions: "Short of abject apology and admission that the defence of the Union was a crime . . . nothing has been left unsaid by our gushing comrades at these pleasant gatherings to express our sorrow at having been compelled to use the bullet and bayonet" (quoted in Davies, p. 267).

14. Buck, p. viii; Davies, p. 249; Gerald Linderman, *Embattled Courage: The Experience of Combat in the American Civil War* (New York: Free Press, 1987), pp. 278–79; Cruce Stark, "Brothers at/in War: One Phase of Post–Civil War Reconciliation," *Canadian Review of American Studies* 6, no. 2 (Fall 1975): 178. In 1869 David McConaughy invited Robert E. Lee, then president of Washington and Lee University, to visit the battlefield and assist in marking the lines of battle. Lee responded on

August 5 that his schedule did not permit him to do so but that he also thought it "wiser . . . not to keep open the sores of war, but to follow the examples of those nations who endeavored to obliterate the marks of civil strife and to commit to oblivion the feelings it engendered" (letter in GNMPL files, 11–30).

15. For information on early reunions, see "Reunions and Various Meetings at Gettysburg," GNMPL files, 11–60. The meeting at the Angle is described in John W. Frazier, *Gettysburg: Reunion of the Blue and Gray* (Philadelphia: Ware Bros., 1906), p. 89; Aylett, a grandson of Patrick Henry, is quoted on p. 103. Frazier also details a similar meeting that took place in September 1906 and was the occasion for the rhetoric of reconciliation.

In February 1887 some survivors of Pickett's division met in Richmond and planned the dedication of a marker to honor Brig. Gen. Lewis Armistead. The marker was to be placed on the Gettysburg battlefield where Armistead had fallen after breaching the Union lines. Bachelder reportedly received "bushels" of letters protesting the erection of such a marker; consequently, the GBMA refused to place the marker at the Angle and Pickett's veterans then refused to attend the reunion in July. Only intense pressure from the Philadelphia Brigade convinced the Confederates to come. On July 12, 1887, the GBMA approved the placement of the marker at the Angle. See Frazier, *Gettysburg;* "Memorable Gettysburg," *Confederate Veteran* 6, no. 1 (1898): 15.

16. Sickles, quoted in Buck, p. 260; Gobin, quoted in *The Cannon's Roar*, July 4, 1988, GNMPL files, A4031.

17. Young and Beers are quoted in Walter H. Blake, *Hand Grips: The Story of the Great Gettysburg Reunion, July 1913* (Vineland, N.J.: G. E. Smith, 1913), pp. 8, 35. For a detailed account of the major reunions, see Stan Cohen, *Hands across the Wall: The 50th and 75th Reunions of the Gettysburg Battle* (Charleston, W.Va.: Pictorial Histories, 1982).

18. Clark, quoted in "Peace Memorial Efforts," GNMPL files, 17–5; his speech was also read into the *Congressional Record* on July 9, 1913. McCreary is quoted in Blake, p. 133.

19. John M. Haines, "The Fiftieth Anniversary Celebration of the Battle of Gettys-

burg," *Lincoln Herald* 55 (Winter 1953): 40–41; Cohen, p. 12. During the reunion Pickett's men wore white silk ribbons six inches long and two and a half inches wide that read, "Pickett's Men 1863–1913." The ribbons quickly became a collector's item in what was already a burgeoning field of Civil War collectibles. One of the participants in the fiftieth anniversary celebration recalled that "stores were filled with pennants, hatbands, flags, etc." (quoted in Blake, p. 2).

20. "Gettysburg's Last Big Reunion," *Literary Digest* 47 (July 12, 1913): 45; Blake, pp. 21–22; "Gettysburg: A Common Ideal," *Outlook* 104 (July 12, 1913): 554.

21. There were two other "final" reunions of Civil War veterans. The GAR held its last encampment in Indianapolis in 1949, and in 1951 the UCV held its final meeting in Norfolk, Virginia. See "Gettysburg Newspaper Cuttings," vol. 2, GNMPL files.

22. The *Christian Science Monitor* and Woodring are quoted in Paul L. Roy, *The Last Reunion of the Blue and the Gray* (Gettysburg, Pa.: Bookmart, 1950), pp. 23, 94.

23. Blake, p. 109; "75th Anniversary and Grand Reunion, 1938," GNMPL files, 11–62. Sentiment for a monument to peace was institutionalized in the Gettysburg National Peace Memorial Association, whose articles of association were adopted in Chattanooga on September 17, 1913. For details on the origin of the idea for a peace memorial during the fiftieth reunion, see Blake, pp. 138; "Peace Memorial Efforts," GNMPL files, 17–5.

24. "75th Anniversary and Grand Reunion, 1938," GNMPL files, 11–62; "Gettysburg Newspaper Cuttings," vol. 2, GNMPL files; unidentified newspaper clipping, "1930s Newspaper Clippings," GNMPL files, D-1.

25. For more information on the "culture" of the Civil War in the 1950s, see "Civil War: Interests and 'Buffs,' " GNMPL files, 18–8b. There are a number of board games focusing on Gettysburg. A sampling of those at Gilbert's Hobby Shop in Gettysburg includes: Terrible Swift Sword (TSR); Gettysburg (Avalon-Hill); Pickett's Charge (Yaquinto); Gettysburg (Phoenix Enterprises); Action Gettysburg (A Toys—Italy); Gettysburg: The Battle (SSI).

26. Robert G. Hartje, *Bicentennial USA: Pathways to Celebration* (Nashville: American Association for State and Local History, 1973), p. 69; Commonwealth of Pennsylvania, *Gettysburg 1963: An Account of the Centennial Commemoration Report of the Commission to the General Assembly,* comp. and ed. Louis M. Simon (Harrisburg, 1964), pp. 3, 6. Edwin C. Bearss, chief historian at the NPS, noted that there had been a "long-standing practice in Charleston to permit Black delegates attending predominately white functions to have rooms and eat at banquets in hotels. . . . but their presence would be low profile, i.e., they would not enter or leave by the front entrance. The National Centennial Commission mistakenly believed that the Black lady member of its New Jersey Commission would adhere to this covert practice and it boomeranged" (letter to the author, Sept. 7, 1989). John Hope Franklin angrily denounced the priorities of some Southern states, where education was the "shabbiest in the country," for spending "incredibly large amounts of money" on centennial events ("A Century of Civil War Observances," p. 103).

27. Quoted in *Gettysburg 1963,* pp. 82, 85.

28. "100th Anniversary of Battle of Gettysburg," GNMPL files, 11–63.

29. Wallace, quoted in "Gettysburg: The Task Remaining," *Newsweek* (July 15, 1963): 18. The other governors' messages are quoted in the *Gettysburg Times* (Centennial Edition of the Battle of Gettysburg), June 28, 1963, GNMPL files, 11–63.

30. "100th Anniversary of Battle of Gettysburg," GNMPL files, 11–63. For these and other details of the centennial celebrations, see *Gettysburg 1963,* pp. 36ff.

31. *Gettysburg 1963,* pp. 117–20. November 19 was officially declared Dedication Day in 1946. Public Law 645 requires that the Gettysburg Address be "read in public assemblages throughout the United States and its possessions, on our ships at sea and wherever the American flag flies" ("Mr. Lincoln Comes to Gettysburg—1952 Reenactment," GNMPL files, 10–28). Dedication Day services were held for many years before the day was officially recognized. See "Dedication Day Ceremonies, 20th Century," GNMPL files, 10–27.

32. Catton was not the only one pondering the meaning of the centennial. The editors of *Newsweek* thought that the words of Lincoln's Gettysburg Address now had a "hollow ring" and asked, "How long will it take Americans of this generation to achieve their own stillness at Appomattox and fulfill 'the great task remaining before us'?" ("Gettysburg: The Task Remaining," pp. 18–19).

33. *Gettysburg Times,* June 28, 1963. A Gettysburg newspaper editorial in 1961 was also critical of battle reenactments, calling the reenactment of First Manassas "silly business" and suggesting that it would have been more useful to portray the field after the battle, "when death and suffering and the indescribable tragedy of war had taken command—as they always have and always will." The editors hoped that Gettysburg would be spared from such reenactments ("Gettysburg Newspaper Cuttings, 1958–61," GNMPL files). Although he does not focus directly on battle reenactments, John Patterson raises interesting questions about the trivialization of the Gettysburg story in his description of the commercialization of the area and the nature of the NPS's presentations. See "Zapped at the Map: The Battlefield at Gettysburg," *Journal of Popular Culture* 7 (Spring 1974): 825–37.

34. While North and South had their own Decoration (or Memorial) Day traditions in the mid-nineteenth century, the origins of this holiday at Gettysburg are unique. On the first day of the battle a fatally wounded Union soldier, Amos Humiston, showed a Philadelphia doctor a picture of his three children. Later, Dr. J. Francis Bourne located Humiston's family and was moved to raise money to build an orphanage next to the cemetery. Humiston's widow moved to the orphanage with her children. In 1867 the orphans paraded to the cemetery and placed flowers on Humiston's grave, and the tradition continues today in only slightly modified form. See *Gettysburg Times,* May 22, 1981, in "Gettysburg Newspaper Clippings, 1981," GNMPL files.

35. Brig. Gen. George A. Custer, U.S. Volunteers, at the time the youngest Union general, fought with Gregg against Stuart on the third day of the battle of Gettysburg. Evaluating Custer's performance at Gettysburg,

Robert M. Utley declares: "Although the steady, capable Gregg deserved much credit, the clear victor of the cavalry fight east of Gettysburg was a twenty-three year-old youth who had been a general less than a week. . . . In one spectacular burst he emerged a general in fact as well as in name. Nor was Gettysburg a splashy anomaly. In the Union cavalry's harassment of Lee's retreat from Pennsylvania and in the subsequent maneuvers of the two armies in Virginia, Custer displayed superior leadership time and again" (*Cavalier in Buckskin: George Armstrong Custer and the Western Military Frontier* [Norman: University of Oklahoma Press, 1988], pp. 23–24).

36. "In the Grip of the Civil War," *U.S. News and World Report* (Aug. 15, 1988): 48. For an introduction to various forms of imaginative entry into history through living-history displays and reenactments, see Jay Anderson, *Time Machines: The World of Living History* (Nashville: American Association for State and Local History, 1984).

37. John Heiser interview, Jan. 19, 1989.

38. Rita Mae Brown, "Fighting the Civil War Anew," *New York Times,* June 12, 1988, pp. 8–9+.

39. "125th Anniversary" (three boxes of material), GNMPL files. Such noble goals conflicted with commercial interest in the drama of the battle. The American Civil War Commemorative Committee, Inc., and local interests in Gettysburg produced and sold a tremendous variety of battle-related items: T-shirts, books, medallions, art, music, and *Pickett's Charge,* a limited edition sculpture by Francis J. Barnum.

40. Sagan's remarks and other details on the activities of the three-day celebration are in "125th Anniversary," GNMPL files.

41. Robert Prosperi, letter to the author, June 8, 1989; Edwin C. Bearss, letter to the author, Sept. 7, 1989.

42. McConaughy, quoted in Georg, " 'This Grand Enterprise,' " p. 38. See also Georg, "A Fitting and Expressive Memorial," p. 3.

43. Quoted in Harlan D. Unrau, *Administrative History of Gettysburg National Military Park and Gettysburg National Cemetery* (Denver: Denver Service Center, Eastern Team—NPS, Department of the Interior, n.d.), pp. 160, 161. For further discussion of the GBMA and the battlefield commission appointed by the War Department, see Georg, "A Fitting and Expressive Memorial," pp. 6–10; Unrau, pp. 160–72.

44. *Gettysburg Compiler,* Apr. 14, 1885. For an analysis of Gettysburg monumentation, see Michael Wilson Panhorst, "Lest We Forget: Monuments and Memorial Sculpture in National Military Parks on Civil War Battlefields, 1861–1917," Ph.D. diss. (University of Delaware, 1988). See also Wayne Craven, *The Sculptures at Gettysburg* (n.p.: Eastern National Park and Monument Assocation, 1982); David G. Martin, "The Gettysburg Battle Monuments," ms., in "Monument Dedication: Dates/Cost, Etc.," GNMPL files, 17–11; Susan P. Staggers, ". . . As Long as Bronze and Granite Lasts . . . Their Memory Will Remain Forever Green . . . ," ms., in "Monuments: General Information," GNMPL files, 17–1. Inside the cornerstone of the Soldiers' National Monument, laid on July 4, 1865, and annointed with oil and corn, are a number of articles in a tin box. These include constitutions from states whose soldiers had fought for the Union, a copy of the U.S. Constitution, a copy of the Emancipation Proclamation, the names of the soldiers buried in the cemetery, and a roster of the Army of the Potomac. The monument was dedicated on July 1, 1869. See *Gettysburg Times,* June 28, 1963.

45. "Minutes of the GBMA, 1872–95," GNMPL files; "Regulations: Gettysburg National Park, 1914," GNMPL files; Stephen Vincent Benét, *John Brown's Body,* intro. and notes by Jack L. Capps and C. Robert Kemble (New York: Holt, Rinehart and Winston, 1968), p. 298.

46. Smith, quoted in Frederick W. Hawthorne, *Gettysburg: Stories of Men and Monuments as Told by Battlefield Guides* (n.p.: Association of Battlefield Guides, 1988), p. 8; Sickles, quoted in New York Monuments Commission for the Battlefields of Gettysburg and Chattanooga, *Final Report on the Battlefield of Gettysburg,* vol. 1 (Albany: J. B. Lyons, 1902), p. 315. While the monuments may have been designed as an immortal rebuke to the indifference of future generations, they were not designed to withstand the ravages of air pollution and acid rain. Faced with monuments that were deteriorating, in the 1980s

the NPS began Project in Preservation, a fund-raising effort to aid in the restoration of many of Gettysburg's monuments. See "Monument Dedication: Dates/Cost, Etc.," GNMPL files.

47. *Gettysburg Compiler* and *Baltimore Sun* articles in "Maryland Monument," GNMPL files, 17–50A; "The Maryland Confederate Monument at Gettysburg," *Southern Historical Society Papers* 14 (Jan.-Dec. 1886): 443, 446. Curiously, the Armistead monument is the only Confederate monument that was erected beyond the line of battle, contrary to battlefield commission policy and GAR sentiment.

Not all GAR members were pleased with the attempts to honor Confederates at Gettysburg. In 1885 the commander of the Colorado GAR angrily declared that there should be "no monuments over the grave of a dead Confederacy." Let the Confederacy lie in its own grave, he said, "unwept, unhonored and unsung." In 1887 the national encampment of GAR posts voted that no local post should support "erection of monuments in honor of men who distinguished themselves by their services in the cause of treason and rebellion" (both comments in Davies, p. 256).

48. In 1901–2 battery and brigade tablets were erected. By 1921 approximately one hundred twenty-five of the two hundred currently existing Confederate monuments were erected. For a thorough history of Confederate monumentation at Gettysburg, see David G. Martin, *Confederate Monuments at Gettysburg* (Hightstown, N.J.: Longstreet House, 1986). See also Kathleen R. Georg, "Confederate Monumentation at Gettysburg," ms., in "Monuments: Confederate Monuments at Gettysburg," GNMPL files, 17–12.

49. George Ripley Stewart, *Pickett's Charge* (Boston: Houghton Mifflin Co., 1959), p. ix.

50. Bachelder's comments on the High Water Mark Monument come from his untitled written report of Feb. 1, 1894. (I wish to thank the New Hampshire Historical Society for providing a copy of this report.) Michael Kernan writes about another piece of wood, placed in a glass case in a "quiet, shadowy hallway of the National Museum of American History," that is being treated as a sacred relic of the war. The wood is all that remains of a tree that originally stood behind the Confederate lines at the battle of Spotsylvania Courthouse and was literally shot to pieces during the fierce fighting of May 12, 1864. After the war Union soldiers learned that the tree stump had been removed and later discovered that a local innkeeper had hidden it. Kernan notes that "in 1876, the War Department let the stump be displayed at the Centennial Exposition, in Philadelphia, after which, in 1888, it was brought . . . to the Smithsonian" ("The Object at Hand," *Smithsonian* 20, no. 2 [May 1989]: 24–28).

51. See Bachelder's Feb. 1, 1894, report.

52. *Gettysburg Compiler,* June 7, 1892. Gen. A. S. Webb of New York, one of the five or six thousand in attendance at the dedication ceremonies, did not agree with the reconciling tone of Beaver's speech. The *Compiler* reported that the general "considered treason the same under whatever title it might appear." Before 1905 the High Water Mark Monument was the sole major monument dedicated to reconciliation. The only other monument to speak to this theme was the one erected by the Sixty-sixth New York, dedicated on October 9, 1899. On it is a small relief of a Confederate soldier and a Union soldier shaking hands, below a banner that reads, "Peace and Unity."

53. *Philadelphia Times,* June 7, 1906, in "Gettysburg Newspaper Cuttings," vol. 2, GNMPL files; *Gettysburg Compiler,* Jan. 28, 1903, in "Virginia Monument," GNMPL files, B–67.

54. Stuart and Robinson are quoted in "Virginia Monument," GNMPL files, B–67. The image of Lee in Southern monument rhetoric has remained unchanged. For example, at the rededication of the Virginia monument on April 25, 1987, Mills E. Godwin, Jr., a former governor of Virginia, said that the "legacy for this revered figure can be counted only by the millions whose lives came under his influence" (GNMPL files, 3–67).

55. Tilberg, quoted in "Confederate Soldiers and Sailors Monument, #1–3," GNMPL files; Emery, quoted in "Mississippi Monument," GNMPL files, 17–54; visitor from North Carolina, quoted in "Gettysburg Newspaper Cuttings," GNMPL files.

56. *Ceremonies of the Dedication of Monuments Erected by the Commonwealth of Pennsylvania to*

Major General George G. Meade, Major General Winfield S. Hancock, Major General John F. Reynolds and to Mark the Positions of the Pennsylvania Commands Engaged in the Battle, vol. 1 (Harrisburg: n.p., 1904), p. 417.

57. Chief Justice Walter Clark, "North Carolina at Gettysburg and Pickett's Charge a Misnomer," ms., GNMPL files. The rivalry between Virginia and North Carolina persisted even in the battle reenactment on the 125th anniversary. Kevin Young, who was the technical director of and a historical reenactor in the film *Alamo . . . The Price of Freedom,* took part in the reenactment at Gettysburg. He mentioned that there was visible "animosity" between Virginians and North Carolinians, including bumper stickers that declared, "I charged with Pickett" (letter to the author, Aug. 17, 1989).

58. "Gettysburg Newspaper Clippings, 1986," GNMPL files. North Carolina was not the only state to claim it had advanced farthest at Gettysburg. At the dedication of the Mississippi monument Sen. James O. Eastland said that Mississippians deserved that honor. See "Mississippi Monument," GNMPL files, 17–54.

59. At least one Civil War monument engenders reflection on the meaning of Union sacrifice in the Civil War: the Shaw Memorial on the Boston Common, dedicated in 1897. That memorial commemorates the death of Col. Robert Gould Shaw, who led the Fifty-fourth Massachusetts (a black regiment) into battle at Fort Wagner in Charleston, South Carolina, on July 18, 1863. Shaw and almost half of his command were killed or wounded, and the Confederates, to show their contempt for a white man leading black troops, threw Shaw's body into a mass grave with the bodies of his men.

In the early part of the twentieth century the black poet Paul Lawrence Dunbar bitterly disputed the belief that the men of the Fifty-fourth had died meaningful deaths. In "Robert Gould Shaw," Dunbar wrote: "Since thou and those who with thee died for right / Have died, the Present teaches, but in vain!" (*The Complete Poems of Paul Laurence Dunbar* [New York : Dodd, Mead and Co., 1968], p. 360). Similarly, Robert Lowell's "For the Union Dead," recited at the Boston Arts Festival on

the Boston Common on June 5, 1960, intimates that the ideals for which Shaw died were as far from realization as they had ever been and that "the monument sticks like a fishbone / in the city's throat" ("For the Union Dead," *Atlantic* 206, no. 5 [Nov. 1960]: 54–55).

Over the years the Shaw Memorial has been damaged by vandals. After money was raised in 1981 to restore it, several blacks objected to the plan to include the names of members of the Fifty-fourth on the monument, suggesting that their omission would symbolize the persistence of racism. Henry Lee, past president of the Friends of the Public Garden and a great-grandson of Col. Henry Lee (a member of the original monument committee), would not have agreed. Two decades earlier he declared that the "monument honors black and white men who served together in common cause," and he hoped that "in drawing attention to this, we could do a little bit toward healing some of our present conflicts" (quoted in David Mehegan, "For These Union Dead," *Boston Globe Magazine,* Sept. 5, 1962, p. 33). For an introduction to the history of the Shaw Memorial, see Stephen J. Whitfield, "Sacred in History and Art: The Shaw Memorial," *New England Quarterly* 60, no. 1 (Mar. 1987): 3–27. For an introduction to the poetry engendered by the memorial, see Steven Axelrod, "Colonel Shaw in American Poetry: 'For the Union Dead' and Its Precursors," *American Quarterly* 24, no. 4 (Oct. 1972): 523–37.

60. Suggestive remarks concerning the function of boundaries are made by John B. Jackson, *Discovering the Vernacular Landscape* (New Haven: Yale University Press, 1984). Establishing boundaries was not sufficient in itself, for sight defilement could take place by looking beyond the boundaries to modernity. Two notable controversies erupted as a result of the NPS's desire to keep adjacent land as farm land: one involved a plan to construct a vocational-technical school near the park in 1973; the other, in 1979, dealt with the proposed location of a sewage treatment plant within sight of the park.

61. The GBPA was formed in 1959 to "prevent non–government owned lands within Gettysburg's famed battlefield proper from disappearing in a welter of housing de-

velopments and commercial structures" ("Early Visitation," GNMPL files, 11–50). It grew out of a meeting of students and Civil War buffs attending the second annual Civil War Study Group at Gettysburg College. In its centennial issue the *Civil War Times Illustrated* called readers' attention to the need for the preservation of the battlefield. Its editor, Robert H. Fowler, noted, "We would like to pay a special tribute to a handful of people who are doing most to preserve these hallowed fields" ("Editorially Speaking," *Civil War Times Illustrated* [July 1963]).

62. Assorted letters to the editor and articles about citizen complaints regarding park expansion are in "Gettysburg Newspaper Clippings, 1980," GNMPL files. Goodling's statement appears in the *Gettysburg Times,* Mar. 18, 1980.

63. Quoted in Harlan D. Unrau, *Administrative History of Gettysburg National Military Park and Gettysburg National Cemetery* (Denver: Denver Service Center, Eastern Team—NPS, Department of the Interior, n.d.), p. 19.

64. *Gettysburg Times,* Mar. 10, 25, 27, 1980. Numerous letters regarding this particular incident are found in "Gettysburg Newspaper Clippings, 1980," GNMPL files. The construction in 1962 of the visitors center (now known as the Cyclorama Center), built near the scene of the Pickett-Pettigrew charge, was also cause for debate. See John S. Patterson "From Battle Ground to Pleasure Ground: Gettysburg as a Historic Site," in *History Museums in the United States: A Critical Assessment,* ed. Warren Leon and Roy Rosenzweig (Urbana: University of Illinois Press, 1989), pp. 149–51. There are scattered references in area newspapers to other restoration activities. For example, on May 31, 1981, the York (Pa.) *Sunday News* informed its readers that the Biglerville High School chapter of the Future Farmers of America had planted 130 peach trees in the famous Peach Orchard area of the battlefield to restore it to its 1863 condition.

65. Unrau, pp. 440, 489 (emphasis added); *General Management Plan for Gettysburg National Military Park and Gettysburg National Cemetery* (n.p.: Mid-Atlantic Regional Office, National Park Service, U.S. Department of the Interior, 1982), p. 57.

66. Letter from Davis to Daniel S. Lamont, May 25, 1893, in GNMPL files. I thank Kathleen Georg Harrison for bringing this material to my attention.

67. This brief, a copy of which appears in the GNMPL files, was presented at the October 1895 term of the U.S. Supreme Court. Kathleen Georg Harrison again deserves the credit for bringing this material to my attention.

68. Quoted in Unrau, p. 168.

69. *Gettysburg Times,* Apr. 29, 1939; Michael Frome, "Historic Gettysburg," *American Forests* 65 (Oct. 1959): 36; *Cleveland Plain Dealer,* July 14, 1963; *New York Times,* Dec. 31, 1970. A similar sense of outrage at the pollution of a sacred martial site was expressed by a visitor in 1961 who wrote to Sen. Hugh Scott of Pennsylvania that he was "amazed" at the number of stores in Gettysburg that sold items made in Japan, adding, "You would think that Japan had won the Civil War." Furthermore, the visitor declared, "I think the citizens of our country making a living at our National Shrine would be patriotic enough to handle merchandise made in America" (in "Gettysburg NMP," box 1–12, historical correspondence files, National Park Service).

70. Baker, quoted in John S. Oyler, "Pickett Charges, Everyone Else Pays: The Story of the Gettysburg Tower Controversy," senior thesis (Department of Politics, Princeton University, 1972), the most comprehensive analysis available of the tower controversy; Frederick (Md.) *Post,* July 25, 1974; Will, quoted in *Philadelphia Inquirer,* May 9, 1974. In response to the various preservation struggles at Civil War battlefields, the Association for the Preservation of Civil War Sites, Inc., was founded in the summer of 1987. According to Prof. Gary W. Gallagher of Pennsylvania State University, there are now more than twelve hundred members in all fifty states as well as Canada and Australia (letter to the author, Apr. 17, 1989).

71. Frederick Tilberg, a former park historian, notes that by the 1890s "a dozen individuals made a substantial part of their living by guiding visitors for a fee." As a result of occasional complaints about the honesty and competence of the guides during the early

part of the century, the War Department established guidelines for guides in 1915. In 1927–28 guides were required to wear service uniforms; in 1928 regular trip itineraries were given to the guides. The guide system flourishes today. Visitors to Gettysburg can request a guide for a several-hour tour of the battlefield, or they can take a self-guided automobile tour. See Tilberg, "Gettysburg in 1954," *Reading Railroad Magazine* 19, no. 3 (Aug. 1954): 5, in "Gettysburg: News Articles," GNMPL files, 18–8.

72. Coleman, quoted in Unrau, pp. 527–29. The Gettysburg cyclorama is an example of panorama painting, which was patented in 1787 by the Irishman Robert Barker and popularized during the nineteenth century. Of the twenty cycloramas still known to exist, twelve deal with war; in the United States they are the Gettysburg cyclorama and the *Battle of Atlanta*.

According to John Patterson the Gettysburg cyclorama has provided "dramatic amusement and patriotic instruction for substantial urban audiences that included thousands of viewers who would never actually leave the city to make the trip to Gettysburg" (letter to John Ernest, Aug. 5, 1986, in GNMPL files). It was painted in Paris by Paul Philippoteaux, who visited Gettysburg in 1882, and then shipped to Chicago in 1883, where it was housed in a huge amphitheater until 1895. *Frank Leslie's Illustrated Newspaper* of July 5, 1884, speaks of the power of the cyclorama as a form of imaginative entry into the battle, noting that when viewing the painting it is "impossible to discover where reality ends and illusion begins." In 1884 a second cyclorama of Gettysburg (the one now housed on the battlefield) was exhibited in a special cyclorama building in Boston until 1892, when it was replaced by a cyclorama of Custer's Last Stand. Severely damaged while in storage, the second Gettysburg cyclorama was bought by a department store owner and displayed in Newark, New Jersey, for a few months in 1911, then displayed in New York, Baltimore, and Washington, D.C. It arrived in Gettysburg on May 8, 1913, in time for the fiftieth anniversary celebration, and is still one of the main attractions at the battlefield.

For a general history of cycloramas and the Gettysburg Cyclorama in particular, see Alfred Mongin, "The National Park Service Gettysburg Cyclorama," ms., July 1968, in "Gettysburg Cyclorama Information," GNMPL files; letter from Patterson to Ernest, Aug. 5, 1986, in GNMPL files; Robert Wernick, "Getting a Glimpse of History from a Grandstand Seat," *Smithsonian* 16, no. 5 (Aug. 1985): 68–84.

73. *General Management Plan*, pp. 5, 62.

74. Patton, p. 173.

75. Scott Hartwig interview, Jan. 25, 1989.

76. Robert Prosperi, an NPS historian who has conducted tours of the battlefield for many distinguished visitors, including (during the Camp David meetings) Anwar Sadat of Egypt, Menachem Begin of Israel, and Pres. Jimmy Carter, related this story to show the universal appeal of Lincoln's words: In 1979 the army chief of staff of the People's Republic of China visited Gettysburg with approximately twenty-five junior officers and several translators. When Prosperi met the group in the visitors center, the Chinese general let it be known that he first wanted to visit the Soldiers' National Monument. Once there he recited the Gettysburg Address in halting English and through one of the translators told the astonished group that he had always admired Lincoln. In fact, he said that he had carried a book of Lincoln's speeches, which he thought outlined the "kind of China he envisioned," while on the Long March with Mao Tse-tung (telephone interview, June 8, 1989).

4

"A Sore from America's Past
That Has Not Yet Healed"

The discovery of gold in Idaho and Montana in the 1860s, the advance of the railroads, and the popularity of the Bozeman Trail as a westward route all served to spark bloody conflicts between whites and Indians. In an attempt to bring peace to the area, the United States government signed the Fort Laramie Treaty in 1868, thereby closing all forts on the trail and establishing a huge reservation that encompassed present-day South Dakota. The treaty also established an "unceded territory" in the Powder River country that was to remain free of whites.

In the early 1870s stories began to circulate about gold in the Black Hills, on part of the Great Sioux Reservation. Lt. Gen. Philip H. Sheridan, commander of the department of the Missouri, sent a military expedition led by Lt. Col. George Armstrong Custer into the area in 1874 to determine whether these stories were true. Custer returned with the news that they were, and by 1875 the army was ready to give up its half-hearted efforts to stop thousands of prospectors from venturing into the Black Hills. In December of that year the commissioner of Indian affairs ordered that any Indians who remained outside the reservation as of January 31, 1876, would be considered "hostile" and forcibly removed from unceded land.

Lt. Gen Philip H. Sheridan ordered three army columns of approximately twenty-five hundred men into the Montana Territory to carry out the government's directive. Gen. George Crook's column was defeated by Sioux and Cheyenne at the battle of Rosebud on June 17, 1876. That left troops under the command of Col. John Gibbon and Gen. Alfred H. Terry to search for the band of Indians, estimated to include no more than a few hundred warriors. On June 21, Terry, Gibbon, and Custer met to plan their strategy. The object, Gibbon later declared, was "to prevent the escape of the Indians, which was the idea pervading the minds of all of us." Terry and Gibbon were to approach the Little Bighorn Valley from the north, and Custer's Seventh Cavalry was to move south, trapping the Indians between the two columns. On the morning of June 25, Custer received word that Sioux scouts had seen his men. Consequently, he decided to find the village and attack it immediately to prevent the Indians from scattering.

While still some miles from the Indians' village, Custer split his troop into three battalions, one under the command of Maj. Marcus A. Reno, one under the command of Capt. Frederick W. Benteen, and one under his own command. Benteen and his men were told to reconnoiter before rejoining the other battalions. By mid-afternoon the large village, comprised of some two thousand Indian warriors, had been located. Reno led the attack and was met by fierce resistance and heavy casualties, which eventually forced him and his men to retreat across the river and up the steep bluffs to what is now Reno Hill. Later that day and for much of the next, Reno's command, since joined by Benteen's, suffered withering fire from the Sioux and Cheyenne. Eventually the Indians moved away toward the Bighorn Mountains.

But what of Custer? Giovanni Martini, his orderly and trumpeter, who was sent to deliver a message to Benteen ordering him to quicken his pace, last saw Custer "going down into [Medicine Tail Coulee]. The gray horse troop was in the center and they were galloping." Shortly thereafter on that hot Sunday afternoon, Custer and five companies of the Seventh Cavalry—approximately two hundred twenty-five men—met their fate on the hills above the Little Bighorn River, at the hands of Teton Sioux and Northern Cheyenne warriors led by Gall, Crazy Horse, and Two Moon. The bodies were not discovered until June 27, when one of Gibbon's scouts came upon the grim scene.

The battle of the Little Bighorn was the greatest single triumph for the Sioux and Cheyenne in their futile attempt to remain free from the shackles of white civilization. A few weeks later, on July 12, 1876, the New York Herald declared that "the story that comes to us to-day with so much horror, with so much pathos, will become a part of our national life." More than a century later most Americans have some inkling of the epic drama that took place in the Montana hills, but the questions how and why will continue to entrance generations of Custerphiles.

The Little Bighorn

LIKE SO MANY BOYS growing up in the 1950s there was little question in my mind who the "good guys" and the "bad guys" were when I was watching movies or reading books about "cowboys and Indians," or, more specifically, the cavalry and the Indians. The cavalry heroes were like us, or like who we wanted to be. They were brave, they were handsome, and they left beautiful women back at the fort every time they rode off to make life safe for the innocent families on the frontier. They spoke our language and wore our clothes. I vividly recall the pride I felt each time I put on my dark blue Cub Scout shirt with the yellow bandanna. That garb connected me, somehow, with those brave cavalrymen.

The Indians, needless to say, were not like us. They were bloodthirsty, not brave. They were willing to risk their lives only to inflict horrible death on besieged whites. They uttered fierce guttural noises. Occasionally, but only occasionally, movies depicted them as the tragic pawns of greedy whites, as innocent, passive victims who elicited in us the same kind of sympathy we felt for a mistreated pet. The Indians' plight did not register as a human tragedy but served instead as the backdrop for the celebration of the westward march of Anglo-American civilization. Injustices done to the Indians were regrettable footnotes to an otherwise happy story. If we mourned, it would be for heroes like Davy Crockett, who died in glory at the Alamo, or for George Armstrong Custer, whose last stand came at the Little Bighorn.[1]

A singular honor came my way as a young boy, when I was given the chance to portray Custer in an outdoor play at Camp Green Acres. Adults may be enthralled with the drama of battle reenactment, but a child can live out the sacred stories more innocently, for history is very much a story, and a simple story at that. To me the message was clear: Custer died for *us*. I can still see myself dressed in a modified Cub Scout uniform, riding a small horse (the only one of my command so honored), waiting for the inevitable. I had been instructed by a counselor to wave my cardboard sword at the attackers and then, after all the soldiers were "dead," to slip off my horse and die a hero's death, the way we "knew" Custer had died. My intentions were good. I was prepared, as I thought Custer must have been. But the power of other, happier endings overcame me, and at the appointed time my horse and I trotted away from the outdoor theater. I returned only grudgingly, after I glanced back and caught the withering glare of the director—which told me that there might be worse things in store for me than glorious make-believe death.

These memories rushed back to me during my first visit to the Little Bighorn on a sweltering day in August 1979. As a student of American culture it was my job to study and understand such myths, but over the years I had convinced myself that I no longer believed them. However, as I approached the battlefield on I–90, I strained to see Custer Hill before anything else—before the valley where the Indian village stood, before the hills up which the remnants of Maj. Marcus A. Reno's troops retreated to defensive positions, to await relief from Brig. Gen. Alfred H. Terry's soldiers. Instinctively, I looked toward the hilltop, where the heroic last stand was made. Here was one of the sacred spots in the nation's patriotic landscape, as important as Lexington Green, the North Bridge, the Alamo chapel and Long Barrack, the Angle at Gettysburg, and the USS *Arizona*. As the hill came into view, outlined against the impressive Montana sky, the simple monument with the white marble headstones clustered around it seemed to capture the essence of the Custer myth. I understood well the words of Ben Blackburn, of the *Rocky Mountain News,* who wrote that visitors to this place will "view a battlefield unlike any other in the land. And . . . they will leave here strangely quieted, hushed by the constant starkness of the place. . . . Callous indeed is the visitor who will not be moved by the sight."[2]

As with the Alamo, the traditional patriotic orthodoxy associated with the Little Bighorn remained essentially unchallenged for a century, drawing countless people into its web. It was not until the centennial commemoration in 1976 that Native Americans made a frontal attack on the symbol of Custer and the Anglo-American interpretation of the battle. They understood completely the power of the Custer myth and carried out their form of symbolic guerrilla warfare where it would have the greatest impact—at the sacred site itself. Far from being a placid tourist attraction amid the rolling prairies of Montana, the Little Bighorn remains the site of an ongoing clash of cultures that is less violent but just as spirited as the military clash that took place there in 1876. Patriotic guardians of the Custer myth have reacted angrily to what they perceive as various forms of desecration: attacks on Custer himself, attacks on the supposed injustice of army activities during the Plains Indian wars, attempts to change the name of the battlefield, the placement of an unauthorized Indian plaque on the grave of the soldiers, anger over a quote from the Sioux holy man Black Elk located on an outside wall of the visitors center, and discomfiture at the marked shift in rhetoric and ritual at anniversary celebrations. Seeking to mediate the struggle for ownership of the Custer symbol is the National Park Service (NPS), itself engaged in the process of redefinition at the Custer battlefield. The NPS is struggling to transform a shrine into a historic site, even as it attempts to open the symbol to diverse interpretations.

Veneration of Custer and the martyrs of the Seventh Cavalry began almost immediately after the battle with their transformation into mythological figures: creators and saviors. By killing the enemy in a sacred cause, these men had preserved the life of the nation; indeed, the blood spilled during their redemptive sacrifice made possible the formation of a new world. Custer's sacrifice has long been celebrated in American culture as the crucial event in the "opening" of the American West for Anglo-American civilization. Gen. William T. Sherman expressed this sentiment several years after the battle in a letter to Mrs. Elizabeth Bacon Custer: "I say that the Indian wars are as much wars as conflicts with foreigners or our own people. . . . the Regular Army of the United States should claim what is true and susceptible of demonstration, that it has been for an hundred years ever the picket line at the front of the great wave of civilization."[3]

Well into the twentieth century Custer was celebrated as having played a crucial role in the creation of civilization on the frontier. In 1920 the Custer Memorial Highway Association designated the road from Omaha, Nebraska, to Glacier National Park as a memorial to the hero of the Little Bighorn, enabling visitors to follow, "in the main[,] the trail covered by General Custer in his last campaign." Furthermore, they would find the ".historic and scenic Custer Battlefield Highway a constant source of surprise and pleasure." On the fiftieth anniversary of the battle in 1926, a reporter for the *Boston Globe* conjured up this image: "As Custer's widow turns her face toward the setting sun she sees the field of bloodshed come to flower. . . . she reads the record of her hero's patriotic service, written in terms of peace and plenty."[4]

Popular literature has portrayed Custer as a sacrificial hero and provided readers with an enduring cultural model of how Americans should face death in battle. The earliest and most influential biography of Custer was written by Frederick Whittaker in 1876, shortly after the battle. Whittaker dramatized the heroism of the sacrifice by suggesting that at the last moment Custer's Crow Indian scout, Curly, had offered a way to escape. Custer "weighed in that brief moment of reflection all the consequences to America of the lesson of life and the lesson of heroic death, and he chose death." Consequently, in cultural memory a great Indian victory was transformed into both a "massacre," in which Custer and his men were victims of "hordes" of Indians, and a great moral victory, surpassing the epic heroism of other last stands at Masada, Thermopylae, and the Alamo.[5]

Certainly, the popular memory of the Little Bighorn has been a model for the transformation of other defeats into moral victories. For example, shortly after watching Errol Flynn portray Custer in *They Died with Their Boots On* (1941), Americans were able to interpret defeat at Wake Island, Bataan, and Corregidor as great moral victories. Lt. Col. Warren J. Clear, one of the last soldiers to escape after the fall of Corregidor, spoke on the "Army Hour" radio program about the bravery of the American troops. The surrender was portrayed as "defeat without despair. . . . The nation had the example of those 'grim, gaunt men of Bataan' to serve as an incentive to greater home effort." Like Custer's troops, the heroes of these battles provided a generation with models of enduring bravery and sacrificial death. Often celebrated in last-stand movies such as *Wake Island* and *Bataan*, these men were the twentieth-century incarnation of the men of the Seventh Cavalry, dying for timeless ideals in the face of overwhelming odds.[6]

As heroic interpretations of Custer and the battle became popular quite soon after the battle, so did plans to sanctify the battlefield and the fallen army heroes. On July 11, 1876, only a few weeks after the battle, the *New York Herald* reported that during a meeting of Custer's "old comrades in arms" plans were made to form the Custer Monument Association. In addition to early interest in a monument to Custer, public pressure focused on establishing a cemetery at the battlefield, due in large part to stories that the hastily buried remains of America's heroes were scattered about the field. Although some observers mistook horse bones for human remains, there was an element of truth to these stories, as relic hunters, predatory animals, and shallow graves combined to leave the unsupervised field in poor condition.

After Brigadier General Terry's soldiers relieved the battered remnants of the Seventh Cavalry on Reno Hill, his chief scout brought the news of the debacle on Custer Hill. Major Reno's troopers buried the dead on the morning of June 28. Lt. Edward S. Godfrey described the scene as one of "sickening ghastly horror." There were few tools available for proper burial and little time to carry out the gruesome task, for the wounded required immediate transportation to the steamer *Far West*, which had proceeded to the mouth of the Little Bighorn River. Consequently, the first graves consisted of a covering of sagebrush or a small amount of dirt. In 1877 enlisted men were reburied on the field and officers' remains were reinterred throughout the nation. Custer was laid to rest at the United States Military

Academy at West Point. In 1878 Col. Nelson A. Miles, commanding officer in the district of Yellowstone, visited the battlefield in the company of a number of Indian veterans of the battle. Miles desired "the attainment of the Indian narrative of the engagement." Even then, two years after the battle, "there were plenty of bones lying about the site. . . . Burying parties were often sent from Fort Custer to collect and bury scattered bony fragments, carried hither and thither by the prairie wolves and coyotes, but they were exhumed after each interment by the rapacious animals."[7]

Since tourists were already visiting the battlefield, such conditions were intolerable. In 1879 an army detail from nearby Fort Custer remounded the graves scattered throughout the field and erected a log memorial on Custer Hill into which they placed the horse bones that littered the site. That same year, on January 29, the secretary of war ordered the establishment of a national cemetery on the field and also authorized the establishment of a permanent monument. In 1881, after a two-year trip to the battlefield by barge, rail, and mule team, a 36,000-pound granite monument arrived from the Mt. Auburn Marble and Granite Works of Cambridge, Massachusetts. After it was erected the soldiers' remains were gathered up and placed in a common grave at the monument's base. During the reinterment troopers "planted a stake, [at each former gravesite] well in the ground, so that future visitors could see where the men actually fell." In April 1890 these markers were replaced by white marble headstones.[8]

The Custer Battlefield National Cemetery was established on the battlefield on August 1, 1879, and army casualties from various Indian conflicts were brought there for burial. The *New York Times* reported on December 8, 1905, that "old Indian fighters, who gave their lives that the white man's civilization might replace the savagery of the Indian," were brought to the Little Bighorn and buried "under the hills hallowed by the blood of Custer and his men of the 7th Cavalry." Eventually, casualties from numerous American wars were buried at the cemetery.

Early commemorative events at the Little Bighorn were rather informal affairs. Some, like the visit of Miles in 1878, were designed to gather information about the battle from Indian participants. In 1886 several cavalry veterans, including Capt. Frederick W. Benteen and Lieutenant Godfrey, returned to witness a skirmish line of troops firing a tribute to Custer on the morning of June 25. Several Sioux and Cheyenne veterans attended, and Chief Gall of the Hunkpapa Sioux took photographer David F. Barry and several other whites on a tour of the battlefield. There were no major ceremonies for the rest of the nineteenth century, leading one observer to remark that while a few friends came to the field to deposit wreaths, "the

Custer Battlefield today is one vast cemetery, neglected and almost forgotten."[9]

Battle reenactments were popular in Montana in the early years of the twentieth century, and in 1902 Custer's Last Stand was reenacted near Sheridan, Wyoming, with Crow Indians playing the roles of the Sioux and Cheyenne, battling the Wyoming militia. Don Rickey, a former National Park Service historian, notes that this was a "gala affair, and ranchers and homesteaders came in from miles around to see the show."[10] In 1909 a reenactment took place on the battlefield and was captured on film by a Chicago movie company. It was not until 1916, however, that the first elaborate commemoration took place.

The great anniversary events of the twentieth century clearly articulated the major themes of patriotic orthodoxy at the Little Bighorn. As they celebrated the heroism and sacrifice of Custer and the Seventh Cavalry, they also described, in quite revealing terms, popular and enduring perceptions of American Indians. In anticipation of the fortieth anniversary in 1916, invitations were sent to all battle survivors, including notable Indians. The *Hardin Tribune* reported on June 23, 1916, that a crowd of approximately six to eight thousand people was expected to arrive on June 25 in the "greatest number of autos ever gathered together in one place in the state of Montana." Special trains ran from Billings and Sheridan to the battlefield. The principal speaker, Brigadier General Godfrey, and a small group of veterans followed Custer's route on horseback. They were met on the battlefield by Two Moon, a Cheyenne chief and veteran of the battle, and other Cheyenne representatives. A Crow band played Custer's battle song, "Garryowen."

Godfrey read from a speech prepared by Elizabeth Bacon Custer, who could never bring herself to visit the battlefield. He then remarked that he was glad to "meet and extend in peace the hand of friendship to a representative of the Indians." Godfrey also expressed the hope that Custer's sacrifice would motivate all who followed him to "defend the country we opened up for your occupancy." Col. Frank Hall, a self-proclaimed authority on American Indians, delivered a speech in which he expressed orthodox views of Custer and the Seventh Cavalry. He noted that the battle and the great sacrifices lived on among Americans and that the forty years since the battle "spanned the gulf between barbarism and civilization, paganism and Christianity." Custer was, of course, a mighty warrior, and "no more gallant soldier, nor more stainless knight, ever drew sword. . . . those who fell with him shared his courage and devotion as they shared his fate." Hall also gave the Indians their due, albeit grudgingly. "Call them savages if you will," he said, "but they were warriors, true leaders" and must be shown "respect, forbearance and patience," for they had been led to "ways of pleasantness." Such patriotic rhetoric continued to look approvingly on the power of Anglo-American civilization to transform wayward "savages" into the cultural progeny of that civilization.[11]

No major ceremonies took place between 1916 and 1921, when the themes of the fortieth anniversary were repeated. With fifteen thousand people in attendance, the most significant event that year was the unveiling of the Custer Monument in Hardin, about fifteen miles from the battlefield. Gov. Joseph Moore Dixon of Montana spoke of the great advances in civilization since the battle and the continued need for sacrifice. He asked that the flags that covered the statue be raised in "salute to the man of '76."[12]

The largest and most elaborate commemoration ever staged at the Little Bighorn took place on June 24–26, 1926, on the fiftieth anniversary of the battle. Don Rickey notes that "as much publicity as possible was disseminated concerning the event, old Indian Wars soldiers and warriors were contacted and invited to attend, and there [were] processions, parades, sports events, speeches, and the memorial ceremonies on Custer Ridge." Publicity brochures from the state of Montana and from the Chicago, Burlington and Quincy Railroad spread news of the celebration to potential tourists. A brochure from the Montana Department of Agriculture, Labor, and Industry, entitled *Carrying On for 50 Years with the Courage of Custer*, declared that the state owed its prosperity to Custer's sacrifice in an "age of savagery." As a reminder of the human face of such savagery, tourists were informed that "warlike Sioux and Cheyenne [will] have a part in the commemoration of the battle in which their people made a last and vicious stand," after which they were soon "herded back to their reservations." The battle, however, should not be seen as a "massacre," for "various representatives of the white race died fighting with weapons in their hands."[13]

Anniversary activities were planned by the National Custer Memorial Association headed by General Godfrey. The overall themes were the continued celebration of Custer and the Seventh Cavalry as creators and saviors and paternal pride with regard to the evolution of American Indians from a condition of savagery to grateful participation in Anglo-American civilization. An association brochure declared that the violent end of the Plains Indians was the Indians' fault, brought about by "hostile Sioux who could not recognize the benevolent attitude of the American government." They only knew that "they could not roam at will without respect to the rights and privileges of their white brother, and they revolted."[14]

Col. J. M. T. Partello recalled the spectacle of the fiftieth anniversary events. "Quite seventy thousand were gathered at the Crow Indian Agency, and beyond twenty thousand autos covered the surrounding hills. In addition heavily loaded trains poured in hourly bringing visitors, frontiersmen, scouts, cowboys, the Governors of the two states . . . and veterans from Indian wars from all over the U.S. Many Army officers were also present and the National Geographic Magazine, Pathé-News from Hollywood, and hundreds of private cameras made pictures of the different events. Fully ten thousand Indians were there. It was indeed a huge affair."[15]

On June 20, shortly before the onslaught of other participants and spectators, troops from the Seventh Cavalry at Fort Bliss, Texas, arrived for the ceremonies. Capt. George J. McMurry, chaplain of the Seventh Cavalry, wrote that "in the evening of the first day the strains of martial music wafted across the hills and echoed among the far-flung ravines as the sun slowly sank behind the Montana hills—for the first time in fifty years the Seventh was standing . . . in the shadow of Custer Ridge. It was a solemn, impressive moment, laden with profound emotions and vivid memories of the past."[16]

Formal ceremonies began on June 24. Aerial exhibitions by army and marine aviators were followed by a parade of cavalrymen and Indians. McMurry recalled that "at the close of the parade the Squadron staged a spectacular charge over a high, steep bank into and across the Little Big Horn River. . . . This was a thrilling scene with real action." The highlight of June 25 was a huge parade, described by McMurry in solemn terms:

> The Squadron, representing the five troops . . . which rode with Custer . . . proceeded up Custer Ridge from the south while the Sioux and Cheyenne warriors, garbed in their war regalia . . . approached from the north. The heads of the columns met at the Custer Monument and General Godfrey and White Bull exchanged peace signs and clasped hands in token of friendship. General Godfrey presented the Chief with a mounted flag and then White Bull reciprocated with a white Hudson Bay blanket. . . . [Troops fired three volleys, and then the] thousands who thronged the ridge uncovered and bowed their heads in silence as "Taps" echoed and re-echoed among those historic hills and ravines, hallowed by Custer and his heroic troopers.[17]

To symbolize the "friendship" between the Anglo-American and American Indian cultures, cavalry veterans and Indian warriors rode off the field in pairs, where "a half century ago, Sioux and Cheyenne on one side and United States troopers on the other . . . had met as deadly enemies." McMurry commented on the historic nature of the event, "a scene which will never again be enacted: it is with the ages now." The *Billings Gazette* noted that during the entire spectacle "not a speech was made, hardly a word spoken in the commemoration of the sacrifice made by the Seventh Cavalry . . . to clear the path for civilization." That night Gov. J. E. Erickson remarked that the Indians had slowly come, since that fateful day, to recognize the advantages of civilization and had proved their sincerity with gestures of peace offered during the ceremonies.[18]

On Saturday, June 26, the most significant event was the reburial of an unknown trooper under Reno's command; his remains had been found only a few weeks earlier during road construction west of the Little Bighorn River. Colonel Partello wrote that the remains were to be placed in a "granite sarcophagus with a crypt in the center to hold relics, newspapers, telegrams and various articles for the benefit of future generations. . . . Red Tomahawk then stepped forward, and with each of us on either side of the sarcophagus, the Indian held one end of the tomahawk, myself the other end, then both reached down, and plucked a small bunch of native grasses, and sprinkled it in the crypt, shook hands across the opening and thus symbolized by the burying of the hatchet, the end of all wars between the two races." Cavalry veterans then placed a marker at the Reno-Benteen battlesite, after which the Seventh Cavalry reenacted the retreat of Reno and his men from the valley and up the steep hills to their defensive positions.[19]

Following these events, several speeches reiterated traditional themes and clarified the nature of the "friendship" between the races that had been so carefully ritualized. Chief Red Hawk of the Sioux spoke of his desire to live in peace and hoped that the Indians' sacrifice in World War I had proved their patriotism, for "thousands of our young men fought, bled and died under the American flag, beside their white comrades." Lieutenant Godfrey responded by acknowledging wrongs inflicted on the Plains Indians but added that the battle was only a "temporary victory of the Red man's savagery" and that this "vengeance only hastened the doom that awaited." The inevitability of the triumph of Anglo-American civilization and the elevating impulses of that civilization softened the effects of such "doom," he declared. Furthermore, modern times had witnessed the "merging of both whites and reds into a common citizenship and everlasting peace." James Marquisee, chairman of the executive committee of the National Custer Memorial Association, reiterated these commemorative themes. According to Marquisee the field no longer echoed with the sounds of battle, for the Indians had "adopted a life with new rights and new opportunities which the relentless march of civilization demands that [they] assume."[20]

Ceremonies in 1936, the sixtieth anniversary of the battle, also were designed as Anglo-American celebrations of the God-given benefits white civilization had brought to American Indians. Ten thousand visitors witnessed parades similar to those of 1926 and heard Gov. Elmer Holt of Montana praise Custer and his men, now resting in "fame's eternal camping ground." Editors of the *Billings Gazette* spoke approvingly of the harmony between the races and remarked that all about them they saw nothing but "the homes of a contented and happy people." They also discerned a providential hand behind the Plains Indian wars: "While the white man's treatment of the Indian has not always been such as to win the admiration of those who believe in justice to all men, may it not be that there was back of all this strife and bloodshed some great plan that was to have its fulfillment in a day when the red, the black and the yellow, were to dwell together in peace, in a harmony such as we have today achieved?"[21]

The symbolic dominance of Custer in battlefield commemorations persisted into the post–World War II years. The seventy-fifth anniversary was celebrated on June 24–25, 1951, with Gen. Albert Wedermeyer as the guest speaker. The Hardin American Legion Post invited the Seventh Cavalry to attend, noting that the "wounds of Custer's time had healed in freedom, not the galling salt of Communism." Since the Seventh was fighting in Korea, Edward S. "Cap" Luce, the superintendent of Custer battlefield, read a letter from the regiment commander: "Since we are heavily engaged in destroying the Chinese Communist forces, we can but send you our best wishes [and assure you that the battle has been] well-fixed in the minds of each officer and man upon joining this regiment." Wedermeyer proceeded to characterize the battlefield at the Little Bighorn as a tribute not to war but to the spiritual strength that motivated sacrifice. He cited the importance of keeping faith with the "ghostly assemblage" present and suggested that the occasion was an appropriate one during which to examine one's commitment to God and country. Clearly, the sacrifice and moral victory of Custer and his men were designed to serve as an inspiration for a new generation. Custer's actions exemplified allegiance to American ideals and, as Gov. John Bonner noted, awakened American patriotism "when our fighting men are again being called upon to make supreme sacrifices."[22]

Ceremonial veneration of Custer was not limited to anniversary activities at the battlefield. Beginning in the 1890s, Memorial Day activities and reinterment ceremonies at the cemetery were regular occurrences. Monuments to Custer were erected at West Point and in his hometown of Monroe, Michigan. The dramatization of the Last Stand was the highlight of Buffalo Bill Cody's Wild West Show, which toured Great Britain in 1887. In 1976 a more intimate form of veneration took place when a man dressed as Custer rode a horse down Main Street to the city hall in New Britain, Connecticut, and read a proclamation honoring the courage of the Seventh Cavalry. Similar acts of folk reverence are recorded in small-town newspapers and long since forgotten brochures, each event bearing witness to the power of the Custer myth.[23]

Battle reenactment during commemorative occasions was another form of veneration of Custer and the Seventh Cavalry. Although reenactments were allowed to take place on the battlefield while it was under the guardianship of the War Department—the last, major reenactment occurring in 1936—once the National Park Service assumed responsibility for the field in 1940 reenactments were discontinued for fear that they would permanently scar the battlegrounds. However, fascination with the battle led some people to persist in their attempts to re-create the drama of the Last Stand. In the late 1950s Bruce Hanson, a producer of historical pageants, informed the Park Service of his interest in such a reenactment. The NPS historian at the battlefield, Don Rickey, wrote to the regional director that he was "anxious to learn of [Hanson's] plans so that we can reduce the possibility of the proposal becoming a reality on Monument lands." In 1959 Stanley Thomas of Aberdeen, South Dakota, requested NPS assistance to put on a pageant, which would include a reenactment of the Last Stand, with the Sioux of the Standing Rock Agency. This plan attracted the attention of the regional director of the NPS, who informed Rickey to "steer [the] group away from any idea of a production at the Monument." It would be better, he thought, if the reenactment took place on the reservation, since that would minimize "the more agonizing episodes involving conflicts with the whites."[24]

As Montana approached its territorial centennial in 1964, further attempts were made to secure permission for a battle reenactment. However, the Park Service remained adamant in its refusal to allow any reenactments on the field. In 1963 the director of the NPS wrote of the "very substantial cultural advances that have been made by the descendants of the Indians involved in the original fight. . . . We believe that staging the battle would be in bad taste." Although the NPS was successful in thwarting attempts to have reenactments on the field itself, in 1964 a popular reenactment was presented by members of the Crow tribe, supported by local interests in the nearby town of Hardin. The reenactment, which was staged for the next ten years to coincide with the annual Crow Fair, a major tourist attraction, was praised for bringing Native Americans and whites together.

This particular pageant was significant because it claimed to tell the story of the Little Bighorn from the Native Americans' point of view. The script was written by Joe Medicine Crow, who, after earning a master's degree in anthropology at the University of California at Berkeley, returned to work for the Bureau of Indian Affairs in Crow Agency. His grandfather had been a scout for Brig. Gen. George Crook; his step-grandfather had been a scout for Custer. Joe Medicine Crow had heard a version of the battle story from Brave Bear, a Cheyenne participant. The pageant dramatized the westward movement of white civilization, beginning with the explorations of Lewis and Clark. It then showed how increasing danger to the Indian way of life and numerous broken treaties led inexorably to the climactic Sun Dance of Sitting Bull and the battle of the Little Bighorn. Custer does not appear as a great hero, nor as a villain. According to Joe Medicine Crow, "I didn't do anything to Custer to offend his followers. I just left him out, and we played Sitting Bull as the big star." Still, the power of the Custer myth pervaded even this pageant, for at one point the narrator said, "Many of us of the Crow tribe will mourn for him. . . . Many of us thought of him as a great man—a mighty genius."[25]

When I spoke with him in 1980 Joe Medicine Crow was convinced that he had managed to tell the battle story "objectively." "It worked," he said. "Nobody was offended." However, the pageant made no demands on tourists to alter traditional perceptions of Custer or the battle. Native Americans appeared as they so often had in portions of patriotic rhetoric: as tragic figures swept up in the inevitable push of history. While they were not portrayed as savages, their story was only preparatory for the climax—the Last Stand at the Little Bighorn. Tourists could leave with their conceptions of Custer and the Indians of yesteryear intact, buttressed by the final reflections of the narrator, who suggested that the blood of the participants shed on that day was responsible for the current strength of the nation: "We live in a United Fortress of Democracy . . . the United States of America." The pageant concluded with the national anthem.

Except for Joe Medicine Crow's production, the elaborate celebrations at the Little Bighorn dramatized traditional perceptions of Custer and the battle. The Last Stand was portrayed as the pivotal battle between barbarism and civilization, and patriotic rhetoric celebrated the opening of the Anglo-American West as the most tangible outcome of the battle. Anniversary events provided participants and spectators with a chance to rededicate themselves to the God-given virtues and ideals for which Custer had died. The fact that Anglo-American civilization had blossomed since the Last Stand proved that God was indeed pleased with the American experiment and made Custer's sacrifice even more worthy of commemoration.

As whites celebrated their own good fortune in anniversary events, the ceremonies at the battlefield also defined their perception of the "evolution" of Native Americans since Custer's time. Rhetoric offered token praise to the skilled but barbaric enemy who had been guilty of a general and undefined "savagery." Luckily for the Indians, however, a benevolent United States government had sternly reprimanded them for their violent outbursts and they were brought slowly to "ways of pleasantness" by the power of Anglo-American ideals, even inspiring some of them to make the

This Otto Becker lithograph was based on *Custer's Last Fight* (1895) by Cassilly Adams, the most famous of the hundreds of paintings of the Last Stand. (National Park Service)

In 1877 horse bones still littered the field and wooden stakes marked temporary graves of members of the Seventh Cavalry who had died in the battle. (National Park Service)

The 1879 log memorial to Custer. (National Park Service)

The Custer Monument in 1886, on the occasion of the tenth anniversary of the battle. (National Park Service)

American Indians and cavalry veterans of the Plains Indian wars ride in pairs to symbolize racial harmony, June 25, 1926. (National Park Service)

The cover of a Burlington Route brochure advertising special rates for train travel "from Billings and Sheridan to Crow Agency—the latter being within easy walking distance of the battlefield." (Burlington Northern)

One of Leonard Baskin's controversial drawings of Custer. Baskin said that he was fascinated by Custer's "sense of posturing, his sense of dressing up . . . and by his incredible mania about himself" ("A Haunting New Vision of the Little Big Horn," *American Heritage* [June 1970]: 102). (National Park Service)

This Leonard Baskin drawing of a nude, dead Custer was pulled from the first edition of an NPS battlefield handbook, due in part to objections expressed by members of the Custer Battlefield Historical & Museum Association, but was restored to later editions. (National Park Service)

ultimate sacrifice for the nation in World War I, World War II, the Korean War, and the Vietnam conflict. Yet, as whites celebrated "harmony" between the races, they failed to appreciate the difference between the enervating effects of military defeat and passivity in the face of a dominant culture and the cultural pluralism and distribution of power that is a requirement for truly equitable social relations between different races. What patriotic rhetoric called harmony, Native Americans called grudging accommodation.

Native Americans became less accommodating in 1976, the centennial year of the battle of the Little Bighorn, when the American Indian Movement (AIM) challenged the symbolic dominance of George Armstrong Custer. At a time when critical examination of the dark side of America's past was underway, when Native American voices were no longer mere accessories to the celebration of Anglo-American patriotic orthodoxies, an unprecedented assault was launched against the Custer myth.

Like any controversial historical figure, the popularity of Custer had waxed and waned since 1876. What had never been publicly proclaimed at the battlefield, however, was the notion that Custer and the battle were symptomatic of a disease within the nation itself. Such a heretical interpretation suggested that the opening of the Anglo-American West was not simply a triumphant story but might symbolize an exterminationist impulse that had permeated the American frontier with regard to people of color. In the 1970s Custer became symbolic of white racism and genocidal expansionism. During this period Robert Utley, an NPS assistant director, noted that "on bumper stickers and lapel buttons . . . Custer reproaches white America for four centuries of oppression." The centennial commemoration at the Little Bighorn became a singular opportunity for Native Americans to intentionally dramatize their dissatisfaction with the current situation. Hence, as Brian Dippie points out, as a "symbolic rallying point for modern Indian dissent, Custer is not just useful, but essential." After the occupation of Alcatraz and the drama of Native American protest at Wounded Knee, South Dakota, the confluence of the centennial of the battle at the Little Bighorn and the nation's bicentennial offered a perfect opportunity for Native Americans to dramatize the sins of Anglo-American culture by focusing on the infamy of one of the nation's great martial heroes.[26]

By 1976 the National Park Service was painfully aware of the fact that it was managing what many perceived to be an ill-advised shrine to Custer. It was equally aware that disruption at the centennial services was a real possibility. Planning for the ceremonies began in 1969, with NPS personnel at the battlefield proposing numerous events: a reenactment of Custer's march from Fort Lincoln to the battlefield; a living-history encampment of cavalry groups; commemorative postage stamps, coins, and firearms; and special invitations to descendants of Seventh Cavalry and Indian participants in the battle.

In 1972, as concern over potential centennial protest grew, a member of Pres. Richard M. Nixon's staff warned the NPS that the "consequences of an unsophisticated treatment of that occasion could be portentous." Now would be "an unusually good time to recapitulate the whole new direction in Indian policy since 1876 . . . and 1970." In response, Raymond Freeman, an acting associate director of the Park Service, declared that the centennial commemoration "must not emphasize the Indian-whiteman conflict that existed in 1876 *and still exists today* [emphasis added]." He suggested discretion to assure that the battle be seen as a "historical event, rather than a racial conflict." The director of the Big Horn County Centennial Committee suggested to the superintendent at the battlefield that a "peace" or "religious" theme, along with festivals including arts and crafts programs, would be "absolutely noncontroversial." In 1974 centennial objectives emphasized better interpretive programs, including a "parade of history," bus tours of the battlefield, various commemorative items, and emphasis on the need for preservation of the site. Some found these plans unsatisfactory because no battle reenactment was planned, although many feared violence if this were to take place.[27]

Much of the correspondence of the time reveals the naive belief that the National Park Service could carry out interpretation at the Custer Battlefield in a neutral manner. The very concern over the delicacy of the centennial program makes it clear, however, that *no* national symbol, especially the potent symbol of Custer, evokes neutral responses. The Park Service's stated goal in opening the Custer symbol to diverse interpretations was sometimes "objectivity" and neutrality—in other words, practicing good and dispassionate descriptive history—and sometimes balance—that is, telling both sides of the story. Proponents of the latter approach at least recognized that there were not only "cultures in conflict" at the Little Bighorn but cultural memories in conflict, struggling to protect, revise, or overturn patriotic orthodoxy.

The centennial approached amid dire warnings of bloodshed. Recalling the events at Wounded Knee in 1973, Paul Swearingen of the National Bicentennial Committee advised against a helicopter flyover to honor Custer, because it might be a dangerous tribute. "The facts still aren't in," he warned, "about the helicopter the FBI lost on the Pine Ridge." From May 1976 through the anniversary an FBI Regional Special Events Team carefully monitored all movement in the area (especially activities of Native American political figures). Consequently, a siege mentality took over as the centennial approached. The official services were shifted to June 24 to discourage large crowds. Speeches were given by the park superintendent, Richard T. Hart, and by Robert Utley. Roughly eight hundred people attended—a far cry from the thousands once expected—including Custer's grandnephew, Col. George A. Custer III.[28]

In his desperate attempt to find language that would satisfy Custerphiles, Custerphobes, and all those in between, Superintendent Hart declared that the commemoration honored all those who died in the battle. He argued that the existence of the Custer Battlefield National Monument was not designed to be divisive but to help members of both races "grope together . . . in our own separate ways, for a better common future." Such tortured rhetoric certainly could not function effectively as a language of reconciliation. Utley, who began his long and distinguished career in the National Park Service as a summer employee (1947–52) at the Custer battlefield, delivered a thoughtful speech, pointing out the shifting public images of the cavalry and of Native Americans since 1876. He called for members of both cultures to liberate themselves from archaic stereotypes and recognize that the battle was a "vivid feature of a long and tragic episode in our country's history, one whose consequences to the victims require public recognition and redress." Utley asked that the battle and the participants be viewed in their own terms and not be used "artificially to serve contemporary needs and ends, however laudable."[29]

Of course, for a century patriotic orthodoxy at the battlefield had done precisely that: it had helped shape a culturally constructed—hence, an "artificial"—interpretation of the battle. A century of commemorative activity not only borrowed from but nurtured the dominant Anglo-American ideology that had defined the nature of Custer and his men, the nature of their opponents, and the meaning of the battle. In fact, commemorations had *always* been used to serve contemporary needs and ends. In 1976, however, traditional needs and ends were being challenged to symbolic combat by those who formerly played a useful, but powerless, role in the commemorations. Utley's caution about twisting history for political purposes certainly meant little to protestors who saw this as *their* opportunity to overturn symbolic domination by winning the symbolic battle of the Little Bighorn.

During the centennial ceremonies 100 Sioux held their own services around the memorial, singing "Custer Died for Your Sins" while carrying the American flag upside down. AIM spokesman Russell Means, who has consistently expressed a visceral hatred of Custer, said that such an act was not meant as a sign of disrespect but rather as an "international signal of distress, because the red man of the Western Hemisphere is in distress." On June 25 the Sioux held a sunrise ceremony at the monument and spoke bitterly about the civilization for which Custer had died. Virgil Kills Straight said that in the "supposedly enlightened age of civilization our people are still being hunted, herded and killed under circumstances that challenge all laws." Many speakers suggested that times had not really changed. Means declared, "Custer came in and invaded us over gold. Today we have a much more sophisticated invasion by the corporate giants of America over mineral wealth, but this time it is for coal." He directly attacked the heart of patriotic orthodoxy, claiming that the battle was not part of a heroic saga and that for a century white Americans had been celebrating an act of genocide. Means scoffed at the very *idea* of a Custer monument. Reminding Americans of more recent atrocities against people of color, he declared, "I can't imagine a Lt. Calley National Monument in Vietnam."[30]

Native Americans not only attacked the symbol of Custer at its source but planned their own ceremonies that were designed to celebrate a different reading of the battle. A brochure for the Lakota Treaty Council announced that on June 22–25, 1976, a "spiritual gathering will pay homage to our forefathers who fell a hundred years ago defending a way of life . . . which is being defended on many fronts today." The invitation asked Native Americans to come and "stand in unity to prove to the world that we have survived 200 years of genocidal policies." The ceremonies were held at the nearby ranch of Austin Two Moons, a descendant of a Cheyenne warrior who fought in the battle. The *Billings Gazette* reported that the four-day event included "a victory dance, speeches, and feasting." The tepees of descendants of warriors who had fought against Custer were arranged in a semicircle, and each tepee had "its own flag at half-mast in honor of Cheyennes who died in all wars."[31]

The various official and Native American ceremonies ended with no outbreaks of physical violence, although the assault on the sacred symbol of Custer and the battle did bring forth a vehement counterattack from guardians of the patriotic faith. Many of those displeased with the nature of the centennial events were members of the Little Big Horn Associates (LBHA), a group founded in 1966 by Robert J. Edge of Great Falls, Montana. Edge had proposed to friends that they begin a monthly newsletter that would "air . . . views, seek information and volunteer information to other serious historians of General George A. Custer, the 7th United States Regiment of Cavalry and the Battle of the Little Big Horn." By May 1967 the LBHA counted 136 members; the first newsletter was sent out in 1968. For at least some of the members, however, veneration and guardianship of the Custer myth and the sacred site were more important than dispassionate historical investigation.[32]

The immediate object of their wrath was the Park Service, which they accused of appeasing a special interest group at the expense of the integrity of the centennial ceremonies. Michael Koury, an LBHA member and editor of the Old Army Press, wrote to the NPS that the "vast majority" of Americans were deprived of the same kind of traditional commemoration that took place at Lexington, Concord, and Bunker Hill because of "pandering . . . to [a] pressure group." He went on to detail the complicity of the Park Service in the sabotage: no Crow battle reenactment; no reride of Custer's route by living-history buffs; no invitation extended to the Seventh Cavalry; and no invitation to Custer's grandnephew, who attended unofficially, had no part in the program, and was not even given a reserved seat. Koury concluded, "It is a sad state of affairs when the parties responsible for the wanton destruction at Wounded Knee are provided a platform, and a man who served his country in its armed forces is ignored and insulted."[33]

For many, such shabby treatment of Custer's relative was especially galling and was indicative of cowardice within the Park Service. Bryce Nelson of the *Los Angeles Times* highlighted this particular issue in his report on the centennial. Custer's relative, he wrote, was "given no chance to tell his family's side of the story. . . . Instead he took his own floral wreath to the burial monument." Colonel Custer himself expressed hurt and anger. "It has been an awkward day for the Custer family," he said. "Twenty-five years ago my father and mother were invited to stay with the monument superintendent. Now, I'm not even allowed to participate." A Vietnam veteran, Custer argued that anger should not be aimed at the Seventh Cavalry or at American troops who had served in Vietnam: "The American public does not understand that the military is merely the instrument of government policy. They blame the military for Vietnam and the Army for what happened with the Indians."[34]

Numerous letters to the National Park Service expressed similar complaints and asked similar questions: Why was the ceremony so "Indian oriented?" Why should the government "at this day and age . . . have a guilt complex about this event in American history?" LBHA member John Carroll, publisher and editor of numerous books about Custer and the battle and one of the leading collectors of Custeriana, informed the director of the Park Service that "Custer would not have tolerated that kind of blackmail, nor would he have tolerated the use and abuse of the American flag." A woman from Banning, California, declared that "sinister powers" were at the root of the attack on the gallant "Indian fighters," and she urged the Park Service to "stand firm." Another letter writer argued that Custer's transformation from hero to scapegoat was the "price military men have had to pay for doing what they thought was their patriotic duty."[35]

Newspaper editorials joined in the chorus of complaints about the centennial. The *Los Angeles Times* remarked that while condemnation of Custer was evident, "the Custer viewpoint and that of the U.S. Army were not expressed." The *Hardin Tribune* called critics of Custer hypocritical because they judged him from the modern luxury that was "the fruit of the sacrifices of men . . . who died . . . on the banks of the Little Big Horn." The Park Service's response to the varied criticism was regret over the expressed displeasure, "respect" for critical comments, and "high praise" for the battlefield staff for "their handling of a volatile and potentially dangerous situation."[36]

Guardians of the patriotic faith were troubled by more than the centennial protests, which they believed provided one more piece of evidence that the NPS had joined in the attempt to revise radically the orthodox interpretation of Custer and the battle. The centennial year's activities also engendered a new controversy, centered on the Park Service's placement on an outside wall of the visitors center a quotation from the Sioux medicine man Black Elk: "Know the Power That Is Peace." A youngster at the time of the battle, Black Elk reportedly had killed a wounded trooper, and some Custerphiles accused him of participating in the mutilation of the dead. The resulting attack against the NPS was led by John Carroll, who sought to have Park Service employees whom he considered unfaithful to the patriotic orthodoxies removed from administrative positions at the battlefield.

Another issue the centennial controversies brought to the surface had simmered since at least the early 1970s, namely, the question of whether to change the name of the battlefield. The possibility of a name change first arose as the Park Service continued to explore ways to open the symbol of the Custer battlefield to diverse interpretations. In 1971 William L. Harris, the battlefield superintendent, reminded his superiors that Pres. Grover Cleveland had named the cemetery the National Cemetery of Custer's Battlefield Reservation and that name had, unfortunately, aided in what Harris believed was an inappropriate fixation on Custer. Harris was uncomfortable with the current name—Custer Battlefield National Monument—and proposed a change to the Little Big Horn National Battlefield to "demonstrate that the National Park Service, the Federal Government, and the American public recognize both sides of the issue equally. The site commemorates the event[;] the name of the area should reflect that attitude." Harris further noted that the battlefield should be a place of pride for Native Americans, but currently it was only "another example of [the] white man's oppression of their culture and heritage." Changing the name, he felt, would "give the Indian equal billing with the military and might help to overcome any initial negative feeling he may have regarding the general purpose of the site."[37]

David A. Clary, an NPS staff historian, agreed with Harris and recommended that the name be changed, for "neutrality would demonstrate to all that the park exists to tell the story of a battle—and not just of one individual at the expense of others with equally important stories to tell." Clary also mentioned that the fixation on Custer and his tactics had resulted in neglect of the "manner in which the Indians took control of the situation, seized the initiative from their opponents, and thereafter molded the course of the battle"—a strategy that was "exemplary," he said, of the "best that Napoleon could have wished in a general." Robert Utley, at that time acting director of the NPS's Office of Archaeology and Historic Preservation, commented that Harris had made a "convincing case." The idea lived on in the battlefield's *Statement for Management* in 1975, which declared that "consideration should be given to a name change such as 'Little Big Horn National Battlefield.'" In that same year, however, Utley expressed misgivings to the NPS's Rocky Mountain regional director, warning that history reveals "few undertakings are more perilous than tampering with established nomenclature." Utley's words were prophetic, as the proposal generated fierce opposition in 1976.[38]

The LBHA asked its members to vote on the desirability of a name change and then informed the Park Service of the overwhelmingly negative response. Several members wrote personal letters to make sure the message was clearly received. W. Donald Horn, a New Jersey restaurateur and former president of the LBHA, remarked that such ill-advised action would "pacify a few misguided people who think that by eliminating the Custer name from the battlefield it will change the actual course of past events." John Carroll wrote that this idea was a "kind of historical revisionism which is more common in the Soviet Union than in the United States of America." The Park Service responded that it would accept the parallel with Soviet revisionism "only if the name change were to be accompanied by a deliberate effort to suppress or otherwise misrepresent Custer's role." A resident of Toluca Lake, California, objected to the change and wondered if Gettysburg would then become the "NAACP Memorial Park"? Another opponent perceived the threatened name change as part of the nation's regrettable infatuation with the undermining of national heroes. "A noisy minority," he wrote, was trying to dictate its wishes to a weak-willed government, but the NPS should not capitulate to "trendy, left-wing, guilt-ridden reverse racism."[39]

After the centennial, no serious discussions about the name change occurred until 1987. In June of that year Jerry L. Russell, the self-appointed national chairman of the Order of the Indian Wars, wrote to William Penn Mott, Jr., director of the NPS, about the Park Service's current plan to rename the site the Custer National Battlefield (as part of a plan to standardize NPS battlefield names throughout the country). Russell argued that if the battlefield were going to be named for anyone, it should be named for Sitting Bull, because it "goes against the grain of historical accuracy to name any battlefield for the losing commander." Because the "continuation of the tradition of glorifying Custer even in his loss is obviously offensive to large numbers of Native Americans who view Custer as the symbol of their perceived mistreatment by the U.S. Government," and because most battlefields are named "for their location," he believed that " 'Little Bighorn (or Bighorn) National Battlefield' would be a much more appropriate designation." Mott responded on July 7, 1987, that he personally agreed with Russell's ideas but did not wish to jeopardize the bill currently before Congress to designate all battlefields as national battlefields. "The removal of 'Custer' from the title would surely engender controversy," Mott declared, "perhaps enough controversy to jeopardize the entire bill."[40]

In a similar vein, Robert L. Hart, deputy director of the Lincoln County Heritage Trust, informed Mott that the proposed name change "[did] not go far enough" and that the fixation on Custer was inappropriate. While "emotional arguments are made for retaining the Custer designation," he declared, "ultimately they refuse to accord the American Indian the due that Confederate 'enemies' earned on many a field of battle." Edwin C. Bearss, the NPS chief historian, responded to Hart's letter. Bearss noted the sensitive political climate surrounding the proposed legislation and expressed hope that Hart and others "of like opinion will wait for a later opportunity when the Montana battlefield can be addressed by itself." Bearss added, "We in the History Division are somewhat ambivalent about the merits of 'Little Big Horn' in lieu of 'Custer.' " Although it made sense "rationally," he wrote, "so much of the public fascination with the battle has stemmed from its association with the colorful, controversial character of Custer. . . . there is something to be said for retaining his name in the site's title. If there is any battlefield that deserves to be personalized in this fashion, this is surely the one."[41]

The struggle over the proper name for the battlefield was an important ongoing battle in the war for symbolic dominance at the Little Bighorn. For those who did not perceive the place as a shrine to Custer, and who believed that the unfortunate fixation on him for the past century had contributed to continuing tension between cultures, the name change symbolized the beginning of the end of the age of Anglo-American dominance of the battlefield. For patriotic guardians, the attempt to change the name was one further example of the weakening of nurturing and sustaining American traditions, another in a series of perhaps irreparable blows to the cultural heroes of the nation.

Guardians of the patriotic faith also perceived the Black Elk quote on the visitors center as a form of pollution of the sacred ground. In a letter to the National Park Service in August 1976, John Carroll complained about the centennial services but objected especially to the quote. While he certainly did not condemn the sentiment expressed, Carroll noted the absence of a quote by General Custer on the exterior wall of the center. He also remarked that Black Elk did not put into practice his own words when he "killed and scalped a trooper." Consequently, the "very existence of the quote is a silent and subtle insult to the many 7th Cavalry heroes who died that day." If Black Elk were to be honored, Carroll thought, that honor should consist of an "appropriate tribute on Sioux reservation land," or perhaps the Crow could donate some of their land near the battlefield for a monument. In a March 1977 letter to Pres. Jimmy Carter, Carroll declared that the existence of the Black Elk quote was "much like awakening one morning to find a quote by Tojo at Pearl Harbor National Cemetery [*sic*]."[42]

The park superintendent, James V. Court, responded to the attacks by Carroll and the LBHA in March 1983, arguing that "to many Americans [Black Elk's statement] is probably an apt phrase to decry the brutality of war." He also offered a rebuttal to those LBHA members who said that there was no place in a military cemetery for comments from the "enemy": "Finally, lest it escape everyone, the so-called enemy was protecting their own right to live on their land in a manner of their own choosing. It was the United States Government who chose to make war and relocate the Indians to 'Reservations.' " By 1985 Court appeared to be fed up with the controversy and told the LBHA that after the new restrooms at the visitors center were finished "the saying will come down . . . and not be replaced."[43] His statement notwithstanding, the quote remains.

For John Carroll, a most formidable guardian of the patriotic faith, the complicity of the Park Service in the symbolic desecration of the Custer Battlefield could not be tolerated. When Court, who became the park superintendent in 1978, took the trouble to attend the LBHA's annual meeting in 1979, Carroll wrote the second of two complimentary letters to the director of the Park Service: "Jim has done an outstanding job at the battlefield. . . . It has given me great pleasure to write this letter for in 1976 I thought I would never go back there again, much less write such a letter as this. Jim also knows to expect much cooperation from me as long as it benefits the Custer battlefield." By 1981, however, Carroll was complaining to Rep. John Seiberling of Ohio about several issues, including the failure of the NPS to erect a marker to Isaiah Dorman, the only black who served with Custer; the failure of the NPS to honor the Indian scouts with a memorial; and what Carroll considered to be the "arbitrary" nature of the book selection process at the battlefield, a process he felt symbolized the "anti-Custer" bias of the staff.[44]

Carroll was sufficiently distressed over the issue of book selection to call for removal of the park superintendent and the park historian, Neil Mangum, as well as the establishment of a "democratic" system of book selection and a watchdog committee to oversee park operations and policy decisions. He also asked for congressional investigation of his many charges. In April 1983 the deputy director of the National Park Service wrote to G. Ray Arnett, assistant secretary of the Department of Fish and Wildlife and Parks, that "several investigations and reports have been prompted by Mr. Carroll's letters and allegations. These have included a field investigation by WASO staff [Washington NPS staff], a Congressional inquiry by the Subcommittee on Public Lands and National Parks, [and] several consultations with the Solicitor's Office." However, "not one investigation has produced evidence of wrong-doing or mismanagement by the NPS at Custer Battlefield."[45]

On June 28, 1983, Arnett traveled to the battlefield for a meeting with Carroll and the park staff. Edwin Bearss reported to the NPS's associate director for cultural resources in August 1983 that all parties had agreed that interpretation should be "balanced and non-partisan," that "inconsistencies" in museum collection policies would be resolved, and that a new review board for publications would be established. The LBHA also reported to its members that Court had promised "to eliminate any anti-Custer bias displayed by his . . . employees during their oral presentation." These pronouncements did little to satisfy some LBHA members, including W. Donald Horn, who wrote, "It is my opinion that a book favorable to . . . Custer cannot pass the book review committee." Others, like Michael Koury, were disturbed by the widely publicized controversy. Koury wrote to the LBHA Board of Directors that, just as he had opposed the Park Service's "catering" to AIM in 1976, he was now troubled by a group "no less biased, vocal, nor it appears, less unreasonable," adding, "We are that group." He went so far as to state emphatically that the LBHA "never required, nor intended" its members to "worship" George Armstrong Custer.[46]

The guardians of patriotic faith were certainly correct in their perception that the National Park Service was trying to undo the symbolic dominance of Custer and allow the story of the battle of the Little Bighorn to be told in other ways. When the cemetery was established in 1886 its function was clear. Executive Order 337443, issued by Pres. Grover Cleveland on December 7, 1886, stated that the cemetery existed to "commemorate this engagement and perpetuate the memory of those gallant men who fought valiantly against tremendous odds." Early visitors to the cemetery often employed guides from nearby Fort Custer to take them on tours of the battlefield. In 1893 a superintendent began living at the cemetery and occasionally offered guide service. But Fort Custer was abandoned in 1897, and by the time the Park Service began to administer the battlefield in 1940, the only guides available, according to a former park historian, were "local youths, generally incompetent and misinformed." In his administrative history of the battlefield, Don Rickey also notes that from 1941 to 1943 Crow tribesman Max Big Man established a museum just outside the entrance to the battlefield. "From this log shack . . . Indian relics and souvenirs were sold to tourists and a garbled history of the Battle was 'explained' to visitors."[47]

There was no systematic, official interpretation of the battle during the War Department's administration of the cemetery from 1879 until 1940. Interestingly, however, early army brochures that describe the cemetery not only celebrate the traditional orthodoxies but provide several phrases that the Park Service used many years later in its attempt to redefine the Custer battlefield. For example, a 1937 brochure speaks of the cemetery as a place where people might "visualize the tremendous struggle and the odds against which the brave Custer and his men fought until death." In 1943 and 1944 brochures added more sober commentary, informing readers that the battle was a "reminder of that long struggle, more than three centuries in duration, between the whites and the Indians for possession of the American continent." The battle represented the last armed resistance to the "everthreatening, never-ceasing, westward march of white man's civilization." Similar themes were used by "Cap" Luce, who had served with the Seventh Cavalry and became the first NPS superintendent of the battlefield in 1941. In his talks on the battlefield to local groups and in the handbook he wrote for the Park Service, Luce spoke of the "long struggle" and characterized the battle as one instance of the "warfare that marred our relations with Indians who took up arms in defense of their land and nomadic free way of life. It also memorializes Custer and his men as symbols of that traditional devotion to duty and love of country which govern all actions of the United States Army." Under Luce's superintendency the Little Bighorn became an NPS shrine to Custer and the Seventh Cavalry.[48]

Luce understood the heroism of the Seventh Cavalry at the Little Bighorn to be enduring, even inspiring the unit in World War II. "It would seem," he wrote,

> that Custer Battlefield, instead of living on its past glorious history, has a continuity which we must perpetuate. There is hardly a week that passes but what we have questions asked by visitors, such as "where is the Seventh Cavalry now, and [in] what part of World War Two has the regiment been engaged." To this, we are pleased to remark that the heritage handed to the regiment . . . has been the

motivating force that has made it the most famous regiment in the United States Army. That the Seventh Cavalry earned the distinction of being the one single unit which saw the most combat service in the South Pacific theatre of war. . . . It was for this combat service that General MacArthur designated the Seventh Cavalry to be his Guard of Honor at the time of his entrance into Tokyo on September 6, 1945.[49]

The first NPS park superintendent also oversaw the realization of one of Elizabeth Bacon Custer's wishes, the construction of a museum on the battlefield. The effort began in 1923 when Sen. Thomas Walsh of Montana introduced a bill into Congress calling for "an office for the custodian and for the convenience and comfort of the public." But Custer's widow wanted more than this. In a 1924 letter to Montana newspaperman David Hilger, she declared, "I have had in mind some sort of a memorial hall on the Battlefield of the Little Bighorn to commemorate the frontiersmen as well as our soldiers." Mrs. Custer enlisted the help of Maj. Gen. Nelson A. Miles, who wrote to various congressmen that "a commodious Memorial Building that would store the trophies and shelter the thousands of friends who visit the grounds is much needed and would be a fitting tribute from our people and government, to the heroes who have given their lives to the welfare of both." Undaunted by her failure to bring this about in her lifetime, Mrs. Custer stipulated in her Will that the government could take possession of the considerable collection of her husband's belongings only when a museum was built. While the necessary legislation passed Congress in 1939, funds for building the museum were not provided until 1951. The museum was finally dedicated on the seventy-sixth anniversary of the battle, in 1952. According to the enabling legislation, the museum was intended as a "memorial to Lieutenant Colonel George A. Custer and the officers and soldiers under his command at the Battle of the Little Big Horn River." A diorama of the final moments of the Last Stand serves to symbolize the continued dominance of Custer in the early years of NPS administration. As one visitor described it, "Custer stands in the foreground beside his battle flag and within a rough semi-circle of dead horses." The museum also contained exhibits about Native Americans: "The Hostile Indians," "Indian Warriors," "Indian Medicine," "The Crow Indians," and "Warriors Who Fought Custer."[50]

Custer's dominance in the interpretive programs of the Park Service in this early period did not go unnoticed. In his visit to the battlefield in 1956, Roy E. Appleman, an NPS staff historian, called attention to museum exhibits that portrayed an "extremely unbalanced story of the events." In his opinion they contained "many inaccurate statements of fact" and paid little attention to the full scope of the battle. There was, he concluded, "far too

much space given in the museum to the personal history of . . . Custer."
Appleman recommended, among other things, that the exhibit containing
Capt. Miles Keogh's famous horse, Comanche, the only cavalry "survivor"
of the battle, presently stuffed and on display at the University of Kansas,
be moved to the battlefield museum. "I can think of no single exhibit that
would excite and retain the public interest at Custer Battlefield as much as
the display of this animal," he declared.[51]

Custer dominated the Park Service's early interpretive literature as well.
A 1956 battlefield brochure characterizes the battle as Indian "resistance"
to the "westward march of civilization." The army is praised for its crucial
role in conquering the frontier, while Custer is described as a "daring and
gallant Indian fighter." Robert Utley has accurately summarized the enduring themes of this early interpretation at the Little Bighorn. The site,
he says, was "handled as a battlefield where an American Army fought";
and the interpreters were the "lineal descendants of Errol Flynn."[52]

Although the National Park Service did not begin in earnest to bring
an end to the dominance of Custer at the battlefield until the early 1970s,
by 1967 it was clear that the process of redefinition was underway. For
example, battlefield brochures returned to some of the more sober themes
that had appeared in cemetery pamphlets of the 1940s. They spoke not of
the glory of Custer's heroic sacrifice but of the "long struggle for possession
of the continent." By 1973 the statement praising the army had been de-
leted; in its place more recent brochures present a small section entitled
"Conflict of Cultures." Appearing at the beginning of each brochure is a
statement that the battlefield memorializes not Custer but "one of the last
armed efforts of the Northern Plains Indians to preserve their ancestral
way of life."[53]

In the 1969 NPS historical handbook Custer shares photographic space
with important American Indian figures in the battle. This attempt to balance the account was not free of controversy, however, thanks to the enduring heroic perceptions of Custer. Among Leonard Baskin's drawings,
which were intended to convey "mortality, brutality, and futility," was an
unheroic, controversial drawing of a dead, nude George Armstrong Custer.
Utley and some members of the Custer Battlefield Historical & Museum
Association (CBHMA), sponsors of the handbook, judged the drawing to
be unsuitable and had it removed; hence, the original edition contains a
blank page, a silent tribute to the enduring symbolic domination of the
heroic figure of Custer.[54]

The Park Service's management plans have also reflected the struggle
to redefine the interpretive mission at the battlefield. Proposed revisions
of the master plan in 1949, for example, used "Cap" Luce's language to
talk about Custer and his men as "symbols of . . . traditional devotion to

duty and love of country" and the battle as a step in the "ultimate solution of the Indian problem." The purpose of interpretation during this period was therefore to tell the "story of the westward advance of our settlements." By the early 1970s this patriotic orthodoxy was completely overturned. Most interesting is a preliminary draft of an early 1970s master plan that pointed to the approach of the centennial as a propitious time for the "nation [to be] reminded that the Indian question is yet unresolved. Once again the battle can be a leading banner in the appeal for a re-examination of our relationship to Red America." The plan offered provocative suggestions: that interpretation at the battlefield begin with a program on the Custer myth; and that the focus of *all* programs be the "clash of cultures." Under this plan battlefield tours would begin near the site of Major Reno's attack on the Indian village, not at the climax of the battle on Custer Hill. In recognition of the need to appreciate the battle through Native American eyes, it was also suggested that visitors walk the field of the Indian village, where they would see a newly constructed "historical encampment site"; and tourists would be encouraged to visit Indian reservations. Park rangers would also read Native American interpretations of the battle. *All* programs, the plan stated, should address three basic questions: What became of the Plains Indians? What did the nation gain in the Plains Indian wars? Can violence in cultural conflicts be avoided? These programs were, of course, dependent on the Park Service's willingness and ability to purchase privately owned land on which the Indian village stood.[55]

In January 1973 David Clary, an NPS staff historian, responded to the latest plan, noting that some "good ideas" unfortunately had disappeared behind an "interpretive jihad." In other words, the authors of the plan were engaged in a symbolic holy war, trying to "right social wrongs" through their reinterpretation of the Custer battlefield. Clary believed that the Park Service "must not take sides in historical events" and that the "Custer Battlefield is not the proper place to attempt to discuss 400 years of white-Indian conflict in North America." The NPS assistant director for historical preservation also disapproved of the plan, calling such broad interpretation a "grievous error." In Utley's view "site interpretation is what visitors travel to our parks to experience." Furthermore, he did not believe that "[NPS] people and programs . . . are capable of properly addressing the subject of Indian-white relationships."[56]

The Park Service's *General Management and Development Concept Plans* (1986) did incorporate some of the ideas from the earlier, stillborn plan. The primary purpose of the battlefield, the new plan stated, was to "preserve and protect the historic and natural resources pertaining to the Battle . . . and to provide visitors with a greater understanding of those events which lead up to the battle, the encounter itself, and the various effects the encounter had on the two cultures involved." To accomplish this the NPS needed to add more land, move the visitors center away from its proximity to Custer Hill, and begin tours at the site of the opening of hostilities in the valley. The effect would be to alter the ideological message conveyed by the layout of the park itself. As the park is presently configured, visitors go first to Custer Hill, the site of the Last Stand; only some of them visit Reno Hill, which affords a good view of the beginning of the battle in the valley and is itself the site of Major Reno and Captain Benteen's defensive position. The proposal to move the focal point of the battle away from Custer Hill would lessen popular fixation on Custer and give visitors "the opportunity to tour the battlefield in a correct, chronological sequence." Also, according to the plan, "museum exhibits should be restructured to emphasize more aspects of the national monument's secondary theme, *A Conflict of Cultures.*" Finally, the Park Service needed to be "more sensitive to Indian visitors and Indian attitudes about the fight."[57]

For Native Americans, Sioux and Cheyenne especially, the Custer battlefield has been perceived as alien land. In her study of Native American perspectives of the battle, Mardell Plainfeather, an NPS historian and member of the Crow tribe, notes that only about 2 to 4 percent of the visitors to the Little Bighorn are Native Americans—despite the fact that the battlefield is in the middle of a Crow reservation and near a Cheyenne reservation. Plainfeather reports that Native Americans do not like the fact that the battlefield is named for Custer or that the interpreters are usually white. Some Native Americans also think that if the battle were forgotten, their relations with whites would improve. In her years at the battlefield Plainfeather has seen members of numerous tribes visit, including Cherokee, Seminoles, Hopi, Apache, Seneca, and Menominee. While these visitors have been able to detach themselves somewhat from the story being recounted, they react with anger when words such as "savage," "buck," or "squaw" are used in interpretive programs.[58]

Royal G. Jackson's oral history of the battle from a Cheyenne perspective also reveals Native American dislike of Custer's dominance at the site. Several Cheyenne mentioned to him that they had heard the "real" story of the battle but that it had never been told to whites, or else what *had* been told to whites was a version distorted by other whites. "What did emerge," Jackson comments, "was a widely held belief that whites were seeking to glorify Custer and his men and diminish the major battlefield victory achieved by the Indians." In addition to complaints about the name and the use of the word "massacre" by interpreters, many Cheyenne did not like the fact that members of the Crow tribe worked at the battlefield. According to Jackson, they saw this as a "continuing attempt by the members of that tribe to preempt the Cheyenne and Sioux in capitalizing on this historic event." A Cheyenne woman told Jackson: "The Crows, they come and took over because it happened over there; they think that's theirs, see. But really it's the Cheyenne."[59]

Occasionally, controversies regarding Park Service interpretation have burst into public view. In the July 2, 1971, issue of *Life* magazine, Alvin Josephy describes his visit to the battlefield and says he listened to a park ranger speak about the denigration of Custer as part of a "scheme to undermine our traditions and our beliefs in the American army." In addition, the ranger used the phrase "hordes of savages" in his account of the battle. What he saw and heard at the Little Bighorn led Josephy to characterize the battlefield as a "sore from American's past that has not yet healed." In response, Bennie F. Irvin, a seasonal ranger at the battlefield and a school principal at the nearby Crow Agency, wrote to Robert Utley that Josephy's account was a "fine mixture of half-truths, untruths, and emotionalism." Not only had the "bigoted" ranger been fired at midseason but, Irvin told Utley, books sympathetic to Native Americans were on sale at the bookstore. Irvin also declared, "I know of no historic site that gives an unbiased account of an event as [does] Custer Battlefield." He nonetheless admitted that NPS staff members seemed "far removed" from their Crow neighbors, and the fact that they sent their children to school in Hardin rather than in Crow Agency was, he acknowledged, one of the "sore spots with the native Indian population."[60]

Characterized as anti-Custer by guardians of the patriotic faith and anti-Indian by those who took umbrage at the content of this faith, the National Park Service was caught in the crossfire of the battle for ownership of the Custer symbol. As it struggled to find a way to do justice to all who claimed this story as part of their tradition, it was also besieged by threats to the integrity of the land itself. Superintendent Luce wrote to the NPS in 1947 that as a result of a boundary study done during World War II, the battlefield was in need of more land for "proper interpretation." There were, he said, "two battlefields connected by a road over private land. Neither area includes all the significant points in the battle actions." In 1953 he noted potential sources of physical defilement: a proposed bar outside the entrance to the battlefield and placement of a hot dog stand near the Reno-Benteen site. Unlike Gettysburg, at the Little Bighorn the threatened encroachment by modern development did not seem urgent during the middle decades of the twentieth century, for the battlefield retained its unspoiled appearance. In the 1980s, however, several Crows who owned land immediately adjacent to the battlefield talked about building homes near the road leading from Custer Hill to the Reno-Benteen site. This would represent a radical intrusion into pristine land and serve to energize preservationist impulses.

James V. Court, who retired as park superintendent rather than accept a transfer to another site, had joined in 1982 with Harold Stanton, a Hardin attorney, to form the Custer Battlefield Preservation Committee (CBPC). In the committee's promotional literature Court described the threat of physical defilement and noted that the NPS owned less than one-tenth of the land associated with the battle. The committee therefore needed to raise more than eight million dollars to purchase nine thousand acres of threatened, private land, which it would then donate to the Park Service. Court called attention to the fact that the battlefield still appeared much as it did in 1876: "Today the Custer Battlefield and Reno-Benteen National Monuments give a person an intimate sense of history. Beyond the National Park Service paths and fences enclosing the Monument sites, there is little evidence of man or industry. It is as though the din of war whoops and the dust of the embroiling commotion had just settled." In consequence, he remarked, the preserved environment allowed for profound personal reflection. "It is quiet here and anyone can commune with the past and reconstruct to personal satisfaction the events surrounding Custer's defeat." But the potential for development of the surrounding area could spell permanent aesthetic defilement of the site. "Once this land has been altered," Court insisted, "the personal interpretation of the montage of fact and conjecture will be unattainable. . . . This place must be preserved as it is, as it has always been."[61]

In 1988 Dennis Ditmanson, a battlefield superintendent, highlighted the immediate physical threats to the sacred environment at the Little Bighorn: a Quik-Mart convenience store chain planned to develop "a 40-unit mini-mall and 100 plus–unit recreational vehicle park" near the site; and the Custer Battlefield Trading Post was being constructed adjacent to the park entrance. "Development has reached the Little Bighorn," he declared, "and for the most part it is heartily supported by the local populace which is seeking relief from the collapse of the energy industry . . . and by an Indian community which registers an unemployment rate in excess of 80% by some estimates." Ditmanson cautioned that the "extremely controversial nature of the park story is at least as great a threat to the park as is the more tangible potential for development," but he was compelled to add that " 'park values' are not a prime topic of conversation at the local coffee shop." For these and other reasons, Ditmanson noted, in 1988 the National Trust for Historic Preservation placed the Custer battlefield on the list of "endangered nationally significant historic places."[62]

The controversial work of the CBPC added to the charged environment of the Little Bighorn. During the 111th anniversary celebration in 1987, for example, "some 25 Crow Indians began demonstrating in opposition to the area's land protection plan," using a public address system to "denounce" Jim Court. NPS officials, including Director William Mott, met with Crow tribal chairman Richard Real Bird to assure him that the NPS "had no intention of kicking Native American landowners off their land." For most Native Americans, of course, the goal was not to preserve the patriotic landscape but to transform it into a shrine that reflected *their* concerns. For them the monument on Custer Hill was a part of the alien landscape, a monument to Custer and the Seventh Cavalry. Charlie Black Wolf, a Cheyenne, declared, "There should be a monument there, you know, Cheyennes, Arapahos, Siouxs, there should be a monument there for the people. 'This is where it took place' . . . stuff like that. . . . These crosses over here and [Custer National Forest], you know everything is Custer, everything."[63]

Interest in erecting an Indian monument at the battlefield has been sporadic. Gov. William L. Guy of North Dakota wrote to J. Leonard Volz, the Midwest regional director of the National Park Service, in January 1971 that "history had been written and was still being interpreted by the white man for and from the white man's point of view." In his opinion it was time "to memorialize the Indian Americans in their struggles in a way at least equal to the memorials already lavished on the white Americans of Indian war fame." Guy suggested the centennial year as the "appropriate target date for the completion of something long overdue" at the Little Bighorn. A few weeks later, in response to a letter from Volz, he repeated his desire to memorialize the American Indian's role in the battle and again offered to support any request for Congressional funds for this purpose. Sen. Quentin N. Burdick of North Dakota wrote to the NPS to express his support of the governor's call for an Indian monument on the battlefield, and Rogers B. Morton, secretary of the Interior Department, also received correspondence that called attention to the lack of such a memorial. For example, a New Jersey couple wrote in 1972 that they were disappointed not to see a monument, erected in a "conspicuous location," to the "warriors who fought so valiantly to preserve their land."[64]

The official response of the Park Service was that the battlefield was a "historical area designed to interpret a major event in American history and not a memorial to either the white man or the Indian. This matter was considered at length some years ago, when a movement was instigated to erect a monument to Custer on that same field. Then, as now, the determination was made to avoid any development that would tend to memorialize an individual or a specific group." Although technically correct, such

Members of AIM protested at the centennial celebration at
the Little Bighorn, June 1976. (R. N. Wathen, Jr.)

Threats of violence led to a relatively small audience at the
official centennial ceremonies. (R. N. Wathen, Jr.)

AIM spokesman Russell Means demanded and received permission to address those gathered for the centennial ceremonies. (R. N. Wathen, Jr.)

Robert M. Utley, representing the NPS, also spoke at the centennial ceremonies. (R. N. Wathen, Jr.)

Col. George A. Custer III and his son, virtually ignored throughout the proceedings, laid a wreath at the Custer Monument after the official ceremonies had ended. (R. N. Wathen, Jr.)

An announcement for the Centennial Victory Dance Celebration that was held on land owned by Austin Two Moons. (R. N. Wathen, Jr.)

A scene from the Centennial Victory Dance Celebration. (R. N. Wathen, Jr.)

On June 25, 1988, the 112th anniversary of the battle, a group led by Russell Means dug up part of the ground near the Custer Monument and erected a plaque honoring Native Americans who had fought in the battle. (*Billings Gazette*)

The controversial plaque erected by Native Americans near the Custer Monument. (National Park Service)

arguments were also quite beside the point. The battlefield *and* the monument on Custer Hill were clearly perceived by the public as memorials to Custer and his men. Indeed, how could that not be the case, since the remains of the dead troopers are buried beneath the monument and their names are inscribed on it. Native Americans most certainly viewed it as an army memorial, despite the NPS's claim that it honored all who had fought in the battle.[65]

During this period Native Americans called attention to the need for an Indian memorial, but like the others their requests were denied. In October 1972, for example, Eldon Reyer, superintendent of the battlefield, refused to let members of the American Indian Movement erect a cast-iron plaque that read, "In memory of our heroic warriors who defended our homes and laws against the hostile aggression of the United States government." In 1973 the director of Indians for Equality wrote to Rogers B. Morton that the group wanted a memorial to be built by "as many tribes as might wish to participate." Responding for the Park Service, Robert Utley argued that the battlefield was a "memorial to the participants of both sides" and that another monument would "diminish the historical integrity of the site and . . . lessen the honor done to the victorious Indians and the defeated Cavalrymen and Indian scouts."[66]

The controversy simmered until 1988. On the 112th anniversary of the battle, following a prayer service held on the battlefield in conjunction with American Indian International Peace Day, Russell Means "spoke for approximately half an hour during which he took issue with most accepted notions of the history of the Battle, and lambasted American society in general for the treatment afforded Indian people." According to the park superintendent, as the AIM leader was speaking "a small group emerged from the crowd with [a] plaque and shovels. They removed the sod from a square-yard area and poured a frame of pre-mix cement onto which they laid the plaque." The inscription on the plaque read: "In honor of our Indian Patriots who fought and defeated the U.S. Calvary [*sic*]. In order to save our women and children from mass-murder. In doing so, preserving rights to our Homelands, Treaties and sovereignty. 6/25/1988[,] G. Magpie[,] Cheyenne." Means asked the NPS not to remove the plaque, situated on the grassy area next to the monument that serves as the burial site for the enlisted men of the Seventh Cavalry. And he again expressed his hatred of Custer and the monument. The troops "came to kill our women and children," Means declared. "Can you imagine a monument listing the names of . . . Nazi officers erected in Jerusalem? A Hitler national monument?"[67]

Clearly, Means and his group understood that such a provocative act of defilement would gain public attention. They had escalated symbolic guerrilla warfare beyond protest at ritual events to physical intrusion at a patriotic gravesite. Most visitors, Dennis Ditmanson reported, were "generally supportive of the idea of an Indian monument while finding both the location, and the wording, of the plaque inappropriate." However, William Wells of the Little Big Horn Associates was grievously offended. In a June 30, 1988, letter to the NPS Wells decried the "sad and disgusting" actions of a "group of thugs comprised mostly of professional Indians," led by a "megalomaniacal convicted felon." Although he complained bitterly about the Park Service's passivity in the face of this illegal activity, he also emphasized that he was not opposed to an Indian memorial. Indeed, "If a legitimate, responsible group representing Indian Americans wants to place an unbiased and historically correct monument to their forebearers who fought and died at the Little Bighorn, it is my feeling that they should get all the help they need, including full government funding."[68]

Others who supported the idea of an Indian monument agreed with Wells that the Park Service should have stopped Means's intrusion on the sacred site. Writing in the *American Spectator,* Wayne M. Sarf berated the park superintendent, for whom "controversy, and not the continued defilement of graves in his care, seemed . . . the worst imaginable catastrophe." Yet according to Ditmanson there was "an atmosphere of uncertainty and tension which prevailed throughout the event. Inflammatory rhetoric marked most of the speeches and it seemed apparent that a confrontation could easily occur. The decision to not interfere with the placing of the plaque was made based on our analysis of what was occurring at the time. Actual damage to the lawn on the mass grave was very minor when compared to the potential for problems should a melee occur."[69]

Sarf had harsh words as well for those who caused the controversy, a group of "burn-outs led by the shameless Means—smug jackals content with 'counting coup' on bones a century dead." James Court wrote to the NPS in June 1988, "I have always felt that we should pay more respect to the Native Americans who fought at Custer Battlefield. I chose to do that by hiring more of them and putting more emphasis on the Indian side of the story. That is the positive approach. Russell Means' approach sets back our past attempt to work together harmoniously." Michael Koury insisted that any "intelligent and informed person knows it is long past time that a fitting monument be erected to the Indian warriors. . . . All of us that truly care about that place share in the guilt of this slight. Regardless of that, *no one* should be allowed to place a marker at his or her whim."[70]

To dramatize their outrage at this act of desecration, some people used inappropriate historical analogies. In *National Parks,* a publication of the National Parks and Conservation Association (NPCA), a short column about the plaque controversy and the Park Service's plan for an "appropriate" Indian monument engendered one response that "putting up a monument at the Custer Battlefield to honor the several thousand Indians who killed the 261 American soldiers is a wonderful idea. Maybe we can get the idea to spread. The Jews could put up a monument to the Nazi SS, the Armenians could put up a monument to the Turks, and the Irish could put up a monument to Cromwell." A respondent took issue with this analogy: "Need I remind [the writer] that Native Americans were not the oppressors in the conflict between immigrants from Europe and themselves." Another response noted that "Custer and his men were no innocent victims of a massacre; they were soldiers who went looking for a fight and got more than they bargained for."[71]

A number of people shared the opinion that the NPS's alleged timidity had set a dangerous precedent for acts of symbolic terrorism at other American memorials. For example, a Syracuse resident wrote to the NPS, "If this marker is allowed, what is to prevent . . . the 'Sons of Union Veterans' from placing a marker at the foot of General Lee's statue at Gettysburg saying he was a traitor to the United States?" A Ft. Lauderdale resident asked, "Could not the Vietnamese place their marker at the base of the Mall in Washington stating the same sentiments? We can wonder what kind of precedent this has set for any others who wish to place their personal sentiments on other mass grave monuments such as the Arizona Memorial at Pearl Harbor."[72] At issue, of course, was not only the distasteful act of defilement but a growing concern that such an act signaled the death knell of traditional patriotic orthodoxies. After all, if sacred places could be attacked, the destruction of the message must not be far off.

The defilement of any grave is a powerful symbolic expression, and it is therefore difficult not to sympathize with those who were outraged by this particular act. Still, Russell Means managed to succeed where others had failed. Almost singlehandedly, he forced the Park Service to address the question of an Indian monument at the Little Bighorn.

On August 26, 1988, William Penn Mott, Jr., director of the NPS, wrote to the Rocky Mountain regional director: "You and the park must swiftly take the initiative and exert strong, positive leadership to organize the [Indian] memorial committee and support its mission. . . . I urge you to communicate your intentions without delay not only to the groups involved in the June 25 event but to the Tribal Chairmen of all the directly affected Indian Nations." The plaque was subsequently removed from the gravesite, on September 6, 1988, and placed in the visitors center where, Ditmanson wrote, it would serve as a "temporary symbol of our intent to develop a memorial that will represent the shared perspectives of the tribes involved in the battle. It also [would serve] to represent certain contemporary native American attitudes about the National Monument." The Park Service quickly produced an informational brochure for the proposed Native American Memorial at Custer Battlefield National Monument. The brochure included possible themes for the monument: to "memorialize Indian participants who fell in the Battle of the Little Bighorn"; or to "address Native American perspectives relating to the Battle . . . in the context of the U.S. Cavalry's 1876 campaign"; or to "address native American perspectives in the 'Conflicts of Cultures' for the previous two decades which culminated in the Battle of the Little Bighorn."[73]

Robert Utley and Russell Means, among others, were named by the Park Service to a committee whose purpose was to select a theme for the monument, to plan a national competition for the design of the monument, and to determine possible locations for the monument on the battlefield. While the committee did not face daunting opposition from the guardians of patriotic faith, certain members of the Crow tribe were not happy that Sioux and Cheyenne were placing a plaque in the middle of Crow land. Mardell Plainfeather explained the dilemma: "If it's a monument only to the Sioux, Cheyenne, and Arapaho victors, where does that leave the Crow and Arikara allies? Their involvement in the battle story is relevant to proper interpretation and must be considered in the design and dedication of a monument if it is to be for ALL the Indians involved in the battle story. If it is a monument for the victors only . . . we will have yet another future dilemma to deal with soon."[74]

Only two years earlier, at the 110th anniversary celebration, both Native Americans and Anglo-Americans had taken part in the reburial of the remains of troopers from the Seventh Cavalry uncovered during archaeological investigations in the summers of 1984 and 1985.[75] A morning service on the Northern Cheyenne World Day of Peace was led by Austin Two Moons, who in 1976 had hosted the Cheyenne centennial victory celebration on his ranch. He asked the crowd to join hands and then declared, "We don't want no nuclear war. We must come together realizing that one God made us and pray for the future of all people and their children." Enos Poor Bear, a former chief of the Oglala Sioux, reminded Native Americans that the battlefield was not alien land, for there was "no spot on earth more steeped with Indian tradition and pride." He also tried to draw a contemporary lesson from the battle, insisting that Native Americans do more than remember it as a great victory. They must, he said, "accept [the] unconquerable spirit of our forefathers, and if we seek to emulate their virtues, such as determination, adherence to traditional values, and the desire to overcome obstacles at all cost, then we . . . can build on the victory that was ours at the Little Bighorn, and . . . by applying these same virtues to our modern day circumstance fashion . . . a better day and a brighter future."[76]

The reburial services began at 4:00 P.M. According to a report in the *Denver Post,* the "three flag-draped canisters containing 411 bones were reburied with full military honors." John D. McDermott, representing the President's Advisory Council on Historic Preservation, reminded spectators that those who "fought against each other in 1876 fought together at Iwo Jima, in the Yalu Valley and at Kehsanh [*sic*]." An honor guard from the Seventh Cavalry carried the canisters to the gravesite in the cemetery, and six American Legionnaires, several of them Native Americans, fired a salute. Rev. Vincent Heier utilized the rhetoric of reconciliation when he offered a prayer that the "clash of cultures should give way to the calming ways of peace."[77]

It is difficult to imagine the "clash of cultures" at the Little Bighorn giving way to the "calming ways of peace" in the near future.[78] Such a transformation cannot be accomplished by turning Custer into the martial madman of the film *Little Big Man.* And it certainly cannot be accomplished by celebrating traditional patriotic orthodoxies, which have long failed to recognize Native Americans as anything but recalcitrant children guilty of barbaric behavior, or as people finally coming to realize the virtues of Anglo-American civilization. The Little Bighorn will continue to be a place where cultures clash through acts of symbolic warfare, primarily because it is the site of the clash of two kinds of patriotism: the patriotism of power and the patriotism of pain. David Chidester writes, "In American history, the patriotism of power has resonated through the commitments to a divine covenant and a sacred destiny that have animated both the self-understanding and territorial expansion of a nation." The Custer battlefield has always been one of the central places in this celebration of power, for the man and the battle symbolize the cultural dominance of Anglo-American patriotic orthodoxies. In more recent years, however, a different patriotic voice, a voice expressing the patriotism of pain, has been heard at the battlefield. It is, in Chidester's words, "a patriotism . . . arising in the hearts of the defeated, dispossessed, and disenfranchised"; it is a "patriotism of the land, but not of the alien architecture that has been constructed on the land." At the Little Bighorn, Native Americans have sought to resurrect their story from an alien patriotic landscape and an alien orthodoxy that has excluded them for a century. Often the only form of power available to those who are excluded from the ownership of important cultural symbols is symbolic guerilla warfare.[79]

Certainly, the National Park Service is struggling to mediate between these two patriotisms, to ensure that both voices are heard at the battlefield. To date, these voices remain uneasy in each other's presence, as the symbolic war for the exclusive ownership of the Custer battlefield rages on. The cease-fire of 1986, though short lived, nonetheless illustrates that the rhetoric and rituals of inclusion may yet lead to a critical, mature patriotism, one that is neither jealous nor exclusive. In intent and in execution, activities like the construction of the Indian monument can act as symbolic salve. One hopes that such acts signify the gradual acceptance of the patriotism of inclusion at the Little Bighorn.

Notes

Portions of this chapter appeared in an earlier form in Edward T. Linenthal, "Ritual Drama at the Little Big Horn: The Persistence and Transformation of a National Symbol," *Journal of the American Academy of Religion* 51, no. 2 (June 1983): 267–81.

1. I also recall watching *They Died with Their Boots On,* in which Errol Flynn's Custer faced his last moments with a look of fierce determination on his face. Such defiance conveyed the message that the ideals for which the cavalry fought were honorable ones that would endure despite the loss of Custer and his men. Recall, too, the Anheuser-Busch print of F. Otto Becker's last-stand lithograph, which presents a fearless Custer at the center of the maelstrom, sword upraised, a tragic hero for the ages.

2. Ben Blackburn, "On Last Stand Hill a Civil War Passes in Review," *Rocky Mountain News,* May 25, 1986.

3. Quoted in Boston Cyclorama Co., *Cyclorama of Custer's Last Battle or the Battle of the Little Big Horn,* comp. and ed. A. J. Donnelle (n.p., n.d.), p. 19.

4. Nora B. Kinsley, "Custer Memorial Highway," *American Review of Reviews* (Aug. 1921): 186; *Boston Globe,* June 20, 1926.

5. Frederick Whittaker, ed., *A Complete Life of General George Armstrong Custer* (New York: Sheldon and Co., 1876), p. 600. For a provocative interpretation of last stands, see Bruce A. Rosenberg, *Custer and the Epic of Defeat* (University Park: Pennsylvania State University Press, 1974).

6. Quoted in Edward M. Kirby and Jack W. Harris, *Star-Spangled Radio* (Chicago: Ziff-Davis, 1948), p. 31. In a similar vein, after the fall of Wake Island, Arthur Upham Pope, chairman of the National Committee for National Morale, wrote, "They lifted our chins, they squared our jaws and stiffened our backs . . . they gave us morale" ("How Can Individuals Keep a Healthy Morale in Wartime," *America Organizes to Win the War* [New York: Harcourt, Brace and Co., 1942], p. 251). In the film *Wake Island,* the final defeat is never shown. Rather, Robert Preston and William Bendix are seen fighting to the last, like Walt Disney's Davy Crockett and Errol Flynn's Custer. In the 1943 film *Bataan,* Robert Taylor, a member of a doomed squad, declares, "It doesn't matter where a man dies, so long as he dies for freedom." See Richard R. Lingeman, *Don't You Know There's a War On? The American Home Front, 1941–45* (New York: G. P. Putnam's Sons, 1970), p. 200.

7. Godfrey, quoted in Robert M. Utley, *Custer Battlefield: A History and Guide to the Battle of the Little Bighorn* (Washington, D.C.: U.S. Department of the Interior, 1988), p. 72; Miles, quoted in Fred A. Hunt, "A Purposeful Picnic," *Pacific Monthly* 19, no. 3 (Mar. 1908): 245.

8. Don Rickey, *History of Custer Battlefield* (n.p.: Custer Battlefield Historical & Museum Association, 1967), p. 67.

9. Quoted in ibid., p. 73.

10. Ibid., p. 74.

11. Godfrey, quoted in *Hardin Tribune,* June 23, 30, 1916; Hall, quoted in ibid., June 30, 1916.

12. Ibid., July 1, 1921.

13. Rickey, p. 79. A copy of the brochure is in the author's files.

14. National Custer Memorial Association, *The Fiftieth Anniversary of the Custer Battlefield,* historical files, Custer Battlefield National Monument (hereafter, CBNM).

15. Partello's account is reprinted in *Little Big Horn Associates Newsletter* 22, no. 8 (Sept. 1988).

16. George J. McMurry, "The 7th Cavalry at the Fiftieth Anniversary of the Battle of the Little Big Horn," *Cavalry Journal* (Oct. 1926): 543–44.

17. Ibid., passim.

18. Ibid., p. 551; *Billings Gazette,* June 25 and 27, 1926.

19. Partello, pp. 7–8; see also Rickey, pp. 79–83.

20. Red Hawk, quoted in *Billings Gazette,* June 27, 1926; Godfrey and Marquisee, quoted in A. B. Ostrander, *The Custer Semi-Centennial* (Casper, Wyo.: Casper Printing and Stationery, 1926), pp. 42, 47.

21. Holt and the *Billings Gazette* are quoted in "Throngs Attend Custer Battlefield Ceremony," *Winners of the West* 13, no. 8 (July 1936): 1–2.

22. The Seventh Cavalry is quoted in *Hardin Tribune,* June 28, 1951; all other quoted material in this paragraph is in the historical files, CBNM.

23. There are occasional references to these intimate ceremonies in the historical files, CBNM. For example, on June 26, 1907, the *Buffalo Enquirer* noted that the Knights and Dames of Malta held a memorial service on the thirty-first anniversary of the battle. During the service patriotic rhetoric reviewed Custer's life and portrayed him as a national martyr.

Residents of Monroe, Michigan, Custer's hometown, were also sensitive to appropriate acts of veneration. Lawrence A. Frost reports that after twenty years the state highway commission gave the Monroe County Historical Commission permission to erect signs informing visitors that Monroe is the "Hometown of General Custer." This, he reported, "led to an increase in tourism to Custer exhibits and [the] Custer trail," not to mention a controversy in 1988 when the city council ordered the Custer signs removed and replaced with signs honoring the new Miss America. With the help of its state representative, Monroe⁻ was granted an exception to a state rule that cities are allowed only one "special designation" sign. According to Frost the Miss America signs would be up for a year, but the "Custer sign is permanent" ("On the Trail of a Tourist," *Little Big Horn Associates Newsletter* 22, no. 2 [Feb. 1988]).

24. All quoted material in this paragraph is from the historical files, CBNM. According to Douglas McChristian, the current NPS historian at the battlefield, Don Rickey's tenure as the battlefield historian (1956–60) was marked by his desire to "balance" the story of the Little Bighorn. He was, McChristian says, one of the first to recognize that there is "another side to the story" (interview, Apr. 29, 1989). In *Forty Miles a Day on Beans and Hay: The Enlisted Soldier Fighting the Indian Wars* (Norman: University of Oklahoma Press, 1963), Rickey writes about the life of enlisted men in the Plains Indian wars.

25. Joe Medicine Crow, quoted in Anne Chamberlain, "Bad Days Ahead for America's Greatest Loser," *Saturday Evening Post* (Aug. 28, 1966): 72; a copy of the transcript of the pageant is in the author's files. Other material referred to in this and the preceding paragraph is from the historical files, CBNM.

26. Robert Utley, "Custer: Hero or Butcher," *American History Illustrated* 5, no. 10 (1971): 4; Brian Dippie, *Custer's Last Stand: The Anatomy of an American Myth* (Missoula: University of Montana Press, 1976), p. 135.

27. All quoted material in this paragraph is from the historical files, CBNM.

28. Ibid.

29. Ibid.

30. Virgil Kills Straight, quoted in *Great Falls Tribune,* June 26, 1976; Means's comment on the flag is in Bryce Nelson, "After 100 Years Wounds of Bighorn Still Festering," *Los Angeles Times,* June 25, 1976; Means's other comments are in Nelson, "Custer Relative Has No Role in Helping Mark 100th Anniversary of 'Last Stand,'" ibid., June 26, 1976.

31. *Billings Gazette,* June 24, 1976; a copy of the brochure is in the author's files. The unnamed participant is quoted in Michael Koury, ed., *The Custer Centennial Observances: 1976.* Source Custeriana Series, no. 10 (Ft. Collins, Colo.: Old Army Press, 1978), p. 55.

32. The origin of the LBHA is discussed in Lawrence A. Frost, "The Beginning of the LBHA," *Little Big Horn Associates Newsletter* 11, no. 1 (Jan. 1987): 3–4. I recognize the danger in indiscriminately labeling any group, but I am compelled to say that when I attended the annual meeting of the Little Big Horn Associates in 1983, it seemed that a goodly number of the attendees took a dim view of the Park Service's attempts to "balance" the story. For many of these people it was clearly the figure of Custer at the Little Bighorn that stirred their imaginations. In 1980 LBHA members attending their annual convention held a patriotic worship service for Custer at the Old Cadet Chapel and Custer gravesite on the grounds of the United States Military Academy at West Point, New York. Billed as "A Service of Reflection in Memory of George Armstrong Custer and Elizabeth Bacon Custer," it consisted of an invocation, hymn, and litany from Ecclesiasticus ("Let us now praise famous men, and our fathers in their generations. The Lord apportioned to them great glory, his majesty from the beginning" [44:1–5]). A tribute was offered to the courage of Custer and the Seventh Cavalry. The "Battle Hymn of the Republic" followed another hymn, which was followed by the recessional and the Seventh Cavalry's famous "Garryowen." Worshipers then processed to Custer's gravesite to lay a wreath, followed by taps and a benediction.

33. Koury's letter to the NPS director, Aug. 12, 1976, in the historical files, CBNM.

34. Nelson, "Custer Relative." Custer's grandnephew expressed his displeasure over the "disturbing program" in a letter to Pres. Gerald Ford on July 12, 1976. He was particularly incensed that Russell Means had been invited to speak but a military spokesman had not. The Park Service offered its "regret" at any offense taken from Means's speech but defended the "appropriate" nature of Native American participation at the ceremony. "To deny recognition in this potentially and possibly dangerous situation would have risked confrontation and possibly even violence," it declared. The Park Service also insisted that the Seventh Cavalry *had* been invited but had declined to attend (Custer's letter to Ford and the NPS's response are in the CBNM files,

National Park Service, Washington, D.C. [hereafter, NPS]). Robert Utley notes that Custer's grandnephew was finally allowed to lay a wreath at the monument late in the day: "I linked arms with George III and his son . . . and together we walked up the hill to the monument. I stood next to George III as he placed the wreath" (letter to the author, Oct. 18, 1989).

35. Numerous letters of complaint about the centennial are in the historical files, CBNM, and in the CBNM files, NPS.

36. *Los Angeles Times,* June 26, 1976; *Hardin Tribune,* June 25, 1976; NPS response is in the historical files, CBNM, and also in the CBNM files, NPS.

37. Memorandum from Harris, Dec. 12, 1971, in "Historical Correspondence, Custer Battlefield National Monument," box 1, NPS. When the administration of the battlefield passed to the Park Service in 1940, the site was still known as the Custer Battlefield National Cemetery. In 1946 the name was changed to the Custer Battlefield National Monument because, as Don Rickey notes, "far more people came to visit Custer Battlefield [for] its historic interest rather than because it included a national cemetery" (p. 90).

38. Memoranda from Clary, Feb. 9, 1972, and Utley, Feb. 10, 1972, and June 3, 1975, are in "Historical Correspondence," CBNM files, NPS.

39. The LBHA and NPS correspondence on the name change is in the historical files, CBNM, and in the CBNM files, NPS.

40. Russell's letter, June 17, 1987, and Mott's response are in the CBNM files, NPS.

41. Correspondence from Hart, Aug. 16, 1987, and Bearss, Sept. 18, 1987, is in the CBNM files, NPS. In 1987 the LBHA again polled its members about the wisdom of a name change and again sent the results to the NPS: 308 opposed, 21 in favor.

42. Carroll's correspondence is in the CBNM files, NPS.

43. Court's letter, Mar. 11, 1983, is in the CBNM files, NPS; see also Court's letter to the LBHA in "A Special Report to the LBHA Membership," *Little Big Horn Associates Newsletter* 19, no. 3 (Apr. 1985). Roger Clawson, in "Custer Buff Fails in Bid to Oust Battlefield Boss," *Billings Gazette,* June 29, 1983, notes

the LBHA's complaints about "enemy" in-scriptions at the battlefield.

44. Carroll's letter, June 29, 1979, is in the CBNM files, NPS. A marker honoring Dorman was placed near the site of his death, outside of NPS property, on land managed by the Bureau of Indian Affairs. As for the book controversy, in 1983 the book committee of the Custer Battlefield Historical & Museum Association (CBHMA), the cooperating asso-ciation that runs the bookstore at the visitors center, refused to stock Lawrence A. Frost's *Custer Legends* (Bowling Green, Ohio: Bowling Green University Popular Press, 1981). Both the park superintendent and the park histo-rian concurred in the decision.

At the Custer Battlefield National Monu-ment there are written guidelines for book selection. They state, "One of the most im-portant tasks of any park area and cooperating association is deciding on what publications are appropriate for sale." The superintendent has the final decision, assisted by the historian and the chairperson of the book committee. At the Custer battlefield primary and second-ary themes guide the selection process: 30 percent of acquisitions should focus on the history of the battle; 20 percent on biogra-phies and the Plains Indian wars; 15 percent on "acquiring knowledge and . . . sensitivity toward the Indian culture, particularly the Crows, Cheyennes, and Sioux cultural heri-tage"; 15 percent should focus on the impact of white culture on the frontier; 10 percent on regional history, and 5 percent each on natural history and the National Park Service. See "Guidelines: Criteria for Book Review Selection, Custer Battlefield National Monu-ment," historical files, CBNM. For a brief introduction to the role of cooperating asso-ciations, see "Superintendent's Notes," *Bat-tlefield Dispatch* 7, no. 2 (Spring 1988): 6.

For Carroll, the committee's failure to ap-prove the sale of Frost's book, even though other titles of his had been sold at the battle-field, reflected a deeper ideological problem, namely, that the NPS staff at the battlefield was hostile to Custer. LeAnn Simpson, the executive director of the CBHMA, informed me that *Custer Legends* was currently on sale at the battlefield bookstore (interview, Apr. 29, 1989).

45. See Edwin C. Bearss's briefing paper, "History of Mr. John M. Carroll's Concerns and Conflicts with the Managers of Custer Battlefield National Memorial, 1976–82," CBNM files, NPS. There are also numerous letters from Carroll in these files.

46. Memorandum from Bearss, Aug. 1983, in CBNM files, NPS; Horn, quoted in *Little Big Horn Associates Research and Review* 1, no. 2 (June 1984): 5; Koury's letter, Aug. 24, 1984, is in the CBNM files, NPS.

47. The executive order is quoted in Rob-ert L. Hart, *Interpretive Beginnings: Custer Bat-tlefield, 1879–1952* (n.p., 1986), in the histor-ical files, CBNM; see also Rickey, p. 46.

48. Copies of these early brochures are in the historical files, CBNM. In the National Archives there is a copy of a talk Luce deliv-ered on March 27, 1947, which he sent to his superiors in the Park Service as as example of the themes he used when he spoke to various groups. Monthly reports, also found in old Park Service records in the Archives, suggest the kinds of public activities the superintend-ent was involved in: for example, speaking engagements included the Hardin chapter of the American Legion, a "young people's" meeting of Native Americans at Crow Agency Baptist Church, and a talk to children visiting the battlefield on Memorial Day (files 207–1, 207–3, National Archives, Washington, D.C.). See also Edward S. Luce and Evelyn S. Luce, *Custer Battlefield National Monument, Montana*. National Park Service Historical Handbook Series, no. 1 (Washington, D.C.: n.p., 1955).

49. Luce also mentions that during MacArthur's entry the Seventh Cavalry Band played Custer's famous battlesong, "Gar-ryowen" (memoranda from Luce, Sept. 10, 1945 [quoted in a memorandum from the superintendent of Yellowstone National Park to the NPS director of Region 2, Sept. 18, 1945] and Mar. 31, 1946, file 201–7, National Archives). Bearss pointed out that the Thirty-second and Forty-first Army Infantry divisions and a number of marine divisions saw consid-erably more combat in World War II than did the Seventh Cavalry (telephone interview, Aug. 31, 1989).

50. All quoted material in this paragraph is from Harry B. Robinson, "The Custer Bat-tlefield Museum," *Montana: The Magazine of*

Western History (July 1952): 11–29. See also Robert L. Hart, *Changing Exhibitry and Sensitivity: The Custer Battlefield Museum, 1952–86* (n.p., 1986), in the historical files, CBNM.

51. Roy E. Appleman, "Report on Visit to Custer Battlefield National Monument, Montana, July 10–12, 1956, and Recommendations," in the historical files, CBNM. After the battle Comanche was found near death, but he survived and was treated as a sacred animal, parading with Troop 1 of the Seventh Cavalry. When Comanche died his body was stuffed and put on display at the National History Museum at the University of Kansas. The Park Service has tried unsuccessfully to bring Comanche back to the Custer battlefield.

52. The brochure quoted in this paragraph, along with numerous related brochures, is in the historical files, CBNM; Utley, quoted in Hart, *Interpretive Beginnings*.

53. The brochures quoted in this paragraph are in the historical files, CBNM.

54. Vincent Gleason, chief of NPS publications, remarked that this controversy was a "silly" one, not even qualifying as a tempest in a teapot. Gleason had clashed with Utley on this issue because he believed that Baskin's drawings captured the "essence" of Custer, who was, in Gleason's opinion, a "fatuous" person. Gleason also mentioned that Baskin's depictions of Native Americans portray them as noble (telephone interview, Nov. 29, 1989). Utley based his objection to Baskin's drawings on the belief that "this sort of impressionism is inappropriate in a park guidebook, which should be full of literal illustrations and maps" (letter to the author, Oct. 18, 1989). Those who purchased the handbook with the blank page could write to the NPS and ask that a copy of Baskin's drawing of a nude, dead Custer be sent to them in the mail. The drawing was restored in later editions.

55. The 1949 master plan is in the historical files, CBNM. The preliminary draft of the 1970s plan is in "Historical Correspondence," CBNM files, NPS.

56. Ibid.

57. *Custer Battlefield National Monument Final General Management and Development Concept Plans*, Aug. 1986, in the historical files, CBNM. This report treats the Sioux and Cheyenne as members of a single culture rather than as members of distinct cultures that banded together for the strategic purpose of defeating a military opponent. In consequence, even in the 1980s the general category "Indian" still bedeviled interpretive efforts.

In recent years museum displays at the battlefield have moved away from the dominance of Custer. For example, in 1989 the NPS displayed the personal belongings of Laban Little Wolf, a Northern Cheyenne who fought at the Little Bighorn. The NPS consulted with members of the Cheyenne tribe and with Laban Little Wolf's grandson to make sure the display was appropriate. For a description of the items on display, see "Laban Little Wolf Exhibit," *Battlefield Dispatch* 8, no. 2 (Spring 1989): 3.

58. Mardell Plainfeather, "Interpreting the Battle of the Little Bighorn: A Native American Perspective," paper delivered at the Montana State History Conference, Oct. 1988. In a *National Geographic* interview Plainfeather called attention to a revealing inscription—which mentions "clearing the District of the Yellowstone of hostile Indians"—that appears in the cemetery. She commented, "It's offensive. As if those troopers were getting rid of a plague. These were people, this was *their* land. They fought for their families, their homes, their culture, their freedom. . . . I wish these words could be removed" (quoted in Robert Paul Jordan, "Ghosts on the Little Bighorn," *National Geographic* 170, no. 6 [Dec. 1986]: 803–4). When I interviewed Mardell Plainfeather on April 26, 1989, I asked her what would happen if the Sioux and Cheyenne were in charge of interpretation at the battlefield. She thought there would be a lot of talk about massacres of Native Americans at Sand Creek and Wounded Knee and about Anglo-Americans' violent conquest of the frontier. I am indebted to her for sharing her paper with me and for discussing her experiences at the battlefield.

Sensitivity regarding appropriate language also played a key role in the controversy over an Indian monument at the site of the Sand Creek Massacre in Colorado, where approximately one hundred thirty Native Americans were killed by the Colorado Volunteers. Descendants of the victims wanted to remove a plaque that characterized the area as a "battleground." In the spirit of compromise, the Colorado Historical Society agreed to place a new marker next the old granite marker. See *New York Times*, Sept. 22, 1985.

59. Royal G. Jackson, *An Oral History of the Battle of Little Bighorn from the Perspective of the Northern Cheyenne Descendants*. Final Report. University of Wyoming/National Park Service Research Center, 1987, passim. Cheyenne also were curious about the continued high level of white interest in the battle. All of them had "experienced some degree of saturation" on the topic during their childhood, and a number of people told Jackson that younger Cheyenne simply wanted to forget the battle.

60. See Alvin Josephy, "The Custer Myth," *Life* (July 2, 1971): 48–59. Irvin's letter and the letter that appeared in the *Billings Gazette* are in "Historical Correspondence," CBNM files, NPS. Also taking exception to Josephy's account is a letter in the *Billings Gazette* that insists the Custer battlefield staff is not "anti-Indian" and that a "visit to the Battlefield is enough to convince anybody that Indians are not referred to as 'savages' or 'hostiles' in any of the talks, taped or live. Nor do the talks heard by the tourists and others idealize . . . Custer" (ibid.).

61. Copies of this promotional material from the CBPC are in the author's files. The committee noted in its prospectus, "A Legacy of the American West: The Case for Preservation of the Custer Battlefield," the endorsement of its efforts by the Park Service. Donald Paul Hodel, former secretary of the Interior Department, commented, "Preserving historic properties through private efforts is a prime example of the President's policy on private sector initiative" (quoted in Custer Battlefield Preservation Committee, "A Legacy of the American West: The Case for Preservation of the Custer Battlefield," prospectus, 1983, in the author's files). For general descriptive articles on CBPC activities, see *Hardin Tribune*, Dec. 8, 1982; *Rocky Mountain News*, July 21, 1985.

62. Dennis L. Ditmanson, "The Demise of America's Battlefields: Can They Survive?" paper delivered at the Fifth Triennial Conference on Research in the National Parks and Equivalent Resources, Tucson, Arizona, Nov. 15, 1988, CBNM files, NPS.

63. Memorandum from Edwin C. Bearss to the NPS associate director of cultural resources, July 16, 1987, CBNM files, NPS; "Indians Protest Custer Battlefield Proposal," *Billings Gazette*, June 29, 1987; Charlie Black Wolf, quoted in Jackson, p. 69.

64. Letters from Guy to Volz, Jan. 20, 1971, and Feb. 12, 1971; from Volz to Guy, Feb. 9, 1971; from Burdick to Hartzog, Feb. 18, 1971; and from Harthon L. Bill, acting director of the NPS, Feb. 24, 1971, all in CBNM files, NPS. The letter from the New Jersey couple to Morton is in "Historical Correspondence," CBNM files, NPS.

65. The "matter . . . considered some years ago" concerned the proposal of Eugene McAuliffe in 1954 to erect an equestrian statue of Custer on the battlefield. The director of the NPS responded that before her death Mrs. Custer had asked that no statue be erected. The NPS also believed that the proposed statue would be an intrusion on the landscape and would allow Custer to be too "dominating" a figure. See "The Equestrian Statue of General Custer as Proposed by Mr. Eugene McAuliffe" (proposal) and related correspondence in "Historical Correspondence," CBNM files, NPS.

66. For details of Reyer's refusal, see *Hardin Tribune*, Oct. 14, 1972. The correspondence cited in this paragraph is found in "Historical Correspondence," CBNM files, NPS.

67. Dennis L. Ditmanson, "Superintendent's Notes," *Battlefield Dispatch* 7, no. 3 (Summer 1988): 2–3; Means, quoted in Frank Del Olmo, "Activists' Plaque at Little Bighorn Honors 'Patriots' Who Beat Custer," *Los Angeles Times*, July 4, 1988.

68. Ditmanson, "Superintendent's Notes"; letter from Wells, June 30, 1988, in "Historical Correspondence," CBNM files, NPS. I asked Doug McChristian, NPS historian at the battlefield, why there wasn't greater furor over Means's action, which was certainly more provocative than anything that took place at the centennial. In his opinion there had been a change in tolerance for minority viewpoints at such public sites, as well as a change in the perception of the Plains Indian wars. People, he said, "want to make sense of all this"

(interview, Apr. 29, 1989). A bill to establish an Indian memorial at the battlefield was introduced into Congress in April 1990 by Montana representatives Ron Marlenee and Pat Williams and Colorado representative Ben Nighthorse Campbell, the only Native American member of Congress.

69. Wayne Michael Sarf, "Russell Means on Custer Hill," *American Spectator* 21, no. 12 (Dec. 1988): 34; Ditmanson, "Superintendent's Notes," p. 2.

70. Letters from Court to the NPS, June 29, 1988, and from Koury to the NPS, July 12, 1988, in "Historical Correspondence," CBNM files, NPS.

71. The original article about Means's activity and the NPS's plans for an Indian monument is in *National Parks* 63, no. 1–2 (Jan./Feb. 1989): 12; responses appear in ibid. 63, no. 3–4 (Mar./Apr. 1989): 7, and ibid. 63, no. 7–8 (July/Aug. 1989): 7. I am indebted to Bruce Craig of the NPCA for bringing this material to my attention.

72. Both letters are in "Historical Correspondence," CBNM files, NPS.

73. Dennis L. Ditmanson, "Superintendent's Notes," *Battlefield Dispatch* 7, no. 4 (Fall 1988): 4; memo from Mott, Aug. 26, 1988, in "Historical Correspondence," CBNM files, NPS. A copy of the NPS brochure on the Indian monument is in the author's files.

74. Plainfeather, "Interpreting the Battle."

75. The archaeological digs at the battlefield were prompted by a fire in the summer of 1983 that swept the area. Sandy Barnard summarizes the importance of the excavations: "The projects have revealed much about the number and variety of weapons used by the Indians; more about where the Indians took cover and fired at the soldiers; more about how the soldiers were deployed and how they stood and fought; and some about how the troops were dressed and equipped. It's also obvious that the 1881 reburial party did not collect all the parts of the soldiers' bodies" (*Digging into Custer's Last Stand* [Terre Haute, Ind.: AST Press, 1986], p. 61).

There was a great deal of media attention in 1985 when the remains of "Trooper Mike," an almost complete skeleton of one of Custer's men, was dug up. For a detailed report on the results of the excavations, see Douglas D. Scott and Richard A. Fox, Jr., with a contribution by Dick Harmon, *Archaeological Insights into the Custer Battle* (Norman: University of Oklahoma Press, 1987). Several sets of remains were submitted to forensic specialists, two of which were tentatively identified as the remains of Sgt. Miles O'Hara and Mitch Boyer, a scout. See Douglas Scott, Melissa Connor, and Clyde Snow, "Nameless Faces of Custer Battlefield," *Greasy Grass* (a publication of the CBHMA), May 1988.

Controversy also attended the excavations. Navy Comdr. Jerry Spencer of the Armed Forces Institute of Forensic Pathology wanted to exhume some of the remains, while the dig was in progress, and attempt to determine if any of Custer's men had committed suicide (as some Native American accounts claimed). Custer's grandnephew spoke for the guardians of patriotic faith when he said, "It's absurd. We had a more manly generation then." For them, the thought of the "heroes" of the Little Bighorn committing suicide clearly went beyond the boundaries of civilized discourse (Peter Larson, "Maybe the Indians Didn't Shoot Custer," *Bradenton Herald*, Feb. 10, 1982).

76. See "Newspaper articles re: 110 Anniversary Ceremonies," historical files, CBNM. This account is from the Wellsboro (Pa.) *Gazette*, July 16, 1986.

77. *Denver Post*, June 26, 1986; Heier, quoted in *Akron Beacon Journal*, June 26, 1986.

78. The latest controversy at the Custer Battlefield National Monument involves the new superintendent, Barbara Booher, a Native American. After a *People* magazine (Feb. 12, 1990) article mistakenly suggested that she was the source of interpretive change at the battlefield, from plans for an Indian monument to revised museum exhibits, William Wells of the LBHA declared that Booher was guilty of "reverse discrimination." According to Wells, she had obviously forgotten that in the late nineteenth century Indians who would not obey government orders were "considered to be the enemy and they were not Americans" (*Little Bighorn Associates Newsletter* 24, no. 2 [Feb. 1990]: 4). See also *Little Bighorn Associates Newsletter* 24, no. 4 (Apr. 1990): 4; Kit Miniclier, "Custer Battlefield Superin-

tendent Seeks Accuracy in Tangle of Cultures," *Denver Post,* Dec. 31, 1989.

79. David Chidester, *Patterns of Power: Religion and Politics in American Culture* (Englewood Cliffs, N.J.: Prentice Hall, 1988), pp. 301–6.

5

"Rust and Sea and Memory in This Strange Graveyard"

Following the Russo-Japanese War of 1904–5, the United States began to view Japan as a potential threat to its political and economic interests in Southeast Asia. A cataclysmic war between the two countries seemed inevitable, according to "Yellow Peril" fiction, and would likely begin with a surprise attack on Hawaii. The Japanese invasion of Manchuria in 1931, which eventually led to the Sino-Japanese War, sparked American moral condemnation as well as trade restrictions. In response, Japan joined Germany and Italy in the Tripartite Pact, fully understanding that war was inevitable if its vision of a Pan-Asiatic Empire was to be realized.

Adm. Isoroku Yamamoto, the commander in chief of the Japanese Combined Fleet and a former naval attaché in Washington, knew that his country could not win a protracted war with the United States. Consequently, on the heels of faltering diplomatic efforts to resolve the crisis, he prepared to destroy the American Pacific Fleet at Pearl Harbor and leave the United States "so dispirited [it] will not be able to recover." A fleet of thirty-two vessels, including six aircraft carriers, left Tankan Bay in northern Japan on November 26, 1941, under the command of Vice Adm. Chuichi Nagumo. The strike force made its way undetected to within 230 miles of the Hawaiian island of Oahu. On December 7, 1941, at 6:00 A.M., 183 Japanese planes, led by Cmdr. Mitsuo Fuchida, began their fateful flight to Pearl Harbor.

Despite unmistakable signs of impending hostilities, Pearl Harbor was completely unprepared for an air attack. At bases scattered throughout Oahu, planes were lined up wing tip to wing tip, to protect them from ground-level saboteurs. Seven battleships, including the USS Arizona, *were moored on Battleship Row along Ford Island. At 7:53 A.M. Fuchida radioed "Tora, Tora, Tora" to the Japanese fleet, signaling that the surprise attack was about to begin.*

A pharmacist's mate on the USS California *looked up and remarked that "the Russians must have a carrier visiting us. Here come some planes with the red balls showing clearly." Pearl Harbor was soon shrouded in dark, billowing smoke, and the most famous radio message in American history, "Air raid Pearl Harbor, this is no drill," announced the reality of war. A second wave of Japanese planes struck at approximately 9:00. Later that morning, despite strong opposition, Vice Admiral Nagumo concluded that the "anticipated results have been achieved" and there was no need to press forward in an attempt to destroy the naval yard and other crucial facilities at Pearl Harbor.*

Twenty-one American ships were hit during the attack, including five battle-ships sunk and two others damaged. Over three hundred aircraft were destroyed or badly damaged. More than two thousand Americans were dead, over half on the USS Arizona, and another eleven hundred wounded. Japan lost only twenty-nine planes, fifty-five airmen, and five midget submarines with ten crew members. By early afternoon the Japanese fleet was heading toward home. In the weeks and months ahead Americans would frequently be told to "Remember Pearl Harbor."

Pearl Harbor

O N A BEAUTIFUL late June day in 1988 it was my good fortune to be in Honolulu when the second of two famous battleships associated with World War II came into port. The USS *Missouri* was returning from the Pacific, where it had been engaged in war games, and I was invited to tour the ship, an invitation I eagerly accepted. My memories of the *Missouri* stretch back to childhood, when I impatiently waited for the mailman to deliver the first plastic model I ever built, the battleship on which the Japanese surrender was accepted by Gen. Douglas MacArthur. Now, as I conjured up images of defeated Japanese military and diplomatic figures standing stoically on the surrender deck, facing stern and proud Americans, their allies in the background, I found myself actually standing on that deck. As I moved forward to the silver chain that guards the area where the surrender table once stood, now marked by a brass plate covered by a plastic bubble, I recalled MacArthur's hopeful words, that "from this solemn occasion a better world shall emerge out of the blood and carnage of the past."[1] I thought about the curious new world that did emerge, a world that made the *Missouri,* still awesome to behold, a poignant reminder of a world that might have been, had things gone differently in the early postwar years.

From the deck of the *Missouri* I looked across the harbor to the gleaming white memorial structure that spans the USS *Arizona,* sunk in nine minutes when a Japanese bomb penetrated its forward compartments and detonated huge quantities of fuel and ammunition, killing 1,177 crew members and entombing slightly less than one thousand. (Approximately one hundred bodies were recovered and identified; another hundred were recovered but never identified.) Other ships were sunk at Pearl Harbor during the attack, other crews decimated by casualties, but the *Arizona*'s "burning superstructure and canted masts [which] projected from the water" became as recognizable an image of Americans at war as Daniel Chester French's Minute Man Statue, the silhouette of the Alamo, or artistic depictions of the Pickett-Pettigrew charge at Gettysburg and Custer's Last Stand. Here, too, a new world began for Americans, a world at war in new and horrible ways. The *Arizona* symbolized complex memories of that war for those who lived in it and through it, and for others, like me, who were born into a world shaped by the events that brought fame to the *Arizona* and the *Missouri*.[2]

Prior to December 7, 1941, neither the *Arizona* nor Pearl Harbor were household names in the United States. Yet the attack has been widely perceived as one of the pivotal events in contemporary world history. *U.S. News and World Report* reflected in 1966 on the changes that Pearl Harbor helped bring about, noting, "The bombs that hit Pearl Harbor unleashed forces that produced a quarter of a century of the vastest changes the world has known. Since that morning, man has tamed atoms, moved into space, surged ahead in unprecedented prosperity. . . . Empires have vanished, maps changed, centers of power shifted. And a whole new set of problems has replaced problems of the past."[3]

For the few Americans who understood the significance of the Hawaiian naval base, Walter Davenport's June 1941 report in *Collier's* must have been reassuring. Davenport wrote that he was awed by the naval war games he had witnessed during his visit to Pearl Harbor, that the "whole thing was a demonstration of how quickly the billion-dollar fist that America has built in the Pacific could deliver a smash. . . . The Pacific Fleet of battleships, destroyers, cruisers, submarines and carriers are always within a few minutes of clearing for action." He conveyed the image of a lean, hungry fleet, ready for any eventuality: "Battleships, steam up and all but stripped, ride in the harbor or plow the ocean practicing gunnery, wary as lions on the prowl." He could not have anticipated just how bitterly ironic his prediction would prove to be, that the navy was waiting for "the word from Washington or an incident in the Pacific. If the latter comes first, the Pacific Fleet will notify Washington that the war is on."[4]

Word of Japan's attack on Pearl Harbor came on that fateful Sunday in December. Frank Knox, the secretary of the navy, interrupted Pres. Franklin D. Roosevelt's meeting with aide Harry Hopkins to deliver the news. The president called his press secretary, Stephen T. Early, shortly after two o'clock and told him to begin releasing information so that radio stations might inform the American public of the events that had taken place. H. R. Baukhage was among the first to spread the news, during a historic live broadcast from the White House on the NBC Blue Network. Spontaneous patriotic rallies were held on some college campuses, including the University of Illinois, where students marched to the president's house chanting "Beat Japan" and demanding suspension of Monday's classes. Long lines of volunteers stood outside recruiting offices—particularly those of the marine corps and the navy—throughout the night, waiting for them to open on Monday morning.[5]

Throughout the day President Roosevelt worked on his war message, most notably altering "a date which will live in world history" to the memorable line "a date which will live in infamy." When he spoke over the airwaves on December 8, roughly sixty million Americans listened to his six-and-a-half-minute address, the shortest war message in the nation's history. Lee Kennett reports, "In New York City, the stock market suspended bidding at noon, while in corporate offices telephone switchboards and intercoms were set to relay the broadcast from Washington. In a Milwaukee courtroom the judge turned on a radio and adjusted the volume so that the President's words could be heard by the jury, spectators, and thirty-one prisoners. . . . In many towns crowds gathered in the streets to listen to car radios, or to amplifiers set up to play Christmas music for shoppers." For many Americans the attack on Pearl Harbor sparked a long-awaited patriotic reawakening and signaled the end of an awkward period when the nation was balanced precariously between war and peace. "The years between Munich and Pearl Harbor," E. B. White wrote, "were like the time you put in a doctor's waiting room, years of fumbling with old magazines and unconfirmed suspicions, the ante years, the time of the moist palm and irresolution." Only months earlier Stewart Alsop had called for a "crusading faith" that would invigorate the nation's young men to "fight the war which sooner or later we shall be called on to fight," the war often remembered as the last "good" war.[6]

As news of the attack on Pearl Harbor spread, hysteria broke out in several mainland cities and Americans began to deal with the realization that war was at hand. Hawaiians were confronted by "constant and shapeless fears," as well as the awful reality of the attack itself. By late afternoon on December 7 the islands were placed under martial law and the police began to arrest Japanese, German, and Italian immigrants who had been designated as "suspicious." Gwenfread Allen notes that on the islands the customary joys of the Christmas season turned to melancholia, with the "tinkle bells on Salvation Army Christmas kettles [being] the only comforting reality in a world of camouflage, gas masks, barbed wire, and bomb shelters."[7]

The full scope of the disaster at Pearl Harbor would not be made public for some six months. In his first wartime fireside chat several days after the attack, the president reported that there had been "serious losses," but he did not reveal the extent of the damage. It was not until late December that *Life* published dramatic pictures of burning ships and bodies, pictures that the editors hoped would help Americans "remember Pearl Harbor always." Even before *Life*'s riveting pictures were available, however, Americans were being urged not to forget. The news of Pearl Harbor had interrupted bandleader Sammy Kaye's popular show "Sunday Serenade" on NBC radio, and Kaye went home and immediately wrote his best-selling song "Remember Pearl Harbor," released eight days later. In it he implored Americans to recall "as into line we fall, the thing that happened on Hawaii's shore. Let's REMEMBER PEARL HARBOR as we go to meet the foe. Let's RE-MEMBER PEARL HARBOR—As we did the Alamo."[8]

It is largely through the ruins of the USS *Arizona* that Americans have been taught to think about the war, the Japanese, and the opening of the nuclear age. In doing so we have come to accept a patriotic orthodoxy that communicates the traditional lessons of the attack, namely, that the events at Pearl Harbor on that quiet Sunday morning were both tragic and fortuitous, for they propelled the nation into a "good" war against the evil Nazis (in contrast to "good" Germans) and the treacherous Japanese (the entire culture was so categorized).[9] If America had been forced to invade Japan, it would have lost hundreds of thousands of men. Instead, thanks to modern science a weapon of benevolent destruction, the atomic bomb, had been created. Although it was unfortunate that two such bombs had to be dropped, they *did* end the war; and they also served as a final act of righteous revenge for the "Day of Infamy." For many Americans the atomic bomb balanced the scales of justice.

While Americans were reacting to the tragedy at Pearl Harbor with shock, anger, and a thirst for revenge, a memorial service was being planned in Honolulu for New Year's Day, to pay homage to the dead. In response to the Maui Rotary Club's request in 1942 that December 7 be set aside as Pearl Harbor Day, President Roosevelt instead asked for a "day of silence in remembrance of the great infamy." Honolulu newspapers agreed with his decision. The *Star-Bulletin* called the anniversary a time to "redouble our efforts and renew our pledges to carry on . . . till the 'day of infamy' is wiped out by a complete victory over a dishonorable foe." The *Advertiser* informed its readers that the one-year anniversary was "not an occasion for any special celebration or observance" but the "first milestone on the road to Tokyo."[10]

Even as the war raged on, plans were being made to memorialize the victims of the attack. Tony Todaro, a civilian worker at the Pearl Harbor Navy Yard, proposed the erection of a shrine at the nearby volcanic crater known as the Punchbowl. The shrine would serve to inform visitors of the history of the war in the Pacific and also would help to transform wartime Hawaii, a "symbol of might," into a "symbol of peace that postwar Hawaii should again become."[11] Other proposals included: an elaborate monument in Washington, D.C., suggested by another Pearl Harbor civilian worker, Herbert Knowles; a memorial on Oahu, for which the Women's National Patriotic Organization planned to raise five million dollars; and a "Temple of Peace," suggested by the Pacific Memorial Foundation, which the legislature designated in 1946 as the official war memorial agency of the territory. Another short-lived group, the Pacific War Memorial, Inc., called for a "living memorial" to those who had died. Rather than a "monument of stone," it proposed a "vast study [of the] science and peoples of the Pacific."[12]

In 1949 the territory of Hawaii established the Pacific War Memorial Commission (PWMC) "to create and maintain a living war memorial commemorating the sacrifices of our heroic dead of World War Two." From its earliest meetings the PWMC struggled with various proposals. In 1952, for example, a resolution was adopted to establish a "suitable and challenging plan for a system of memorials. . . . These sites encompass the Battleship Arizona; . . . Red Hill, which was the site of the first burials after the Pearl Harbor attack; the Pearl Harbor terminus of a mall or highway between Pearl Harbor and Honolulu; the Honolulu terminus of this same mall; Tripler Military Hospital; and Punchbowl National Cemetery." In 1953 the PWMC included in its long-range plans a "suitable monument at the site of the sunken battleship Arizona." Finally, in 1956 the commission's chairman, H. Tucker Gratz, reported that at a meeting with the commandant of the Fourteenth Naval District at Pearl Harbor, a "decision was reached . . . to sponsor a nationwide campaign for $250,000 to erect a permanent memorial on the U.S.S. Arizona."[13]

During years of planning the commission received suggestions from a number of individuals that focused on the *Arizona* itself. For example, a 1959 proposal envisioned enclosing the *Arizona* in a concrete wall to create a "lasting and fitting memorial" and then burying the ship and its entombed crew in the newly created *Arizona* Memorial Park next to Ford Island. A 1961 proposal asked the governor and the commission to encourage the people of Japan to participate in planning a memorial, which would take the form of a "Hall of Humanities" in an East-West cultural center. The plan called for the "reverent and tender recovery and re-interment of those now lying in the Arizona, side by side with an Unknown Soldier of Japan representing those of his comrades who also lie in ground and waters far from home." Furthermore, the *Arizona* should be removed and broken up and an "auction of the remains" conducted, with the proceeds earmarked for construction of the proposed "Hall of Humanities." Such potential alien intrusion on American sacred space was viewed with horror by many Americans, who wanted the memorial simply to "recall the infamy of Japan and the disgraceful act."[14]

The PWMC received congressional authorization in 1958 to raise funds and donate them to the navy to be used for the construction of a memorial. Fund-raising activities were aided by Ralph Edwards's December 3, 1958, television show "This Is Your Life," which focused public attention on the need for funds, and by an Elvis Presley concert in Honolulu on March 25, 1961, which raised the main portion of what became a $65,000 memorial fund. Still, to complete its task the PWMC needed a congressional appropriation. In 1961 Public Law 87–201 authorized use of public funds and offered a glimpse of Congress's perception of the memorial's function. In essence, the USS *Arizona* Memorial was to be "maintained in honor and commemoration of the members of the Armed Forces of the United States who gave their lives to their country during the attack."[15]

As the PWMC struggled to fund the memorial, citizens expressed anger and shame over the neglect of the *Arizona*. For example, *Collier's* Memorial Day 1950 issue showed a sailor standing forlornly on the rusted platform above the *Arizona*. The editors remarked, "It would be a better picture if the sailor were doing something besides just standing there—saluting a commemorative shaft, perhaps. But there was nothing for him to salute, no memorial, plaque, marker or anything to show that these first American casualties of World War II were even remembered by their countrymen." Readers were asked to consider the possibility that the navy did not *want* to remember the attack on Pearl Harbor because it had been such a shattering defeat for the United States. Nevertheless, they argued, while every effort should be made to ensure that another such attack would never take place, "the absence of a fitting memorial to the men of the Arizona, and to the others who died at Pearl Harbor and Hickam Field, is a symptom of an attitude that should be remedied."[16]

In 1955 Adm. C. E. Olsen, commandant of the Fourteenth Naval District, informed the secretary of the navy that visitors, often relatives of those entombed on the ship, were "shocked" at the condition of the "resting place of friends and loved ones." "Why," asked Olsen, "isn't there a fitting monument here?" He characterized the *Arizona* as a "rusted mess of junk metal in contrast to magnificent battle monuments at other famous battlegrounds." In January 1961 the editors of the *Washington Post* urged congressional funding to complete the memorial, calling the current situation a "poor memorial to these men and an unsuitable focal point for patriotic remembrance of this great disaster." On Memorial Day 1961 Adm. Robert L. Campbell, commandant of the Fourteenth Naval District, told a small gathering that he hoped this would be the "last Memorial Day ceremony on an open platform." And H. Tucker Gratz told Gov. Price Daniel of Texas, in Honolulu for the 1961 Conference of Governors, that "it is our first World War II dead who are the last to be given a suitable marker for their common grave."[17]

Politicians also spoke out against the neglect of the site. Testifying before the Naval Affairs Subcommittee of the House Armed Services Committee on June 28, 1961, Rep. Olin E. Teague of Texas, who had sponsored legislation to fund the memorial, called it "unthinkable" that the memorial would not be completed in time for the twentieth anniversary. He argued that the government had a moral obligation to "help complete the transition of the *Arizona* from a neglected wreck into something worthy of the men who lie forever within it."[18]

In 1959, even before the fund-raising was completed, Alfred Preis was selected by the navy to design the memorial. Michael Slackman notes that Preis was raised in Vienna and had been impressed with the "jewel encrusted crypts of the Hapsburg emperors and the immanent presence of death they conveyed." As a result, Preis initially proposed a structure in which visitors would be able to view "the underwater remains of the ship, encrusted with the rust and marine organisms" that reminded the architect of the royal sarcophagi. This proposal was unacceptable to the navy and Preis therefore proposed the current structure. Kevin Lynch correctly notes that such memorials take "dramatic advantage of destruction."[19]

The USS *Arizona* Memorial is an arched concrete structure, 180 feet long, that straddles but does not touch the sunken ship. When visitors disembark from the boats that bring them to the memorial, they can see the ship's bell in the entryway. There is also a central area from which they can view the remains of the *Arizona* and a room where the names of the 1,177 men who died on the *Arizona* are engraved on a white marble wall. Preis conceived of the memorial as an architectural expression of the rhythm of American wars and the rhythm of World War II in particular. Slackman notes that the architect "viewed the United States as an essentially pacifistic nation, one which inevitably would sustain the first blow in any war," and he wanted to remind Americans of "the inevitability of sustaining the initial defeat, of the potential for victory, and the sacrifices necessary to make the painful journey from defeat to victory." During anniversary services in 1973 Adm. Richard A. Paddock, commandant of the Fourteenth Naval District, recalled Preis's belief that "the form, wherein the structure sags in the center but stands strong and vigorous at the end, expresse[s] initial defeat and ultimate victory."[20]

The construction of the memorial began in 1960. On May 30, 1962, more than one thousand people attended the dedication ceremonies, in "tribute to the men whose lasting resting place has become a symbol for all who fell on December 7, 1941." Marine Attack Squadron 212 staged a flyover at 9:30 A.M., followed by the national anthem and an invocation. Then the chairman of the Veterans' Affairs Committee, Olin E. Teague, reminded the audience that "upon this sacred spot we honor the specific heroes who surrendered their lives . . . while they were in full bloom, so that we could have our full share of tomorrows. They remain imprisoned within this shattered hulk so that we could be free." Teague's speech was followed by a prayer, the navy hymn, the casting of flowers onto the harbor waters, benediction, and taps.[21]

Since its creation the USS *Arizona* Memorial has functioned as a ceremonial center for acts of commemoration and as a place to recall the lessons of the battle. The Pearl Harbor dead have been celebrated as heroes of the first battle of the war and mourned as victims of an inattentive nation. Especially during the bitter years of the Vietnam conflict, when martial memories were under severe assault, these tragic heroes were characterized as cultural models for a nation sorely in need of patriotic revitalization. For example, Adm. Harold G. Bowen, Jr., speaking at Memorial Day services on the *Arizona* in 1968, bemoaned the lack of a "spirit of nationalism" in the country and said that Americans must be prepared to fight "like our forebears that we today here honor." In 1969 Henry W. Buse, Jr., commanding general of the Fleet Marine Force, Pacific, said that the "memory of past greatness has real meaning when it is an inspiration for the present and the future." Pres. Gerald Ford's Pearl Harbor Day message in 1975 emphasized that blood sacrifice is often the price for freedom. "We will," he said, "hold our course for a peaceful Pacific . . . remembering that vigilance, the price of liberty, must be paid and repaid by each generation."[22]

The blood of the dead at Pearl Harbor was perceived to have paid for one vital lesson for the nation: the lesson of preparedness. In 1958 Sen. Carl Hayden of Arizona argued that any memorial at Pearl Harbor should "focus our attention on our most striking example of unpreparedness, so that we may be perpetually reminded of the security that is found in strength." The Conference of Governors, meeting in Honolulu in 1961, adopted a resolution calling for a memorial to serve as a reminder of the need for "eternal vigilance against the dangers of surprise attack." Speaking in support of public funding for the memorial, Harold Russell, commander of the veterans' organization AMVETS, told a congressional committee in 1961 that the men on the *Arizona* died needlessly, "pawns of a nation's folly—a grim example of what happens when a nation relaxes its guard." On December 5, 1976, navy veteran Jim D. Miller, a survivor of the attack, expressed the need for eternal vigilance in an increasingly hostile world: "It would have a different name. It would be a different place. . . . That is the event against which we must remain on guard." And in a 1980 National Park Service interpretive prospectus, Gary Cummins, the first NPS superintendent of the USS *Arizona* Memorial, characterized the crew as victims, "deprived of the opportunity to reflect upon the last inexorable steps to armed confrontation[;] most were denied even the exhilaration of battle and the sense of duty faithfully discharged."[23]

Coupled with the theme of preparedness was the realization that the stakes in future wars would be considerably higher, now that the nuclear age had begun. No sooner had the bombs dropped on Hiroshima and Nagasaki than Americans began worrying about a Pearl Harbor–like nuclear attack launched against them. Only three weeks after Nagasaki the *St. Paul Pioneer Press* dramatized the effects of unpreparedness for its readers: "cities wiped out, millions of its people killed and the survivors made the panic stricken and helpless captives of an invasion force." Many Americans believed that the Russians, like the Japanese at Pearl Harbor, were ready to launch an unexpected attack at the first sign of weakness. On December 8, 1966, at services at the National Memorial Cemetery of the Pacific, Secretary of the Navy Paul Nitze informed the crowd of about five thousand that the United States must not fall into a state of "psychological and military unpreparedness"; rather, it must maintain "effective and ready deterrents" to avoid the "new nightmares of 1941."[24]

Nightmares of surprise attacks merged with cold war tensions to make Pearl Harbor the most relevant lesson for a generation of nuclear strategists. In February 1950 the Weapons System Evaluation Group, a Pentagon think tank for the Joint Chiefs of Staff, warned that the Strategic Air Command (SAC) bases in Europe were in danger of being " 'Pearl Harbored' at the outset of future hostilities." RAND analyst Albert Wohlstetter, one of the most influential defense intellectuals of the early 1950s, also reached the conclusion that SAC forward bases were vulnerable to a Soviet surprise attack. According to Fred Kaplan, the impact of Wohlstetter's thinking was to "reinforce the assumption that once the Soviets acquired a theoretical capability to launch a dazzling . . . first-strike, they might very well launch one despite the many uncertainties and risks involved." Even in the late 1980s the lessons of Pearl Harbor were being used to argue for a nuclear weapons freeze. The Freeze Voter Institute, in an attempt to convince conservative voters of the wisdom of such a plan, warned that "new generations of [Soviet] nuclear weapons [could] wipe out American forces in a nuclear version of Pearl Harbor."[25]

The lessons of Pearl Harbor were not taught only through the exercise of patriotic rhetoric. On almost any day volunteers of the Pearl Harbor Survivors Association (PHSA), the nation's living link to the battle, can be found on the lawn outside the visitors center at the USS *Arizona* Memorial, talking about their experiences of the attack and how important it is to keep those memories alive. The motto of the PHSA is, "Remember Pearl Harbor—Keep America Alert," and every five years the group holds a sunset service at the memorial (the Honolulu-based Aloha chapter holds a private wreath ceremony at the memorial every year). According to the *Pearl Harbor-Gram,* the official magazine of the PHSA, each December 7 at 7:55 A.M. various ceremonies nationwide forge a "common bond" that reaches out "from Wisconsin to Seattle . . . from Florida to California, and from Oregon to New York," reminding Americans everywhere of the lessons of Pearl Harbor.[26]

Memories of Pearl Harbor were kept alive in the aftermath of the attack via celebrations of the triumph of the forces of righteousness in the great moral drama of World War II. The blood that was shed there was popularly perceived as redemptive blood; as such, it motivated America to enter the war and defeat the enemy. The blood that was shed at Hiroshima and Nagasaki was also considered redemptive blood, for it brought the story full circle. In addition, various other military victories during the war were perceived as just retribution for Pearl Harbor. During the Battle of Guadalcanal, for example, Japanese carriers that had launched Pearl Harbor strike planes were attractive targets. William Manchester remarks in *Goodbye Darkness,* his moving memoir of the Pacific war, that at the battle of Midway an American pilot who had been at Pearl Harbor "turned the nose of his Dauntless dive-bomber down toward the *Akagi*" and exclaimed as it blew up, " 'Arizona, I remember you.' " Almost forty years after American air power destroyed sixty Japanese ships and more than three hundred aircraft, and killed nearly eighteen hundred men, at Truk Lagoon, Geraldo Rivera, reporting for the ABC-TV news program "20/20," remarked, "They called it the 'Pearl Harbor payback.' "[27]

The language of righteous vengeance was frequently used during and after the war to justify U.S. military action. For example, following the firebombing of Tokyo in 1945, the *Atlanta Constitution* declared: "And with each city thus attacked, we remember the treachery of Pearl Harbor and find calm satisfaction in the knowledge that the Japanese of one more city have learned that there is a bill, which must be paid, for treachery, that retribution for such a deed is implacable." Pres. Harry S Truman insisted, "Nobody is more disturbed over the use of the atomic bomb than I am, but I was greatly disturbed over the unwarranted attack by the Japanese on Pearl Harbor and their murder of our prisoners of war. The only language they seem to understand is the one we have been using to bombard them. When you have to deal with a beast you have to treat him as a beast." Shortly after Hiroshima was destroyed the *Omaha Morning Herald* declared that "no tears of sympathy would be shed in America for the Japanese people. . . . Had they possessed a comparable weapon at Pearl Harbor, would they have hesitated to use it?" In 1947, reporting on the sixth anniversary of the attack on Pearl Harbor, the *Honolulu Advertiser* remarked that "the Japanese people have food and fuel shortages to remind them that six years ago . . . their radios blared the announcement of the 'spectacular victory.' " In 1966 *U.S. News and World Report* noted that while the United States had been criticized for the use of atomic weapons, "Americans . . . remembered Pearl Harbor."[28]

Believers in the moral symmetry of righteous vengeance have reacted bitterly to the transformation of Hiroshima into a universal symbol of the horror of modern war and human suffering. During his visit to the Peace Museum at Hiroshima, Peter Wyden, author of *Day One: Before Hiroshima and After*, noticed that the museum exhibits engendered quite different reactions from Americans: "Some visitors were ashamed and wept. Some felt angry and wrote in the visitors' book that they remembered Pearl Harbor." J. Richard Nokes, writing in *The Oregonian* in August 1980, expressed his own righteous anger when he asked if antinuclear activists commemorating August 6 (the anniversary of the bombing of Hiroshima) would also be "demonstrating enthusiastically December 7th to condemn the Japanese-attack on Pearl Harbor." The atomic bomb, he added, was a "terrible swift sword that ended a bloody war."[29]

Memories of Pearl Harbor often led the way toward the popular acceptance of the redemptive function of American strategic bombing, including the use of the atomic bomb. This was dramatically expressed in an air-power demonstration staged by the Confederate Air Force (CAF) at various places throughout the country. The CAF began as a group of former military pilots dedicated to acquiring and restoring World War II aircraft that were being scrapped. Chartered as a nonprofit organization in September 1961, the group had acquired sufficient aircraft by 1974 to stage a "dramatic two hour lesson in American history known as the WWII AIR-POWER DEMONSTRATION." The show began with a demonstration of German air power during the Spanish Civil War and ended with the "final assault on the Japanese mainland in 1945." The two-part message of the show was clear: "We must never be caught asleep again as we were on December 7, 1941"; and we must be "as relatively strong as we were in 1945 when these machines were first-line combat aircraft."[30]

The CAF's reenactment of the attack on Pearl Harbor was accompanied by rhetorical images of new birth. The narrator noted that before the attack America was "still asleep." But, he exclaimed, as soft Hawaiian music was drowned out by approaching planes adorned with Japan's Rising Sun, "out of the ashes of early defeat rose the phoenix of future victory."[31] A 1976 reenactment, before a crowd of more than forty thousand, ended with a solemn tribute to the memory of those who brought the nation victory through air power and with the "simulation of the B–29 A-Bomb attack on Japan signifying the allied victory and the end of the War." "As the B–29 approaches," the narrator informed the audience, "the explosion of the

Atomic Bomb goes off[,] ending some of the darkest days of America's history, WWII. And at the controls of the Boeing B–29 Superfortress is Gen. Paul Tibbets, who is the pilot of the Enola Gay that dropped the first Atomic Bomb on Hiroshima."[32]

Reenactment of the atomic destruction of Hiroshima sparked widespread controversy, especially in Japan, and the CAF has discontinued this portion of its show. In response to criticism the group expressed "regrets" that anyone would take offense but added, "The Japanese seem to have forgotten who started that war. We do not believe they apologized for their attack on Pearl Harbor, the Bataan Death March or other atrocities." The group also spoke about the significance of the reenactment of American air power: "We of the Confederate Air Force are going to do our best to see that the American people do not forget Pearl Harbor—and that the Japanese and others do not forget what made it necessary to drop that bomb on Hiroshima and Nagasaki."[33]

For those who felt the need for more inspiration than rhetoric or ritual could provide, Americans have enshrined the sacred relic of the battle, the USS *Arizona.* James P. Delgado, a National Park Service maritime historian, has characterized the *Arizona* shipwreck as unique, because it functions as a patriotic shrine, a grave, a memorial, and a historic site. Yet the *Arizona* is only one of forty-five enshrined warships that populate the American commemorative landscape. The USS *Alabama,* for example, is the "featured attraction of Mobile's 100-acre Marine Park." The Civil War ironclad USS *Cairo* rests in a museum near the Vicksburg battlefield, and the USS *Constellation,* the nation's oldest warship still afloat, is a national shrine in Baltimore. The USS *Constitution,* anchored in Boston's naval shipyard, has been "a favorite frontispiece for school texts since the turn of the century . . . [and was] chosen by the Post Office Department in 1964 as one of the three symbols of our heritage—together with the eagle and Liberty Bell—to appear on a 4-cent blue stamped envelope." The USS *Massachusetts* serves as a memorial to war veterans in Fall River, Massachusetts, and the USS *North Carolina,* which gained fame in the Pacific war, treats visitors to "splendid illumination and animation. . . . guns belching realistic fire and smoke captivate and inform up to 1,000 visitors during a typical 45-minute production." The USS *Texas,* which saw action in both world wars, is the "crowning touch" to the San Jacinto battlefield.[34]

In addition to these "massive metal statements of American might," the ceremonial landscape is also populated with a remarkable variety of relics from famous warships. For example, the "conning tower, bridge, shears, and periscope" from the USS *Flasher,* which sank more than one hundred

The USS *Arizona* burns following the explosion of its forward magazines.
(USS *Arizona* Memorial, National Park Service)

The USS *Arizona* as it appeared on December 10, 1941, after all the fires had been
extinguished. (USS *Arizona* Memorial, National Park Service)

These posters and the items shown on the next four pages illustrate some of the ways in which Americans "remembered Pearl Harbor." (Mariners Museum, Newport News, Va.)

A poster. (James P. Delgado
and the National Park Service)

A cachet envelope. (Ted Przychoda)

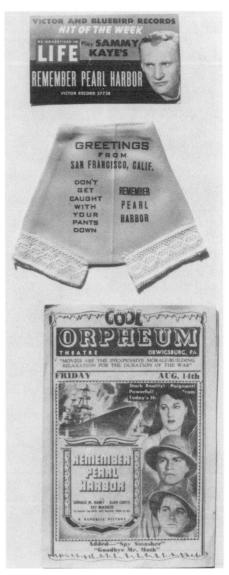

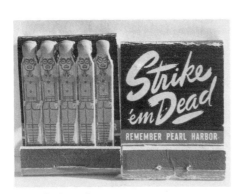

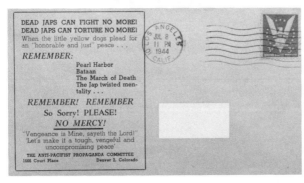

A matchbook, cachet envelope, record label, novelty panties, theater flyer, and assorted stamps and labels. (Ted Przychoda)

A Pearl Harbor remembrance calendar. (Ted Przychoda)

The Japanese minisubmarine *Ha. 19*, which toured the United States during the war, was the feature attraction of the Navy Day ceremonies at the San Francisco Civic Center, October 27, 1942. (James P. Delgado and the National Park Service)

thousand tons of enemy shipping in World War II, make up a "permanent memorial at the U.S. Naval Submarine Base, New London, Conn., to all underseas heroes who lost their lives in World War II." The bridge of the aircraft carrier USS *Franklin,* damaged in World War II, was installed as a permanent memorial in Norfolk, Virginia. The mast of the USS *West Virginia* rests at the University of West Virginia, and the bell, wheel, and other relics of the USS *Washington* are on display at the capitol in Olympia.[35]

Relics of the USS *Hartford,* Adm. David G. Farragut's flagship during the Civil War, are on display throughout the state of Connecticut and elsewhere. "One of the ship's bells graces [Hartford's] new Constitution Plaza. The Navy League placed a bronze plaque with an anchor from the ship in a beautiful setting near the University of Hartford's . . . administration offices. . . . [And] Connecticut Governor Abraham Ribicoff dedicated a second anchor memorial at the entrance to Mystic Seaport's yacht basin." Similarly widespread are relics from the USS *Indiana.* One of the mainmasts and several gun mounts are placed near Indiana University's football stadium, "an anchor is on view at Fort Wayne, and more than a thousand other relics have been placed in schools, museums, and exhibits throughout the State." The mainmast of the USS *Maine,* whose destruction sparked the Spanish-American War, stands in Arlington National Cemetery, and relics of the USS *South Dakota* make up an intricate memorial landscape in Sioux Falls.[36]

At Pearl Harbor, in the immediate aftermath of the battle, the USS *Arizona* was not treated as a sacred relic or a shrine. Although the navy had not yet determined the final disposition of the ship and its crew, navy divers removed the superstructure, armament, ammunition, and any other salvageable equipment—a pragmatic act that took precedence over any sense that a sacred place was being defiled.[37] By the time the battleship was taken off the record of active ships in 1942, its very presence inspired informal acts of veneration. John Martini notes, "Passing warships would muster their crews to the railings and have them render honours to Arizona, as they would to any ship of the fleet. In 1950 the symbolic gesture was made official when the battleship was placed in 'symbolic commission' and again allowed to fly the National Ensign. . . . A small wooden platform was constructed on her exposed deckhouse, and a surplus flagpole tacked onto the stump of her mainmast."[38] Beginning in 1950 the navy operated a popular shuttle boat to the memorial; on March 7, 1950, after ordering the installation of the flagstaff, Adm. Arthur Radford, commander in chief of the Pacific Fleet, also ordered that the flag be raised and lowered daily.

Like relics from other commemorative ships, pieces of the *Arizona* were scattered across the nation, many of them finding a home in the state of Arizona.[39] One of the battleship's bells, which had been dumped in a Bremerton, Washington, salvage yard and left there until someone noticed the inscription on it, eventually made its way to the University of Arizona, where it was housed in the student union, dedicated to those who had died in the war. In 1957 a USS *Arizona* Memorial committee asked the university's president, Richard A. Harwill, to return the bell so that it could become the "speaking heart" of the memorial. Harwill responded that to do so would be "impossible" because the bell was a "permanent part" of the student union. On October 16, 1962, another bell from the ship was placed in the lobby of the First National Bank of Arizona, in Phoenix. The Arizona Historical Foundation offered to return the bell to Pearl Harbor in 1964, and it was installed at the memorial on Memorial Day 1966.[40]

In 1972 one of the *Arizona*'s ten-ton anchors was brought into the state, to eventually serve as the major Arizona memorial to the Pearl Harbor heroes. The *Phoenix Gazette* reported that the "anchor provides particularly appropriate symbolism . . . because its massive weight and its purpose are symbolic of the massive faith thousands of Arizonans have displayed in keeping the American way solidly in place against the tides and currents of aggression." The anchor was housed in a special memorial display constructed after a public campaign during which 440 proposals for an appropriate memorial were received. On Flag Day, June 14, 1976, the USS *Arizona* Anchor Memorial was dedicated on the east mall of the capitol. Pearl Harbor Day services subsequently were held at this site and became the occasion for celebrations of patriotic revitalization. In 1982 Capt. Bruce McCormick, commanding officer of the Phoenix–San Diego naval recruiting district, told a Pearl Harbor Day audience he thanked God that "pride has returned in this last couple of years and the uniform and the insignia of this great country have once again become the symbol of what's right and what is just and honorable in America."[41]

To help Americans remember Pearl Harbor, some organizations and individuals constructed huge models of the *Arizona*. In 1967 the Fleet Reserve Association, a veterans group, presented an exact replica of the ship to the navy, the custodian of the USS *Arizona* Memorial. It weighed 325 pounds and was six feet, three inches long. Some years later Scottsdale resident Charles Berry built a seven-and-one-half-foot scale model of the *Arizona* and, after equipping it with motors and sailing it on a small lake, donated it to the state in 1980. The model was exhibited in a case on the second floor of the capitol, near a display of *Arizona* memorabilia. According to a report in the *Phoenix Gazette*, "The gray, black and rust colored model features intricately carved sailors walking the deck, four gun turrets, 22 smaller guns, anchors and chains and miniature flags, with the Arizona flag flying at the stern." In 1984 Cecil Gates of California completed work on a thirty-four-foot fiberglass replica of the *Arizona*. At the ship's christening he asked that all Americans "remember the sacrifice of these men who gave their lives that we may enjoy the freedoms we have today." Gates envisioned his touring model as a "miniature shrine" that would sail "into the ports and hearts of America." Powered by two fifty-horsepower engines, Gates's *Arizona* was displayed at a Los Angeles boat show and at the state capitol in Phoenix; it also toured many of the nation's waterways and in 1986 took part in the "Tall Ships" display in New York City during Fourth of July festivities.[42]

Like the Alamo chapel, the *Arizona* Memorial was consciously designed to function as a shrine. In addition, it is unique because it was built over a sacred relic that is also a tomb. Certainly, the presence of the remains of almost one thousand men contributes to the charged environment of the memorial and draws visitors for various reasons. In July 1968, for example, a Cincinnati resident who lost two sons on the *Arizona* and had saved for more than twenty-six years to visit their gravesite finally paid an emotional visit to the memorial. Others come in death, their remains placed inside the *Arizona,* for any *Arizona* survivor may request that his ashes be deposited at the bottom of one of the open gun turrets on the ship. George Lang, of KGO-TV in San Francisco, was allowed to film an underwater interment in 1988 and tells the moving story of a dying man's agonizing choice between burial near his family and burial with his shipmates on the *Arizona*. The man's wife helped him decide on the latter, because "his whole life was that day."[43]

As James Delgado notes, those who died on the *Arizona* have, from the beginning, been treated differently from other American casualties of World War II.[44] Instead of remains waiting to be recovered and dealt with appropriately, the bodies of the Pearl Harbor heroes are to be protected from any form of defilement. In 1983 the navy and the Park Service received a proposal from a man who claimed that he had invented a machine that would "get the bodies out without anyone getting hurt." The regional director of the NPS responded that "any attempts to remove the remains of these men and disturb their final resting place would be considered by many, including their families, to be a sacrilege." The navy "respectfully declined [the] offer."[45]

The *Arizona* engenders conflicting emotions in those who revere it. On the one hand there is the urge to preserve the boundary between sacred ship and secular harbor—clearly a more difficult task for the NPS at Pearl Harbor than at battlefields on land; on the other hand there is the urge to know as much as possible about the mysterious underwater tomb-relic. This mixture of veneration and curiosity was expressed in a series of underwater explorations of the *Arizona* carried out by the navy and the Park Service beginning in September 1983. The dives were spurred by visitor curiosity as well as the fact that the NPS was responsible for managing and interpreting a site that it could not see. As Daniel Lenihan, the NPS chief of the Submerged Cultural Resources Unit, remarked, "People stood on the memorial and saw jagged stuff, not a ship. We wanted to make sense of this for the visitors." Lenihan and Gary Cummins, the NPS superintendent, presented their plan to Adm. Conrad J. Rorie, commander of the naval base at Pearl Harbor, who authorized the use of navy divers to assist in the project. "Assessment dives" began in 1983; in 1984 and 1985 the site was surveyed and videotaped, and precise drawings were made of the ship. In 1986 and 1987 divers studied the level of corrosion on the *Arizona* and also surveyed the USS *Utah*, Pearl Harbor's "forgotten" wreck. In 1988 the goal was a "full submerged cultural resources study of World War II remains in Pearl Harbor."[46]

The first dives were carried out simply to provide basic information on the *Arizona*. Underwater visibility in the harbor was poor and, as Cummins wrote, the "mapping project became similar to entering a strange room in the dark with pencil, paper, measuring tape and a flashlight, to make a scale drawing." Video and still cameras brought to the surface images that were, in the words of the NPS's John Martini, "fascinating and haunting . . . an open deck hatch, with its sun awning still in place, exposed floor tiles and broken crockery in the galley, a fire hose stretched out on deck by crewmen who had died minutes later."[47]

Many of the divers were overwhelmed by what they saw. For Lenihan, the difficulty of the task at hand was so great that he did not begin to feel the impact of what he had seen until he was resting in his hotel room after the first dive, looking at the film he had taken as it appeared on Honolulu television. A sense of presence and intimacy came slowly, over a number of dives. Later, he recalled the jarring contrast between the peaceful underwater surroundings and the violence in the twisted wreckage. He also spoke of the awe he felt at the scale of destruction, which impressed upon him the power of conventional warfare. Lenihan remembered asking, "What can we expect from the atomic bomb?"[48]

By contrast, James Delgado, whose job permitted him to "touch the sacred," said that he immediately felt both fear and attraction, the traditional ambivalence human beings sense in the presence of great power—in this case, "a living entity sitting on the bottom." Delgado characterized the scene as one of "fresh death" and remarked that it was like being at the Little Bighorn, with the "bones still sticking out of the ground." He spoke of the "bleeding wounds," referring to the haunting image of the still-seeping oil, which visitors to the memorial can clearly see. He also mentioned the various encrustations that covered the *Arizona,* which could be viewed in one of two ways: either the ship was "fouled" by this growth or it was bejeweled. For Delgado, like Lenihan, one of the messages conveyed by the *Arizona* was the "futility of war."[49]

Cummins, Lenihan, and Delgado all described visitors to the USS *Arizona* Memorial as intensely curious about what the divers were doing and mostly supportive once they understood the reason for the dives. For some, however, the presence of divers anywhere near the *Arizona* represented desecration. In 1983 a constituent wrote to Sen. Sam Nunn of Georgia that the "invasion of divers around the bodies of the men and officers of the USS Arizona I find lacking in sensitivity and shocking." The NPS took extreme care to inform veterans groups, particularly the Pearl Harbor Survivors Association, whose support was politically crucial, of the fact that divers would not enter the wreckage and that the purpose of the dives was to help the Park Service—and therefore present and future visitors—better appreciate the condition of the *Arizona.*[50]

In November 1987 the NPS superintendent at the memorial, William Dickinson, wrote to the remaining survivors from the *Arizona* to inform them of the success of previous dives, which had "contributed significantly to visitor understanding of the USS Arizona, the massive destruction . . . [and] the tragedy and finality of those who lost their lives." He asked for their reaction to a plan to conduct two-way video programs between the underwater site and separate groups of schoolchildren and survivors in San Francisco. "At no time," he assured them, "would the ranger enter the ship," for the program was designed to be "educational, not sensational" and "sensitivity to those killed [would be] of utmost importance." Such a program would reach "a large and diverse audience, many of whom would otherwise know little of the fate of the USS Arizona, her crew and the sacrifices." The program would also provide an "opportunity for survivors to see the Arizona for the first time in over 46 years." Dickinson noted in a letter to Delgado that responses ranged from "support . . . to total disgust." The program was never carried out, in part because many survivors were concerned about the "presence of bodies or bones" and felt that to "open a gravesite for general viewing . . . [would] be a 'commercialization' . . . of the grave site."[51]

From the Park Service's perspective the dives were certainly a success. Based on painstakingly executed underwater drawings, Robert F. Sumrall, curator of ship models at the United States Naval Academy, was able to build an eight-foot model of the modern-day *Arizona,* which was installed in the visitors center at the memorial in April 1987. The NPS also has a more complete picture of the resource it is responsible for and can chart the progress of corrosion more accurately. In addition, the various responses to the dives revealed a great deal about the power of the *Arizona*. The divers experienced fear, awe, intimacy, and a sense of being in the presence of something alive, something holy. Like the divers, a majority of visitors were curious, eager to "see" the *Arizona* with a postbattle immediacy that was not available to those who wished to go back in time and "see" the Little Bighorn or the Angle at Gettysburg. Others expressed shock and outrage at any human presence around (let alone inside) this sacred environment.

Pearl Harbor shares with other battlesites in the ongoing struggle to reconstruct the physical environment as it was at the time of the battle and to establish markers to separate consecrated space from ordinary surroundings. But where are the boundaries at Pearl Harbor? And how can they be defined in underwater space?

The USS *Arizona* Memorial rests in the middle of a harbor that bustles with the daily activity of a major naval base. It is also not the only significant commemorative space in or near the harbor. The USS *Utah* Memorial stands on the far side of Ford Island, accessible only to military personnel. And as James Delgado notes, the "bullet holes in the buildings of Hickam Field and Schofield Barracks comprise a material statement that . . . preserves the reality of World War II in a manner that could never be replicated by books, films or pictures."[52] Yet the presence of these other stark material reminders of the attack has not diminished the role of the *Arizona* Memorial as the sacred center of Pearl Harbor. Thus, various attempts have been made to lessen the risk of defilement by building or maintaining both physical and ideological boundaries around the memorial and its message.

For some, physical defilement is symbolized by the presence of Japanese tourists and Japanese ships at Pearl Harbor, at the visitors center, and at the memorial. In a moving account of his return to various Pacific war battlesites, William Manchester expressed his discomfort at the sight of two Japanese navy ships in Pearl Harbor: "I jerk upright as we dart by one inlet. Moored there are the last ships I expected to see in Pearl Harbor—two spanking-new destroyers of the Empire of Japan." Gary Cummins spoke of the bitter feelings many visitors have toward the numerous Japanese tourists who come to the memorial. He was asked often, he said, "How many Japs work for you?" and he remembered one gentleman who pointed angrily toward a group of Filipinos and asked, "Why are those Japs here?" Similarly, several Asian American NPS rangers mentioned that visitors would occasionally ask them if they were Japanese. In 1983 a visitor wrote to the NPS to express his "shock and anger" at seeing so many Japanese tourists applaud a Park Service presentation that spoke of the brilliance of Japan's tactics at Pearl Harbor. He added, "I wish that I felt better about the loyalty of Americans of Japanese ancestry now in Hawaii," obviously lumping Japanese Americans and native Japanese together. The NPS responded that the Japanese tourists were merely "applauding a speech by a uniformed person, rather than the subject matter, since visitors from Japan usually have no understanding of English, but do have great respect for officials." Cummins concurred. He said that he never heard Japanese tourists applaud during any description of the attack, but they did applaud as a gesture of thanks for the ranger's program.[53]

Angry voices have also protested the presence in Pearl Harbor of things Japanese, from gift shop items in the visitors center and too many Japanese-made cars in the parking lot to the Japanese-owned hotel and golf course in the hills above the harbor. In April 1977 a visitor was outraged when he purchased a paperweight version of the memorial that had been made in Japan. "I think it's kind of a slap in the face at [the] US," he wrote to the *Star-Bulletin*. Those who died at Pearl Harbor "would turn over in their graves if they knew where this thing came from." In 1986 another one of Senator Nunn's constituents complained about purchasing a postcard "printed in Japan. . . . To have such a card for sale at the U.S. Government Memorial is to me a slap in the face of any U.S. veteran of World War II who served or died because of this dastardly deed." The park superintendent informed the senator that "card selection is based upon [an] evaluation of the quality, cost and relationship of each individual card to the USS Arizona Memorial" and that the sale of cards made in Japan did not represent "approval of the Japanese actions on the morning of December 7, 1941." Even Alfred Preis's "tree of life," carved into one wall of the memorial, provoked comments by the occasional visitor who thought that it was composed of Japanese characters.[54]

Of greater consequence for the Park Service were controversies regarding the proposed return to Pearl Harbor of a Japanese midget submarine, captured on the day of the attack, and the planned display of a Japanese airman's personal belongings. The minisub (designated *Ha. 19*) ran aground at Bellows Field beach when its self-destruct mechanism failed to operate correctly. One of the crew members, Kazuo Sakamaki, became the United States' first prisoner of war. The *Ha. 19* was captured by a salvage party and shipped to the mainland in January 1942, where it was mounted "on a trailer and modified for public display." According to James Delgado the submarine "toured the United States in 1942–1945 as a promotion for war bond sales." Beyond its significance as the first American war prize, it served another purpose, becoming the focal point for American anger at the Japanese. After a brief stay in Chicago at the end of the war, the *Ha. 19* was moved to a submarine base in Key West, Florida. In 1964 the navy loaned it to the Key West Art and Historical Association, and it was displayed at the Key West Lighthouse Museum. In 1987, when the museum decided to focus its energies elsewhere, NPS Superintendent Dickinson began to explore the possibility of bringing the *Ha. 19* to the USS *Arizona* Memorial.[55]

As was the case with the underwater exploration of the *Arizona,* the Park Service took great pains to inform veterans groups of its reasons for calling for the return of the *Ha. 19.* An NPS "Issue Briefing Statement" in 1986 noted that "interest among Veterans' groups is very high. Organizations including the Naval Historical Center, Office of Naval History acknowledge the submarine should logically be on display and interpreted at the USS *Arizona* Memorial." The statement also noted that the plan had received the support of the director of the U.S. Navy Submarine Base Pearl Harbor Museum and Sen. Spark Matsunaga. After meeting with representatives of the ad hoc committee of the National Veterans Organizations (representing approximately thirty groups), James Delgado informed the NPS's chief historian, Edwin C. Bearss, that the "only concern voiced was over how much government money would be expended to move and display *Ha. 19* at Pearl Harbor." In response to a congressional query, the executive director of the Veterans of Foreign Wars indicated that the plans "[did] not appear to create a situation which the VFW finds insensitive or [which] detracts from the USS *Arizona* Memorial."[56]

While representatives of the various veterans organizations were not offended by the plans, resistance from some of the rank and file did create problems for the Park Service. A member of the American Legion in Niagara Falls, New York, sent a letter to other legionnaires in which he termed the planned return of the Japanese minisub a "gross insult to all of our Servicemen and Women who died [at Pearl Harbor]." Declaring that "this desecration of the Arizona Memorial must be stopped," he asked that each legionnaire write to his congressional representative to protest the plan. In April 1989 a World War II veteran voiced his objections in a letter to the NPS: "I cannot understand memorializing the Japan War Machine. We have done more than enough to forgive the Japanese people." During that same month the Education and Human Services Committee of the Niagara County legislature passed a resolution against the transfer of the *Ha. 19,* declaring that it would be a "direct insult to those who are entombed on the U.S.S. Arizona and to all Veterans."[57]

Editorial and congressional objections also complicated the Park Service's plans. In April 1989 Bob Curran of the *Buffalo News* reported on the veterans' discontent and informed his readers that one veteran told him he would withdraw his objections "just as soon as Japan puts up a monument honoring the 'Enola Gay.' " On April 26, 1989, Rep. William Paxon of New York wrote to Manuel Lujan, secretary of the Department of the

Interior, about the large number of complaints he had received regarding the minisub. He voiced his *"strong opposition"* to the plan, calling it an "insult to the many brave Americans who fought and died in the service of our country during World War II."[58]

The NPS prepared a standard response to these complaints, offering a brief history of the *Ha. 19* and emphasizing its function at Pearl Harbor. "If we acquire and display the submarine," the NPS declared, "our intent is certainly not to memorialize the Japanese attackers. Rather it will be displayed as the only enemy vessel captured intact . . . and an effective tool for war bond sales, and the role it played as a symbol to help the nation 'Remember Pearl Harbor.' " In responding to Representative Paxon, the Park Service director, James M. Ridenour, declared: "Under no circumstances would the minisub be placed on or near the USS Arizona Memorial itself, which is athwart the sunken vessel. Rather, consideration is being given to displaying the minisub on the shoreside visitor center about a half mile across open water from the memorial. . . . If acquired, the submarine would be displayed along with other tools of war. Their display is intended to help bring home the awful reality of December 7, 1941." Ridenour added that "without such reminders, I fear the meaning of the event will be lost to future generations, Japanese as well as American." In another response the Park Service noted that it was trying to "present all aspects of the attack on Pearl Harbor. . . . The submarine represents a part of that story."[59]

In January 1990 the NPS received a letter from twenty-six members of the Fresno, California, chapter of the Pearl Harbor Survivors Association who supported the plan to bring the *Ha. 19* to the visitors center at the *Arizona* Memorial. In their letter they noted that the capture of the submarine and the taking of the first prisoner of war were "two of the few victories for our side on December 7, 1941." They added, "Many of us . . . plan to attend our 50th Reunion in Hawaii on December 7, 1991. Let us hope the fruits of two of our first victories will be on display." These PHSA members were also critical of opposition to the plan to relocate and exhibit the *Ha. 19,* wondering if "VFW members who voiced the opposition are really so sincere that they have refrained from purchasing Japanese autos, TVs, VCRs, computers, etc." Such support was not, however, sufficient to allow the NPS to risk making an unpopular, politically loaded decision. Consequently, in March 1990 Ridenour asked other NPS officials to review various options for the display of the submarine: at the visitors center, at the USS *Bowfin* (a private nautical museum adjacent to the *Arizona* Memorial), or at the Nimitz Museum in Fredericksburg, Texas. It was eventually decided that the *Ha. 19* would be displayed at the Nimitz Museum until after the fiftieth anniversary ceremonies and then moved to the visitors center at Pearl Harbor.[60]

In 1987 the Park Service also became embroiled in a controversy regarding the planned display of the personal belongings of a Japanese airman who flew in the Pearl Harbor attack. Some thought, mistakenly, that the display would be in the memorial itself rather than in the museum at the visitors center. A New Jersey resident wrote to his congressional representative, "If this atrocity planned by the National Park Service is intended to be included as part of the USS *Arizona* Memorial, it will defile the memory of all Americans who died as a result of that Japanese airman's treachery and [will] desecrate the grave of 1,177 victims thereof who are still buried there." He noted that his wife's brother was entombed in the *Arizona* and that he himself was a combat veteran of the Pacific war. In a rather strident tone he demanded assurances that any Japanese memorial would "get no closer to Pearl Harbor . . . than Tokyo." NPS Director William Penn Mott, Jr., responded that the display was "intended to bring home the awful reality of December 7, 1941. If we omit such items from exhibit, we leave the erstwhile enemy faceless." Mott also declared that such exhibits were important in order to impress upon Japanese tourists the meaning of Pearl Harbor, for what began there "ended at Hiroshima." Mott continued, "To appreciate one it is necessary to acknowledge the other. The people of both Nations must continue to appreciate the terrible price we paid for peace."[61]

Although the vast majority of complaints about Pearl Harbor that were directed to the Park Service dealt with the perceived defilement of a sacred environment by things Japanese, a number of individuals were angered by racial slurs they felt were aimed at the Japanese. In November 1983, for example, a Des Moines, Iowa, physician wrote to Sen. Daniel Inouye about a videotape he had purchased at the gift shop in the visitors center. In it the face of an Oriental woman is superimposed over the burning wreckage of the USS *Arizona*. The physician commented that this ranked with "the 'Yellow Peril' sentiment of World War II." Gary Cummins informed Inouye that the woman in the videotape was Edean Saito, the assistant business manager at the Arizona Memorial Museum Association and a park ranger. The purpose of the scene, Cummins said, was to "demonstrate that oriental, specifically Japanese, visitors are welcome" and that the memorial is for "all peoples, not just Caucasians."[62]

Besides the perceived threat of pollution from the Japanese, other, more traditional forms of disrespect angered visitors to the USS *Arizona* Memorial. In some cases it was the lack of proper behavior and the belief that such irreverence revealed troublesome truths about the nation. A letter to Pres. Richard M. Nixon in 1972 complained about the lack of good boats and sailors in "proper dress and deportment" at the memorial. "Only a

Divers measured the depth of encrustation on the USS *Arizona* during the NPS/navy investigative dives in the mid-1980s. Photograph by Larry Murphy. (National Park Service)

An exposed section of teak decking on the USS *Arizona*. Photograph by Larry Murphy. (National Park Service)

Eating utensils in the *Arizona*'s galley area. Photograph by Larry Murphy. (National Park Service)

A diver points out that the space between this blackout cover and porthole glass is still partially filled with air. Photograph by Larry Murphy. (National Park Service)

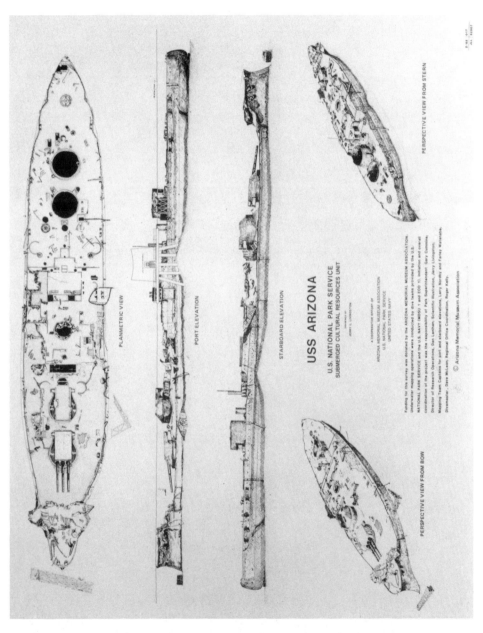

These drawings of the submerged *Arizona*, made by Jerry Livingston, were the basis for a model of the ship now on display at the visitors center. (Arizona Memorial Museum Association)

Scenes from the CAF's reenactment of the attack on Pearl Harbor during a World War II Airpower Demonstration. (Confederate Air Force)

The CAF's controversial reenactment of the dropping of the
atomic bomb on Hiroshima. (Confederate Air Force)

The USS *Arizona* Memorial in December 1956, looking toward Ford Island.
(National Park Service)

Unattended wreckage of the superstructure of the
USS *Arizona*, at Waipo Point. (James P. Delgado
and the National Park Service)

Two views of the USS *Arizona* Memorial. (USS *Arizona* Memorial, National Park Service)

The shrine room at the USS *Arizona* Memorial. (USS *Arizona* Memorial, National Park Service)

U N I T E D   S T A T E S

M A R I N E   C O R P S

THE GALLANT MEN
THEIR SHIPMATES
...IVES IN ACTION
THE U.S.S. ARIZONA
BY AMVETS 1960

The USS *Bennington* salutes the *Arizona,* 1958. (USS *Arizona* Memorial,
National Park Service)

dying disinterested country," the president was told, "disregards its own dead and its own memorials." Several letters in the *Navy Times* in 1987 complained about the concessions being sold at the visitors center and the fact that "this year you could have gone out there [to the memorial] wearing almost nothing." Other tourists disagreed. One wrote, "If a visit to this memorial leaves visitors with a better understanding of why the attack took place and with the strong feeling that we *must not* let this happen again, then surely those entombed will not have died in vain."[63]

As at other battlefields and shrines the *Arizona* Memorial occasionally has been the site of protest—though given the logistical problem of transporting protesters by boat to the memorial, this has happened far less frequently at Pearl Harbor than at other locations. In 1980 a scuffle ensued when members of the Revolutionary Communist party, who understood the memorial to symbolize "America's hypocrisy," tried to put up a red banner. In 1981 members of the same group tore down the American flag at the memorial to call attention to the "guilt" of the United States, which they claimed had provoked the Japanese attack in order to bring the country out of its economic depression.[64]

Another concern at Pearl Harbor has been the nature of ritual activities. A navy regulation issued in 1971 offered guidelines for conducting services at the memorial: "Because of numerous inquiries from service personnel as well as civilian organizations, it is requested that a determination be made as to whether ceremonies such as reenlistments, promotions, retirements . . . fall within the dignity associated with the memorial and whether they should be permitted." The chief of naval operations ruled that they did not. In December 1974 naval regulations stipulated that the commander of the Fourteenth Naval District had the authority to "coordinate all formal and informal observances. . . . wreath layings, plaque presentations and other informal tributes conducted with dignity, such as prayers and flag raisings, are considered appropriate, but no formal ceremony is permitted except the annual services held on Memorial Day." That same year a shipyard employee suggested to the navy that it would be "fitting" if all employees were allowed to "pause for one minute of silent prayer each Dec. 7th at 0750." His proposal was adopted, and a shipyard whistle now sounds to mark the employees' observance of the events that transpired at Pearl Harbor. The commander of the Fourteenth attended the first observance, along with the employee and his family, and honored him for caring about his country and "the memory of those who died."[65]

Just as various forms of physical defilement have threatened to contaminate the sacred environment of Pearl Harbor, so has ideological defilement threatened the venerable patriotic orthodoxies that help Americans remember Pearl Harbor and the Pacific war in heroic terms. At the heart of such orthodoxies is the immutable truth of the treachery and infamy of the attack. Even the faintest suggestion that the Japanese carried out a tactical masterpiece is deemed by some to be unacceptable, for the wounds of war are still not healed sufficiently.

At Pearl Harbor the power of patriotic faith is expressed in vehement reaction to part of the script of a movie shown to tourists at the visitors center prior to boarding the boats that carry them to the memorial. The same heretical words can also be found on an interpretive plaque in a museum display. The culprit is Adm. Husband E. Kimmel, commander in chief of the Pacific Fleet in 1941, who spoke these words, shortly after the battle, in his testimony before the Roberts Commission, the first of many government commissions searching for Pearl Harbor scapegoats: "I must say that this air raid was a beautifully executed military maneuver. [The Japanese] knew exactly where every air field in this place was and they knew exactly where every ship in the harbor was supposed to be." Kimmel's characterization of the attack as "a beautifully executed military maneuver" has led some visitors to complain to their congressional representatives and to the National Park Service. In 1985, for example, a Maryland physician asked Rep. Sidney Yates to investigate the use of this heretical phrase by the NPS. Gary Cummins explained that these were Kimmel's words, not the Park Service's, and that he felt Kimmel had demonstrated "personal integrity and courage" during his testimony. Rather than pass the buck to save his career, Cummins declared, Kimmel had chosen to help make the commission and others aware that the "Japanese were an extremely capable foe."[66]

Cummins also noted in his response to Yates the support of the Pearl Harbor Survivors Association and another veterans organization, the Arizona Reunion Association, neither of which "has had any problem with the museum exhibits." Furthermore, he remarked, people have to face "unpleasant facts from which we learn the lessons of history." Admiral Kimmel's statement "is his own assessment, not mine," the superintendent concluded. Not surprisingly, Yates's constituent found Cummins's careful explanation "unacceptable" and declared that "describing the Japanese attack in these terms smacks of another Bitberg [sic]." The physician also informed Yates that a few hours after reading Kimmel's heretical words at the exhibit he had suffered a coronary attack and, while in the hospital, had heard a nurse "of Japanese descent describe the attack in the same fashion." The director of the NPS responded to Yates that the quotation was not offensive "in context" and that in updated museum displays care would be taken to "insure that . . . visitors will recognize that it was extracted from the Roberts report."[67]

As on other issues, the NPS had a stock response to most complaints about the film, including a 1987 letter in which the writer expressed outrage that "*American* tax money is being spent at an *American* National Park to propagate anti-American propaganda!" The Park Service declared that it was responsible for providing "forthright, honest, and . . . accurate interpretations of the historical events occurring before, during, and after the attack on Pearl Harbor." It felt that the film in question communicated in a "solemn and eerie sort of way . . . the loss of American lives." These explanations aside, Michael Slackman, who served as a seasonal ranger at the USS *Arizona* Memorial for three years, commented that he heard an "overwhelming number of complaints about the lack of patriotism in the film."[68]

In 1989 the NPS's chief historian, a marine combat veteran of the Pacific war, visited Pearl Harbor and reported on the need to "update and improve" the story being presented in the interpretive displays. In particular, Edwin Bearss thought the NPS interpretation should "include events in the Pacific War from the December 7 attack through the Battle of Midway, June 3–6, 1942." Furthermore, the movie at the visitors center should be redone, but not to ensure traditional patriotic purity. "The script needs to be rewritten," Bearss said, "to eliminate elements of racism and inappropriate rhetoric that distorts or makes history too simplistic." He also suggested that the oral-history program be expanded to "include Japanese veterans and participants in the December 7 attack and the operations during the period from December 1941 through the Battle of Midway."[69]

The need to define appropriate physical and ideological boundaries at the memorial continues to present a challenge to the National Park Service. What, for example, should be done with the physical remains of the *Arizona*? "Should we be doing anything to preserve shipwrecks in place? . . . What about shipwrecks that are also grave sites? Should we let the natural processes continue unimpaired? Should we be looking for means to slow or stop deterioration? Should we be retrieving significant artifacts? Should we, for example, remove the [remaining] 14-[inch] guns from the USS ARIZONA so they can be displayed and people can see them before they are lost to corrosion? Should we document wrecks with known dead? Should we merely monitor the deterioration process, noting changes in conditions that occur over time but allowing deterioration to continue? . . . Should we be diving on such submerged grave sites? Should we penetrate them?"[70]

Sensitivities regarding the *Arizona* present the Park Service with a dilemma no matter what decisions it reaches. Acts of preservation, designed to protect the tomb of the *Arizona* dead, could be construed as defilement through intrusion; but leaving the *Arizona* to deteriorate slowly could be construed as defilement through neglect. Part of the *Arizona*'s superstructure, removed during the construction of the memorial, lies rusting in an open field and is easy prey for relic hunters. Gary Cummins recalled individual proposals to profit from the sale of relics made from remnants of the superstructure; indeed, he remembered seeing advertisements for the sale of pieces of the rusted remains. One entrepreneur planned to melt down the superstructure and sell small pieces as religious trinkets. Admiral Rorie, commander of the naval base at Pearl Harbor, addressed the curious neglect of this integral part of the *Arizona* when he approved the plans for underwater exploration in 1983. He asked the NPS to locate a suitable underwater site next to the *Arizona* where these rusting pieces of the superstructure could be placed, for they were too large and too badly damaged to be displayed in the museum. The divers did find such a location, but as yet no action has been taken.[71]

Although Pearl Harbor does not face the same threats from the encroachment of modernity that are faced at other battlesites such as Lexington and Concord, the Alamo, and Gettysburg, the Park Service must nonetheless fend off commercial designs that would pollute the sacred environment around the USS *Arizona* Memorial. In what may be the most tasteless of recent suggestions, former Hawaii senator Hiram L. Fong wrote to Vice Pres. George Bush in 1986 asking him to support a plan to locate a floating restaurant, Oceania, in the harbor for the convenience of visitors to the memorial. Hiram Fong, Jr., who conceived the plan, told Secretary of the Interior Donald P. Hodel and Adm. J. A. Lyons, Jr., commander in chief of the Pacific Fleet, that "many visitors face a long wait at the bus stop and an hour's ride in heavy traffic back to their hotels in Waikiki." His restaurant would change all that, of course. However, he wanted to assure everyone concerned that he would "scrupulously avoid any activities that would possibly detract from or conflict with the Center operations." Furthermore, "prior to mooring . . . the exterior of the *Oceania* [would] be remodeled to provide a subdued appearance in keeping with the area around the Memorial Center." The vice president passed Fong's request along to the Park Service, which responded that "a visit to the USS *Arizona* is a powerful, emotional experience. Therefore, we believe that realizing a profit from the sacrifice of the men aboard the ship would be inappropriate."[72]

The NPS obviously faces an immense task at Pearl Harbor as it seeks to develop "an interpretive program which promotes a clear and objective understanding of the reasons for the December 7 attack; . . . the role of the USS *Arizona* in the attack; how the attack affected the United States, the people of Hawaii; and the course of the Pacific War afterwards." It must carry out these interpretive goals while remaining sensitive to those who do not come to Pearl Harbor seeking a "clear and objective understanding" but to grieve over personal loss at a "family" gravesite.[73] In the view of some Americans Pearl Harbor should remain a shrine, and the story of the Pacific war, including reflection on its horror, should be told elsewhere. Even the NPS's modest attempts at more expansive interpretive programming—attempting to put a face on the enemy through the acquisition of the Japanese airman's belongings, or displaying the *Ha. 19*—have engendered fierce resistance from those who feel that an alien presence has no place in the sacred environment of the *Arizona* Memorial.

As Gary Cummins notes, the various motivations that bring people to Pearl Harbor have placed an "especially heavy burden on the interpretive staff" at the memorial, who try to present programs that are "forthright, honest, totally accurate, and without a spirit of malice." Although the area is perceived as "primarily a military shrine," the least desirable route for the Park Service to take, in Cummins's opinion, would be to maintain the memorial in such a way that it would "perpetuate old attitudes toward another people." He insists that the NPS "must avoid turning this new National Park area into a place to keep alive old hatreds."[74]

Cummins is joined by William Dickinson, another former park superintendent, in arguing that the Pearl Harbor story must be extended beyond what they think is an unfortunate fixation on the drama of the *Arizona*. For example, only the names of those who died on the ship are listed on the wall inside the memorial. The approximately fifty-eight men entombed in the USS *Utah*, a ship with a storied martial past, were memorialized in 1971, yet they have not been commemorated in publicly accessible ways; nor have others who died in the attack. As at the Little Bighorn, the choice of names for the site is significant: *Custer* Battlefield National Monument and the USS *Arizona* Memorial. Dickinson has said that he prefers the name Pearl Harbor Attack Memorial, with various commemorative spots, including the *Arizona*, established in Pearl Harbor and elsewhere on Oahu. Mark Hertig, the former Park Service curator at the memorial, notes that there were plans to develop a "remembrance exhibit," which would have attempted to broaden the story beyond the tragedy of the *Arizona*, but that it was never implemented. Instead, the ship's presence at the memorial is overwhelming, even in the museum and the gift shop. Huge models of the *Arizona* before and after the battle are on display, as is a fifteen-by-fifty-foot mural of the famous battleship. Visitors can purchase toy models of the ship and assorted printed materials in the gift shop.[75]

The interpretive challenge at Pearl Harbor has been magnified as the fiftieth anniversary of the attack approaches. Commemorative events in

Honolulu will inaugurate a half-decade of ritual remembrance of World War II. For some, the fiftieth anniversary will be the occasion for articulation of the traditional lessons of Pearl Harbor. For others, the fiftieth anniversary will provide the opportunity for rituals of reconciliation. Both the rhetoric and rituals of reconciliation have a long history at Pearl Harbor and have focused on "restoring" the Americans of Japanese ancestry to their rightful place as American citizens and recognizing the humanity of the former enemy.

On Pearl Harbor Day in 1946, Gov. Ingram M. Stainback of Hawaii remarked that the "heroic deeds of our citizens of every race should silence for all times those preaching racial intolerance, should forever still the tongues of discord that would divide our people." An editorial in the *Honolulu Advertiser* argued in a similar vein that only international understanding would do away with war. In 1968 a letter published in the *Honolulu Star-Bulletin* on the day before the anniversary of the attack urged the editors to "de-emphasize the 'infamy of the Pearl Harbor attack'" by throwing away "photos of burning, sinking battleships and dive-bombing planes emblazoned with Rising Sun emblems" and focusing instead on "positive exchange." More recent letters to Honolulu newspapers have urged greater attempts at cross-cultural understanding as the key to better economic relations and the most significant factor in avoiding nuclear war.[76]

From time to time in the postwar years it was suggested that any memorial at Pearl Harbor should honor the dead of both the United States and Japan. This sentiment was repeated during congressional hearings in 1972 on the funding of the visitors center at the memorial, when Rep. Julia B. Hansen of Washington argued that "the Japanese have made the center of rebuilt Hiroshima a national shrine, dedicated to peace and the avoidance of further atrocities of war. Our memorial at Pearl Harbor must symbolize the same high goals for the citizens of the United States and it must be accessible to all who wish to reaffirm their commitment to those noble objectives."[77]

Similar rhetoric has been used in sporadic rituals of reconciliation, one of the most interesting having occurred in 1966. Cmdr. Mitsuo Fuchida, who led the attack, had converted to Christianity shortly after the war, and during his five visits to Pearl Harbor he became a close friend of a Hawaiian clergyman, Rev. Abraham Akaka. On the twenty-fifth anniversary of the attack Fuchida was in attendance at Akaka's worship service. After preaching about reconciliation with God, Akaka told his parishioners about Fuchida and called him forward, saying, "I greet you, my brother in Christ." While in Hawaii, Fuchida also presented a bible wrapped in silk to the Pearl Harbor Survivors Association. A more formal ceremony of reconciliation took place at the memorial in 1960, when Prince Akihito of Japan, accompanied by

United States Navy dignitaries, dropped a white carnation lei on the water to honor the dead of Pearl Harbor. And in the 1980s a number of Buddhist monks, including Eiki Ikeda, journeyed to the memorial to pray for the dead. When asked in 1987 why he did this, Ikeda said, "For the past 6 years, every Pearl Harbor day and Hiroshima day, I have been going to the respective places to pray for the souls of the dead. . . . We should all reflect on this and stop fighting war and pray for world peace."[78]

Moving acts of reconciliation have occurred as well between former combatants. On ABC-TV's "Nightline" in 1981, on the fortieth anniversary of the attack, several members of the Pearl Harbor Survivors Association spoke with another "Nightline" guest, Sadeo Yakamoto, who had participated in the attack. The theme of the show was reconciliation. ABC correspondent Ken Kashiwahara reported that "the wounds of war have healed, and Japanese jumbo jets now land near an airfield that was bombed 40 years ago." Anchorman Ted Koppel asked PHSA member Jim Miller how long it had taken him to develop a more "objective" view of the Japanese. Miller responded that in the 1950s, as the commander of a destroyer division, he had entertained a rear admiral from Japan. The exchange led him to see that "working together in this great Pacific area, we could do much better if we worked in a friendly way and helped each other [rather] than . . . combatting each other." William Aupperlee noted that the PHSA wanted to have a reunion of former combatants. "We have a national convention every two years," he said, "and we come back to the islands every five years. . . . and if I could get the names of some of these people, it would be nice to meet 'em. I would think it would be very nice to meet the people." Yakamoto responded, "That would be a wonderful, splendid arrangement."[79]

No formal reunion has taken place since Aupperlee extended his invitation, but in 1984, according to Gary Cummins, several members of the Japan Naval Pilots Association just "showed up" at the memorial to offer flowers and a wreath. Cummins remembers that an American veteran approached one of the visitors, told him that "five of my classmates are at the bottom," and then embraced him. A similar reaction was seen on ABC-TV's "Good Morning America" in 1989, when PHSA member Bill Speer said, "I met six Japanese pilots that bombed Pearl Harbor. They were doing what they were ordered to do and we were doing what we were trained to do. Time heals wounds, and God teaches, the Bible teaches, to forgive, so as they say, it is kind of an eerie feeling to meet somebody—I guess it'd be like the Civil War, brothers fighting brothers and getting together afterwards. And you forgive."[80]

Bill Speer was only partially correct in comparing the reconciliation that took place after the Civil War with that of the Pearl Harbor (or any of the

Pacific war) combatants or assuming that any form of meeting is truly reconciliatory. As at Gettysburg, the danger of trivialization haunts any attempt at reconciliation. Also, the Civil War was, quite literally, brother fighting brother, and combatants therefore shared important cultural inheritances that made reconciliation (such as it was) a relatively easy task. This was not the case at Pearl Harbor, and formal acceptance of such rituals of reconciliation has not, as yet, been forthcoming. Indeed, if reconciliation were forced on veterans not yet ready to make that move, it would certainly be perceived as oppressive.

In the preliminary plans for the fiftieth reunion William Dickinson proposed extending an invitation to Japanese participants in the attack on Pearl Harbor, although he noted the "extremely sensitive emotional and political issues which will need to be addressed." Denis P. Galvin, at the time the NPS acting director, argued against such contamination of the sacred boundaries of Pearl Harbor and declared that the commemoration should be an *"internal American observance."* He felt strongly that Japanese participation should come at ceremonies marking the end of the war and the establishment of the United Nations, not at commemorative ceremonies in Honolulu. Any official invitation to the Japanese to participate in the fiftieth reunion would be, in his words, "inappropriate, possibly offensive, and fraught with problems and incalculable indelicacies."[81]

The anniversary activities at Pearl Harbor in 1991 will inaugurate a series of commemorative events focusing on America's role in World War II that will bring the nation to within five years of a new century. Such timing will ensure that, just as the war imprinted itself on the second half of the twentieth century, remembrance of the war will become part of our entry into the twenty-first century. How will the nation choose to remember World War II? Certainly, it will reiterate evocative patriotic orthodoxies that express powerfully felt emotions regarding the "good" war. And such events might even challenge Japanese and American citizens to "Remember Pearl Harbor" and the war in the Pacific with a greater sense of irony and humility. Such feelings would be most appropriate as people worldwide pause to reflect on the bittersweet legacy of World War II, from the Nazi death camps to the attack on Pearl Harbor and the destruction of Hiroshima and Nagasaki. The USS *Arizona* Memorial can contribute to this reflection by encouraging visitors to stare history in the face with both sorrow and hope. In doing so, future generations might be helped to remember Pearl Harbor in even more profound ways.

Notes

1. MacArthur, quoted in Columbia Broadcasting System, *From Pearl Harbor into Tokyo: The Story as Told by War Correspondents on the Air* (New York: Columbia Broadcasting System, 1945), p. 296.

2. James P. Delgado, "Surveying the Wreckage of the U.S.S. Arizona," *Sea Classics* 22, no. 5 (May 1989): 56. John Martini reports that "nearly 1,800,000 pounds of ammunition was stored there, and it detonated with the force of almost one kiloton. The force of the explosion was enough to peel back the main deck from bow to bridge, and soon pieces of the *Arizona* were raining all over the harbour" ("Surveying the Arizona," *After the Battle* 45 [Aug. 1984]: 39).

3. "25 Years After Pearl Harbor—An Attack That Remade the World," *U.S. News and World Report* 61 (Dec. 12, 1966): 47.

4. Walter Davenport, "Impregnable Pearl Harbor," *Collier's* (June 14, 1941): 75, 78.

5. Lee Kennett provides interesting details on the Illinois students' and others' reactions to the attack on Pearl Harbor in "The Seventh of December," *For the Duration . . . : The United States Goes to War—Pearl Harbor, 1942* (New York: Charles Scribner's Sons, 1985), pp. 1–17.

6. Ibid., pp. 12, 13; Stewart Alsop, "Wanted: A Faith to Fight For," *Atlantic* 167, no. 5 (May 1941): 597; White, quoted in Richard Polenberg, *War and Society: The United States, 1941–45* (Philadelphia: J. B. Lippincott, 1972), p. 1; "When Isolationism Died," *New Republic* 177 (Dec. 10, 1977): 2.

7. Gwenfread Allen, *Hawaii's War Years, 1941–45* (Westport, Conn.: Greenwood Press, 1950), p. 57.

8. "Attack on Hawaii: First Pictures Show Death and Destruction at American Base," *Life* (Dec. 29, 1941): 11. Other songwriters also wrote pieces entitled "Remember Pearl Harbor," but Kaye's became the most famous, selling more than one million copies. The phrases "Remember December 7th" and "Remember Pearl Harbor" were widely used in American popular culture. Lawrence Sherman, in "World War II Patriotic Covers That Remembered Pearl Harbor," *American Philatelist* 95, no. 12 (Dec. 1981): 1121–30, notes that the phrases undoubtedly "must have sprung spontaneously and instantly to the lips of Americans as they heard the news of the attack" (p. 1124). At a Pearl Harbor Day celebration at the Alamo in 1985, Sammy Kaye's song was played by the Fifth Army Band at 10:55 A.M. on December 7. Gene Lamp, a retired army colonel, noted the parallels between Pearl Harbor and the Alamo: both were "devastating defeats"; both were "rallying point[s]"; and "both gave us a battle cry" (quoted in the *San Antonio Express-News,* Dec. 6, 1985; see also ibid., Dec. 8, 1985).

9. "Yellow Peril" themes, present in American imaginative war literature of the early twentieth century, came to life after Pearl Harbor. For a detailed discussion of such literature, see H. Bruce Franklin, *War Stars: The Superweapon and the American Imagination* (New York: Oxford University Press, 1988), pp. 19–53. John Dower's *War without Mercy* (New York: Pantheon, 1986) clearly and convincingly documents the role that race hatred played for both the Japanese and Americans in the Pacific war. Michael Sherry, in *The Rise of American Air Power: The Creation of Armageddon* (New Haven: Yale University Press, 1987), and Ronald Schaeffer, in *Wings of Judgement: American Bombing in World War II* (New York: Oxford University Press, 1985), detail the role that racial attitudes toward the Japanese played in the adoption of the strategic bombing campaigns against Japanese cities.

It is not only in retrospective analysis that the racial dimension of the Pacific war becomes clear. When he arrived in the Pacific in 1945 the beloved war correspondent Ernie Pyle wrote, "In Europe we felt that our enemies, horrible and deadly as they were, were still people. But out here I soon gathered that the Japanese were looked upon as something subhuman and repulsive; the way some people feel about cockroaches or mice" (*Last Chapter*

[New York: Henry Holt and Co., 1946], p. 5). Germans were associated with unequivocal evil and portrayed as sadists, while the Japanese were often portrayed as monkeys. A radio show host declared, "Listen! Have you ever watched a well-trained monkey at a zoo! Have you seen how carefully he imitates his trainer? . . . The monkey . . . actually seems to be human. But under his fur, he's still a savage little beast!" (quoted in William A. Bacher, ed., *The Treasury Star Parade: 27 Radio Plays* [New York: Farrar and Rinehart, 1942], p. 359). Michael J. Yavenditti points out that several polls revealed a considerable minority of Americans wished more atomic bombs had been dropped on Japan before it had the chance to surrender; and a *Fortune* survey of November 30, 1945, revealed that 13.8 percent of those polled thought the Japanese should be exterminated as a race. See Yavenditti, "The American People and the Use of Atomic Bombs on Japan: The 1940s," *Historian* 49 (Feb. 1974): 224–47.

10. FDR, quoted in the *Honolulu Star-Bulletin,* Nov. 20, 1942 (hereafter *Star-Bulletin*); ibid., Nov. 30, 1942; *Honolulu Advertiser,* Dec. 7, 1942 (hereafter *Advertiser*).

11. Todaro, quoted in *Advertiser,* Oct. 29, 1943. The Punchbowl eventually became the site of the National Memorial Cemetery of the Pacific. Construction began in 1948, and in January 1949 an unidentified victim of the Pearl Harbor attack was reburied there. The cemetery, dedicated on VJ Day 1949 with more than twelve thousand visitors from the mainland in attendance, was constructed according to the plans of the American Battle Monuments Commission, founded in 1923 to maintain military cemeteries on foreign soil. Each cemetery has three basic features: a devotional chapel, walls on which the names of the casualties are inscribed, and a "graphic record in permanent form of the achievements and sacrifices of the United States Armed Forces" (quoted from one of the informative plaques at the cemetery).

12. Knowles's proposal is discussed in Michael Slackman, *Remembering Pearl Harbor: The Story of the USS Arizona Memorial* (Honolulu: Arizona Memorial Museum Association, 1984), p. 29. Information on the Pacific Memorial Foundation is in Allen, pp. 372–73,

and in "Pacific Memorial Foundation, 1947," Hawaii State Archives, Honolulu. Private funds were used to build a temporary war memorial on the grounds of the territorial office building, where an "American eagle perched on an olive branch decorates an 18-foot wooden shaft which bears the words 'In honor of all Americans of Hawaii who died in this world war that the beauty and freedom of our land might be preserved for all humanity' " (Allen, p. 373).

13. Minutes, Apr. 16, 1952, July 16, 1953, Oct. 25, 1956, Pacific War Memorial Commission Records, Hawaii State Archives, Honolulu (hereafter PWMCR). The memorial was opened in 1962, but the shoreside visitors center and museum facility were not opened until 1978. In 1980 the increasing number of visitors created a burden for the navy and it agreed to allow the National Park Service to manage the memorial complex.

14. For information about the various proposals, see Minutes, May 7, 1959, PWMCR; "USS *Arizona*: Design, 1957–64," PWMCR. These files contain numerous letters that accompanied small contributions made during the fund drives of 1960–62. Many of the letters suggest that the message of the memorial should reflect remembrance of the "treachery" of the day of "infamy."

15. Slackman, p. 70. The NPS uses the language of such authorizing legislation as a direct guide to its interpretive programs at all battlefields. For a thorough examination of the activities of the PWMC in its struggle to fund the memorial, see ibid., pp. 62–72.

16. "It Is Altogether Fitting and Proper," *Collier's* 125 (June 3, 1950): 74.

17. Olsen, letter of Nov. 23, 1955, in "USS *Arizona*: Military, 1955–63," PWMCR; Campbell, quoted in "USS *Arizona*: Appropriations, Governors Conference, 1961," PWMCR; letter from Gratz to Daniel, June 26, 1961, in ibid.; "The Rusting Memorial," *Washington Post,* Jan. 18, 1961.

18. Teague, quoted in "USS *Arizona*: Appropriations, U.S. Correspondence, 1961, n.d.-July," PWMCR.

19. Slackman, p. 73; Kevin Lynch, *What Time Is This Place?* (Cambridge: Massachusetts Institute of Technology Press, 1972), p. 44.

20. Slackman, p. 74. Paddock's comments are among uncataloged materials in the USS *Arizona* Memorial Archives, Honolulu (hereafter USSAMA).

21. *Pacific Memorial System Newsletter* 1, no. 3 (1962), in USSAMA; see also the program for that day's services, in USSAMA.

22. Bowen, quoted in *Star-Bulletin*, May 30, 1968; Buse, quoted in *Advertiser*, May 31, 1968; Ford, quoted in the *Pearl Harbor-Gram* (Jan. 1976): 1, in USSAMA clippings file. Just as John Wayne's movie *The Alamo* was designed to arouse patriotic fervor, *Tora Tora Tora*, the 1970 drama of the Pearl Harbor attack, complete with a $1.5 million replica of the *Arizona*, was designed to remind Americans of the need to be prepared. Darryl F. Zanuck, the president of 20th Century–Fox, declared that he hoped the movie would help ensure that an attack like the one at Pearl Harbor would never happen again. See Henry Ehrlich, "Tora! Tora! Tora!" *Look* (Sept. 22, 1970): 27.

23. Hayden, quoted in Slackman, p. 60; Russell, quoted in "USS *Arizona*: Appropriations, U.S. Correspondence"; "USS *Arizona*: Appropriations, Governors Conference"; Miller, quoted in Nina Hart, "Arizona Heartbeats," vol. 2, USSAMA; "NPS Interpretive Prospectus, 1980," USSAMA.

24. The *St. Paul Pioneer Press* is quoted in Gordon Prange, *Pearl Harbor: The Verdict of History* (New York: McGraw-Hill, 1986), p. 563; Nitze, quoted in an unspecified clipping in the USSAMA files.

25. Fred Kaplan, *The Wizards of Armageddon* (New York: Simon and Schuster, 1983), pp. 93, 109; *Nuclear Times* 6, no. 5 (May/June 1988): 597. According to Kaplan, Wohlstetter never asked if the "Japanese would have attacked Pearl Harbor if they thought that the United States could retaliate with 600 or even 100 or even 10 Nagasaki-size . . . nuclear explosions" (p. 109). Wohlstetter's wife, Roberta, published her own study of Pearl Harbor (*Pearl Harbor: Warning and Decision* [Stanford: Stanford University Press, 1962]), in which she concludes that amid the barrage of intelligence that was available the military was unable to recognize the real warning signals that the Japanese were going to attack. The prominent strategist Thomas Schelling writes in a foreword to Roberta Wohlstetter's book that *Pearl Harbor* "can only remind us how likely it is that we are in the same kind of rut right now" with regard to nuclear war (p. viii). Gordon Prange reminds readers of his massive work *Pearl Harbor: The Verdict of History* that "in the nuclear age, the United States needs an intelligence system so keenly honed and finely attuned that it can anticipate an attack" (p. 555).

26. *Pearl Harbor-Gram* (Jan. 1969): 2.

27. William Manchester, *Goodbye Darkness: A Memoir of the Pacific War* (New York: Dell, 1980), p. 56; "Pearl Harbor Payback," ABC-TV's "20/20," Dec. 6, 1984, transcript #445, p. 4. James P. Delgado notes that besides the *Akagi* Japan lost three other carriers at Midway that had participated in the Pearl Harbor attack: the *Kaga*, the *Hiryu*, and the *Soryu* (letter to the author, Sept. 27, 1989).

28. The *Atlanta Constitution* is quoted in Sherry, p. 291; Truman, quoted in Peter Wyden, *Day One: Before Hiroshima and After* (New York: Simon and Schuster, 1984), p. 294; *Omaha Morning Herald*, quoted in Paul Boyer, *By the Bomb's Early Light: American Thought and Culture at the Dawn of the Atomic Age* (New York: Pantheon, 1985), p. 12; *Advertiser*, Dec. 8, 1947; "25 Years after Pearl Harbor," p. 47.

29. Wyden, p. 360. Nokes's article "Remember Hiroshima and *Also* Pearl Harbor" is reprinted in the *Pearl Harbor-Gram* (July 1981).

30. Confederate Air Force, *Ghost Squadron of the Confederate Air Force: Wings of Freedom* (n.p., 1987), p. 56; "Narration of the World War II Air Power Demonstration by the Confederate Air Force," ms., author's files.

31. "Narration of the World War II Air Power Demonstration," pp. 5, 6. The image of Pearl Harbor as a creative event, giving birth to "victory" or to a stronger postwar America, is used elsewhere. For example, on the twentieth anniversary of the attack Sen. Hiram E. Fong of Hawaii spoke of modern-day Pearl Harbor as the "phoenix of the Pacific, rising out of the ashes to become the hub of the greatest and strongest naval command in history," its "missile-toting nuclear submarines . . . more deadly than the combined firepower of the seven battlewagons

moored . . . that fateful December morning" (quoted in "USS *Arizona*: Appropriations, U.S. Documents, 1961–62," PWMCR).

On occasion the CAF has reenacted the Pearl Harbor drama at other martial ceremonial centers. In 1982 the PHSA held its annual convention in San Antonio and the *Pearl Harbor-Gram* promised its readers an "epic event that will bring chills to the spines of all who survived. . . . The legendary Confederate Air Force will present the largest reenactment of 'Tora Tora Tora, the Pearl Harbor attack' ever staged" (July 1982). One spectator noted that "the simulated raid on Pearl Harbor had to be the most profoundly moving, scintillating flying act I've ever witnessed (*CAF Dispatch* 14, no. 1 [Jan./Feb. 1989]: 12).

32. *CAF Dispatch* 1, no. 2 (Oct./Nov./Dec. 1976): 4.

33. See ibid., pp. 1–11, for a good summary of the controversy and the CAF's response.

34. Information on these and other enshrined ships is in "Historic Ship Exhibits in the United States," pt. 1: "Enshrined Ships of the Continental, the United States, and the Confederate States Navies," *Dictionary of American Naval Fighting Ships*, 8 vols. (Washington, D.C.: Navy Department, 1968), 3:683–701 (quotations from pp. 683, 686, 694). For a discussion of the different functions of the *Arizona* as symbol, see James P. Delgado, "Significance: Memorials, Myths, and Symbols," in *Submerged Cultural Resources Study, USS* Arizona *Memorial and Pearl Harbor National Historic Landmark*, ed. Daniel J. Lenihan. Southwest Cultural Resources Center Professional Papers, no. 23 (Santa Fe: National Park Service, U.S. Department of the Interior, 1989), pp. 169–91.

35. The phrase "massive metal statements of American might" was used by Daniel J. Lenihan, the NPS chief of the Submerged Cultural Resources Unit, to characterize battleships (telephone interview, July 26, 1989). For further information about the examples discussed in this paragraph, see "Historic Ship Exhibits in the United States," pt. 2: "Major Parts and Commemorative Displays of Fighting Ships of the United States and Confederate States Navies, and Contemplated Major Salvage Projects," *Dictionary of American Naval*

Fighting Ships, 3:703–25 (quotations from p. 705).

36. "Historic Ship Exhibits," pt. 2, 3:703–25 (quotations from pp. 707, 709). When the Sioux Falls Chamber of Commerce and the Navy League learned in 1962 that the USS *South Dakota* was going to be scrapped, the two groups embarked on an ambitious fund-raising campaign, selling admiralships in the South Dakota Navy (!) and coins made from the battleship. Aided by a $100,000 state appropriation in 1965, they were able to construct a memorial and purchase several "freight car loads of artifacts . . . including the ship's bells, anchor and chain, teakwood decking, [and] mainmast." The memorial was completed in 1969. The mainmast stands near a museum, and the ship's lifelines re-create the contours of the ship. For further information, see *The USS South Dakota*, pamphlet, USS *South Dakota* Battleship Memorial Foundation, Sioux Falls.

37. Gruesome scenes were fixed in the memories of some salvage workers. James W. Green remarked: "As you walked along, the air from your diving helmet created a whirlpool. . . . it drew the bodies toward you" (quoted in Ann Jensen, "USS Arizona: The Memories Do Not Die," *American History Illustrated* 23, no. 8 [Dec. 1988]: 14). Salvage work aboard the *Arizona* ended in mid-1942, and James P. Delgado notes that "the barrels, hoisting and handling equipment . . . from *Arizona* were used to build casemated seacoast defense batteries on Oahu; the batteries were completed at war's end and were never fired, except once—on August 15, 1945, to salute the U.S. victory. Thus, the main armament of a ship that did not survive the 'first shots' of the Pacific war, and whose demise symbolized the cause for which the U.S. fought, finally spoke in a symbolic 'last shot' " (letter to the author, Sept. 27, 1989). Daniel J. Lenihan said that he felt the superstructure was removed not only for pragmatic reasons but to "erase the visible, shameful image of what occurred" (telephone interview, July 26, 1989).

38. Martini, p. 40.

39. See *Arizona Republic*, Dec. 12, 1975, for information about other relics of the *Arizona* scattered throughout the state. Fascination with newly discovered relics persists. In Au-

gust 1989, for example, the USS *Arizona* Mast Committee was formed to purchase the ship's signal mast, which had been sent by Fleet Adm. Ernest J. King to his hometown of Lorain, Ohio, to save it from being scrapped during salvage operations. The mast stood for thirty-six years at the Lorain Naval Reserve Training Center. When the building was torn down in 1980 the city refused to purchase the mast. A private citizen of Lorain bought it and stored it in his backyard. During its Second Regular Session, the Arizona Senate resolved that "the department of administration shall accept for erection and thereafter maintain the U.S.S. Arizona mast within the Wesley Bolin memorial plaza at a location in close proximity to the U.S.S. Arizona anchor." The Mast Committee noted that there was some urgency to the purchase, as the owner of an Ohio restaurant was also interested in buying and displaying the anchor—an act that the committee declared "would be the desecration of a national treasure." I am indebted to Jim Delgado for bringing this material to my attention.

40. Letters from the *Arizona* Memorial Fund to Harwill, Oct. 21, 1957, and from Harwill to the *Arizona* Memorial Fund, Oct. 24, 1957, as well as the story of the bell in the Phoenix bank are in "USS *Arizona*: Ship's Bell," PWMCR. The *Phoenix Gazette* reported on December 5, 1969, that the bell in the student union would "toll for the first time since 1958." The only other occasions on which it tolls are after football victories.

41. *Phoenix Gazette*, June 12, 1972; McCormick, quoted in *Arizona Republic*, Dec. 8, 1982; information on the dedication services in ibid., June 15, 1976. Forty "beturbaned" Sikhs were inspired by McCormick's rhetoric to protest their exclusion from American military service, to the consternation of many in the crowd (ibid., Dec. 8, 1982). The *Arizona* Anchor Memorial stands in Wesley Bolin Plaza in Phoenix, along with memorials to Martin Luther King, Jr., Vietnam veterans, and Jewish war veterans. For information on these memorials, see Vicky Hay, "Wesley Bolin Plaza," *Arizona Highways* 65, no. 6 (June 1989): 14–17.

42. For information on the Fleet Reserve Association's model, see *Navy Times*, Dec. 20,

1967; on Berry, see *Phoenix Gazette*, Sept. 6, 1980; on Gates, see Hart, "Arizona Heartbeats."

43. George Lang, telephone interview, July 24, 1989. During the ceremony a navy boat brought the deceased's family and an honor guard to the memorial. The flag on the *Arizona* was lowered, and a flag provided by family members (one they would take with them in remembrance) was raised, then lowered to half-mast. After the mahogany urn bearing the man's remains was handed to navy divers by the National Park Service superintendent, the divers followed a path to the turret that allowed the family to see as much as possible and then placed the urn in the turret. For reports on earlier interments, see *Advertiser*, June 9, 1976, and Apr. 14, 1982. Those who served at Pearl Harbor but not on the *Arizona* may have their ashes scattered from the memorial into the harbor, but they may not be interred on the ship.

44. Other war dead have indeed been treated differently from those who died on the *Arizona*. For example, forty years after their B–24 crashed into the mountains of New Guinea, twenty-two Americans were returned to their families for burial. Consider also that at Truk Lagoon the Japanese eagerly recovered their dead from ships resting on the ocean's bottom in order to cremate their remains. On the subject of the treatment of human remains in ships, see Toni Carrell, "Human Remains and Shipwreck Sites: A Management Issue in the National Parks," ms., maritime historian's files, National Park Service, Washington, D.C. (hereafter NPS).

45. Correspondence about the recovery of human remains from the Arizona is in "Congressional/Controlled Correspondence (1982–83)," NPS files, USSAMA. Delgado, who has taken part in NPS dives at the *Arizona*, commented that the question he is most often asked by tourists is, "Did you see any bodies?" (interview, June 3, 1989). See also Delgado, "Significance."

46. Lenihan telephone interview, July 26, 1989; see also Daniel J. Lenihan, "Introduction," in Lenihan, *Submerged Cultural Resources Study*, pp. 1–12. Such emotions resemble the mixture of veneration and curiosity that was evident in the archaeological dig at

the Little Bighorn. Yet the Little Bighorn has its own clearly defined cemetery; consequently, few people objected to penetration of the battleground in the same way that many would object to anyone entering the *Arizona.* The dives at Pearl Harbor were part of a larger project, Sea Mark, which included underwater exploration of German and Japanese ships sunk at Guam. See Tracy Connors, "Project Sea Mark," *All Hands: Magazine of the U.S. Navy* (Feb. 1988): 19–25.

47. Gary T. Cummins, "U.S.S. Arizona: A Cultural Resource Management Success Story," *CRM Bulletin* 7, no. 1 (Apr. 1984): 4; Martini, p. 42.

48. Lenihan telephone interview, July 26, 1989.

49. Delgado interview, June 3, 1989. He also remarked that the *Arizona* was "carpeted with money" people had thrown from the deck of the memorial and that the money contributed to the corrosive process. For a good description of the wreckage, see Delgado, "Surveying Wreckage," pp. 50–57, 64–65.

50. Letter to Nunn, Sept. 20, 1983, in "Congressional/Controlled Correspondence (1982–83)."

51. Letter from Dickinson to *Arizona* survivors, Nov. 25, 1987, USSAMA; letter from Dickinson to Delgado, Mar. 15, 1988, clippings file, USSAMA.

52. Lenihan, "Introduction," p. 8.

53. Manchester, p. 67; Cummins telephone interview, July 30, 1989. The letters between Col. A. Deane Gough (ret.), Feb. 13, 1983, and the NPS, Mar. 8, 1983, about Japanese applause are in "Congressional/Controlled Correspondence (1982–83)."

54. *Star-Bulletin,* Apr. 16, 1977. The letters between Nunn, his constituents, and the NPS are in "Complaints (1987)," USSAMA. Gary Beito, executive director of the Arizona Memorial Museum Association, commented that he had refused a proposal to sell a plastic replica of the *Arizona,* to be filled with water from Pearl Harbor (interview, June 20, 1988).

55. "National Register of Historic Places Registration Form, *Ha. 19,*" p. 8, in "Maritime Heritage," maritime historian's files, NPS. Delgado notes that the submarine was a powerful symbol of Japanese treachery, exemplified by the insolence of a "little people"

who presumed to attack a Western power (ibid., p. 9). John Dower calls attention to a 1944 report from Gen. Douglas MacArthur of the Southwest Pacific Command: "In every sense of the word, the Japanese are *little people.* . . . Some observers claim there would have been no Pearl Harbor, had the Japanese been three inches taller. . . . Being *little people,* the Japanese dreamed of power and glory, but lacked a realistic concept of the material requirements for a successful world war" (quoted in Dower, p. 143).

56. NPS Western Region, "Issue Briefing Statement," Jan. 1986, USSAMA; memo from Delgado to Edwin C. Bearss, Feb. 22, 1989, and letter from VFW, May 15, 1989, in maritime historian's files, NPS. I wish to thank Jim Delgado for opening his files to me and for bringing the midget submarine controversy to my attention.

57. The American Legionnaire's letter, undated, the veteran's letter, Apr. 20, 1989, and related legislative information are in the maritime historian's files, NPS.

58. Paxon's letter is in ibid.

59. An undated draft of Ridenour's general response to these complaints and other typical letters on this subject are in ibid.

60. PHSA to Ridenour, Jan. 21, 1990, in ibid.

61. The New Jersey resident's letter, Dec. 18, 1987, and Mott's reply, Feb. 10, 1988, are in "USS *Arizona,*" NPS. Sensitivity to the presence of anything that could be construed as a memorial to the Japanese engendered spirited opposition in several places in the Pacific. For example, on the twenty-fifth anniversary of Pearl Harbor the South Pacific Memorial Association (a group of Japanese and German business leaders) planned to erect a monument to the Japanese war dead in Guam. Secretary of the Interior Stewart Udall received a letter in which the writer equated this with "putting a Nazi monument on the soil of Israel." Rep. Richard White of Texas planned to sponsor legislation banning such a monument, or at least requiring that an American memorial also be erected. Guam's envoy to Washington, whose brother had been executed by the Japanese and who was Guam's representative to Washington, disagreed. He said that such a monument would be a symbol

of friendship between the United States and Japan. He also remarked that part of the motivation was the attraction of the Japanese tourist trade. See *Advertiser,* Dec. 7, 1966.

62. Letters from the Iowa physician to Inouye, Nov. 20, 1983, and the NPS to Inouye, Dec. 29, 1983, in "Complaints (1983)."

63. Letter to Nixon, Jan. 18, 1972, in "Correspondence," NPS. See also the exchange of letters on this subject in *Navy Times,* Sept. 7, 1987, and Oct. 5, 1987.

64. *Advertiser,* Apr. 17, 1980; *Star-Bulletin,* Aug. 8, 1981.

65. Proposals and progress reports in navy files, USSAMA.

66. Letter from Cummins to Dr. David Nurco, May 15, 1985, with references to Nurco's earlier letter (which is not in the file), in "Congressional/Controlled Correspondence (1987)." A woman from Virginia, incensed at one presentation by a seasonal Park Service ranger, thought that the NPS should "investigate the training of these men." She worried that the economic power of the Japanese would alter the traditional story. "I know the Japanese have invested millions among the coastal land of the island," she wrote, "but in no way are we to slant history" (letter to NPS, Dec. 7, 1983, in ibid.).

67. Letters from Cummins to Nurco, May 15, 1985, Nurco to Yates, Jan. 7, 1986, and Mott to Yates, Mar. 4, 1987, are in ibid.

68. For the NPS's stock response, see the undated draft letter on this topic in ibid.

69. Bearss's report is in "USS *Arizona* Memorial," NPS.

70. Gary Cummins and Bill Dickinson, "The Management Experience," in Lenihan, *Submerged Cultural Resources Study,* p. 157.

71. Cummins telephone interview, July 30, 1989; Admiral Rorie's actions are described in Cummins and Dickinson, p. 160.

72. This exchange of correspondence is in "USS *Arizona* Memorial," NPS.

73. "USS *Arizona* Memorial Statement for Management," n.d., p. 24, USSAMA.

74. Gary T. Cummins, "Interpretive Prospectus," ms., n.d., pp. 1, 2, USSAMA.

75. Cummins telephone interview, July 30, 1989; Dickinson telephone interview, July 27, 1989; Hertig informal conversation, June 1988.

76. *Advertiser,* Dec. 7, 1946; *Star-Bulletin,* Dec. 6, 1968; *Advertiser,* Dec. 7, 1973; *Star-Bulletin,* Dec. 7, 1981.

77. Hansen, quoted in Slackman, p. 82.

78. *Star-Bulletin,* Sept. 23, 1960, Dec. 7, 1981. Ikeda's comments are in the script of *Pearl Harbor Project,* produced by An American Portrait (a New York film company). I thank the associate producer, Julie Parroni, for sending me copies of a number of interviews conducted for this film at Pearl Harbor.

79. "Pearl Harbor 40 Years Later," ABC-TV's "Nightline," Dec. 7, 1981, transcript #151. In 1981 George Oshida, president of the United Japanese Society of Hawaii, placed a plaque at the memorial honoring the *Arizona* dead. The inscription on the plaque read, "With our hope that there shall be everlasting peace between our country and Japan" (quoted in *Advertiser,* Apr. 2, 1981; also in *Star-Bulletin,* Apr. 3, 1981).

80. Cummins telephone interview, July 30, 1989; ABC-TV's "Good Morning America," Feb. 21, 1989, transcript GMA702.

81. Gary Cummins also thinks that the fiftieth anniversary should be an American "family affair." (My thanks to Jim Delgado and James H. Charleton for permission to read draft documents in their possession on the preliminary planning for the fiftieth anniversary.) On March 27, 1991, Don Magee, superintendent of the *Arizona* Memorial, declared in a news release (a copy of which was provided to me by James H. Charleton) that the NPS planned to "extend a tribute to the returning survivors and relatives of victims, and to provide a dignified commemoration that will inspire all Americans and people everywhere."

The content of this "dignified commemoration" remains the subject of continuing bureaucratic negotiation and growing public curiosity. While discussion over the wisdom or appropriateness of official or even unofficial Japanese participation continues in governmental agencies, newspapers have speculated on the desirability of the presence of other distinguished guests. For example, the editors of the *Honolulu Advertiser* (Mar. 4, 1991) found it "hard to imagine that President Bush and Defense Secretary Cheney would not try to be here for the first . . . of four years of

50th anniversaries of landmark World War II events." Some Japanese, concerned that the anniversary would bring in its wake renewed anti-Japanese sentiment in the United States, urged their prime minister to apologize for the attack on Pearl Harbor. And, while visiting Tokyo, former Assistant Secretary of Defense Richard Armitage suggested that Prime Minister Toshiki Kaifu participate in a wreath-laying ceremony at the commemoration; in return, President Bush could pay homage to Japanese dead in a visit to Hiroshima. This, Armitage suggested, "would put the specter of World War II behind us" (*San Francisco Chronicle*, Dec. 4, 1990). Clearly, lack of consensus over the content of ceremonies reflects widespread uneasiness that reviving memories of the war will further complicate the troubled state of American-Japanese relations.

Conclusion

Lexington and Concord. The Alamo. Gettysburg. The Little Bighorn. Pearl Harbor. The evocative power of a battlefield, like the power of a particular piece of music or poetry, depends on the sensibility of the person who becomes fascinated by a particular site, for whatever reason. Of all the battlefields of the American Revolution and the Civil War, for instance, what makes Lexington and Concord and Gettysburg so important and so revealing? Why not Bunker Hill or Yorktown? Why not Vicksburg or Antietam? My choice of which battlefields to discuss was not based on personal fascination, though I am clearly fascinated by these places. Rather, I chose these battlefields because the American populace, past and present, clearly perceives *these* battles and battlefields from *these* wars as crucial to the life of the nation. Indeed, more than any other battles, these five symbolize national birth from the agony of martial sacrifice.

The prestige associated with origins certainly contributes to the enduring cultural attention—evident in processes of veneration, defilement, and redefinition—given to these battlefields. Yorktown signifies final victory in the Revolution, but Lexington and Concord symbolize the martial birth of the nation. Sam Houston's triumph at San Jacinto, only weeks after the fall of the Alamo, sealed Texas independence, but the Alamo is the shrine that commemorates the sacrificial deaths of the Texas heroes, which, patriotic orthodoxy declares, brought the Republic of Texas into being. Vicksburg may have been strategically just as important—or more so—than Gettysburg, but the "high water mark" of the Confederacy is at Gettysburg. While there are numerous forts and road markers to commemorate the Plains Indian wars, the sacrifices of General Custer and his men at the Little Bighorn have traditionally been credited with opening the West for Anglo-American civilization. Pearl Harbor, the only battlefield of World War II that lies within the fifty states, symbolizes rebirth at a different stage in the national life cycle: namely, when a "mature" nation rose from the immediate prewar years, ready to exercise paternal responsibility for the new world it was destined to help sire. Reflecting on the meaning of Gettysburg—but speaking as well to the significance of each of these battles—J. Frank Hanly exclaimed in 1912, "Out of the baptism of fire and blood and the holocaust of carnage and of woe the Union is rising, rising undismembered and unbroken, sublime in the unity of its forging purpose, glorious with the splendor of future endeavor, and luminous with achievement."[1]

Pathos and no small amount of romance in the story line of each of these battles provide Americans with alluring images of war. Better to think of the last stand at the Alamo than the slaughter at Goliad. Better to be awestruck by the "beauty" of the Pickett-Pettigrew charge than the slaughter at Fredericksburg or Cold Harbor. Better to contemplate the drama of the Little Bighorn than the legacy of Sand Creek or Wounded Knee.

Other wars fought on American soil have not captured the public imagination in quite the same way as the Revolution, the Civil War, or the Plains Indian wars. The War of 1812, for example, is memorialized in a number of ways on the martial landscape: the heroic actions of Capt. Oliver Hazard Perry at the battle of Lake Erie in 1813 are commemorated in Perry's Victory and International Peace Memorial; Fort McHenry, in Baltimore, is renowned as the birthplace of the "Star-Spangled Banner"; Chalmette National Historical Park commemorates Andrew Jackson's victory at the battle of New Orleans in January 1815—a battle that took place after the warending Treaty of Ghent had been signed—and the USS *Constitution* (also known as *Old Ironsides*) is a popular tourist attraction that rests in Boston Harbor. Still, despite these and other material remembrances, there is no evocative sacred ground for the War of 1812. James M. Mayo rightly comments that the " 'Star-Spangled Banner' is the ultimate war memorial. . . . The war's purpose and its territorial consequences seem to be forgotten."[2]

Another war that is almost completely ignored on the martial landscape is the Mexican War of 1846. Many Americans would have a hard time naming a single battle from this war, despite the fact that significant fighting took place in California and Texas. California did not enshrine any of its battlesites, and except for the San Pasqual battlefield, all that commemorates the places of battle in California are road markers. The only national site commemorating the Mexican War is the Palo Alto battlefield near Brownsville, Texas.

Neither the War of 1812 nor the Mexican War plays a significant role in the patriotic canon. Perhaps this is due to the controversial nature of these two wars, each fought for less than idealistic reasons. Or perhaps as interest in the memorialization of the American past gathered momentum in the second half of the nineteenth century, the heroic traditions of the Revolution and the Civil War overwhelmed any enduring images from these other wars.

The five battlefields discussed in this book—Lexington and Concord, the Alamo, Gettysburg, the Little Bighorn, and Pearl Harbor—function as sacred centers in several ways. Traditionally, they are centers of power; that is, the sacred stories celebrated in patriotic rituals at each of these places are stories that "belong" to certain groups. However, these battlefields are also places where power has been, and will continue to be, contested; they are places where the struggle for ownership, for the right to alter the story, is a vibrant part of the site's cultural history.

For the guardians of patriotic faith, the revolutionary heritage celebrated at Lexington and Concord is one of martial valor, to be honored—and, if possible, repeated—by future generations. For others, Lexington and Concord serve to legitimate the contemporary practice of a revolutionary tradition of dissent, including opposition to the unpopular wars of the nation.

At the Alamo, the last-stand saga of the Texas heroes almost immediately engendered a racially exclusive patriotic orthodoxy. Only recently have Mexican Americans entered into symbolic battle with the guardians of patriotic faith, whether to restore Tejano ancestors to their rightful place in the saga or to reject the saga entirely.

Ritual memory at Gettysburg has long ignored or trivialized the continuing oppression of black Americans, whereas commemorative events quickly became occasions for the rhetoric of affection between the Northern and Southern veterans who jointly "owned" the story. Bravery and devotion to duty, no matter what that duty was, have been the measure of heroism at Gettysburg, where visitors are only occasionally reminded by patriotic rhetoric of the conveniently forgotten message of Abraham Lincoln—namely, that martial sacrifice would only take on meaning as Americans addressed the continuing tragedy of racial division. The 125th anniversary of the battle in 1988 brought into sharp relief two contrasting cultural memories of war. The pageantry of battle reenactment offered an imaginative entry into the past, while the sober ceremonies at the Eternal Light Peace Memorial sought to deepen the spirit of reconciliation that had moved veterans to propose this memorial in 1913 and to erect it in 1938. Even as battlefield memories were being used to engender a rhetoric of racial inclusion, Carl Sagan was declaring that these memories should not lead to the romanticization of the battle but should serve as a reminder of the horror of war in the nuclear age.

Perhaps the most intense battle for ownership has taken place at the Little Bighorn. The modern battle there has raged over various issues, including: the changing perceptions of George Armstrong Custer and the Seventh Cavalry; the name of the battlefield; the call for an Indian memorial; the presence of Black Elk's message on an outer wall of the visitors center;

and the ideological message communicated by the physical layout of the battlefield itself. Despite conscious attempts by the National Park Service to fashion a rhetoric of inclusion, acts of symbolic terrorism reveal the enduring differences between practitioners of the "patriotism of power" and the practitioners of the "patriotism of pain."

At Pearl Harbor the NPS faces the difficult task of shaping a commemorative environment acceptable to people who come to Pearl Harbor for vastly different reasons. For some, Pearl Harbor belongs to them because they lost a loved one in the battle. Something of them rests in the USS *Arizona*. Others seek to ensure that the enduring lesson of military preparedness will continue to be emphasized. For still others, Pearl Harbor is a place where commemorative ritual should include gestures of reconciliation in light of contemporary political realities. These people wish to emphasize the need to heal the enduring wounds of war.

Activities at all of these centers of power have helped to define, for numerous generations, those who are "insiders" and "outsiders" in American culture, those who belong in the stories and, equally important, *how* they belong in them. For insiders, or celebrants of patriotic faith, these power points are appropriate places of worship, places where patriotic revitalization can be accomplished through the celebration of the enduring inspiration of the heroic age of the battle. For outsiders, these places are the nerve centers at which they can begin the process of symbolically reshaping the nation's sense of its past, a process that outsiders believe can significantly alter their own marginal status.

These battlefields are also centers of purity, as well as centers where purity is defiled. Frozen in time through preservation and restoration, they are set apart symbolically from the constantly changing secular world; they stand out from the homogeneity of modern space. The urge to preserve and restore these holy places of the nation comes from an intuitive sense that the essence of America can be found in our sacred environments. Just as the sculptured stone of the great cathedrals of the Middle Ages communicated the Christian faith, so too do the monuments, markers, and memorials of these battlefields communicate America's patriotic faith. Just as the cathedrals provided a material threshold across which humankind could approach God, so too do these battlefields provide a conduit through which citizens are able to participate in the power of a heroic past—a past that continues to demand allegiance to its cherished principles.

Like cathedrals, each of these battlefields has a sacred center within a center, a "holy of holies": the line of the minutemen, now marked by a boulder on Lexington Green, or the Revolutionary Monument of 1799, which contains the remains of the minutemen slain that April morning; the North Bridge or perhaps Daniel Chester French's famed minuteman statue, which reputedly stands on the spot where Isaac Davis fell; the Alamo chapel or, for some, the Long Barrack, saved from destruction by the impassioned protest of Adina De Zavala; the Angle at Gettysburg, referred to as the "high water mark" of the Confederacy, or the Soldiers' National Monument, the site of Lincoln's famed address; Custer Hill at the Little Bighorn or, for some, the Indian village in the valley; and the shrine room of the USS *Arizona* Memorial at Pearl Harbor.

At a time in which Americans—often grudgingly and all too haltingly—recognize the strengths of cultural pluralism, no one can be allowed to win the struggle for exclusive ownership of these places. Indeed, no one should. It is certainly a sign of ideological maturity that the wider public has come to accept the fact that there is more than one story to be told, and that these stories convey diverse, often conflicting interpretations of cherished patriotic orthodoxies. With the exception of the Alamo (understood by its caretaker, the Daughters of the Republic of Texas, to be a shrine rather than a battlesite), the National Park Service faces the challenge of orchestrating at each of the other four sites a plurality of public voices. Individuals and groups may come forth and say, "Here is what this place means"; they may even try to convince others that their interpretation is the correct one. But the NPS will allow no single individual or group to claim exclusive ownership of these sacred spaces, or of the stories that are told there. Indeed, the Park Service has been remarkably successful in reminding visitors that symbolic domination by any one person or group is a form of cultural violence and will no longer be tolerated.

Dissonance, not harmony, characterizes the many voices heard at these battlefields. Those who wish to sing in unison the pure song of patriotic faith, to hear voices raised in celebration of Davy Crockett swinging "Old Betsy" at Santa Anna's thousands, or Armistead leading his men into the Angle, or Custer dying a glorious death, must share the choir loft with those who wish to sing a different song. Still, dissonance can be creative. Perhaps from the clashing voices heard at America's sacred ground, new, more complex, more inclusive songs of the nation will one day be sung.

Notes

1. J. Frank Hanly, *The Spirit of Gettysburg* (Cincinnati: Jennings and Graham, 1912), p. 85.

2. James M. Mayo, *War Memorials as Political Landscape: The American Experience and Beyond* (New York: Praeger, 1988), p. 129.

Epilogue

My interest in the cultural life of America's battlefields did not end with the publication of *Sacred Ground* in 1991, for a wide variety of struggles continue to characterize the nation's engagement with these places of memory. When I was told there would be a paperback edition of *Sacred Ground* coming out in 1993, I asked if I might add significant new information to the Little Bighorn and Pearl Harbor chapters. The decision was made to add this epilogue, which updates events at each of the five sites.

Lexington and Concord

After several years of contention between the National Park Service and the citizens of Lexington, Concord, and Lincoln, agreement was reached over a 200-acre expansion of Minute Man National Historical Park, largely along Route 2A. The "invisibility" of the historic route along which the minutemen battled the retreating British soldiers had long bothered those interested in historic preservation. Massachusetts congressman Chester G. Atkins, sponsor of legislation that would appropriate funds for expansion, expressed these sentiments succinctly: "Just as in Gettysburg and in Antietam, people ought to [be] able to feel, palpably, a connection to those who fought on these lands, who farmed on these fields and who died there for principles we still hold dear to this day."[1]

Passed in October 1992, Public Law 102-488 authorized, over a ten- to fifteen-year period, approximately $15 million for park development and more than $7 million for land acquisition. Citizen concern over potential Park Service land acquisition policy and the lack of mapped boundaries of the park convinced NPS officials to scale back their ambitious plans of the late 1980s to restore the highway to its 1775 state. Rather, they decided to ban traffic from elements of the Battle Road that diverged from Route 2A and hoped, thereby, to soften the impact of this major thoroughfare on the patriotic landscape. Superintendent Lawrence D. Gall declared that "signage will be improved and pull-offs provided at strategic interpretive locations. Designed entrance signs and right-of-way landscaping . . . will aim to strengthen the feeling of 'parkway' and reduce the feeling of 'highway.' "[2]

The Park Service hoped that, with some aesthetic modifications, visitors would still be able to connect symbolically with portions of the Battle Road landscape. In his congressional testimony, John Clymer, chairman of the Concord Board of Selectmen, insisted that the resolution of problems between the NPS and the town had already illustrated a symbolic connection with the revolutionary spirit of the minutemen. "Responsible, democratic government," he declared, "is alive, is well, and is as effective in the 1990's as it was in the 1770's."[3]

Also at issue was symbolic ownership of the minuteman image, as well as ownership of French's Minute Man Statue. Recall that in 1984 the Concord selectmen denied the Air National Guard permission to build a replica of the statue for its headquarters building. In September 1992, a similar controversy arose between the town and the Army National Guard, which asked for approval of its plan to reproduce the statue from the Park Service's plaster cast (which had been made in 1975 as insurance against destruction of the statue). Shortly thereafter, the Guard received legal advice that copyright protection had expired in 1929 and French's statue was therefore in the public domain. The Guard was advised that it need not ask the town for permission to copy the statue; and the Guard reasoned that it also was entitled to use the cast since federal funds had been spent on its construction. If the NPS denied the Guard access to the cast, the Guard informed the selectmen, it would proceed on its own with plans to have a replica made.

Maj. Gen. Charles H. Perenick, of the Massachusetts National Guard, argued that the minuteman had been the symbol of the Guard for years and a duplicate statue would help keep the spirit of the minuteman alive. Concord officials "don't own the spirit," he declared. "We will have a replica of the Minuteman statue in Virginia when the complex opens one way or the other. We'd like to do it as a good neighbor."[4] Based on a 1984 letter from then NPS superintendent Robert Nash to the Board of Selectmen, which argued that the "intention of the Park Service in commissioning this model was to be able to re-create the statue as accurately as possible should it ever be damaged in the future," Superintendent Gall responded that, "by implication, any other use of the cast would require the permission of the statue's owners, i.e., the Town of Concord. . . . In other words, the Selectmen must give their approval for use of the cast in our possession by the Army National Guard before the Park Service would permit it to be used."[5]

Even the most vociferous defenders of Concord's right of ownership conceded that the familiar figure of the minuteman had often been used commercially, and in ways arguably less patriotic than that proposed by the Army National Guard. Yet the statue was, for many, inextricably linked to the site where the first minuteman was said to have fallen. Just as Concord zealously guarded its proclaimed location as the site of the first battle of the Revolution, so too did it guard the iconographical essence of the spirit of that battle. French's statue, Selectman Leland Wood declared, "belongs to the people of the world. . . . We share it with the world—when people come to visit." Susan H. Curtin, chairperson of the Concord Historical Commission, also argued for the link among place, statue, and event, stating that the statue has symbolic importance for the nation "precisely because [it] is rooted historically in the place where our eighteenth century militiamen began the American Revolution."[6]

Amid escalating rhetoric—the Army National Guard accusing the town of selfishness, and members of the town accusing the Guard of attempting to "cheapen" the memory of the minutemen and, through the Guard's arrogance, "dishonoring the very spirit of the Minutemen"—and sensing at best a Pyrrhic victory, the Guard decided in December 1992 to settle for a bronze statue of a colonial militiaman by a New Jersey sculptor. The Concord selectmen, who had voted 4–1 to refuse the Guard's request, wrote to Maj. Gen. Perenick that their decision "in no way reflected any lack of respect for, or appreciation of, the Guard and its role" and indicated how pleased they were to have the issue of symbolic—if not legal—ownership resolved once again.[7]

The Alamo

In September 1992, *San Antonio Express-News* editorial writer David Anthony Richelieu berated the Daughters of the Republic of Texas for various acts of contemporary defilement—among them allowing tour buses to "drive up and drip oil . . . right where the Alamo defenders fell"—and grumbled as well about their past sins—for example, altering the environs of the Long Barrack for financial gain. "Doorways that the Alamo heroes ran through to fight to the death were blocked up," Richelieu lamented, "and new doorways were cut in these sacred walls so tourists could run to the DRT Gift Shop." A month earlier, a chain-link fence had been erected to keep visitors at bay after the DRT decided that body oils from people's hands were damaging the structure's outside walls.[8]

Richelieu took a dim view as well of the group's response to a recent apology from the rock musician Ozzy Osbourne, who had urinated on the

Alamo Heroes Cenotaph in 1982. In thanking Osbourne for his $10,000 donation, the DRT applauded "the progress he [had] made in turning his life around in a new and positive direction." Richelieu, claiming that Ozzy "leaves wet spot again," complained that the Cenotaph belonged to the city of San Antonio, not to the DRT, and that the check should have gone to the Alamo Foundation, which hoped to restore "major portions of the Alamo and battleground."[9]

In 1993, Texas state representative Ron Wilson—who vowed, "I'll keep going until I outlive the Daughters"—once again proposed legislation to transfer custodianship of the Alamo from the DRT to the state's Parks and Wildlife Department. He raised familiar complaints about inadequate historical presentation, declaring that the DRT had chosen "not to highlight a number of Hispanics who helped defend the Alamo" and had failed to give "the correct historical perspective of the Mexican government . . . [which] was opposed to slavery, while the Texans endorsed it." Public response was quick and contemptuous. *Express-News* editorial writer Roddy Stinson accused Wilson of offering "politically correct" legislation and responded sharply to his claim that the state could spend considerable funds to better restore and run the Alamo: "No doubt. If Texas legislators know how to do anything, it's 'pump more money.'" Reminding readers that the Alamo was "an irreplaceable symbol of human courage in the face of overwhelming odds," the *Houston Chronicle* declared that as caretakers the DRT had done an "outstanding job."[10]

Gettysburg

The enduring preservation impulse at one of the nation's most sacred battlefields led to a 2,050-acre addition to the Gettysburg National Military Park when Pres. George Bush signed Public Law 101-377 on August 17, 1990. A few months later, on November 28, 1990, Public Law 101-628 was enacted, establishing a Civil War Sites Advisory Commission to identify sites threatened by development and to recommend preservation strategies.

The Gettysburg land acquisition was not sufficient to calm the fears of those who worried about the ever-present threat to the commemorative landscape from various forms of modernity, for despite the additional acreage, more than 70 percent of the battlefield still lay outside the park's boundaries. Any new roads and industrial development in the immediate area would still threaten portions of the landscape that have, according to a 1991 NPS Management Statement, "remained basically unchanged since colonial settlement." An increase in tourist activities—including helicopter tours—also meant "audible and visual intrusions" that threatened the "comparative serenity and contemplative ambience of the park." And Civil War battlefields, including Gettysburg, were more popular than ever, thanks in part to Ken Burns's critically acclaimed Civil War series on PBS in September 1990, which was viewed by an estimated thirty-nine million Americans. NPS staff have remarked that now there is "no down time. There are always lots of visitors."[11]

The Little Bighorn

George Armstrong Custer and the battle of the Little Bighorn were again brought to the forefront of the nation's consciousness with the ABC-TV adaptation of Evan Connell's popular book *Son of the Morning Star,* which aired on February 3–4, 1991, and with the PBS telecast on November 25, 1992, of "Last Stand at the Little Big Horn," as part of its "American Experience" series. While attendance at the battlefield continued to climb, surpassing the 300,000 mark in 1992 (nearly a 30 percent increase over the previous year), Barbara Booher, the battlefield's first female—and, more significant, first Native American—superintendent, bore the brunt of the criticism from some Custerphiles who were losing their fight to keep Custer's name in the official designation of the battlefield. In December 1991, the battlefield was renamed Little Bighorn Battlefield National Monument and the proposed Indian memorial—not nearly as controversial as the name change—moved closer to reality.

Amid these changes, the Park Service continued to distance its interpretive programs from an emphasis on Custer and the Seventh Cavalry. Also, beginning in June 1990, and coinciding with the anniversary of the battle, the nearby town of Hardin, Montana, resurrected Joe Medicine Crow's pageant as part of the commemoration known as "Little Big Horn Days," and the pageant has twice been repeated. The brochure distributed at the June 1992 "Custer's Last Stand Re-Enactment" that I attended proclaimed that the program would be "featured by national and international media including CNN, *Friends Magazine,* and television stations in Denver, Seattle, New York, South Dakota, West Virginia, Virginia and even as far away as Berlin, Germany."[12] Finally, both Indian activists and Custerphiles sought to use the battlefield for ritual purposes, one of their only remaining means of claiming temporary ownership of the free space of the Little Bighorn.

Barbara Booher, who is of Ute and Cherokee ancestry, came to the Little Bighorn battlefield in July 1989 from the Bureau of Indian Affairs in Alaska. She was catapulted into the public eye in 1990 when *People* magazine ran a story entitled "General Custer Loses at Little Big Horn Again as an Indian Activist Becomes Keeper of His Legend." Booher was said to be "uncomfortable" standing next to the marker where Custer fell, and she was quoted as saying, "I don't like the man." But she also stated quite clearly, "I don't have to like him to do my job." In the same article, Jerry Russell, a member of the Little Big Horn Associates, remarked, "I don't want to sound racist and chauvinist . . . but I want the lady out of there. She's not qualified." Native Americans had different reactions. Janine Windy Boy, president of Little Big Horn Community College in Crow Agency, Montana, pronounced the new superintendent a "breath of fresh air. . . . Superintendents prior to her were consistently more interested in military history from the Custer point of view."[13]

Both the *People* article and an Associated Press wire story in August 1990 that was carried by many newspapers portrayed Booher as the instigator of major historical revision in NPS interpretation and characterized her as "leading a drive" for an Indian memorial. These publications clearly had no idea that Booher was working within Park Service interpretive mandates to help bring about changes that had begun to take hold in the 1960s and early 1970s and had gathered momentum as the NPS sorted out the consequences of the centennial events of 1976 and the demonstrations of 1988. The Park Service's response to those who questioned Booher's qualifications was to emphasize that "she has made no decisions that do not reflect the policy of the National Park Service, and there has been no noteworthy change in the interpretive message that visitors receive."[14]

Letters soon began to pour into Booher's office. Many of them began, "I am not a letter writer, but . . ."; most of them were supportive; the majority expressed acceptance of the fact that Native Americans deserved full inclusion in this sacred American narrative. For example, a constituent of Illinois senator Paul Simon wrote that he was glad the Indian point of view would now be heard: "We should now, finally, pay homage to those Americans, more than one hundred years later, by equal recognition of the participants, without overtones of racial superiority and intolerance." A teacher wrote that after visiting the battlefield in 1988, her family was "emphatically in favor of your efforts to bring a new honesty about the past and a better cultural balance to the public presentation of this important site. . . . If Americans are sophisticated enough to listen to point-counterpoint on television and to cut through campaign ads to understand complex issues, they can surely begin to hear the untold perspectives of Native Americans on key historical episodes."[15]

Jack Manion, the chairman of the LBHA Board of Directors, wrote to disassociate the organization from some of Jerry Russell's comments. Other LBHA members, also incensed at the boorish public pronouncements of several of their colleagues, wrote Booher to express their support. And, in a thoughtful letter that put the interpretive issue at the Little Bighorn into comparative perspective, Kathleen Georg Harrison, the Gettysburg National Military Park historian, remarked that "the original proprietors of [Gettysburg] (in this case, the victors) presented a one-sided story for over thirty years. It was not until the intervention of the Federal Government in 1895 that Confederate positions began to be routinely monumented and made accessible. I am chagrined to see that we still haven't reconciled ourselves to another dark era in our history, that of the wars against the Indian nations. . . . All I can say to you is to never lose sight of our responsibilities to the resource, to the law, to the generation of Americans and Native Americans who gave the site its original significance, and to those generations of Americans and Native Americans who must learn of and from that significance."[16]

Through Booher's appointment, the National Park Service had sent a clear message that the interpretive momentum sparked by the centennial would not be halted. The public trust, it said, did not require that the site superintendent be fixated on Custer, or be a military historian, or even be a white male. Yet for some Custerphiles, Booher was an intruder into the inner sanctum. Those who refused to see nineteenth-century Native Americans as Americans, but instead characterized them as "enemies," now saw a descendant of the enemy within and found it intolerable.

Part of their ire, of course, came about because of Booher's enthusiastic support for the Indian memorial and the name change—although for her, as for a number of Native Americans, the memorial project was clearly more important. Legislation designed to establish an Indian memorial was introduced in April 1990 during the 101st Congress by Montana representative Ron Marlenee and cosponsored by Colorado's Ben Nighthorse Campbell, a Northern Cheyenne whose great-grandfather fought in the battle, and Montana's Pat Williams. Prior to this—and largely in response to the Indian plaque controversy in 1988—the NPS had established the National Indian Monument Committee, an advisory group that included Russell Means and Robert Utley, which was charged with recommending possible locations for a memorial. The committee also established a memorial theme: "Peace through Unity."

Despite the political ramifications of a memorial honoring Sioux and Cheyenne on Crow land, Crow tribal chairwoman Clara Nomee endorsed the project in testimony before a House Interior subcommittee. "It is fitting," she said, "for other American Indians to see this as a show of Indian solidarity. . . . We thought it . . . was long overdue." However, the Crow did not agree with the monument committee's recommendation that the memorial be placed on Custer Hill but preferred a ridge near the Little Bighorn River that offered a good view of the site of the Indian encampment of 1876.[17]

The legislation died unexpectedly when, shortly before Congress adjourned, Rep. Williams tried to attach a name change provision to the bill. Rep. Marlenee was opposed to the name change and refused to accept Williams's amendment, calling instead for public hearings. Although there was little substantive public or congressional opposition to the Indian memorial, Bill Wells, an LBHA member, did ask, "What's next? Do we build a monument to the Japanese that died at Pearl Harbor and to the Mexicans that died at the Alamo? Both ideas make as much sense as an Indian monument at the Little Big Horn." George Armstrong Custer IV, while not opposed in principle, argued that "no memorials to past enemies of the United States have ever been financed by the Federal Government. . . . I fail to see why this memorial should be treated differently." Speaking in favor of a monument, Jerry Rogers, the NPS's associate director for cultural resources, remarked during congressional testimony that "as the 7th Cavalry monument, *funded by Federal appropriations* in 1881, records commemorative sentiment of earlier generations, so too a memorial constructed with Federal funds honoring the Indian participants is appropriate to record a later generation's recognition."[18]

Those who argue against federal funding for the Indian memorial because tribes who fought in the battle were enemies of the government overlook the fact that Civil War national military parks, including Gettysburg, Vicksburg, Chickamauga-Chattanooga, Shiloh, and Antietam, are federally funded and that *both* Union and Confederate lines of battle are marked. Indeed, as Kathleen Georg Harrison has noted, in the last decade of the nineteenth century the majority of federal funding at Gettysburg "was directed toward opening avenues along Confederate lines and erecting markers and reproduction cannon carriages along those same lines." Gettysburg is "a national memorial to the victor and the defeated 'enemy' paid for by the Federal goverment and is still a national memorial maintained and preserved by the Federal government." Mindful of critics' charges of favoritism in the use of public funds for construction of the memorial, various tribes have contributed more than $8,000 to the project at the Little Bighorn.[19]

Numerous letters to Superintendent Booher recall interest in the commemorative balance so eagerly sought at Civil War battlefields as a precedent for evaluating the appropriateness of an Indian memorial. For example, a Missourian wrote, "We respect and honor Confederate generals and soldiers who gave their lives at Shiloh, Antietam, Chickamauga . . . fighting for slavery and/or state sovereignty. This is palatable. However, are native Americans who fell in defense of *their* freedom, *their* way of life and *their* ancient homeland less worthy of respect given by fair historical treatment?" Understanding the Indian memorial as a significant step not only in the interpretive evolution of the Little Bighorn but also in the ongoing cultural conversations regarding multicultural education, Dr. J. Edson Way, interim director of the New Mexico Museum of Natural History, wrote that "modifying the message of that historic location . . . betokens a maturing perspective on American history that needs to be encouraged if this nation is to successfully meet the challenge of a multi-cultural future within and even between our nation and the rest of the world."[20]

Letters of support came also from those connected with the Seventh Cavalry. Proud of the fact that his father served with the Seventh in Mexico and then in France during World War I, a Bostonian wrote the letter he believed his father "would have written were he alive today. . . . Be assured that millions in this land honor you [Booher] for the courage, born of your ancestors, to make right a small part of an unrightable wrong. I wish you a monument as wide as the prairies and as tall as the Rockies." A relative of Lt. Col. Charles A. Varnum, Custer's chief of scouts, wrote that an Indian monument was "long overdue. . . . Many people died that day for what they believed in. . . . Let us not forget the ones that fought to save (what they believed was) their land and to preserve their way of life."[21]

With the exception of Rep. Marlenee, whose attempts to focus legislative action solely on the Indian memorial were unsuccessful, congressional supporters of the name change and the Indian memorial refused to let the two issues be separated. Dr. Heather Huyck, a staff member of the House Subcommittee on National Parks and Public Lands whose job it is to shepherd bills through Congress, felt that the link was essential. "If you did the memorial by itself," she said, "the name change would never happen."[22]

To name something is, in some sense, to own it, and Custerphiles raised their voices in protest. Rep. Campbell held public hearings in Billings, Montana, on June 10, 1991. Former park superintendent James Court argued against a name change for historical reasons: Lt. Edward Maguire, Gen. Alfred Terry's field engineer, had used the name "Custer's Battlefield" on a map prepared for the annual report to the secretary of war in 1877. "This official usage," said Court, "would seem to set the record straight that it was officially called the Custer Battlefield from the very first days after the battle."[23]

Court was aware, of course, that no other National Park Service battle site is named for a person. For him, this was not an argument for change; it simply made the Custer battlefield unique and provided "more of a reason to keep the name as it is." Court also utilized arguments that had become standard with other opponents: removing Custer's name would be an inappropriate act of scapegoating, making Custer guilty for the sins of national Indian policy in the nineteenth century; and renaming the battlefield smacked of historical revisionism, that is, "changing the name to suit a current political or social cause." Representatives of the Custer Battlefield Historical & Museum Association (the Park Service's cooperating association) and the city council of Hardin spoke against the name change on economic grounds. The CBHMA worried that the site would not be as popular if renamed—and a decline in visitation would place a further burden on "an already economically depressed area." City council members were concerned about the cost of reprinting all the "books, pamphlets, brochures and information put out by promotional entities" and also mentioned the cost to the state for changing road maps and highway signs.[24]

During congressional deliberations, Sen. Malcolm Wallop of Wyoming offered a minority report on the name change, which agreed with the LBHA and other critics that this was an attempt "to alter history" and that it did "considerable damage to the historical context." Taking pains to point out that he was neither criticizing the interpretive programs of the Park Service nor trying to "glorify Custer," Wallop argued that the site only became famous *because* Custer died there, an argument not altogether different from one made by the NPS chief historian Edwin C. Bearss in 1987.[25]

Supporters of the name change reiterated the fact that NPS sites are not named for individuals and that this change would be an appropriate act of interpretive balance. Even Robert Utley, longtime opponent of a name change, offered congressional testimony supporting the legislation. Also, in a speech at the Montana History Conference on October 25, 1991, he acknowledged that the Custer name was "part of the battlefield ever since it was set aside as public property" and that such a change should not, in principle, be made "to appease a sentiment that may be only a fad." Nevertheless, he observed, the Custer name was as offensive to many Native Americans as was the Confederate flag to many African Americans, and usage of both "should be sharply examined and limited as necessary to remove the offense." Hence, according to Utley, "the time has come to embrace the more neutral, and the more accepted usage in naming battlefields."[26]

What of the argument that such an act would be a blatant disregard of the *intent* of an earlier generation of military men who had named the battlefield? A careful response came from Douglas C. McChristian, the NPS's chief historian at the battlefield, who argued that there was "compelling historical evidence to support the name change." Although Gen. Terry's field engineer had used Custer's name on a map prepared for the secretary of war, McChristian noted that an earlier report filed by Terry did not name the site, nor did the field engineer's earlier maps. In fact, these earlier maps "reveal that Maguire considered the whole area fought over as the Little Bighorn battlefield."[27]

According to McChristian, Custer's name was used on the 1877 map largely for political purposes, as Gen. Terry "had his own reasons . . . for focusing as much attention as possible upon the late Custer and away from himself and other officers." Other army documents led McChristian to conclude that the army clearly distinguished the "Custer battleground" from "Maj. Reno's first battle-field." In other words, there were various names assigned to different sites *within* the area where the "Battle of the Little Big Horn" had been fought. McChristian also noted that when Mrs. Custer willed her priceless collection of her late husband's effects to the battlefield museum, she referred to the "battle of the Little Big Horn." So, concluded McChristian, " 'Custer Battlefield'. . . is but one aspect of the Little Bighorn battlefield administered by the National Park Service, just as the Reno-Benteen battlefield is another."[28]

After much debate, legislation sponsored by Rep. Campbell passed both houses during the 102nd Congress, and on December 10, 1991, Public Law 102-201 was enacted. It not only changed the name of the battlefield to the Little Bighorn Battlefield National Monument but also established an advisory committee, still in the process of formation as of June 1993. The committee's charge is to "advise the Secretary [of the Interior] that the memorial is appropriate to the Monument, its resources and landscape, sensitive to the history being portrayed, and artistically commendable."[29] As soon as the committee is formed, a nationwide design competition will take place.

It is difficult to take seriously the argument that the name change will hurt visitation to the battlefield or will seriously damage area tourism. Montana's *Regional Tour Guide* for that part of the state is subtitled "Custer Country." National forest lands within the state are named after Custer, stores and motels carry his name, and his face adorns a variety of tourist brochures. In short, Custer remains a powerful symbolic presence in southeastern Montana, and he is memorialized throughout the nation as well. During the June 1992 LBHA conference in Monroe, Michigan, for example, the unveiling of the completely restored Custer equestrian statue—erected in 1910—took place, and a state historical marker was installed at the site. Clearly, however, the name change at the battlefield is significant because it indicates that Americans can approach the battle of the Little Bighorn without Custer as the sole or even the primary memory category. And the name change may portend further name changes in "Custer Country."

In what sense *is* it appropriate to characterize this part of Montana as "Custer Country"? Crow tribal member Barney Old Coyote offered a different reading of the land in his testimony at the name change hearings in

Billings, Montana. "The fact is," he said, "that this has always been, is now, and will always remain Crow Country. In the treaties with the USA, Crow leaders declared this to be 'Crow Country for as long as there are Crow Indians, even if there be only one Crow left.' . . . Custer 'lived' (alive) here less than 36 hours! His remains have been removed to West Point, New York. The remains of Crow Indians through the ages are still here, hence our position that this is Crow Country, not Custer Country."[30] In early 1992, different groups of Native Americans asked the state's regional tourism organization to change the designation. Angela Russell, a state representative and Crow tribal member, suggested "Indian Country" or "Buffalo Country." Custer Country executive director Edythe McCleary responded that the image of Custer was "unique" and that they had "gotten results with the name."[31]

Both those who supported a name change at the park and who want to rename "Custer Country" and those who opposed removing Custer's name from the battlefield share the conviction that these acts are significant revisions of memory. Unlike Custerphiles, however, those who questioned not only the name of the battlefield but the dominant symbol of "Custer Country" see the changes as acts of *corrective* memory, undoing a dominant cultural construction that had endured for far too long, rather than as heretical alterations of a sacred narrative. The story of Custer at the Little Bighorn, revisionists claim, did not open with the words, "In the beginning . . ."[32]

While the Indian memorial and name change issues were being resolved, NPS interpretation continued to move away from an emphasis on Custer. The second draft of a 1992 "Interpretive Prospectus" notes that, despite the fascination with the symbol of Custer, "changing times and perceptions are bringing a more holistic approach to modern interpretations of the Little Big Horn." Visitors are now introduced to the history of the cultural clash over the battlefield itself, as well as to the history of the Plains Indian wars, including intertribal warfare, and the role of the army as an instrument of government policy—perceived by many as a buffer between white society and Native Americans. Visitors are also asked to view the battle of the Little Bighorn as a high-water mark in the clash of cultures begun with European arrival in the New World.[33]

Impetus for a shift in interpretive emphasis has led to significant changes in museum displays and continued attempts to shift attention away from Custer Hill. Now present in the museum are photographs of Native American survivors of the battle, taken at a September 1948 reunion. Erected in 1991, this permanent display has prompted some negative comments and some graffiti. The center wall of the museum, which, according to Superintendent Booher, expressed a "them versus us" atmosphere, has been removed. Mural-size portraits of Ulysses S. Grant and Sitting Bull greet visitors to the museum, further reducing the aesthetic domination of Custer and offering a needed historical corrective. Douglas McChristian notes that while Grant and Sitting Bull occupied positions of leadership, Custer was a "tactical commander. . . . Too often we have seen him misrepresented as everything from the expedition commander up to the architect of the government's Indian policy." The change, McChristian hopes, will "create a public awareness that this battle was the result of factors far beyond the Custer personality." As another way of helping visitors see the battle through different eyes, there are several bus tours daily to the Little Bighorn Valley, the site of the Indian encampment. These tours emphasize Plains Indian life and changes brought about by white movement into and through the area.[34]

Neither resolution of the Indian memorial issue or the name change nor more balanced programs at the battlefield will transform the site into a placid memorial environment, for Custerphiles and Native Americans—having perhaps given up frontal assaults on the Park Service—still seek to claim ownership through ritual incursions. On June 11–14, 1992, for example, Russell Means, of the American Indian Movement, held a Sun Dance on Crow land immediately adjacent to the battlefield after Superintendent Booher had rejected his request to hold it *on* the battlefield. Despite the fact that the ceremonial site was readily visible from the road to the Reno-Benteen site, Means was reportedly "offended" by visitors who stopped to photograph the ceremony. He arranged to have the road closed, claiming his right to religious privacy under the American Indian Religious Freedom Act. Booher decided that while Means's action was inappropriate, it was in the public's best interest to avoid conflict. Consequently, she decided that the NPS would take charge of the road closure to avoid violence.

This prudent judgment was bitterly attacked by Custerphiles in the pages of the *Little Big Horn Associates Newsletter* as yet another example of the NPS's attitude of appeasement. One Custerphile was heard to say that he thought the Park Service should go in and "wipe them [the Indians] out." Clearly, Means's actions were designed to embarrass Booher. Could it be that a more inclusive message at the battlefield posed symbolic problems for Indian political activists who needed Custer and the Little Bighorn as a symbol of evil? Or was this simply a tactical irritant, a way of staking claim to Indian ownership of the land? Or, more alarming, was it an attempt to force the Park Service to potentially violent enforcement of its right to keep the road open, which could lead, once again, to public images of Native American blood being spilled at the Little Bighorn?[35]

Determined to take credit for the successful passage of the Indian memorial and name change legislation—in 1990 he said, "I was the first guy to push for the monument"—Means released to the press a June 1, 1992, letter to Booher in which he claimed that AIM "led the call over the past nineteen years to have the Custer Battlefield renamed." He also bitterly attacked the Park Service for omitting AIM representatives from the ceremonies to receive formally the Indian memorial and name change legislation, scheduled for the weekend of July 4, 1992, which he characterized as an "attempt to write out of the story those people without whom the story never would have unfolded. Without the agitation of AIM . . . the name change that is about to be celebrated would never have happened." Once again, Means used words of intimidation to underscore the importance of his message: "Various chapters of the American Indian Movement plan to attend and participate in the celebration in July; the nature of that participation will be determined by the level of respect and consideration that is given this correspondence."[36]

While the staff at the Little Bighorn was ready to proceed, Park Service officials in Washington, D.C., postponed the ceremony until Veterans' Day, November 11, 1992. On a cold, snowy day, approximately one thousand spectators gathered at the battlefield. Among them were Delores Mills, a descendant of Crazy Horse; Emmanuel Red Bear, Jr., great-grandson of Sitting Bull; Claudia Iron Hawk, whose grandfather fought in the battle; and Celane Not Help Him, whose grandfather Dewey Beard was the battle's last surviving warrior. Various Sioux and Cheyenne groups planned the ceremonies, which were dominated by the presence of numerous Native American military veterans. The keynote speaker was Lionel Bordeaux, president of Sinte Gleska University, located on the Rosebud Sioux Reservation in South Dakota. He said that the name change represented the Native Americans' second victory at the Little Bighorn, "the victory of the people who worked so hard to see that this place is called by its rightful name." That evening, Senator-elect Ben Nighthorse Campbell, who spoke at a buffalo meat dinner provided by the Oglala Sioux, declared that the name change was an act of inclusion, "to give our people equal time . . . so that our part in history could be written for the first time." Now, said Campbell, "I feel I'm welcome." Earlier, at the conclusion of the ceremonies, Austin Two Moon, a Northern Cheyenne, held a pipe that belonged to his grandfather—a veteran of the battle—and an eagle feather owned by Red Cloud and offered a closing prayer: "I've prayed here every June 25. We need to pray together, ask the Creator for peace throughout the country and throughout the world. I don't want any other war here." AIM members took part in a procession of veterans groups before the ceremonies began but complained publicly about being ignored during the ceremonies.[37]

Custerphiles have also held ceremonies at the battlefield. Before Barbara Booher became superintendent, a small group that called itself "The Committee of American Traditions" was regularly allowed on the battlefield at midnight to conduct a ceremony at Custer Hill to honor the Reno-Benteen water carriers—men who had made the perilous trip down the bluffs from the Reno-Benteen defensive position to bring water to their comrades. Once she became superintendent, Booher angered Custerphiles by insisting that the ceremony take place during regular park hours. Reluctantly, they agreed. The ceremony consisted of setting up a card table on which they placed paper cups filled with water, observed a moment of silence, then poured the water over the fence onto Custer Hill.[38]

Many personal memorial expressions also give shape to this contested landscape. For example, Brian Pohanka, an LBHA member and senior researcher for *Time-Life*'s multivolume history of the Civil War, as well as a consultant for the film *Glory*, wrote to Booher on November 3, 1990, describing acts that reveal the intimate relationship between people and place. Pohanka noted that there were already three stone markers at places where Indian warriors fell during the battle. "Two commemorate the Cheyenne warriors Lame White Man and Noisy Walking. . . . The third . . . commemorates the warrior who was shot while trying to 'count coup' on one of Reno's men, and stands on the Reno/Benteen battlefield on the slope below the site of Benteen's 'charge.' Many times I have walked down to them with other students of the battle, and rebuilt the little piles of stone so these important sites are not lost to history."[39]

The Indian memorial will ensure that various American memories will be represented at the Little Bighorn and not "lost to history," but monument planning itself is often a highly contested process. If reasonable consensus is reached, the memorial's dedication ceremony will be an opportune—and much-needed—occasion for further expression of ritual reconciliation at the Little Bighorn.

Pearl Harbor

On December 3, 1991, I joined Edwin Bearss (NPS chief historian), James Charleton and Harry Butowsky (two members of Bearss's staff), and James Delgado (former NPS maritime historian) in Honolulu, Hawaii. Bearss had invited me to work for four days as a volunteer for the Park Service at the USS *Arizona* Memorial, providing me with the priceless opportunity to be a participant-spectator at the kind of event I had only written about at other battlefields: a fiftieth anniversary. Beginning on December 4, I attended the Park Service's programs at the memorial, offered a number of talks on the USS *Arizona* as a sacred relic at the museum in the visitors center and on boats returning from the memorial, and spoke about the legacy of Pearl Harbor at a conference held in Honolulu on December 9–11.

The fiftieth anniversary of any great battle is a poignant occasion, for it is the last time large numbers of participants have the opportunity to put their unique stamp on the interpretation of the event and to claim that *their* memory should govern the way coming generations understand the significance of the battle and their sacrifice. In 1991, Pearl Harbor survivors did not have the interpretive field to themselves. Historians were not satisfied with simple explanatory constructions regarding the attack, namely, that it happened because the Japanese were by nature "sneaky" people. As with new perspectives on the necessity of the use of atomic weapons to end the war, certain memories of the veterans' generation were being contested. This anniversary gave some veterans a chance to reiterate traditional patriotic orthodoxies. It also gave some of them a chance to meet their former enemies face to face.

The fiftieth anniversary of Pearl Harbor took place in the context of cultural friction—largely but not solely based on economic issues—between the United States and Japan. For the Japanese, it brought often unwelcome attention to the troubling and unresolved issue of World War II in their own national memory and raised fears of a new wave of anti-Japanese feeling in the United States. For the United States, the anniversary was an evocative patriotic moment, a time of intense remembering of every detail of the attack and of equally intense forgetting of the context of war in which the attack took place. It was a time to celebrate and mourn those men and women Pres. George Bush called "heroes of the harbor." It was a time for some to emphasize that the Japanese character that had revealed itself in the attack was again endangering the United States through an "economic Pearl Harbor" and a time for others to warn against the dangers of using the language of warfare to characterize modern American-Japanese relations. For many, it was a time to celebrate the legacy of Pearl Harbor: fifty years of a real—if sometimes strained—alliance between the two nations.[40]

Although the question of Japanese participation in the commemorative events was settled in August 1991 when the State Department simply announced that no representative of *any* foreign government would be invited, other controversies intensified as the anniversary drew near. There were many perceptions of the lessons that appropriate commemoration could bring, yet Pearl Harbor survivors—and, indeed, many Americans of the World War II generation—were adamant about the need to keep faith with patriotic orthodoxy, a faith that would tolerate no alteration. Caught in the path of this passionate commitment was the National Park Service, which tried to walk the razor's edge at the USS *Arizona* Memorial between commemorative grave site, where certain interpretive voices were not appropriate, and historic site, where those same voices were necessary for historically dispassionate interpretation. According to Bearss, his office received "more questions and complaints about the historical interpretation and management of this site than about all the other historical areas of the National Park System put together."[41]

The most serious criticism was that the Park Service was not an appropriate guardian of the sacred memory of those Americans who died in the attack on Pearl Harbor. Accusations came from various quarters: individuals wrote to their congressmen, to the president, and to the staff at the memorial itself to complain that the NPS was being "soft" on the Japanese. The text of the film shown at the memorial (made not by the NPS but by the navy) was repeatedly questioned for stating, among other things, that the United States had "forced" the Japanese to attack. (The single line in the script that has caused such consternation is: "Japan felt that her back was to the wall.") In *Betrayal at Pearl Harbor,* James Rusbridger and Eric Nave lambaste the Park Service for this "sanitized film," which they claim plays down "the treacherous nature of the attack that morning . . . made while diplomatic negotiations were still in progress. President Roosevelt's 'infamy' speech," they declare, "has been excised and is shown only mute, thus robbing it of its dramatic impact. Even the final surrender of the Japanese on board the USS *Missouri* in 1945 has been delicately edited so that there is only a fleeting glimpse of the defeated enemy. Revisionist history is commonplace in communist countries, but it is bizarre to find it so grotesquely displayed at one of America's great national shrines."[42]

Based partly on Rusbridger and Nave's harsh interpretation of a film incorrectly attributed to the Park Service, some members of the American Ex-Prisoners of War undertook a letter-writing campaign in which they accused the NPS of an act of unconscionable defilement. "An Open Letter to All Chapter Commanders" quoted the above passage from *Betrayal at Pearl Harbor* and called for the termination of the Park Service's involvement at the memorial, a return of the memorial guardianship to the navy, and removal from the film of the "glorification of Admiral Yamamoto's sinister tactics and . . . any allegation of the United States forcing Japan to attack Pearl Harbor." Clearly, *any* attempt to claim that Japan was motivated by geopolitical concern and saw some strategic wisdom in the attack is heretical to some.[43]

The Park Service was still receiving letters from American tourists complaining that Japanese visitors applaud when Yamamoto's name is mentioned in the film. However, Al Frumkin, commander of the Hawaii chapter of the American Ex-Prisoners of War, wrote to the group's national commander that he had seen the film "many times" and "never . . . have I ever heard of any ethnic group laughing, clapping in glee, or in any way being disrespectful." He added that the NPS rangers' introductions to the film are "in good taste and well done." In a letter to a self-proclaimed "historian and author" from Gardena, California, who claimed she had *heard* Japanese tourists clapping at Yamamoto's mention, Superintendent Donald Magee wrote: "I have also spoken to many of the park rangers, staff, and volunteers (that includes five Pearl Harbor survivors among their number) here at the Memorial. Three of the individuals, including the film projectionists, have been here since the facility opened in 1980 and they collectively have seen thousands and thousands of programs. They were unable to recall a single incident of Japanese visitors applauding, clapping, or cheering. If such behavior has happened, it must be very rare indeed." Magee notes too that "Roosevelt's speech has not been muted as it was never in the movie. . . . Admiral Yamamoto is not glorified and is but mentioned briefly in a single sentence, 'The Commander-in-Chief of the combined Japanese fleet was the brilliant strategist, Admiral Isoroku Yamamoto.' "[44]

A Maryland physician named David Nurco continued his crusade, begun in 1985, to have Adm. Husband E. Kimmel's "offensive" remark about Japan's "beautifully executed military maneuver" removed from a museum exhibit. "What better time could there be but right now," he wrote in a letter to Pres. Bush on December 4, 1990, "for a concerted effort to be made toward turning the Memorial into a more fitting tribute to the many who made the supreme sacrifice and who lie entombed in the USS Arizona." Nurco not only objected to the "poor taste" of placing the quote in a visitors center exhibit but to its proximity to the "men entombed just a few hundred yards away." Magee responded that the visitors center was an appropriate place for educational exhibits that might include such a quote, and the three-quarter-mile distance to the memorial "creates an emotional as well as a physical distance" between the two. Nurco's persistence paid off, however, when the exhibits underwent alteration in 1991. In a letter to Michael Dugan of the American Legion, Bearss said that the statement—which he agreed appeared "out of context"—would be removed and that any future use of the quote would place it "in the context of the occasion on which Kimmel made it."[45]

Concern about ethnic purity at the USS *Arizona* Memorial became intense as the fiftieth anniversary approached. One angry tourist suggested in a letter to his congressman that "no visitors from areas of the Far East be allowed to visit this area during the first two weeks of December 1991." Park Service staff of Asian ethnicity but United States nationality experienced tense moments with hostile visitors, and there were accusations of irreverent behavior by Japanese tourists, including complaints that Japanese teenagers were wearing headbands decorated with the Rising Sun. Thurston Clarke offered a spirited rebuttal to such accusations in his book *Pearl Harbor Ghosts*. Clarke wrote of his visit to Pearl Harbor in 1990: "while most Japanese wore sober suits, modest skirts, or polo shirts, Americans came in tank tops, tube socks, and sweatshirts, in cutoff blue jeans, jogging shorts, and bathing shorts. They wore plastic visors that turned their faces green, and novelty t-shirts with four-letter words. I watched them pick up tickets for the shuttle boat, and saw looks of amazement and disgust at those turned away for failing to meet the minimal requirement of 'shirts, shorts, and footwear.' " He concluded: "The more I compared the Japanese to the American visitors, the better the Japanese looked, and the more obvious it became that if anyone was desecrating this place, it was us."[46]

Criticism peaked shortly before the commemorative events in a widely publicized argument between the NPS staff at the memorial and Ray Emory, a retired naval chief petty officer who had served aboard the USS *Honolulu* and was now a Pearl Harbor Survivors Association volunteer and the group's historian. Emory wrote lengthy letters to Bearss and other NPS officials detailing his numerous complaints. Among them was his belief that the Park Service did not properly and accurately honor American heroes of the attack and that the interpretive programs made it appear as if the United States had forced the Japanese to attack. He bitterly complained about "untrained" rangers offering "revisionist" history, all the while ignorant of what he believed were basic, crucial "facts" about the attack. Emory's complaints were made public in the *Wall Street Journal* and the *Honolulu Advertiser* and became the basis for an attack by the syndicated columnist Thomas Sowell, who angrily accused the National Park Service of turning "its back on patriotism." Sowell declared that "people who are squeamish about telling the truth and apologetic about being Americans are the last people to be left in charge of a national shrine like that at Pearl Harbor."[47]

At the 7:55 A.M. December 7 services at the USS *Arizona* Memorial—with room for only about two hundred guests—Ray Emory was seated between Pres. and Mrs. Bush, a symbolic positioning not lost upon television reporters or Park Service staff. By contrast, one of the two surviving Medal of Honor recipients, John Finn, was relegated to a seat farther back; and Gerald Glaubitz, the mayor of Morningside, Maryland, and president of the PHSA, was also seated in an obscure location. In the coming days, however, the heartfelt gratitude directed toward the memorial's staff by individual veterans and by the PHSA president made Emory's complaints about lack of patriotism and sensitivity less persuasive among many of the veterans in attendance.

Planning the major commemorative events involved a complex process of jousting for position, particularly between the Park Service and the navy.

Eventually, the navy took complete responsibility for Pres. Bush's three speeches on December 7, and the NPS planned four days of programs at the visitors center. In charge of NPS planning was James D. Harpster, a former public affairs officer for the Park Service who continued to volunteer his services at various national parks after his retirement. Harpster worked with Blanca Stransky, the memorial's public affairs officer, and Kam Napier, an assistant to the museum's curator. This team—and the whole staff at the memorial—struggled with shortages of funds, a curious lack of interest and support from the NPS's western regional office, a physical plant in need of refurbishing, and a lack of personnel.

Despite these daunting logistical problems, Park Service planners sought to connect visitors to the Pearl Harbor story in an intimate manner by inviting various participants in the battle to take part in commemorative events. Personal recollection was the dominant voice of the planned activities and the symposium. Hence, the invitation extended to Lenore Rickert, who had witnessed the attack while serving as a nurse in the Pearl Harbor Naval Hospital and would have the honor of introducing Pres. Bush at one of his December 7 speeches. The NPS was responsible for inviting the two surviving Medal of Honor recipients, John Finn and Capt. Donald Ross (since deceased), and it also invited Franklin Van Valkenburgh, son of the USS *Arizona*'s captain, who had never been to the memorial, and Carl Christiansen, the youngest crewman to survive the attack.

Given the presence of more than five thousand members of the PHSA and thousands of other tourists in Honolulu for the commemoration, a disappointingly small crowd witnessed the opening ceremonies on December 4, which had been designated "Hawaii Remembrance Day" to honor civilian victims and the people of Hawaii. The Park Service had conducted a painstaking search for relatives of such victims and sent personal letters of invitation to the event, receiving over ninety responses. At 9:30 A.M., thirty-one *Arizona* survivors were greeted with a standing ovation as they made their way to a large covered stage, adorned with floral arrangements, that had been set up in the spacious parking area between the visitors center and the USS *Bowfin* museum. In the early afternoon, after a colorful procession by the Aloha Week Royal Court, which celebrated the ethnic traditions of native Hawaiians, Rev. Abraham Akaka offered an invocation asking that "something good . . . come out of the fiftieth anniversary." Echoing Lincoln, he called for those in attendance to be "on God's side" rather than asking "that he is on ours." The mayor of Honolulu, Frank F. Fasi, who came to Hawaii as an American serviceman during World War II, spoke of a "far different Honolulu" but reassured the audience that the "same American people" were still "willing to go to war . . . to sacrifice . . . to die." Gladys Ainoa Brandt, one of Hawaii's most distinguished educators and a regent of the University of Hawaii, set a very different tone in her speech, declaring that "we must always be more willing to live for our ideals than to die for them." She argued that memories of the attack should not be a "justification for racism" and that we must "actively shun the glorification of war."[48]

December 5 was designated "Survivors Day." At 9:45 A.M. a tribute was offered to the sailors and marines on the nine battleships that were in Pearl Harbor at the time of the attack; the event was hosted by Hawaii's governor, John D. Waihee III, who was joined by representatives from states after which the ships were named. In the afternoon, Capt. Jim D. Miller, the highest-ranking survivor from the USS *Arizona,* offered welcoming remarks to an audience which then listened to personal reminiscences of the battle from Assistant Secretary of the Navy Joseph K. Taussig, Jr., who had been awarded the Navy Cross for his heroic actions during the attack, and from Capt. Donald K. Ross and Lenore Rickert. The audience warmly greeted Van Valkenburgh, who wore his father's 1909 Naval Academy ring, recovered from the bridge of the *Arizona* shortly after the attack. According to Van Valkenburgh, the worker who found it had "cleaned it up and gave it to Admiral Traine, a classmate of my Dad's from the academy. Today I wear that ring with pride." After these moving recollections, Capt. Ross led the audience in an enthusiastic rendition of "God Bless America."[49]

December 6 was designated "Reflections of Pearl Harbor." Military music and an exercise from the Presidential Honor Guard entertained visitors in the morning. In the afternoon, a concert by the United States Navy Pacific Fleet Band preceded the introduction of John Finn to an enthusiastic audience, followed by speeches by Alfred Preis, the Austrian-born designer of the USS *Arizona* Memorial who had been interned in Sand Island on Oahu during World War II due to his classification as an enemy alien, and by Edward H. Ichiyama, a retired Honolulu attorney who had served with the much-decorated Nisei 100th Battalion, 442nd Regimental Combat Team, during the war. Ichiyama recounted that while he was fighting in Europe, his brother Katsuji, a crew member on a Japanese destroyer in the Pacific, was wounded. Katsuji Ichiyama's wife still suffered from radiation sickness as a result of the attack on Hiroshima. According to Ichiyama, his brother had declined the Park Service's invitation to participate in the ceremonies.

Last to speak on that afternoon was the acclaimed author James Michener, himself a navy veteran, who told the audience: "I come before you today as one who was modified by our national experience in fighting Japan. For four long years I battled her empire with every shred of energy I had, and watched with pride as we slowly drove her from the oceans and assailed her on land. . . . For the next few years, I lived in Japan, studied her ways, grew to love her art, and wrote six books about things Japanese. From a dedicated enemy I slowly transformed myself into a devoted friend, with help from the Japanese themselves, who were becoming my friends." It was from this "devastation and cruelty," Michener said, that a "miraculous friendship developed, . . . and it is that human triumph that we honor today." Michener's Japanese-American wife was with him. A fitting end to the day came after the program, while Michener was resting on the patio outside the Park Service offices at the visitors center and signing autographs. Finn, wearing his Medal of Honor, approached (he had expressed a desire to meet Michener more than Pres. Bush). Spying Finn's medal, Michener reached for his cane and, struggling to his feet, said, "For you sir, I will stand."[50]

On December 7, Pres. Bush, a former navy pilot whose plane had been shot down by Japanese anti-aircraft fire in 1944, spoke at 6:30 A.M. at a PHSA ceremony at the Punchbowl National Cemetery. Characterizing America's role in the war as "just and honorable," the president nonetheless recalled a more uncomfortable memory of war, the memory of veterans—Americans of Japanese ancestry—buried at Punchbowl "whose love of country was put to the test unfairly by our own authorities. . . . They . . . and other natural born Americans were sent to internment camps simply because their ancestors were Japanese." He also tried to connect the heroic legacy of World War II with more recent conflicts. His generation, the president declared, "saw its younger brothers go to Korea, its sons to Vietnam to resist communism. . . . [And its] grandchildren answered the call to reverse Saddam's aggression against Kuwait."[51]

By 7:30, the president was aboard the freshly painted memorial, where several hundred dignitaries had gathered. At 7:55, the exact moment of the attack, the USS *Chosin* sailed past the *Arizona* and sounded its whistle; then, after a moment of silence, four F-15s flew overhead in the missing-man formation. After the president and Mrs. Bush dropped leis into the harbor and "Taps" was played, he was introduced to the television audience and to those listening and watching on shore by Capt. Ross, who said of the president, "he knows what we went through and like us, he remembers." The president's speech focused on preferred memories of the "good war." He told stories about individual sailors who had been in the harbor that fateful morning, Americans of "all races and colors, native-born and foreign-born." He told of those who had died, those for whom "heroism came as naturally as breath."

I watched the ceremony aboard the memorial on a television that had been set up on the patio outside the NPS offices, directly behind the gift shop. Interestingly, except for the precise time of the attack, many visitors were more concerned with purchasing items that offered evidence of their participation in the event than with participating via loudspeaker and television in the ceremony itself. Veneration and consumption blended together as the feverish sale of books, T-shirts, slides, videotapes, maps, and photographs illustrated the desire to "own" the fiftieth in material ways.

Pres. Bush delivered his third morning speech at Kilo 8 Pier in the shadow of the USS *Missouri*, which was docked near the *Arizona* Memorial. The president underscored words spoken earlier by Hawaii senator Daniel K. Inouye, a World War II veteran and member of the 442nd Regimental Combat Team, who had said, "Fifty years have passed since that tragic day. Let the healing process begin." The president told the audience that he had wondered, prior to arriving in Hawaii, whether or not he would "feel the remnants of that intense hatred we all felt for the enemy 50 years ago. . . . I wondered: what will my reaction be when I go back to Pearl Harbor?" His response was a fitting benediction for his participation as veteran and commander in chief: "I have no rancor in my heart towards Germany or Japan—none at all. I hope you have none in yours. This is not the time for recrimination." With these words of reconciliation the president left Hawaii, soon followed by fifteen hundred media people, one-third of whom were Japanese.

Commemorative events continued throughout the day at approximately thirty separate public and private events. And, as was the case with previous Pearl Harbor commemorations, the web of memory spread throughout the nation in communities large and small. There was, for example, a commemorative ceremony at the Alamo, and in Baltimore there was a ceremony on board the Coast Guard Cutter *Taney*, the last ship afloat from December 7, 1941. The USS *Indianapolis*—the namesake of the World War II vessel—tolled its bell once for each of the victims of the attack, and "memorial wreaths were tossed into waters from the decks of battleships in New York City; Buffalo, N.Y.; Pittsburgh; Charleston, S.C.; and Portland, Ore." Fifteen hundred people took part in a wreath-laying ceremony at the Tomb of the Unknowns in Arlington National Cemetery. In Philadelphia, a moment of silence was observed at the Liberty Bell, and a "24 foot stage that replicated the Arizona Memorial" was the centerpiece of halftime festivities at the army-navy football game.[52]

Memories of Pearl Harbor and Hiroshima were ritually linked as well. For example, the Wesley United Methodist Church in Honolulu and Nagarekawa Church in Hiroshima held concurrent services. In Honolulu, Bhp. Joseph Ferrario joined with Bhp. Joseph Misue of Hiroshima—Honolulu's "sister city"—in a joint call for "reconciliation and forgiveness."[53]

Ceremonies continued throughout the day at the visitors center. At 11:00 A.M., the Emmy Award–winning composer John Duffy's "Time for Remembrance" premiered, performed by the Honolulu Symphony Orchestra. This work was commissioned as part of a commemorative intent by the National Park Service to "break dramatically with the stereotypical all-military format of bands, banners and bombast." Duffy wrote that he sat down to compose the piece "on the day the Persian Gulf War began . . . [and] finished on Hiroshima Day." "Time For Remembrance" was, he said, his "testament to the victims of war: my dearest sister Agnes, a Navy nurse; my cousin who died aboard the USS Shaw; the men entombed on the USS Arizona and other countless men, women and children across the earth. May peace reign for their sake."[54]

Far more than any of the commemorative speeches, Duffy's music expressed the human cost of war. He had woven his composition around four texts, the first three of which were sung by the acclaimed mezzo-soprano Clamma Dale. Duffy selected Rupert Brooke's World War I poem "The Dead," his own lyric composed after reading letters penned by sailors on the USS *Arizona,* and lyrics from a Negro spiritual, "I Want to Die Easy." The final section consisted of two speeches by Pres. Franklin D. Roosevelt, his fourth inaugural address and a speech written on the eve of his death, words that conveyed an urgent plea for peace, which were movingly read by Sen. Inouye.

Although this performance gave a sense of appropriate closure to the official ceremonies, there was more to come. In the afternoon, the Honolulu Boy Choir performed on the lanai of the visitors center, joined by twenty-five young women dressed in white, each with a bouquet of red flowers. Hawaii's first lady, Lynne Waihee, told the audience that the "true legacy of those who sacrificed so much . . . lies in the peace and the longstanding democratic alliances that followed—alliances . . . that made peace more than just a temporary interlude between wars." Then, the choir members and young women walked in pairs to the newly finished Remembrance Exhibit—panels near the shore on which are engraved the names of American civilian and military dead from the attack—and placed floral tributes. Shortly after this program ended, the USS *Arizona* survivors made one last trip to the memorial for an emotional service, finishing with the "Navy Hymn." Then these men and their families joined in the concluding program at the visitors center stage area. A large crowd heard brief comments from Gerald Glaubitz, PHSA president, and from Gen. Colin Powell, chairman of the Joint Chiefs of Staff.

The preservation of memory took place in many other ways during these eventful days. More than sixty oral histories of the attack were gathered by Park Service historians. After the ceremonies, on December 9–11, a number of American and Japanese survivors gathered with military, academic, and

NPS historians, radar operators, nurses, pilots, NPS underwater archaeologists, and others in Honolulu's Blaisdell Center for the Performing Arts for "The Storm Unleashed," a symposium cosponsored by the Arizona Memorial Museum Association and the Navy Historical Institute. Japanese participants included Lt. Zenji Abe, a flight leader from the carrier *Akagi;* Takeshi Maeda and Lt. Cmdr. Hirata Matsumura, two pilots who had participated in the attack; the World War II historian Masataka Chihaya, who had served on the staff of Adm. Yamamoto; Cmdr. Tadakazu Yoshioka, who had helped develop the shallow water torpedo used in the attack; and Tomatsu Yoshida, a Japanese Navy veteran and distinguished peace educator.[55]

There were many kinds of voices in evidence at the symposium's twenty-six different sessions: voices of recollection in sessions entitled "Gallant Ladies: The Women of Pearl Harbor," "The First Shot: The USS *Ward* Incident," and "Tora! Tora! Tora! The Japanese Aviator Experience over Pearl Harbor"; voices of history, with John Costello and John Dower leading sessions entitled "Climbing Mt. Niitaka: A Historian's Review of the Pearl Harbor Attack" and "War without Mercy: A Review of Japanese and American Attitudes in 1941"; voices of infatuation with the machinery of war in sessions such as "Wings of the Samurai: Japanese Naval Aircraft Used at Pearl Harbor"; and voices of fascination with battleships in sessions entitled "End of an Era: The Destruction of the Battleline at Pearl Harbor," "Death of a Battleship: The Loss of the USS *Arizona,*" and "Diving into History: Pearl Harbor as an Archeological Resource." A panel of Japanese and American participants also offered reflections on the meaning of the Pearl Harbor attack after fifty years.

By the end of the conference, the audience—never as large as had been expected—had thinned. But the approximately one hundred people still in attendance got to witness, quite unexpectedly, an extraordinarily moving event.[56] The Punahou School Chorale ascended the stage and sang the beautifully haunting Civil War song "Tenting on the Old Camp Ground." As the refrain "many are the hearts that are weary tonight, wishing for the war to cease; many are the hearts that are looking for the right, to see the dawn of peace" hung in the air, American and Japanese veterans walked slowly—some with canes—to the stage area to stand together and exchange farewells as the audience joined the choir in singing "God Bless America." It was a majestic moment in our commemorative history. No reporters from the mainland were there to record it for posterity, but I suspect that it was something I and everyone else present that day will never forget.

On December 12, only a few hours before returning to the mainland, I joined Larry Murphy of the NPS's Submerged Cultural Resources Unit for a 2½-hour dive around the USS *Arizona.* I was privileged to bid farewell to Pearl Harbor by touching history in a special way: entering the underwater world in which the USS *Arizona* lives. The ineffable power of the ship was intensified by physical contact, and I felt an intimate connection with the legacy of this once majestic battleship.

Conclusion

Tradition is both handed down and taken up at places of memory, with each generation constructing and contesting the significance of act and site. Symbols are invested with new meaning. Rituals convey new messages. Sacred stories are open to revised interpretation. Events and objects can be uncovered, recalled, and put to contemporary use—as they were by Margit Nagy at the Alamo—to widen the impact of commemoration and to expand the boundaries touched by emplaced memory.

Understood in this way, the various forms of contestation continue to reveal resistance to forgetfulness. It is *still* important to many in Concord that *their* statue stand unique. It is *still* important to both Custerphiles and Custerphobes that the Little Bighorn battlefield remain central to the story of a violent encounter of cultures. That each side wishes to take up that story in crucially different ways underscores the investment that many are willing to make in the construction of, and resistance to, altered sacred national narratives.

At Pearl Harbor, survivors and relatives came together at the fiftieth anniversary ceremonies to remember and to mourn the loss of life. Clearly, it was still too soon for many to view the attack in a broader commemorative context. Thirteen months later, however, the grim reminder that the first week of December 1941 was not just about those killed at Pearl Harbor was brought home to me. In January 1993, in the hauntingly beautiful forest near Chelmno, Poland, I stood at the mass graves of over three hundred thousand Jews, victims of an extermination process that began while battleship row at Pearl Harbor still smoldered. To one day link in commemorative ceremonies those who died in Honolulu with those who died half a world away would not dilute the message of either site. Rather, it would expand our vision and allow us to register each death in our memory of this most global of wars.

Notes

1. "Statement of Congressman Chet Atkins," Subcommittee on National Parks and Public Lands, Sept. 17, 1991, copy in author's files. I am grateful to Superintendent Lawrence D. Gall for copies of this and other documents pertaining to current issues at Minute Man National Historical Park.

2. Lawrence D. Gall, "Minute Man National Historical Park," undated ms., author's files.

3. "Testimony to House Interior Subcommittee on National Parks and Public Lands on HR 2896, September 17, 1991," transcript, copy in author's files. Thomas Boylston Adams, in an editorial in support of the restoration of the Battle Road area to farming use, states that such agrarian visions hold the possibility of more fundamental transformation: "this will excite the imaginations of rising generations to the heroic actions of ordinary people who brought to birth the Great Republic. It will wake us up—the people—to what we can do when we get mad enough. . . . It will excite us all—politicians included—to act now, and fast, to save our Earth and the air" (*Boston Globe,* Apr. 28, 1990).

4. Perenick, quoted in Jack Sullivan, "Limitation of Statue," *Boston Globe,* Nov. 26, 1992. See also Jason Dickey, "Battle Looms over Statue," *Concord Journal,* Nov. 19, 1992.

5. Letters from Nash to Board of Selectmen, May 18, 1984, and from Gall to Walpole, Nov. 16, 1992, copies in author's files. The selectmen had notified Maj. Gen. Perenick that approval of the town would be necessary and that the decision would be made at a meeting on Dec. 14, 1992 (letter from Walpole to Perenick, Nov. 23, 1992, copy in author's files).

6. Suzanne Alexander, "Minuteman's Heirs Want to Clone Him; How Revolutionary!" *Wall Street Journal,* Dec. 10, 1992; letter from Curtin to Board of Selectmen, Dec. 3, 1992, copy in author's files.

7. David Stephens, a member of the modern Minutemen, commented on the arrogance of the Guard in "Limitation of Statue," *Boston Globe,* Nov. 26, 1992; letter from Walpole to Perenick, Dec. 21. 1992, copy in author's files. See also Sharon Britton, "Minuteman of Concord to Remain Unique," *Boston Globe,* Dec. 18, 1992.

8. *San Antonio Express-News,* Sept. 4, 1992, and undated clipping in author's files. For a discussion of the Alamo's defilement by body oils, see *San Antonio Light,* Aug. 11, 1992.

9. *San Antonio Light,* Sept. 11, 1992; *San Antonio Express-News,* Sept. 11, 1992. Richelieu continued his criticism of the commercialization of the Alamo and the need for a restoration of the original site in *San Antonio Light,* Dec. 27 and 29, 1992. I wish to thank Kevin Young for bringing these articles to my attention.

10. *San Antonio Express-News,* undated clipping in author's files; *Houston Chronicle,* Mar. 3, 1993; *San Antonio Express-News,* Mar. 4, 1993; *Houston Chronicle,* Mar. 6, 1993. For letters in support of the DRT, see *Houston Chronicle,* Mar. 3 and 6, 1993.

11. For thorough documentation of the threats to the park, see "Statement for Management, Outline of Planning Requirements, May 1991," p. 34, Gettysburg National Military Park Library. I am indebted to James C. Roach, chief, Interpretation and Visitor Services, for a copy of this document.

12. A copy of the promotional brochure for the June 1992 re-enactment is in the author's files.

13. Booher, Russell, and Janine Windy Boy are quoted in *People,* Feb. 12, 1990.

14. The AP story appeared in, among other newspapers, the *Los Angeles Times,* Aug. 12, 1990, under the headline "New Boss at Little Bighorn Monument Draws Fire from Fans of Custer." On the Park Service's response, see, for example, the letter from NPS Rocky Mountain Regional Director Lorraine Mintzmyer to Sen. Bill Bradley, June 21, 1990, superintendent's files, Little Bighorn Battlefield National Monument (hereafter LBHS files; referred to in chap. 5 as CBNM files). Don Rickey, Jr., in *History of Custer Battlefield* (Billings, Mont.: Custer Battlefield Historical & Museum Assocation, 1967), cites a letter

from Mrs. Thomas Beaverheart to the super-intendent of the battlefield on July 27, 1925. Mrs. Beaverheart wrote: "My father Ve-hoenxne was among the Cheyennes who was killed at the Custer Battle. He was a Cheyenne Chief, and there are two Cheyenne men living who know where he fell and where he was buried. We would be glad if you could help us get the places marked, so that the place might be remembered on the next anniver-sary." (Barbara Booher has a copy of the letter from which this quotation is taken. The letter also appears in "Superintendent's Notes," *The Battlefield Dispatch,* 9, no. 4 (Fall 1990): 2.) Booher notes: "There is a great contrast be-tween Mrs. Beaverheart's humble letter and the demonstrations [in 1976 and 1988] but both actions carry the same message: a me-morial to recognize the Indians has been a request for a long, long time" (ibid.).

15. Miscellaneous letters to Booher, Apr. 5, 1991, Sept. 12, 1990, LBHS files.

16. Letters from Manion to Booher, Feb. 10, 1990, and from Harrison to Booher, Sept. 14, 1990, LBHS files.

17. See "Marlenee Offers Bill for Indian Memorial," *Billings Gazette,* Apr. 27, 1990; " 'Peace through Unity' " Is the Theme be-hind Monument at Battlefield," *Glacier Re-porter,* June 21, 1990; "Nomee Backs Plan for Indian Monument at Battlefield," *Billings Ga-zette,* Sept. 12, 1990; "Bill OK'd for Indian Memorial," *Billings Gazette,* Sept. 13, 1990. In 1989, ten people submitted comments to the NPS on four sites considered by the Indian Memorial Committee. All comments favored Last Stand Hill (Booher interview with the author, June 29, 1992; "Battle Memorial Comments End," *Billings Gazette* Oct. 11, 1992).

18. Bill Wells, "Little Big Horn Diary," *Little Big Horn Associates Newsletter* 25, no. 4 (May 1991): 4; see also "Custer Park Name under Siege," *USA Today,* Apr. 23, 1991. Cus-ter quoted in *Little Big Horn Associates News-letter* 25, no. 7 (Sept. 1991): 8. Rogers's tes-timony is in "Little Bighorn Battlefield National Monument," 102d Cong., 1st Sess., Senate Report 102-173, Oct. 3, 1991, p. 6 (emphasis added). See "Indian Memorial Bill Dies," *Billings Gazette,* Oct. 31, 1990; "Congressional Feud Angers Indians," *Bill-*ings *Gazette,* Nov. 1, 1990; "Name Dispute Blocks Memorial to Indians," *Boston Globe,* Nov. 4, 1990; "Ambush at Little Big Horn; or George Custer Revisited," *Big Horn County News,* Nov. 7, 1990.

19. Letter from Harrison to the author, Jan. 12, 1993; Booher interview, June 29, 1992.

20. Letters from a Missourian to Booher and from Way to Booher, Oct. 15, 1990, LBHS files.

21. Letters from a Bostonian to Booher, Oct. 16, 1990, and from Varnum to Booher, Oct. 17, 1990, LBHS files.

22. Huyck interview with the author, July 24, 1992. I wish to thank Heather Huyck for allowing me to read written statements from the Billings hearings. For a summary of the arguments for and against the name change offered at this hearing, see "Battlefield Name Divides Opinion," *Billings Gazette,* June [11], 1991.

23. Court's comments were made during the Billings hearings, June 10, 1991, and are quoted from Huyck's files.

24. The statements from the CBHMA and the city of Hardin come from position papers titled, respectively, "The Association's Posi-tion on Changing the Name of the Custer Battlefield National Monument" and "Name Change for Custer Battlefield." Heather Huyck allowed me to read these papers during our interview, July 24, 1992.

25. Wallop's report is in "Little Bighorn Battlefield National Monument," pp. 8–9. Bearss's argument is summarized on p. 148 of this volume.

26. Robert M. Utley, "Whose Shrine Is It?: The Ideological Struggle for Custer Battle-field," *Montana: The Magazine of Western His-tory* 42, no. 1 (Winter 1992): 70–75.

27. Quoted material in this and the follow-ing paragraph from Douglas C. McChristian, "In Search of Custer Battlefield," *Montana: The Magazine of Western History* 42, no.1 (Win-ter 1992): 75–76.

28. There is also a murky history regarding the name "Reno-Benteen" for that battle site. The government purchased the land in 1928 and, according to several War Department documents of 1937 (General Orders, no. 6, and General Legislation, Oct. 25, 1937),

named the site the "Sioux Indian Battle Monument Site" (I am grateful to Andrew Stock, a volunteer at Little Bighorn Battlefield National Monument, for bringing this to my attention). However, a congressional act approved Aug. 7, 1946, providing funds for road repair, used the name "Reno Monument site" (letter from Edwin Bearss to the author, Jan. 5, 1993).

29. See "Marlenee Plans 2 Bills on Custer Battlefield," *Billings Gazette,* Dec. 6, 1990; "Marlenee Will Sponsor Separate Memorial, Name Change," *Big Horn County News,* Dec. 12, 1990; "Indian Memorial Bill Introduced," *Billings Gazette,* Feb. 1, 1991.

30. "Testimony of Barney Old Coyote before the Sub-Committee on Public Lands and Parks, Interior Committee, United States House of Representatives, June 10, 1991," transcript, copy in author's files.

31. *Billings Gazette,* Feb. 16, 1992. A modest alteration of memory is present in Hardin's "Custer's Last Stand Re-Enactment": after the national anthem, the announcer asks visitors to remember that they are "always welcome in Crow land."

32. Places outside "Custer Country" are also beginning to ask whether the names of certain institutions should be changed as a way of altering memory systems. For example, school board members in Detroit, Michigan, debated renaming George Armstrong Custer Elementary School because "Detroit has one of the largest Native American populations in the state—and there is presently no school named for a Native American in the city"— and because of the "negative historical connotation" of the Custer name (*Little Big Horn Associates Newsletter,* 26, no. 3 [Apr. 1992]: 7. The name they eventually chose was Thurgood Marshall Elementary School (*Boston Globe,* Mar. 12, 1993, p. 3). For others, the Custer name and memory live on, as with members of the Seventh Cavalry, deployed in Saudia Arabia in 1990, who "gathered desert rocks and arranged them to spell out 'Garry Owen' on a hillock" (*Little Big Horn Associates Newsletter,* 25, no. 1 [Feb. 1991]: 8).

33. Quoted material in this and the following paragraph is from "Interpretive Prospectus: Little Bighorn Battlefield National Monument, Montana, 1992," second draft, copy in author's files. Program descriptions for summer 1992 reveal the implementation of these themes: "Road to Little Bighorn," "Battle of Little Bighorn," "Plains Indians," "U.S. Cavalry," "Unveiling the Battle through Archeology," "Weapons and Tactics," "Reno-Benteen Entrenchment Trail." I am grateful to Superintendent Barbara Booher for copies of this and other documents pertaining to recent events at Little Bighorn Battlefield National Monument.

34. Booher interview, June 29, 1992; McChristian, quoted in "Historian's Corner," *The Battlefield Dispatch* 11, no. 4 (Fall 1992): 6; author's observations on bus tour, June 28, 1992. Some of Custer's personal items that were part of Elizabeth Custer's donation to the museum will be displayed in a twelve-foot-long case.

35. Booher interview, June 29, 1992; *Little Big Horn Newsletter* 26, no. 6 (Aug. 1992): 3. Means had less success in convincing the Crow and Cheyenne to boycott the Hardin re-enactment. Crow tribal member Arlo Dawes, the Indian cast coordinator, said that the event was *not* disrespectful to Indians, and John Pretty on Top, the Crow cultural director, characterized Means as a "self-ordained medicine man who has no authority to hold sun dances" (*Big Horn County News,* June 17, 1992, p. 3).

36. Means, quoted in *Rocky Mountain News,* Aug. 5, 1990; letter from Means to Booher, June 1, 1992, LBHS files. Note that Means released the letter to the press before Booher received it. Also note that in March 1991, Means told Booher that he opposed the name change because he wanted his son to grow up hating Custer as much as he did—a revealing example of the difference between public and private persona.

37. Campbell, quoted in "Solemn Celebration Where Custer Fell," *New York Times,* Nov. 12, 1992, and *Denver Post,* Nov. 15, 1992; Austin Two Moon, quoted in *Rocky Mountain News,* Nov. 12, 1992; Bordeaux, quoted in *Billings Gazette,* Nov. 12, 1992. The participation of AIM members in the procession and their public complaints are cited in *Billings Gazette,* Dec. 6, 1992.

38. Booher interview, June 29, 1992.

39. Letter from Pohanka to Booher, Nov. 3, 1990, LBHS files.

40. For a variety of perspectives on the legacy of Pearl Harbor, see "Remembering Pearl Harbors: A Journalist's Guide to Reporting the Multiple Meanings of the Fiftieth Anniversary," *Deadline: A Bulletin from the Center for War, Peace, and the News Media* 6, no. 3 (Fall 1991).

41. "Pearl Harbor Anniversary Commemoration: History Division Report," memo from chief historian to associate director of cultural resources, Apr. 6, 1992, USS *Arizona* Memorial Association files (hereafter, USSAMA files). I am grateful to Superintendent Donald E. Magee for a large packet of materials about the fiftieth anniversary.

42. James Rusbridger and Eric Nave, *Betrayal at Pearl Harbor* (New York: Simon and Schuster, 1991), p. 155.

43. The "open letter" and other correspondence from this veterans' group is found in USSAMA files.

44. Letters from Frumkin to Francis W. Agnes, Oct. 22, 1991; from Magee to John J. Krejci, Nov. 1, 1991, and from Magee to Lillian Baker, Nov. 18, 1991, all in USSAMA files. A new film has recently been completed with the approval of Assistant Secretary of the Navy Joseph K. Taussig (a Pearl Harbor survivor), three historians from the Naval Historical Center, Gerald Glaubitz (national president of the PHSA), and Michael Duggan (of the American Legion). Comments were also solicited from John Finn and the late Capt. Donald Ross. See History Division File, National Park Service, Washington, D.C.

45. Letters from Nurco to Bush, Dec. 4, 1990, from Nurco to Magee, Dec. 19, 1989, from Magee to Nurco, Dec. 28, 1989, and from Bearss to Dugan, Mar. 25, 1991, all in USSAMA files.

46. Letter from Norman G. Tellier to Pete Geren, June 26, 1991, USSAMA files; Thurston Clarke, *Pearl Harbor Ghosts: A Journey to Hawaii Then and Now* (New York: William Morrow, 1991), p. 198.

47. Letters from Emory to James Ridenour, director, NPS, Jan. 4, 1991, and Feb. 20, 1991, USSAMA files; *Wall Street Journal*, Nov. 29, 1991; *Honolulu Advertiser*, Sept. 16, 1991; Sowell, "Park Service Turns Its Back on Patriotism," *Honolulu Star-Bulletin*, Dec. 11, 1991. Emory's opinion was also solicited regarding the new film, but according to Bearss, Emory provided only a few factual corrections to the script (memo from Bearss to Magee, Apr. 5, 1992, USSAMA files).

48. Except where otherwise noted, quoted material in this section comes from the author's notes of the fiftieth-anniversary ceremonies and the symposium that followed.

49. The most thorough "insider" account of the fiftieth is James D. Harpster's unpublished 148-page narrative history, a copy of which is in the author's files. Van Valkenburgh is quoted on p. 123 of the Harpster ms.

50. Harpster ms., pp. 126, 127.

51. Excerpts from the president's Punchbowl speech are in *Star-Bulletin & Advertiser*, Dec. 8, 1991, pp. B1, B3.

52. See *Boston Globe*, Dec. 8, 1991; *Star-Bulletin & Advertiser*, Dec. 8, 1991, p. A13.

53. *Star-Bulletin & Advertiser*, Dec. 8, 1991, p. A13.

54. Harpster ms., p. 40; John Duffy, "Time for Remembrance," printed program, copy in author's files.

55. James Delgado, former NPS maritime historian, participated in the oral history project and wrote: "I found it interesting that most journalists focused on the events in Honolulu and not on the nearby reunion of the thousands of 'shipmates' in Waikiki. That reunion assembled groups of men who had not seen each other for fifty years, and was for me the emotional 'magic moment'" (letter from Delgado to the author, Feb. 24, 1993). The "Storm Unleashed" symposium followed up on a May 1991 symposium "The Gathering Storm," held at the Admiral Nimitz State Historical Park in Fredericksburg, Texas, where the *Ha. 19* midget submarine was being temporarily exhibited (it was due to be moved to Hawaii in 1994, perhaps to the *Arizona* Memorial). At the earlier conference, Kazuo Sakamaki, the skipper of the *Ha. 19*, was reunited with his vessel and with Lt. Steve Weiner, who had questioned him after his capture at Bellows Point, Oahu. See Mary-Love Bigony,

"The Gathering Storm: Symposium Relives Pearl Harbor Attack," *Texas Parks and Wildlife Magazine* 49, no. 11 (Nov. 1991): 4–15.

56. As Edwin Bearss notes in his "History Division Report" (see note 41), many of the most emotional events of these days were not announced on the formal program. Among them he includes: "the meeting of Japanese pilot Zenji Abe with Gerald Glaubitz, the president of the Pearl Harbor Survivors Association, at the conference's final banquet at the Royal Hawaiian Hotel," where Glaubitz, whose strong opposition to Japanese participation in the commemorative events had been widely quoted, embraced Abe in a simple and powerful individual act of reconciliation; "the standing ovation for the Medal of Honor winners at the 'Storm Unleased' Symposium; [and] the 'Promise of Aloha' program where Hawaiian primary school children honored with flowers and songs those who perished in 1941."

Index

Acuña, Rodolfo, 73, 75
Adair, A. Garland, 65
Adams, John Quincy, 35
Adams, Josiah, 38
Adams, Samuel, 37
Adams, Thomas Boylston, 35
Adams, Rev. Zabdiel, 20
Akaka, Abraham, 202
Akihito (prince of Japan), 202
Alamo: defilement of, 56–57, 64, 65, 67–69;
  Japanese interest in, 79–80; monument
  building at, 61, 64, 66–67, 79; patriotic
  rhetoric about, 54, 57–64, 80–81, 215; and
  patriotism during other wars, 59–60, 63;
  preservation of, 56–57, 64–70; redefinition
  at, 6, 58, 74–78; reenactments at, 56, 61,
  84n.49; relics from, 48n.57, 65; role of
  Mexican Americans at, 6, 57, 70–78, 215; as
  site for political protest, 68, 80; veneration
  of, 55–62
Alamo, The (film, 1960), 71, 75, 207n.22
Alamo: Thirteen Days to Glory, The (television
  movie), 55
Alamo Day (March 6), 58
Alamo Heroes Cenotaph, 67, 68
Alamo Monument Association, 66–67
Alamo . . . The Price of Freedom (film, Merrill),
  61, 64, 75–78
Alexander, Peter, 110
Alleman, Tillie, 92
Allen, Gwenfread, 177
Allred, James V., 58, 59
Almaráz, Félix D., Jr., 72, 76
Alsop, Stewart, 177
American eagle, 3, 186
American Indian International Peace Day, 159
American Indian Movement (AIM), 141, 150,
  159
Anderson, John, 90
Andros, Edward, 21, 44n.7
Appleman, Roy E., 152–53
Arizona, USS. *See* USS *Arizona*

Arizona Reunion Association, 198
Arlington National Cemetery, 3
Armistead, Brig. Gen. Lewis A., 88, 106, 109,
  120n.15, 123n.47, 217
Armitage, Richard, 211–12n.81
Arnett, G. Ray, 150
Association for the Preservation of Civil War
  Sites, Inc., 125n.70
Aupperlee, William, 203
Aylett, Col. William R., 94

Bachelder, Col. John B., 93, 94, 104, 107
Baker, Amos, 14, 23
Baker, Russell, 115
Barker, Eugene C., 72
Barnett, Ross, 99
Barrett, Col. James, 9, 16
Barry, David F., 133
Bartlett, Samuel Ripley, 23, 24
Baskin, Leonard, 153
Battleships, as memorials, 186–87
Baukhage, H. R., 176
Beach, Douglas, 76
Bearss, Edwin C., 103, 148, 150, 194, 199
Beaver, James A., 108
Becker, F. Otto, 164n.1
Beers, Alfred B., 95
Begin, Menachem, 126n.76
Benét, Stephen Vincent, 105
Benteen, Capt. Frederick W., 128, 133, 155
Beretta, J. K., 61
Berriozabal, Maria, 75
Berry, Charles, 188
Berry, Adj. Gen. Kearie L., 59
Biggs, Casey, 61
Big Man, Max, 151
Billings, Hammett, 38
Blackburn, Ben, 130
Black Elk, 131, 146, 148–49, 215
Black Wolf, Charlie, 158
Blake, Walter H., 96
Board games, of Civil War battles, 98

Bonaparte, Charles J., 27
Bonham, James, 53, 57, 60, 62, 67, 77, 85n.59
Bonner, John, 138
Boston Massacre, 17
Boston National Historic Sites Commission, 14
Bourne, Dr. J. Francis, 121n.34
Bowen, Adm. Harold G., Jr., 182
Bowie, Jim, 53, 57, 59, 60, 67, 68, 73, 75, 76, 77
Boyer, Mitch, 170n.75
Brave Bear, 139
Briggs, Lt. Gen. James E., 73
Brigham, Charles H., 31
Brown, Edmund G. (Pat), 99
Brown, Richard, 17
Brown, Rita Mae, 102
Buck, Paul, 93
Buckley, William F., 37
Bueno, Anastacio, 71–72
Bullard, F. Lauriston, 29
Bunker Hill Monument Association, 29–30
Burdett, Lt. Gen. Allen, Jr., 62
Burdick, Quentin N., 158
Burns, Lt. Gen. Robert W., 62
Buse, Henry W., Jr., 182
Bush, George, 200, 211–12n.81
Buttrick, Maj. John, 9–10, 23, 30
Buttrick, Stedman, 30

Cabot, Frances, 35
Cabot, Henry B., 27
Campbell, Adm. Robert L., 180
Capers, Bishop William T., 58
Captain Parker/Lexington Minuteman Monument (Lexington Green), 14, 15, 17, 29, 49n.68
Carrington, Evelyn M., 59
Carroll, John, 145, 146, 147, 149, 150
Carroll, Thomas, 39
Carter, Jimmy, 126n.76, 149
Carver, John A., Jr., 98
Cassidy, Gen. Patrick F., 73
Cataldo, Robert, 40
Catton, Bruce, 100, 102, 103
Chamberlain, Gen. Joshua L., 87
Chavira, Cruz, 77
Cheney, Dick, 211–12n.81
Chidester, David, 6, 163
Children of the American Revolution (CAR), 39
Chomsky, Noam, 41
Cisneros, Henry G., 63, 74, 77
Civil War Centennial, 5, 98–100, 114
Clark, Champ, 95
Clark, Walter C., 110
Clark, William, 140
Clarke, Rev. Jonas, 9, 13, 20

Clary, David A., 146, 147, 154
Clear, Lt. Col. Warren J., 132
Cleveland, Grover, 104, 146, 150
Cobb, Donald B., 13, 14
Cody, "Buffalo Bill," 138
Coins, commemorative, 16, 142
Cole, Abraham, 2
Coleman, J. Walter, 116
Collins, John H., Jr., 62
Colquitt, O. B., 64
Comanche (horse), 153
Commemoration: and National Park Service, 217. *See also* Veneration
Concord (Mass.). *See* Lexington and Concord (Mass.)
"Concord Fight" (poem, Bartlett), 23
"Concord Hymn" (poem, Emerson), 16, 30
Confederate Air Force (CAF), 185–86
Confederate Soldiers and Sailors Monument (Gettysburg National Military Park), 109
Conservation, 4. *See also* Preservation
Coppini, Pompeo, 67
Cós, Gen. Martín Perfecto de, 53
Court, James V., 149, 157, 158, 160
Cowan, Andrew, 97
Cox, Joseph, 66
Crazy Horse, 128
Crockett, Davy, 53, 57, 58, 59, 60, 65, 67, 68, 72, 73, 76, 77, 78, 129, 217
Cronkite, Walter, 29
Crook, Brig. Gen. George, 127, 139
Cruz, Dr. Gilbert R., 74
Cummins, Gary, 182, 190, 191, 192, 193, 196, 198, 200, 201, 203
Curly (Indian scout), 131
Curran, Bob, 194
Curtin, Andrew, 89
Curtis, George, 19, 21, 25
Custer, Mrs. Elizabeth Bacon, 131, 134, 152
Custer, Lt. Col. George Armstrong, 121–22n.35, 127, 129–35, 137–41, 143–55, 157–59, 161, 163, 213, 215, 217
Custer, Col. George A., III, 143, 145
Custer Battlefield Historical & Museum Association (CBHMA), 153, 167n.44
Custer Battlefield National Monument, 143, 146–48. *See also* Little Bighorn
Custer Battlefield Preservation Committee (CBPC), 157
Custer Memorial Highway Association, 131
Custer Monument (Hardin, Mont.), 135
Custer Monument Association, 132

Dana, Richard Henry, 18, 20, 36
Daniel, Price, 180
Daughters of the American Revolution (DAR), 39

Daughters of the Republic of Texas (DRT), 56,
58, 64, 65, 69, 70, 74, 78, 217
Davenport, Walter, 176
David, Capt. Isaac, 10
Davies, Wallace, 93
Davis, Gen. Bennie L., 62
Davis, Maj. George B., 113
Davis, Capt. Isaac, 30, 38–39, 217
Dawes, Charles G., 16
Dawes, William, 16
Dawn of Liberty, The (mural, Sandham), 38
Dedication Day (November 19), 99–100,
121n.31
Defilement: of the Alamo, 56–57, 64, 65, 67–
69; of Gettysburg National Military Park, 69,
111, 113–15; ideological (heresy), 5, 216; at
Lexington and Concord, 12, 22–23, 33–35,
37, 43–44; of the Little Bighorn, 148–50; of
Pearl Harbor, 192–96, 200; physical, 5; of
sacred spaces, 1, 5; of USS *Arizona*, 189,
191, 192–99
De León, Arnoldo, 70, 72
Delgado, James P., 186, 189, 190–91, 192,
193, 194
DePugh, Robert, 28
De Zavala, Adina, 64, 217
Dickinson, William, 191, 194, 201, 204
Dippie, Brian, 141
Disney, Walt, 50–51n.83, 84n.51
Ditmanson, Dennis, 157, 160, 161
Dixon, Joseph Moore, 135
Dobie, J. Frank, 61, 67
Doolittle, Amos, 32, 37
Dorman, Isaiah, 149
Douglass, Frederick, 91
"Drama of Concord: A Pageant of Three
Centuries, The" (play, French), 21
Driscoll, Clara, 64
Dukakis, Michael, 20
Dunbar, Paul Lawrence, 124n.59
Dwight, Timothy, 20

Early, Stephen T., 176
Edge, Robert J., 144
Edgren, Charles, 78
Edwards, Jonathan, 20
Edwards, Ralph, 179
Eisenhower, Dwight D., 98, 100
Elizondo, Fr. Virgil, 74
Ellis, Rev. George E., 38
Ellis Island (N.Y.), 3
Emerson, Ralph Waldo, 11, 15, 16, 24, 30, 32,
36
Emerson, William, 17, 29, 31
Emery, George F., 109
Emmons, William, 23
Erickson, J. E., 136

Esparza, Francisco, 76
Esparza, Gregorio, 76
Eternal Light Peace Memorial (Gettysburg
National Military Park), 97, 102, 103, 118,
215
Everett, Edward, 15, 18, 19, 20, 22, 30

"Fall of the Alamo, The" (heroic account,
Potter), 66
Farragut, Adm. David G., 187
Fehrenbach, T. R., 63, 74
Flag, veneration of, 3
Flynn, Errol, 84n.51, 132, 153, 164n.1
Flynn, Paul, 42
Fong, Hiram E., Jr., 200, 207–8n.31
Fong, Hiram L., 200
Ford, Gerald, 42, 182
Ford's Theatre (Washington, D.C.), 3
Foreman, Gary L., 56–57, 64, 69
Forgie, George G., 22, 24
Forney, Brig. Gen. W. H., 104
"For the Union Dead" (poem, Lowell),
124n.59
Franklin, John Hope, 91
Frantz, Joe B., 74
Frassanito, William, 112
Freeman, Raymond, 142
French, Allen, 21
French, Daniel Chester, 15, 17, 26, 30–31, 32,
36, 42, 49n.68, 175, 216
Frome, Michael, 114
Fuchida, Cmdr. Mitsuo, 173, 202

Gage, Gen. Thomas, 9
Gall (Indian chief), 128, 133
Gallegly, Joseph, 67
Galvin, Denis P., 204
Garrison, George P., 60
Gates, Cecil, 188–89
Geere, Maj. Frank, 49n.68
Gettysburg Battlefield Memorial Association
(GBMA), 90, 93, 104, 106, 107, 109
Gettysburg Battlefield Preservation Association
(GBPA), 111
Gettysburg National Military Park: battle art
commemorating events at, 116, 122n.39,
126n.72; burial of the dead at, 89, 92–93;
defilement of, 69, 111, 113–15;
interpretation at, 116–17; monument
building at, 4, 99, 104–11, 161; National
Park Service at, 98–99, 102–3, 109, 111,
112–13, 115–16; patriotic rhetoric at, 90,
95, 110–11; preservation of, 89–90, 103–4,
111–15; and reconcilation of the Union, 90–
91, 93–97, 106, 109, 203–4, 215;
redefinition at, 6, 215; reenactments at, 97–

98, 99, 100–103, 117, 124n.57; relics from, 48n.57, 107, 123n.50; reunions held at, 93–97, 101; veneration of, 89–91
Gibbon, Col. John, 127, 128
Giles, Alfred, 67
Gobin, Bvt. Brig. Gen. J. P. S., 95
Godfrey, Brig. Gen. Edward S., 132, 133, 134, 135, 137
Gold, Vic, 43
Good, Francis J., 27
Goodling, William F., 112
Graham, Don, 71
Grand Army of the Republic (GAR), 91, 93, 95, 104–5, 120n.21, 123n.47
Grant, Ulysses S., 14, 31
Grant, Maj. Gen. Ulysses S., III, 98
Gratz, H. Tucker, 179, 180
Greene, Bob, 68
Gregg, Brig. Gen. David M., 100, 121–22n.35
Grills, Maj. Gen. H. L., 55
Guerra, Henry A., 72–73
Guy, William L., 158

Hall, B. H., 39
Hall, Col. Frank, 134
Hancock, John, 36
Hanly, J. Frank, 214
Hansen, Julia B., 202
Hanson, Bruce, 139
Harlan, Doug, 68
Harmon, Maj. Gen. E. N., 20
Harrington, Jonathan, 14, 22, 23
Harris, William L., 146, 147
Harrison, Benjamin, 58
Harrison, Kathleen Georg, 104, 112
Harrison, Walter, 94
Hart, Richard T., 143
Hart, Robert L., 148
Hartwig, Scott, 117
Harwill, Richard A., 188
Hayden, Carl, 182
Hayes, Rutherford B., 94
Hayward, Deacon, 38
Heier, Vincent, 163
Heiser, John, 101
Helms, Col. Fred, 32
Herter, Christian, 27, 33
Hertig, Mark, 201
High Water Mark Monument (Gettysburg National Military Park), 106–8, 123n.52
Hilger, David, 152
Hillsman, Chuck, 101
Hinojosa, Gilberto, 72, 77
Hoar, George Frisbie, 18, 23, 25
Hoar, Samuel, 36
Hodel, Donald P., 200
Hogue, Lt. Gen. William L., 60

Holt, Elmer, 137
Hood, Brig. Gen. John Bell, 60
Hooper, Dr. Jack, 63
Hopkins, Harry, 176
Horn, W. Donald, 147, 150
Hosmer, Abner, 10
Houston, Gen. Sam, 60, 213
Howard, Sidney, 16, 19
Hubbard, Ebenezer, 30
Hudson, Alfred Sereno, 32
Hudson, Charles, 14
Hughes, Harold E., 99
Humiston, Amos, 121n.34
Hunt, Maria Davis, 39
"Hymn of the Alamo" (poem, Potter), 66

Iithete, Immanuel, 102
Ikeda, Eiki, 203
Independence Hall (Philadelphia), 3
Indiana War Memorial Plaza (Indianapolis), 3
Indians for Equality, 159
Inouye, Daniel, 196
Interpretation: at Gettysburg National Military Park, 115–18, 116–17; and National Park Service, 217
Irvin, Bennie F., 156
Isaac Davis Monument (Acton, Mass.), 38
Isaac Davis Trail, 39

Jackson, Andrew, 214
Jackson, J. B., 31
Jackson, Royal G., 155–56
Janacek, Rev. Balthasar ("Father Balty"), 57, 74, 75
Jark, Lt. Gen. Carl H., 60
Jefferson, Thomas, 44n.3
Jeffries, Charlie, 59
Jester, Beauford H., 59
Jesus Christ, and sacred imagery, 4, 11, 20, 21
Jimenes, Damacio, 72, 75
Johnson, Edith Mae, 56, 57, 73
Josephy, Alvin, 156

Kaifu, Toshiki, 211–12n.81
Kaplan, Fred, 183
Kashiwahara, Ken, 203
Kaye, Sammy, 177
Kelly, J. R., 4
Kennedy, John F., 3, 28, 98
Kennett, Lee, 177
Keogh, Capt. Miles, 153
Kerr, Capt. William, 109–10
Kerry, John, 40
Keyes, John S., 21, 24
Keyes, Prescott, 15
Kills Straight, Virgil, 143

Kimmel, Adm. Husband E., 198
King, Rev. Dr. Martin Luther, Jr., 3
Kitson, Henry H., 14, 49n.68
Knowles, Herbert, 178
Knox, Frank, 176
Koppel, Ted, 203
Korell, Jason H., 43, 45n.14
Koury, Michael, 144–45, 150, 160

Lafayette, Marquis de, 15, 36
Lamont, Daniel S., 104
Lang, George, 189
Lara, Jose Garcia de, 78
Last Command, The (film, 1955), 71
Last Reunion of the Blue and the Gray, 96–97, 101
League of United Latin American Citizens (LULAC), 77, 78
Lee, Robert E., 87, 108, 119–20n.14, 161
Lenihan, Daniel, 190, 191
Lewis, Meriwether, 140
Lexington (play, Howard), 16
Lexington and Concord (Mass.): battle art commemorating events at, 32, 37–38; ideological defilement (heresy) of, 12, 22–23, 37, 43–44; and imagery of the minutemen, 11, 16–28; invented traditions at, 37–40; monument building at, 4, 12, 13, 14–15, 24, 28–33, 36–37, 38; National Park Service at, 12, 21, 33–35, 42, 45n.14; and patriotic rhetoric, 11–12, 13, 17–28, 215; and patriotism during other wars, 11, 23–26, 27–28; physical defilement of, 33–35; preservation of, 33–35; redefinition at, 12, 40–43; reenactments at, 13–14, 15–17, 20, 29, 37, 45n.14; relics from, 48n.57; rivalry between, 12, 35–37; rivalry with other towns, 38–40; veneration of, 11–16; Vietnam antiwar protests at, 12, 40–41
Lexington Green. *See* Lexington and Concord (Mass.)
Liberty Bell, 3, 186
"Liberty Boys of '76, The" (book series), 26
Lincoln, Abraham, 2, 3, 47n.34, 87, 89, 91, 94, 97, 99–100, 102, 103, 117, 118, 126n.76, 215, 217
Lincoln Memorial (Washington, D.C.), 2
Linderman, Gerald, 94
Linn, John B., 92
Little, David B., 14
Little Bighorn: archaeological investigations of, 162, 170n.75, 209–10n.46; battle art commemorating events at, 164n.1; burial of the dead at, 132–33, 137, 162–63; commemorative events at, 133–40, 162–63; defilement at, 148–50; monument building at, 133, 149, 158–62; and name of the

battlefield, 146–48, 201; National Park Service at, 131, 139, 141–42, 144–46, 149–50, 152–55, 156, 163; and Native American interpretations, 130–31, 136–38, 139–46, 148, 153–54, 155–56, 158–62, 163–64, 170n.78, 215–16; patriotic rhetoric about, 130, 134–35, 140; and patriotism during other wars, 132; preservation of, 132, 156–58; and redefinition, 6, 131, 146–48, 150–56, 163–64, 215–16; reenactments at, 129, 133–34, 139; relics from, 48n.57; veneration of, 131–33
Little Big Horn Associates (LBHA), 144–45, 150
Little Big Man (film), 163
Little Wolf, Laban, 168n.57
Longstreet, Gen. James, 87
Losoya, Toribio D., 75
Lothrop, Mrs. Daniel, 39
Lowell, James Russell, 15, 19, 21
Lowell, Robert, 124n.59
Lowery, Dr. Joseph E., 102
Luce, Edward S. ("Cap"), 138, 151, 153, 156
Lujan, Manuel, 194
Lynch, Kevin, 181
Lyons, Adm. J. A., Jr., 200

McAlister, George, 75–77
McAlister, Hill, 58
MacArthur, Gen. Douglas, 175
McBirnie, Dr. W. S., 62–63
McCarthy, Eugene, 41
McConaghie, James R., 112
McConaughy, David, 89, 90, 92, 103
McCormick, Capt. Bruce, 188
McCreary, James B., 96
McDermott, John D., 163
McGiffert, Lt. Gen. John R., 63
McGreevy, Patrick, 2
McLean, Angus W., 90
McMurry, Capt. George J., 136
McPherson, Edward, 107
Magee, Don, 211–12n.81
Magpie, G., 159
Mammoth Cave (Ky.), 2
Manchester, William, 184, 192
Mangum, Neil, 150
Marine Corps War Memorial (Iwo Jima Memorial), 3
Marquisee, James, 137
Marshall, Thomas, 95
Martinez, Walter, 75, 76, 77, 78
Martini, Giovanni, 128
Martini, John, 187, 190
Martyrs of the Alamo (film, 1915), 71
Matsunaga, Spark, 194
Mayo, James M., 214

Meade, Gen. George C., 87

Means, Russell, 143–44, 159, 160, 161, 162, 166n.34

Medicine Crow, Joe, 139–40

Memorials, forms of, 3

Menetrey, Lt. Gen. Louis Charles, 73

Merrill, Kieth, 61, 75, 77

Mexican War, 214

Milam, Benjamin Rush, 53, 58

Miles, Maj. Gen. Nelson A., 133, 152

Miller, Jim D., 182, 203

Minuteman intercontinental ballistic missiles (ICBMs), 11, 31

Minute Man National Historical Park, 33–35

Minute Man Statue (Concord, Mass.), 15, 16, 17, 27, 29–32, 36, 42, 49n.68, 175

Minutemen, imagery of, 16–28

Montejano, David, 71–72

Monticello (Va.), 3

Monument building: at the Alamo, 61, 64, 66–67, 79; at Gettysburg National Military Park, 4, 99, 104–11, 161; at Lexington and Concord, 4, 12, 13, 14–15, 24, 28–33, 36–37, 38; at the Little Bighorn, 133, 149, 158–62; in Pearl Harbor, 178–82; and veneration, 4

Monument Drive (Richmond, Va.), 3

Mormons, 2

Morton, Rogers B., 158, 159

Mott, William Penn, Jr., 147, 148, 158, 161, 196

Mount Vernon (Va.), 3

Munroe, James Phinney, 19

Munroe, William, 13

Murdock, Harold, 37

Nagumo, Vice Adm. Chuichi, 173–74

Nagy, Margit, 79–80, 81

Nangle, William B., 66

Napoleon Bonaparte, 147

National Custer Memorial Association, 135

National Memorial Cemetery of the Pacific (Hawaii), 206n.11

National Parks and Conservation Association (NPCA), 160

National Park Service: and commemoration, 217; and interpretation, 217

National Trust for Historic Preservation, 157

Nelson, Bryce, 145

Niagara Falls (N.Y.), 2

Nicholson, Col. John P., 104

Nimitz, Adm. Chester W., 59

Nitze, Paul, 183

Nixon, Richard M., 142, 196

Nokes, J. Richard, 185

North Bridge (Concord, Mass.), 32–33. *See also* Lexington and Concord (Mass.)

Northern Cheyenne World Day of Peace, 162

Noyes, Frederick, 39

Noyes, Lucy Emily, 39

Nunn, Sam, 191, 193

Oakley, Don, 43

"Ode to Concord" (poem, Lowell), 21

O'Hara, Sgt. Miles, 170n.75

Olsen, Adm. C. E., 180

Osborne, Patricia E., 70, 73

Osbourne, Ozzy, 68

Oshida, George, 211n.79

Oswald, Lee Harvey, 3

Ottenstein, Thomas R., 115

Pacific Memorial Foundation, 179

Pacific War Memorial, Inc., 179

Pacific War Memorial Commission (PWMC), 179–80

Paddock, Adm. Richard A., 181

Paradise, rhetoric of, 1, 2

Parker, Capt. John, 9, 11, 13, 14

Parmenter, J. M., 71

Partello, Col. J. M. T., 135, 137

Patriotic rhetoric: about Pearl Harbor, 176–78, 182–83, 199; about the Alamo, 54, 57–64, 80–81, 215; about the Little Bighorn, 130, 134–35, 140; at Gettysburg National Military Park, 90, 95, 110–11; at Lexington and Concord, 11–12, 13, 17–28, 215; and veneration, 1, 2–4, 5

Patriots' Day (April 19), 14, 26

Patterson, John S., 92

Patton, George S., Jr., 89, 116

Paxon, William, 194–95

Payson, Rev. Phillips, 17

Pearl Harbor: commemorative events at, 201–4; defilement of, 192–96, 200; Japanese attack on, 173–74, 175–78; Japanese relics from attack on, 193–96; monument building in, 178–82; and patriotic rhetoric, 176–78, 182–83, 199; and patriotism during other wars, 182, 183; and reconciliation between Japan and U.S., 202–4; redefinition of, 6, 200–204, 216; reenactment of attack on, 185–86, 207–8n.31; revenge for attack on, 184–86; survivor memories of attack on, 183–84; veneration of, 178. *See also* USS *Arizona*

Pearl Harbor Day (December 7), 178, 182, 184, 188, 202, 205n.8

Pearl Harbor Survivors Association (PHSA), 183–84, 191, 195, 198

Peckham, Rufus W., 114

Peña, José Enrique de la, 84n.51

Pendleton, John, 38

Pennybacker, Anna M. J. Hardwicke, 60
Peoples Bicentennial Commission (PBC), 6, 12, 41–43
Percy, Sir Hugh, 10
Perez, Severo, 76
Perry, Capt. Oliver Hazard, 214
Pershing, Gen. John J., 16
Pettigrew, Brig. Gen. James J., 88, 94, 95–96, 99, 100, 101, 103, 106, 109
Phinney, Elias, 36, 38
Pickett, Brig. Gen. George E., 88, 94, 95–96, 99, 100, 101, 103, 106–7, 109, 110, 114
Pitcairn, Maj. John, 9
Pius IX (pope), 2
Plainfeather, Mardell, 155, 162
Plymouth Rock (Mass.), 2
Poor Bear, Enos, 162
Potter, Reuben Marmaduke, 66
Poyo, Gerald E., 72
Preis, Alfred, 181, 193
Prescott, George, 47n.36
Prescott, Dr. Samuel, 9, 16
Preservation: of the Alamo, 56–57, 64–70; of Gettysburg National Military Park, 89–90, 103–4, 111–15; of Lexington and Concord, 33–35; of the Little Bighorn, 132, 156–58; motivated by veneration, 2, 4, 5; of Pearl Harbor, 192–96; of the USS *Arizona*, 199–200
President's Advisory Council on Historic Preservation, 163
Presley, Elvis, 180
Pride, Mary, 26
Private John (Alamo defender), 76
Prosperi, Robert, 103
Puck, Col. Armin F., 60
Puffer, Dr. Raymond L., 31
Pullen, Doris L., 13, 14
Puritans, 1

Quimby, Ian M. G., 37

Radford, Adm. Arthur, 187
Rainey, Reuben M., 89
Rantoul, Robert, 23
Rash, Martha, 61
Real Bird, Richard, 158
Redefinition: at the Alamo, 6, 58, 74–78; at Gettysburg National Military Park, 6, 215; at Lexington and Concord, 12, 40–43; of the Little Bighorn, 6, 131, 146–48, 150–56, 163–64, 215–16; of Pearl Harbor, 6, 200–204, 216; of sacred spaces, 1, 6, 217
Red Hawk (Indian chief), 137
Red Tomahawk, 137
Reenactments: at the Alamo, 56, 61; of the attack on Pearl Harbor, 185–86, 207–8n.31;

at Gettysburg National Military Park, 97–98, 99, 100–103, 117, 124n.57; at Lexington and Concord, 13–14, 15–17, 20, 29, 37, 45n.14; at the Little Bighorn, 129, 133–34, 139; and veneration, 4, 5, 42
"Remember Pearl Harbor" (song, Kaye), 178
Reno, Maj. Marcus A., 128, 130, 132, 137, 154, 155
Revere, Paul, 9, 14, 16, 28, 40
Revolutionary Monument (Lexington Green), 4, 14, 22, 29, 33
Reyer, Eldon, 159
Reynolds, Rev. Grindall, 18, 21, 29
Reynolds, Maj. Gen. John Fulton, 104
Rhodes, E. Washington, 100
Ribicoff, Abraham, 187
Richardson, Charles A., 104
Rickey, Don, 134, 135, 139, 151, 165n.24
Ridenour, James M., 195
Riecke, H. S., 28
Rife, Capt. Tom, 58
Rifkin, Jeremy, 41, 42
Ripley, Ezra, 29, 30, 36, 38
Rivera, Geraldo, 184
Robbins, Roland Wells, 30
Robbins, William M., 104, 106
Robertson, Pat, 56, 57
Robinson, George Dexter, 20
Robinson, Leigh, 108
Rogers, Mrs. Floyd V., 65
Roosevelt, Franklin D., 59, 97, 176, 177, 178
Rorie, Adm. Conrad J., 190, 200
Rose, Moses, 60
Russell, Ezekiel, 18
Russell, Harold, 182
Russell, Jerry L., 147, 148

"Sabbath at Niagara, A" (poem, Cole), 2
Sadat, Anwar, 126n.76
Sagan, Carl, 102–3, 215
Saito, Edean, 196
Sakamaki, Kazuo, 193
Saltonstall, Leverett, 27
Sanchez, Ray, 71–72
Sanchez, Ricardo, 76
Sandham, Henry, 38
Santa Anna, Gen. Antonio López de, 53, 62, 70, 71, 74, 76, 77, 217
Sarf, Wayne M., 160
Saunders, William, 93
Schouler, William, 25
Scranton, William W., 98
Scudder, Townsend, 25
Sears, John, 2
Seguín, Juan, 77
Seiberling, John, 149
Shakers, 2

Shattuck, Lemuel, 38, 49n.67
Shaw, Col. Robert Gould, 124n.59
Shaw Memorial (Boston Common), 124n.59
Shepperd, John Ben, 60, 62
Sheridan, Lt. Gen. Philip H., 127
Sherman, Gen. William T., 131
Shiga, Shigetaka (Juko), 79, 80
Sickles, Maj. Gen. Daniel E., 95, 104, 105–6, 111
Sitting Bull, 140, 147
Slackman, Michael, 181, 199
Smith, Bvt. Maj. Gen. Charles H., 105
Smith, Lt. Col. Francis, 9
Smith, Mrs. Marian, 115
Soderman, Danuta, 56
Soldiers, imagery of, 11. *See also* Minutemen, imagery of
Soldiers' Monument (Concord, Mass.), 24
Soldiers' National Monument (Gettysburg National Military Park), 104, 117, 122n.44, 126n.76, 217
Speer, Bill, 203
Stainback, Ingram M., 202
Stamps, commemorative, 16, 98, 142
Stanton, Harold, 157
Stark, Cruce, 94
Statue of Liberty (N.Y.), 3
Stewart, George, 106
Stinson, Roddy, 68
Strong, Bernice, 76
Stuart, Henry Carter, 108
Stuart, J. E. B., 100
Sul, Aristeo, 71
Sumrall, Robert F., 191
Swearingen, Paul, 142
Sweeney, Rodney, 101
Szarka, Fred, 35, 41

Taylor, Col. Charles, 105
Teague, Olin E., 181
Terhune, Brig. Gen. Charles J., Jr., 28, 31
Terry, Brig. Gen. Alfred H., 127, 130, 132
Terry, Samuel L., 59
"Texas Hymn" (Parmenter), 71
Texas School Book Depository (Dallas), 3
They Died with Their Boots On (film), 132, 164n.1
Thomas, Capt. George, 106
Thomas, Isaiah, 17
Thomas, Stanley, 139
Thornton, William, 35
Tibbets, Gen. Paul, 186
Tilberg, Frederick, 109
Todaro, Tony, 178
Tomb of the Unknown Soldier (Arlington National Cemetery), 3
Tora Tora Tora (film, 1970), 207n.22

Travis, Lt. Col. William Barrett, 53, 57, 59, 60, 61, 62, 64, 65, 66, 67, 68, 73, 77, 78
Trees: as monuments, 29, 33, 107, 123n.50; and restoration of historic spaces, 112
Trimble, Brig. Gen. Isaac R., 88
"Trooper Mike" (skeleton), 170n.75
Truman, Harry S, 184
Two Moon, 128, 134
Two Moons, Austin, 144, 162

Udall, Stewart, 210–11n.61
United Confederate Veterans, 91, 120n.21
United States v. *Gettysburg Electric Railway Co.*, 113–14
USS *Alabama*, 186
USS *Arizona*: defilement of, 189, 191, 192–99; divers' exploration of, 189–92, 200; established as a war memorial, 179–82; Japanese attack on, 173–74, 175–76; preservation of, 199–200; relics from, 187–89; veneration of, 178, 179–82, 187–89. *See also* Pearl Harbor; USS *Arizona* Memorial
USS *Arizona* Anchor Memorial (Phoenix), 188
USS *Arizona* Memorial: burial of dead at, 175, 189; development of, 181–82; Japanese interest in, 192–93; name of, 201; and National Park Service, 182, 190, 191, 192–96, 198–99; and patriotic rhetoric, 4; preservation of, 192–96; as site of protests, 197. *See also* USS *Arizona*
USS *Bowfin*, 195
USS *Cairo*, 186
USS *California*, 173
USS *Constellation*, 186
USS *Constitution* (*Old Ironsides*), 186, 214
USS *Flasher*, 186–87
USS *Franklin*, 187
USS *Hartford*, 187
USS *Indiana*, 187
USS *Maine*, 187
USS *Massachusetts*, 186
USS *Missouri*, 175, 176
USS *North Carolina*, 186
USS *South Dakota*, 187, 208n.36
USS *Texas*, 186
USS *Utah*, 190
USS *Utah* Memorial, 192
USS *Washington*, 187
USS *West Virginia*, 187
Utley, Robert, 141, 143, 147, 153, 154, 156, 159, 162

Valdez, Lalo, 73, 75
Valley Forge (Pa.), 3
Vanderslice, John, 91
Varney, George, 37

Vasquez y Sanchez, Ramon, 78
Velasquez, Willie, 77
Veneration: of the Alamo, 55–62; and battlefield reenactments, 4, 5; and concept of sacred space, 1–2, 5, 215; forms of, 4; of Gettysburg National Military Park, 89–91; of the Little Bighorn, 131–33; and monument building, 4; as motive for preservation, 2, 4, 5; and patriotism, 1, 2–4, 5; of Pearl Harbor, 178; of USS *Arizona*, 178, 179–82, 187–89. *See also* Patriotic rhetoric
Vicksburg (Miss.), 213
Vietnam Veterans Against the War (VVAW), 12, 40–41
Vietnam Veterans Memorial (Washington, D.C.), 3
Vincent, Col. Strong, 105
Volpe, John A., 28
Volz, J. Leonard, 158

Wald, George, 42
Wallace, George, 99
Walsh, Thomas, 152
War of 1812, 214
Warren, Gen. Gouverneur K., 87
Washington, George, 4, 17, 50–51n.83
Washington, D.C., 2
Washington Monument (Washington, D.C.), 2
Washington's headquarters (Newburgh, N.Y.), 4
Watson, Francis, 42
Wayne, John, 55, 68, 69, 75, 207n.22
Weaver, Samuel, 93
Webb, J. E., 79
Webster, Daniel, 46n.30
Wedermeyer, Gen. Albert, 138

"Welcome Home Concord" (poem, Pride), 26
Wells, William, 160
Wert, J. Howard, 4
West, Felton, 78
White, E. B., 177
White, Richard, 210–11n.61
Whittaker, Frederick, 131
Wilderness, rhetoric of, 1
Will, George, 115
Willard, Solomon, 30
Williams, Clayton, 82n.17
Williams, Gen. Edward T., 73
Wills, David, 93
Wilson, Henry, 14
Wilson, John F., 2
Wilson, Ron, 85n.56
Wilson, Woodrow, 96
Wohlstetter, Albert, 183
Women's National Patriotic Organization, 178
Wood, Michael B., 27
Woodring, Harry H., 97
Wyden, Peter, 185

Yakamoto, Sadeo, 203
Yamamoto, Adm. Isoroku, 173
Yancey, William L., 23
Yates, Sidney, 198
Yellowstone National Park, 2
York, Sgt. Alvin C., 47n.39
Yorktown (Va.), 213
Yosemite National Park, 2
Young, Capt. Bennett H., 95
Young, Kevin, 61, 124n.57

Zelinsky, Wilbur, 2, 3
Zuber, William P., 60

A Note on the Author

Edward Tabor Linenthal, professor of religion and American culture at the University of Wisconsin-Oshkosh, is also the author of *Changing Images of the Warrior Hero in America* (1982) and *Symbolic Defense: The Cultural Significance of the Strategic Defense Initiative* (1989).